PORTRAITS OF THE ARTIST IN EXILE

*James Joyce. Drawing by Adolf Hoffmeister
(courtesy of Lilly Hoffmeister)*

Portraits
of the Artist
in Exile

✿

*Recollections
of James Joyce
by Europeans*

Edited by WILLARD POTTS

UNIVERSITY OF
WASHINGTON PRESS
SEATTLE AND LONDON

Library of Congress Cataloging in Publication Data
Main entry under title:

Portraits of the artist in exile.

   Includes bibliographical references and index.
   1. Joyce, James, 1882–1941—Biography—
Addresses, essays, lectures. 2. Authors, Irish—
20th century—Biography—Addresses, essays,
lectures. I. Potts, Willard, 1929–
PR6019.09Z7823   823'.9'12   78–4367
ISBN 0–295–95614–3

The text is set in linotype Janson with Monotype Janson display and
printed letterpress on 60 lb. Warrens Olde Style at Heritage Printers, Inc.,
Charlotte, North Carolina.

J89ZPO

Portraits of the artis
   exile

Acknowledgments

VARIOUS DEGREES OF COLLABORATION have been involved in preparing
the translations of the recollections by Nino Frank, Philippe Soupault,
Adolf Hoffmeister, Ole Vinding, Jan Parandowski, Dr. Carola Giedion-
Welcker, and Paul Ruggiero. The principal translator of each is indicated in the text, but others who have assisted significantly are Ronald
Notto, Benjamin Murdzek, Tharald Borgir, Brookes Spencer, Tove
Bodvarsson, Blanka Wright, Gigi Lynch, and Lea Jaroškovà. Special
problems presented by Francini Bruni's two recollections made their
translation more of a collaborative effort than the others. Those chiefly
involved were Camilla Rudolph, Thomas F. Staley, Aldo Andreotti,
and Lido Botti, with valuable assistance from Eva Millemann. Since I
have had a hand in the final version of all these recollections, responsibility
for any faults in the translations must be mine.

I owe thanks to Dr. Carola Giedion-Welcker, Jacques Mercanton,
Nino Frank, Philippe Soupault, and Ole Vinding for generously
granting me permission to use their recollections; to Joseph Prescott
for permission to use his translation of Georges Borach's recollection;
and to Fritz Senn for providing me a copy of Paul Ruggiero's previously
unpublished recollection. I also wish to thank Mme Lilly Hoffmeister
for permission to use the recollections by her husband, Adolf Hoffmeister, and to reproduce his caricatures of Joyce; the Humanities
Research Center, University of Texas, Austin, for permission to reproduce the drawing of Joyce by Desmond Harmsworth: Sir Caspar John,
for permission to reproduce a drawing of Joyce by Augustus John;
Fred B. Dennis, for permission to reproduce Constantin Brancusi's
drawing of Joyce; and Jane Lidderdale, receiver for Lucia Joyce, for
permission to reproduce Lucia's sketch of her father.

Further thanks are due for permission to use the following material:
Oxford University Press for extracts from Richard Ellmann's *James
Joyce*; the Viking Press, Inc., and Faber and Faber Ltd. for extracts
from the *Letters of James Joyce*; and the Society of Authors, as the
literary representative of the Estate of James Joyce, for extracts from
unpublished letters in the Harriet Weaver Collection in the British

284448

Library and for extracts from the Gorman papers in the Croessman Collection at Carbondale.

In addition to those who worked on the translations, many others have given me invaluable assistance, particularly Robert Deming, K. C. Gay, Alan Cohn, Kenneth W. Duckett, Patricia Brandt, Robert Frank, and Chester Garrison. I am grateful for their help and for Sharon Springer's skillful preparation of the manuscript.

For financial support while working on this volume, I am obliged to the Oregon State University Foundation, the Oregon State University Research Council, the Oregon State University Graduate Research Fund, and the Penrose Fund of the American Philosophical Society.

The publication history of the recollections is given below:

Alessandro Francini Bruni's *Joyce intimo spogliato in Piazza* was originally published by La Editorale Libraria (Trieste) in 1922. The translation appeared previously in *James Joyce Quarterly*, 14 (Winter 1977): 127–59. Those chiefly involved in the translation were Camilla Rudolph, Thomas F. Staley, and Aldo Andreotti, with valuable assistance from Eva Millemann. Francini Bruni's "Ricordi su James Joyce" was published in *Nuova antologia*, 441 (Sept.-Dec. 1947): 71–79; the translation appeared previously in *James Joyce Quarterly*, 14 (Winter 1977): 160–68.

Silvio Benco's recollection appeared originally as "James Joyce a Trieste," *Pegaso*, 2 (Aug. 1930): 150–65, and was reprinted as "Ricordi di Joyce," *Umana*, 20 (May–Sept. 1971): 6–12. The translation published here comes from the *Bookman*, 72 (Dec. 1930): 375–80 (no translator designated).

The translation of August Suter's recollection is taken from *James Joyce Quarterly*, 7 (Spring 1970): 191–97, where it bears the prefatory remark, "August Suter left the following notes, written in German and translated here for the first time."

George Borach's recollection appeared originally as "Gespräche mit James Joyce," *Die Neue Zürcher Zeitung*, no. 827, May 3, 1931. The translation was originally published in *College English*, 15 (March 1954): 325–27. The translation also has appeared in *Meanjin*, 13 (Spring 1954): 393–96; and *London Magazine*, 1 (November 1954): 75–78.

Nino Frank's recollection, "L'Ombre qui avait perdue son homme," appears in his *Memoire brisée* (Paris: Calman-Lévy, 1967), pp. 29–64. It is an expanded version of "Souvenirs sur James Joyce," *La Table ronde* (Paris), 23 (Nov. 1949): 1671–93, part of which was published in an Italian translation as "L'ombre che aveva perduto il suo Uomo,"

Il Mondo, 2 (June 3, 1950): 11–12; (June 10, 1950): 11–12. A portion of the recollection appears as "La joyeuse partie de campagne de James Joyce," *Figaro litteraire*, May 8, 1967, p. 27.

Philippe Soupault's recollection comes from his *Profils perdus* (Paris: Mercure de France, 1963), pp. 49–70. A portion of the recollection was published as "Portrait de l'artiste à Paris," *Lettres françaises* (Feb. 16–22, 1961), pp. 1, 3. An earlier version, with some additional matter, is contained in *Souvenirs de James Joyce* (Paris: Charlot, 1945). A brief excerpt from the latter volume was translated in the *James Joyce Yearbook*, ed. Maria Jolas (Paris: Transition Press, 1949), pp. 126–29.

Adolf Hoffmeister's "James Joyce" and "Osobnost James Joyce," appear in his *Podoby: Napsal a Nakreslil* (Prague: Ceskoslovenský Spisovatel, 1961), pp. 71–78, 118–26. An Italian translation of "Osobnost James Joyce" was published as "Un incontro con James Joyce," *Europa letteraria*, 2 (Feb.–Apr. 1962), 55–63. Both recollections appear in the French translation of Hoffmeister's book, *Visages écrits et dessines*, trans. Francois Kerel (Paris: Les Editeurs Français Réunis, 1963), pp. 39–47, 48–60.

Ole Vinding's "James Joyce i København" appeared in his *Vejen til den halve Verden* (Copenhagen: Gyldendal, 1963), pp. 198–209. The translation appeared previously in *James Joyce Quarterly*, 14 (Winter 1977): 173–84. Vinding published shortened versions of the recollection as "Et Interview med Joyce," *Forum* (Copenhagen), no. 1 (Feb. 1941), pp. 21–22; and "James Joyce," *Perspectiv*, no. 8 (Summer 1959), pp. 14–16. Copies of Vinding's original typescript are located in the Joyce collections of the universities of Cornell, London, SUNY/Buffalo, and Yale. A translation of the typescript, with several pages missing, is at SUNY/Buffalo.

Jan Parandowski's "Spotkanie z Joycem" appears in his *Dziela wybrane* (Warsaw: Czytelnik, 1959), 3:468–77. A German translation, minus the first paragraph, was published as "Begegnung mit Joyce," *Deutsche Rundschau*, 83 (1957): 279–84. A portion of the recollection, with an English extract, appeared in *Umana*, 20 (May–Sept. 1971): 46–48.

Louis Gillet's "Adieux a Joyce," first appeared in *Paris-Soir* on January 15, 1941. The following recollection by Gillet, "Joyce vivant," with some additional material, appeared as "Recuerdos de James Joyce," in *Sur* (Dec. 1941), pp. 28–42; (Jan. 1942), pp. 53–65. Both recollections were included in Gillet's *Stele pour James Joyce* (1941: rpt., Paris: Editions du Sagittaire, 1946). The translations published here come from the English translation of that volume, *Claybook for*

James Joyce, trans. Georges Markow-Totevy (London: Abelard-Schuman, 1958), pp. 75–79, 80–119.

Jacques Mercanton's recollection appeared as "Les heures de James Joyce," *Mercure de France*, 348 (1963): 89–117, 284–315; rpt. with slight changes (Lausanne: Editions l'Age d'Homme, 1967). The translation published here comes from the *Kenyon Review*, 24 (Autumn 1962): 700–30; and 25 (Winter 1963): 93–118.

Cardo Giedion-Welcker's "Begegnungen mit James Joyce," appears in her *Schriften 1926–1971: Stationen zu einem Zeitbild*, ed. Reinhold Hohl (Cologne: M. DuMont Schauberg, 1973), pp. 53–74. A shortened version of the recollection appeared in English translation as "James Joyce in Zurich," *Horizon*, 18 (Sept. 1948), 207–12; rpt. *The Golden Horizon* (London: Weidenfeld and Nicholson, 1953).

Paul Ruggiero's previously unpublished recollection of Joyce "James Joyce's Last Days in Zurich," is based on a typescript left by Ruggiero. The original is in French.

The translation of Paul Léon's "In Memory of Joyce" comes from *A James Joyce Yearbook*, ed. Maria Jolas (Paris: Transition Press, 1949), pp. 116–25. The original appeared in *Poesie*, no. 5 (1942), p. 35.

Contents

Introduction

THE REPRINTING OF JOHN BYRNE'S ECCENTRIC BOOK *The Silent Years* and of other Irish recollections about James Joyce reflects the persistent interest in his relations with Ireland.[1] In many ways continental Europe, where he found his chief literary inspiration, wrote all his major work, and spent most of his adult life, had a greater significance to him than did Ireland. He indicated this significance in a blunt note on the typescript of Herbert Gorman's biography. Alluding to Stephen Dedalus' search in *Ulysses* for his spiritual as opposed to his physical or "consubstantial" father, Gorman asked rhetorically, "Of whom was [Joyce] the spiritual son and where would he find the Mystical Father?" In the margin Joyce wrote, "His spiritual father is Europe . . ." (*JJ* 737). Of the biographical sources bearing on Joyce's relationship with his spiritual father, the most important are the recollections of Europeans who knew him in "exile," as he somewhat misleadingly called his life abroad. Richard Ellmann drew from these recollections in writing his biography of Joyce. But like the recollections of Joyce's English-speaking friends, Padraic and Mary Colum, Sylvia Beach, Constantine Curran, Robert McAlmon, and Frank Budgen, they have an intimacy and vividness uncapturable in excerpts or summaries.[2] Moreover, several of them apparently escaped Ellmann's attention, while others were published after he had completed his work.

The European recollections that follow, seven of which appear here for the first time in English, span Joyce's exile, from his arrival in Pola in 1904 at the age of twenty-two until his death in Zurich nearly thirty-seven years later. Some are by close friends of his, others by more or less casual acquaintances, a few by people who knew him only

1. *The Silent Years: An Autobiography with Memoirs of James Joyce and Our Ireland* (1953; rpt., New York: Octagon Books, 1975).
2. The principal recollections of these acquaintances are, Padraic and Mary Colum, *Our Friend James Joyce* (Garden City, N.Y.: Doubleday and Co., 1958); Sylvia Beach, *Shakespeare and Company* (New York: Harcourt, Brace and Co., 1956); Constantine Curran, *James Joyce Remembered* (New York: Oxford University Press, 1968); Robert McAlmon, *Being Geniuses Together: 1920–1930* (1938; rev. with supplementary chapters by Kay Boyle, London: Michael Joseph, 1970); and Frank Budgen, *James Joyce and the Making of "Ulysses"* (1934; rpt., with "Other Writings," London: Oxford University Press, 1972).

briefly. Together they describe or give instances of his response to nearly every aspect of European life. They show that he felt much more at ease with Europeans than with his fellow Dubliners, that he came to know the chief cities of his exile—Trieste, Zurich, Paris—almost as well as he did Dublin and that he found them much more to his taste. They also show that his admiration for European writers, above all Ibsen and Dante, remained as great as it had been in Dublin, while his pre-occupation with learning European languages became even greater, now that occasions offered themselves on every side. In 1937 Joyce wrote Constantine Curran turning down another of many invitations to visit Ireland. "But every day in every way," he added, "I am walking along the streets of Dublin and along the strand" (*Letters* I, 395). Such remarks, coupled with the predominantly Irish matter in his work, easily lead to the impression that though he lived on the continent he thought of nothing but Ireland. The European recollections make the error of that impression emphatically clear. They portray a man intent on transforming himself into that ideal person Joyce once referred to as "the Good Terrafirmaite," who was "equally at home" anywhere in Europe (*Letters* I, 284), and almost as intent on transforming his books into the literary equivalent by having them discussed in European journals and translated into European languages.

But the recollections are not tracts on Joyce's response to Europe. They present him from many points of view, each emphasizing some different facet of his character or experience. Philippe Soupault focuses on Joyce the dedicated writer; Louis Gillet, on Joyce the friend and companion. August Suter and Ole Vinding stress his self-centeredness; Dr. Giedion-Welcker and Paul Léon, his sensitivity to others. Francini Bruni shows him as clownish, irresponsible, and inclined to drunkenness; Silvio Benco, as industrious, sober, and reliable. The tones vary, too, from Francini's high-spirited zaniness to the often somber tones of those who knew Joyce later on during the years of his near-blindness and anguish over his daughter's insanity. In the resulting composite portrait certain traits appear prominently. Some of these traits, such as his devotion to his family and work, love of music, habit of celebrating anniversaries, and indifference to politics, are well known. Others, such as his fondness for telling stories, persistent youthfulness, intense energy, wide-ranging curiosity, and almost manic-depressive fluctuations from despair to gaiety or taciturnity to talkativeness are perhaps not so well known.

"There never was a good biography of a good novelist," F. Scott Fitzgerald thought. "There couldn't be. He is too many people."[3]

3. *The Stories of F. Scott Fitzgerald*, ed. Malcolm Cowley (New York: Charles Scribner's Sons, 1951), p. xviii.

In showing Joyce from different points of view the recollections give a sharper sense of his many facets than is likely in a biography. They have the additional advantage of being unencumbered by the multitude of dates, addresses, and other such factual material that a biography is obliged to provide. For the most part they contain descriptions of Joyce as each acquaintance saw him and accounts of his conversations. The descriptions give vivid glimpses of him in a wide range of moods and circumstances: standing in a bar full of tipsy Triestines singing Italian drinking songs at the top of his lungs; striding about Trieste on compass-pole legs to give another English lesson; strolling along the shores of the Lake of Zurich discussing *Ulysses* with the crippled Georges Borach; sitting silently in his darkened Paris flat while the young Nino Frank on his first visit fails in desperate attempts at starting a conversation; calling Adolf Hoffmeister's attention to a vase of small Greek flags on the piano and remarking proudly that each one represents a new edition of *Ulysses*; walking along a Paris street, whistling under his breath and twirling his stick as though it were the ashplant of his youth rather than the white cane of a blind man; urging Jacques Mercanton after a late night out to come listen to a few pages of "Work in Progress"; climbing on top the Giedions' car after another late night, stretching out flat, and commanding Giedion to drive on; passing along a snowy Zurich sidewalk hand in hand with his grandson Stephen. The vividness of these glimpses gives them a value apart from any character traits they reveal.

Many of Joyce's conversations are recorded in remarkable detail, often on the basis of notes kept at the time. Some concern himself, especially his life in Europe, seldom touching on Dublin or Ireland except in response to direct questions. Another major topic is European writers, with Ibsen and Dante predominating. The many references to the latter support Ellmann's observation that "Dante was perhaps Joyce's favorite author" (*JJ* 2), and show in addition a strong sense of identification with the Italian poet. But the most extensive and detailed conversations deal with his own work, making the European recollections one of the richest sources of his authorial remarks. The comments, most of which concern *Ulysses* and *Finnegans Wake*, explain particular passages and general techniques as well as his intentions, hopes, and fears regarding his work.

The readiness with which Joyce spoke to Europeans about himself and his work indicates his close and sympathetic relationship with them, from the bank clerk Paul Ruggiero to the businessman Georges Borach or the French Academician Louis Gillet. In addition to providing him a vital contact with his spiritual father, they responded to his work with an appreciation and willing helpfulness that he could not have expected from many of his fellow Dubliners. Their recollections show that they found him strongly appealing and remained attached to him in spite of burdens he sooner or later placed on most of them. In general they write of him not only with great fondness but also with admiration and respect. In a strange little biographical study of Joyce, Edna O'Brien asks, ". . . Was he neurotic?"[4] More recently the chief question seems to be, Was he syphilitic? Such questions have their interest but are limiting and in any event have been explored adequately. The European recollections do not ignore Joyce's clay feet, but, to a greater extent even than the accounts of such friendly observers as Frank Budgen, they bring out his vitality, warmth, sensitivity, and intelligence.

The European recollections are far too numerous to be included in a single volume; consequently, I have aimed at selecting the most substantial of those not readily accessible. The only major one not included is Lucie Noël's recollection of her husband's friendship with Joyce, which already has been published separately as a book.[5] Of the remainder, the most interesting are by Italo Svevo, Dario de Tuoni, Carlo Linati, Simone Téry, Alfred Kerr, and Heinrich Straumann.[6] Aside from Svevo's, which contains only a few brief personal references, these are based on casual or single encounters with Joyce. Though published as a book de Tuoni's recollection consists mainly of digressions, including a long one about Joyce's painter friend Tullio Silvestri and his painting technique. Maria Jolas' fine account of Joyce at Saint-Gérand-le-Puy, "Joyce en 1939–1940," has not appeared in English, thus giving possible grounds for including it; however, permission was unobtainable.[7] Eugene Jolas' recollection, "My Friend James Joyce," was omitted since it has already been reprinted.[8]

As nearly as possible the pieces have been arranged according to the

4. "Dear Mr. Joyce," in *A Bash in the Tunnel: James Joyce by the Irish,* ed. John Ryan (Brighton: Clifton Books, 1970), p. 43.

5. *James Joyce and Paul L. Léon: The Story of a Friendship* (New York: Gotham Book Mart, [1950]).

6. Italo Svevo, *James Joyce,* trans. Stanislaus Joyce (New York: New Directions, 1950); Dario de Tuoni, *Ricordi di Joyce a Trieste* (Milan: Insegna del Pesce d'Oro, 1966); Carlo Linati, "Ricordi su Joyce," *Prospettive,* (February 15, 1940), p. 16; Simone Téry, *L'Ile des bardes* (Paris: Ernest Flammarion, 1925), pp. 213–17; Alfred Kerr, "James Joyce in England," trans. Joseph Prescott, in *A James Joyce Miscellany,* ed. Marvin Magalaner (New York: James Joyce Society, 1957), pp. 37–43; and Heinrich Straumann, "Last Meeting with Joyce," in *A James Joyce Yearbook,* ed. Maria Jolas (Paris: Transition Press, 1949), pp. 109–15.

7. *Mercure de France,* 109 (May-Aug. 1950): 45–58.

8. *Partisan Review,* 8 (March-April 1941): 82–93; rpt., *James Joyce: Two Decades of Criticism,* ed. Seon Givens (New York: Vanguard Press, 1948), pp. 3–18.

chronology of Joyce's life rather than in the order they were written, though the two chronologies often correspond. Except for one instance noted later on, the complete texts are given. In a series of recollections such as this a certain amount of repetition is inevitable, but eliminating that slight annoyance would have involved the greater one of a text marred with ellipses. Joyce complained constantly and joked occasionally about blunders people made in writing about his life. "Nobody," he said, "seems to be inclined to present me to the world in my unadorned prosaicness."[9] Though boners occur in the European recollections, they usually are the result of small failures in memory rather than of attempts at exaggerating his life, which in any event was not as prosaic as he liked to maintain. In the introductions and footnotes to the individual recollections I have attempted to correct these inaccuracies as well as to identify allusions, fill in biographical gaps, and supply additional information bearing on points raised in the recollections or Joyce's relationship with their authors. I also have used the introductions and footnotes as a means of incorporating some material from the European recollections not included in the volume. A few silent changes have been made in those translations that have been previously published, to supply inadvertent omissions from the originals, to clarify meaning, and to standardize the spelling of proper names and the references to Joyce's works. Throughout I have inserted identifications of passages from Joyce, using the following abbreviations.

CW	Joyce, James. *The Critical Writings of James Joyce*, ed. Ellsworth Mason and Richard Ellmann. New York: Viking Press, 1959.
D	Joyce, James. *"Dubliners": Text, Criticism, and Notes*, ed. Robert Scholes and A. Walton Litz. New York: Viking Press, 1969.
E	Joyce, James. *Exiles*. New York: Viking Press, 1951.
FW	Joyce, James. *Finnegans Wake*. New York: Viking Press, 1939; London: Faber and Faber, 1939.
JJ	Ellmann, Richard. *James Joyce*. New York: Oxford University Press, 1959.
Letters I, II, III	Joyce, James. *Letters of James Joyce*. Vol. 1, ed. Stuart Gilbert. New York: Viking Press, 1957; reissued with corrections, 1965. Vols. II and III, ed. Richard Ellmann. New York: Viking Press, 1966.

9. *Selected Letters of James Joyce*, ed. Richard Ellmann (New York: Viking Press, 1975), p. 287.

P   Joyce, James. *"A Portrait of the Artist as a Young Man":*
           Text, Criticism, and Notes, ed. Chester G. Anderson. New
           York: Viking Press, 1968.

SL   Joyce, James. *Selected Letters of James Joyce*, ed. Richard
           Ellmann. New York: Viking Press, 1975.

U   Joyce, James. *Ulysses.* New York: Random House, 1934 ed.,
           reset and corrected 1961.

PORTRAITS OF THE ARTIST IN EXILE

Alessandro Francini Bruni

ACCORDING TO JOYCE *his father urged him to go to Europe, but he would have needed no urging* (JJ 737). *Like his boyhood hero, Ulysses, he was always a restless searcher for new adventures and as a young man doubtless shared the conviction of the precocious boy in "An Encounter" that "real adventures . . . do not happen to those who remain at home" but "must be sought abroad" (D 21). He had in addition a deep interest in European languages and literature that hardly could have been satisfied in an Ireland where, under the leadership of William Butler Yeats and others, his compatriots were focusing intensely on their own language, literature, and history. In a brief essay, "The Day of the Rabblement," the nineteen-year-old Joyce took his stand against this stifling provincialism. "A nation which never advanced so far as a miracle play," he said, "affords no literary model to the artist. . . ." The artist, he went on to say, "must look abroad" (CW 70). His decision to go abroad, however, was precipitated by his attachment to Nora Barnacle and his desire that their matrimony be completely personal, without the intervention of, as he said later on, "a clerk with a pen behind his ear or a priest in his nightshirt."[1] Such a matrimony would have been difficult in Dublin even for a man of Joyce's moral courage.*

On October 8, 1904, a date he later regarded as his marriage anniversary, Joyce and his bride left Dublin for Europe. He had been assured a job teaching English at the Berlitz School in Zurich, but on arriving there, after a short stop-over in Paris, he found the position did not exist. In pursuit of another supposed opening, he went to Trieste, and from there was sent to a post at the Berlitz School in Pola. Now in Yugoslavia, Pola was then part of the Austro-Hungarian Empire, its harbor serving as a base for the empire's navy. Because of its out-of-the-way location on the tip of the Istrian peninsula, Joyce referred to it disgruntledly as a "naval Siberia" (Letters I, 57). But he had to remain there only four months, after which he returned to Trieste and began teaching in the Berlitz School there. Though at

---

1. Unpublished portion of letter from March 11, 1931, in the Harriet Shaw Weaver Collection at the British Museum.

*the time also a part of the Austro-Hungarian Empire, Trieste was
populated mainly by Italians, the principal language being a Triestine
dialect of Italian. Except for three visits to Dublin and a year in Rome
as a bank clerk, Joyce remained in Trieste until the fall of 1915, when
the war forced him to take refuge for four years in Switzerland.
He returned to Trieste for eight months following the war and then
moved to Paris.*

*The years in Trieste were not easy for Joyce or his wife. Having
arrived without any money except the little that he could borrow, they
always quickly dispensed the little he earned, so that they were perpetually on the verge of destitution. Knowing only a few words of
Italian, she was forced to lead an isolated life. When she became preg-
nant matters worsened to the degree that Joyce found her in perpetual
tears (Letters II, 95). Her unhappiness was only one of his various
problems, among which were frequent quarrels with his brother
Stanislaus, who arrived in 1905, and the heat. Used to the cooler climate
of Dublin, he complained, "I hate a damn silly sun that makes men
into butter" (Letters II, 109).*

*In spite of the difficulties, Joyce later recalled Trieste with pleasure,
and Nora remembered it as a time of much laughter. One ameliorating
circumstance was their friendship with the twenty-six-year-old Florentine, Alessandro Francini Bruni (1878–1964) and his young wife. (He
had added his wife's last name, Bruni, to his own, but Joyce ignored
the addition.) Francini, who was director of the school in Pola when
Joyce arrived, became not only the first but also for a decade the
closest of his European friends. The two men along with their wives
spent many evenings together, for a time even sharing an apartment,
first in Pola and later in Trieste.*

*Francini wrote two recollections of Joyce, both of which are in-
cluded. The first was a lecture, "presented," according to the title page
of its published version, "under the auspices of the Triestine Press
Association in the Dramatic Society's Hall on the evening of February
22, 1922." The publication of* Ulysses *not quite three weeks earlier
made the moment one of special interest in Joyce. Shortly before giving
the lecture Francini wrote to him about it, and Joyce, always eager to
assist efforts in behalf of his work, asked Harriet Weaver to send
Francini reviews of the book. "He is giving a lecture on me . . .," he told
her, "and I want him to have as many notices as possible."[2] But Francini
intended to talk about Joyce, not about* Ulysses.

Earlier articles by Padraic Colum and Silvio Benco contain bio-

2. Unpublished letter from February 17, 1922, in the Harriet Shaw Weaver
Collection. See also *Letters* III, 55–56.

graphical material about Joyce,[3] but Francini's lecture is the first intimate
look at the man as well as the first to have received separate publication.
Written in a highly colloquial Tuscan, with smatterings of Triestine
and Venetian dialect and numerous puns, double-entendres, outrageous
figures of speech, and digressions, it contains obscure expressions
that challenge even native speakers. The difficulty of its style, coupled
with the rarity of copies, has kept the lecture from being widely known,
except for passages quoted in Ellmann's biography. But the style is
significant in other respects as well. It reveals an antic humor that helps
explain Francini's strong appeal to Joyce, who worried that domestic
life was making him too solemnly conventional (Letters II, 75). It also
suggests the linguistic daring and caprice of Joyce himself. Though
the first impulse would be to conclude that he had influenced Francini,
Nora thought the influence flowed in the opposite direction, to the
detriment of her young husband's verbal manners. "Since you've come to
know Francini," she told him, "I can't recognize you anymore (JJ 224).

The lecture begins with a long, whimsical description of the Berlitz
School, its staff, and its students, relevant details considering that the
school was an important part of Joyce's life for three of his first four
years in exile. Never one to understate his misfortunes, Joyce complained
in letters home about the long hours and low pay at the school but
even more about the tyranny of its owner, Almidano Artifoni, whose
name he later used in Ulysses for Stephen Dedalus' Italian teacher.
Artifoni "gave me to understand one day very pointedly," Joyce reported, "that whenever he found a teacher trying to get a post elsewhere
he packed him off." He also took Joyce's B.A. certificate and locked
it in a safe, apparently as a means of keeping tabs on him (Letters II,
94). While making the grim side of the school perfectly clear, Francini
shows that there was a great deal of laughter and joking in which
Joyce participated fully.

In connection with his sketch of the school Francini recalls at length
a series of vignettes that he says Joyce used in classes. These vignettes,
most of which Ellmann quotes, are personal comments on various
topics, including the Catholic Church, Ireland, government, and his
private life. It is surprising that he should have used such personal
material in a class open to the public. It is equally surprising that Francini,
whose memory is demonstrably fallible, should have been able to
recall them in detail after nearly twenty years. Yet echoes of the vignettes occur repeatedly in Joyce's letters from the period and in his

3. Padraic Colum, "James Joyce," *Pearson's Magazine*, 44 (May 1918): 38–42;
and Silvio Benco, "Un illustre scrittore inglese a Trieste," *Umana*, 1 (July 1,
1916): 1–3.

work, so that whatever the exact story behind them, the evidence of their authenticity is strong. As Ellmann says, "Here, in Chaplinesque caricature, are most of Joyce's central preoccupations . . ." (JJ 227).

Moving to the Joyce he knew from their long conversations and evenings together, Francini tries to make sense out of a personality where he found in baffling combination an admiration for the profound Dante as well as the "ephemeral" Verlaine, a thorough knowledge of the church coupled with a total lack of faith, a powerful intellect in the service of denial, and a talent of great promise threatened by destructive bouts of drinking. Finally, with an honesty unusual among those who have written about Joyce, Francini admits that he cannot understand his friend. He is equally candid about his feelings, which range from love and admiration for Joyce, to disgust, to a religiously based note of disapproval and concern.

Though highly personal and admittedly a caricature, Francini's lecture identifies many traits now associated with Joyce, largely because of his own self-portraits. Displaying a similar turmoil of emotions, appearance of self-possession, esoteric knowledge, skepticism, and skill in argument, the Joyce Francini recalled closely resembles the Stephen Dedalus of A Portrait and Ulysses, only now seen from a comic perspective as the young husband in exile.

Stanislaus, who was present at this first public examination of his brother's character, considered the lecture an outrage. He wrote to Joyce that Francini "swore to me before the lecture that it was a caricature in good taste and 'worthy of the subject.' Instead it was vulgar and silly . . ." (Letters III, 59; see also III, 102). At first Joyce laughed it off, remarking, "I'm sure it was very funny and quite suited to the distinguished audience" (Letters III, 61). But after reading it he came around to Stanislaus' point of view, ultimately regarding the lecture as another instance of betrayal,[4] though the only apparent betrayal lay in Francini's assuming the right to caricature Joyce, who preferred reserving that right to himself.

Whereas verbal high-spiritedness thrived in Joyce, it withered in Francini, so that stylistically his second recollection, written in 1947, bears little resemblance to the lecture. However, it adds an interesting account of Joyce's manner of exchanging language lessons with Francini and of celebrating Saint Patrick's Day. In the exchange, Francini says, Joyce took but did not give. Such was the young Joyce's habit in other

4. See the footnotes on pp. 265 and 267 of Herbert Gorman's *James Joyce* (New York: Farrar and Rinehart, 1939). Except for two slight changes these footnotes reproduce Joyce's dictated comments written on the typescript of the biography in the Croessmann Collection at Carbondale. See also Jacques Mercanton's recollection, p. 243 and note.

relations as well, particularly with his brother, from whom he demanded a variety of personal favors, giving little in return. The Saint Patrick's Day celebration is an early instance of Joyce's devotion to anniversaries and his habit of involving family and friends in the devotion. Many other instances will turn up in later recollections.

Joyce Stripped Naked in the Piazza

By *Alessandro Francini Bruni*

WHAT CHARACTERS THESE IRISH ARE! Oscar Wilde, Bernard Shaw . . . , but the elusive personality of James Joyce surpasses them all.

This chaotic fellow is on the point of becoming a scandalous celebrity; he seems to have a passion for causing turmoil in the press and the public opinion of half the world. I can't figure out whether they are going to stone him; it is possible. At any rate I can tell that they will come to blows. Oh! if they would!

Let us wait until after that English sailor, *Ulysses,* has embarked from the Seine and lands, translated, on the coast of Europe; then we will see.

But this evening I am not talking about Ulysses; I am talking about James Joyce.

I found him a man after my own taste. Joyce is ours—that is our pride and his. He grew up beside our hearths. We can share him. I even have a right to dissect him. I will show him to you stark naked, as I have seen him. I will make you a present of him.

I have exquisite personal memories of him dating from the beginning of our friendship in the years of our stay in Pola and Trieste. Before and after the war.

It was a lazy November in 1904.

We met in Pola—we came from opposite poles—Joyce from Dublin and I from Florence, hired by the same outfit, a language school. For a bit of bread.

Not too bad for me. But for that crust of bread Joyce had traveled many miles. On embarking he had said, like Charles V: "I will visit my realm, on which the sun never sets."

And via many stages, landings, mountain passes, and bivouacs, he had crossed half of Europe. He had visited England, Holland, Germany, France, Switzerland, Austria, Italy, and then Austria again. Finally he had arrived.

Now our paths and our destinies crossed.

We became friends.

Having become fed up with the Irish swamp and its croaking frogs, Joyce one day decided to take the great leap. Without making a fuss, he turned on his heel, leaving his father's house and all family ties. He took the woman of his heart, the shirt on his back, a basket of provisions so that on their honeymoon they wouldn't have to kiss each other with hungry mouths, and a trunkful of learning. All this to come and pound on the pumpkin heads of some imbeciles with ape-like mimicry:

"What is this?"

"It is a chair."

"Is this a man or a woman?"

"A woman."

"Are you sure?"

"Very sure."

"Well, shall we see?"

"Yes, it is a woman. It is a woman."

"Very good."

Such a school must be as much like a zoo as possible; that is, the teacher has to behave like a bloody monkey. The students are vain and dull apes of every imaginable kind: coquettish women, cashiers about to abscond, single girls with no hope of ever being otherwise, officers as ignorant as donkeys, jobless waiters, ship's officers ready to embark, and more. I had, besides, the janitor and the cat, both of whom had gotten it into their heads to learn Tuscan in a hurry. They competed in murdering the language. The janitor was a pale young man with large, protruding ears and thick lips, which reminded me of the ears and lips of the King of Spain when he was young. The young man's name was Svoboda. The cat had more language facility than Svoboda, but Svoboda learned blasphemies better. That swindler had learned them so well that I had to intervene promptly to restrain his ardent enthusiasm.

"No, Svoboda," I told him. "I don't like such manners. You can have your blasphemies at home for lunch, but we don't need them here, and even then, water them down."

"What, Mr. Director?"

"Water them down, I said."

Shortly, the news spread around Pola that the director had taught that cabbage head to water down the saints: "Diluted Christ," "Immersed Mary," "Dunked Saint Joseph," "Soaked Saint Anthony and his pig," and all the rest. In sum, a general drowning. No one seemed left in Paradise.

Oh, me! Oh, me! I tell you, you can never do anything right with imbeciles! "Enough," I told him. "You will be a success in the world; whether you water your curses or not is up to you, but it would be better if you left here." So I got rid of the bas——, you understand?

The curtain was raised and the comedy had begun.

Was Berlicche[5] crazy or had we been tricked? We had been tricked. No crazy person had ever been cleverer—he had found the magic key for making a successful enterprise out of nothing.

He had managed to patent an American-style gimmick for filling skulls with modern languages and then making these languages come out through the mouth sounding like a big belch. Then using American high pressure, he gathered an army of stray dogs from every place imaginable and unleashed them on the surface of the globe, saying to them: "*Ite in civitates*[6]—run around, break your neck, bruise your feet, your ankles, your shins, and your ass; go wherever you want, but ballyhoo my business like the devil. Tell all the baboons in Europe that my remedy is better than all those sticking plasters that have ruined their corns and their souls, that my method is the real panacea for ignorance. Nothing to those who do not pay, understand! Because, though you who have to mingle with the mob must stay as hungry as the Apostles, I, who stay here and wait far away, I don't intend to play the Teacher of Galilee's role."

Here they are, the wretched ones, with no other inclination but to line the pockets of the Wizard, not only eating their lungs and livers out but also showing the holy image of the Venerable to ignorant and devout humanity.

"Who is this?"

"It is Mr. B."

"Am I Mr. B?"

"No, (unfortunately). You are Mr. Joyce."

I haven't really told you anything yet. But if you are to be amused by the following farce, you must know a little more about the comic complications of the plot, that is to say the stipulations of our contract.

It is well known that the teachers in those schools are a species of stray dog, licking here today and gnawing there tomorrow the bones thrown to them from the Wizard's table. They run around the world, fatalistically struggling to avoid disaster, now under this job label, now under that, but always either unsuccessful or rejected, indifferent

5. An unflattering reference to Berlitz. Berlicche is the name of an Italian clown figure.

6. Echoing Christ's words to the Apostles (Matt. 26:18), "Go into the city. . . ."

to everything and prepared to be everything: hotel waiters, interpreters, cicerones, tourist guides, middlemen, and so forth. The specialty of these teachers is really their ability to transform themselves, to appear and disappear, turning up in different masks, but really always unchanged, always remaining in that category which is spread all over the world and which is called the category of the Desperate.

Listen to the awful things that could happen to us in those days.

Among the many clauses and general conditions in the contract for the "Signori Professori" were two cynical and appalling affronts: "The Signori Professori (written in capital letters) must be single and have clothing."

Good God! What nonsense! I understand single, but with clothes? Had anyone ever appeared only in a fig leaf? "Just imagine," I said to myself when a copy of the contract arrived in Florence for my signature, "just imagine what kind of ragamuffins these people must employ!" But enough, I'll sign.

Now, you can imagine the disappointment—but what am I saying—the consternation—even more, the grimace—of the assistant, the trusted servant, Mr. B.'s factotum—a nice-looking, plump young fellow, dressed like a peacock—when, on the day of arrival, instead of a dressed Irishman—Oh, thank God, his shame was covered!—he found himself confronted by an avalanche in an indescribable state. It was that blockhead Joyce. And with the little lark of a bride along! And in what a condition! A bunch of rags tumbling out of a third class car—too bad that in Austria there were no fourth class cars as in Germany—like two sacks of spoiled beans.[7]

You should know that two weeks before one of the papers had begun to blow the horn of publicity about us, introducing Joyce to the public pompously and with a string of exaggerated adjectives. Here he was, the long-expected one, bewildered and shivering, naked as Jesus, waiting for someone to reclothe him from head to foot so that he could enter the ring decently and begin the performance.

The Professor of English! Mr. Joyce! Graduated with highest honors from Cambridge University! and other such inflated mish-mash. My name was included too, followed by a string of adjectives as long as a lady's train, dragged in the mud by a bunch of scoundrels who had a lot of fun jumping on it and grinding it under their feet.

The meeting of the two—someone who had the good luck to be there at the moment told me later—was spectacular.

Joyce's arrival left only two possible solutions for the assistant,

7. Actually, Joyce and his wife arrived by boat from Trieste. They were met by Artifoni, who owned the Pola school as well as the one in Trieste (*JJ* 192).

suicide or assassination. No other solutions existed. A moment's weakness would have compromised everything, turning the tragedy into farce and covering the protagonists with ridicule. If only someone would die to distract everyone's attention. But no one did. There they were, three shamed dogs. Joyce didn't think for even a minute about the state of his clothing. The problem of sartorial harmony never crossed his mind. On the contrary, Joyce in his greatness was so aloof, so aware of his role, that he waited motionlessly for the others to approach and welcome him on behalf of the city. When they were face to face they began to measure one another, each trying to spy in the other's eyes what he was thinking. The clear-eyed, poised Joyce stared into the puffy eyes of Mr. B.'s factotum, as if he really were Charles V surveying his realm.

Ragged and tattered as a beggar, he dragged along nonchalantly a hyena of a suitcase that had lost its fur but not its vice of laughing immoderately at the distress of its owner and master. From every rent in it things hung dangling in the breeze, but he did not trouble himself to tuck them in. On the contrary he dragged it behind him with absolute poise, hobbling along as if it were the most natural thing in the world. Mrs. Joyce, a little to one side, almost lost in a wide-brimmed straw hat and a man's overcoat that hung below her knees, looked like a pile of rags. Erect and motionless, she shifted her glance from one man to the other, without a trace of expression on her face.

The assistant was beside himself. He looked like an angry Jupiter emitting thunder and lightning. Unfortunately he was dressed incongruously in a boater and a light overcoat. At first he was pale and dismayed, but little by little became scarlet, like a cooked lobster.

He didn't dare make a scene. He was seething with rage; however, he didn't want it noticed for fear of ridicule. He wanted to remain still, but he couldn't. He wanted to appear indifferent and taciturn, and he was melting in bows and compliments. He couldn't keep silent. He kept talking and talking, mechanically. He tried to distract himself and forget his troubles by raising the tone of his voice excessively. He tried hard to laugh, though he wanted to cry. His whole body was shaken by a thousand tremors. He had St. Vitus dance; he made abrupt and ridiculous gestures, like a marionette when the puppeteer simultaneously jerks the head, trunk, arms, and legs.

I believe the unfortunate man was asking God then to let him sink beneath the earth rather than be present at that scene. The other two creatures, they were standing there, impassive and poised as two members of royalty. Joyce especially—cool and collected, as though the whole world were a pleasant joke. He had the nonchalance of a bored dandy returning from a surfeit of pleasure at the seashore. Since, after all, everything was useless and the situation couldn't be remedied, the assistant submitted himself to the ineluctable.

At that time Joyce talked a strange species of Italian. It is better to say archaic than strange, a crippled Italian full of ulcers. It was, if you can imagine such a thing, like an only-child language, and that child the deformed daughter of a buxom wet nurse and a diseased old dwarf. At any rate, it was a dead language, which joined the babble of living languages coming out of that pit of poor devils at the school.

Joyce was not aware of the ulcerations but, on the contrary, spoke them with great naturalness. The beautiful thing was the confidence with which he uttered those heresies. He came out with certain abortions that, as God is true, could not be allowed either in heaven or on earth. In heaven God in all his mercy could not have accepted them. On earth they existed only because Joyce did and because he kept them alive. He spoke them with brazen indifference to people's opinions. This virtue was not lacking in that spirited man. It is true that five years later the Italian language—the real language—was much more familiar to him than to me. He was a valuable and powerful contributor to our newspapers. And even though Benco,[8] with false humility, exaggerated in saying that Joyce had taught him Italian, it is certain that many of us would have been happy to write Italian as skillfully as that Irishman did. But at first, I assure you, it was another story.

Then, in order to ingratiate himself with this bear, the assistant decided to ask him a question. Trying to recall all the English he knew, he inquired with graceful unctuousness,

"Do you speak Italian, Mr. Joyce?"

Joyce replied, "Tu dici."[9] And not a word more.

("What kind of Italian does this tramp speak?") "Did you have a good trip, Mr. Joyce?"

"Tu dici." And nothing more. Pause and bewilderment of the questioner.

("What a hell of a way this Lutheran has of expressing himself! Bah! Let's ask him another question.")

"How do you like Italy, Mr. Joyce?"

"Che è quel ch' i' odo. Sere, issa vegg'io. Pola oppo del Carnaro."[10] Spoken in a tone as if to say, give me time to breathe, you fool.

The situation, as one can see, was highly dramatic. Mr. B.'s factotum was at the pitch of desperation. He didn't know what to do. Just for a

8. Silvio Benco, whose recollection follows.
9. Roughly, "You are saying it."
10. Roughly, "What do I hear? M'lord, what do I see? Pola on the Carnaro." "Che è quel ch' i' odo" comes from the *Inferno*, canto 3, line 32.

minute he toyed again with the idea of killing the two visitors. Finally, however, a less sanguinary idea prevailed. And as if a flash of genius had given him the solution, he seized both of them by the clothes and threw them one after the other into the first passing cab. Then he breathed a sigh of relief. But his relief was only temporary. The best was yet to come. You can imagine the anguish of the poor fellow in having to go through such a provincial, gossipy town in the company of those zoological rarities.

🙰

The farce reached its climax. It wasn't easy to tell who was the biggest clown in that cage of lunatics. Everyone joined in with devilish glee. Only Joyce responded differently to the mockery. He remained aloof, offering his person to mockery as he would have offered his body to torture. The rebellion inside him turned into a yielding meekness. He drooped like a rag. He looked around as if he were lost. He was as passive as a repentant sinner and exuded humility. Walking the streets with his head in the clouds or entering the classroom with a pious bow, pinched face, and sheep's eyes, he looked like the Grand Black Knight in the Lodge of Benevolent Death.

Moving listlessly and disjointedly and without paying any attention to the blockheads, he would approach the first stool his eye fell on, collapse on it like a deflated balloon, and begin to lecture. But inside him he must have had such a compound of contempt for Mr. B.'s damned creation that I bet the Venerable One would not have liked to hear it expressed from that skilled mouth.

"Here is an exercise. A head of cabbage or the head of a pr——k. Take your choice, gentlemen."

In the room next door a stolid, dim-witted German with glasses perched on the end of his up-tipped nose—a man infatuated by his position—was demonstrating an idiotic sentence in German with lavish care. He discussed the sentence pompously and with all the flowers of rhetoric, as though he were Theodore Momsen explaining to the world the history of ancient Rome. That simpleton had a spectacular imagination. You can see an example of it in the following dialogue, a poetical masterpiece invented by him as part of his teaching method.

It is a farcical dialogue in which the characters are the teacher and the pupil. Here it is:

"Wer ist hier?"

"Herr Professor."

"Wer ist da?"

"Herr Collessor."[11]

"Wer ist hier, wer ist da, Herr Professor, Herr Collessor"—once he got started, the simpleton would never stop; he would go on and on chanting in his dismal, melancholy tone. In the meantime he was measuring the effect it had on the students.

At the right moment, when he sensed the general trance his mellif-luousness had induced in those poor fellows, he would suddenly shake them up and bring them back to reality with another explosive trick of immeasurable effect.

"Hier ist eine gnädige Frau. Diese gnädige Frau ist die Frau B."

And then without stopping to catch his breath:

"Bin ich eine gnädige Frau?"

"You? Anything is possible. But you look to me more like a big ape, mein lieber Herr Professor."

The bomb, you see, had its effect, causing general hilarity and a burst of Homeric laughter. Not knowing Italian, that dullard had not understood a thing, but he was nevertheless happy and would go on with his restless chanting.

"Wer ist hier?"

"Herr Professor."

"Wer ist da?"

"Herr Collessor."

Then there was a little French fellow, a midget gallant, with as many vices as a monkey. He used to walk quickly, on tiptoes, wagging his rear end and clattering his heels on the floor. Aside from smelling of garlic, he hoisted bottles and even more frequently skirts, so the administration sent him off.

And then there was an Englishman, an authentic Englishman, who was Joyce's despair.[12] He was a rather dull-witted young man with no manners and insipid as cork. He must have been a plumber at home before becoming an English teacher, since he corrected sentences the way a plumber fixes toilets. If they worked, fine; if they didn't, let the students fix them themselves.

The farce was hilarious but it could not continue without beginning to annoy the respected audience. Still, between one thing and another we went on like this for a year. There wasn't anyone who hadn't gone through the school. All had laughed enough to pop their navels. It was

11. Ellmann says Joyce himself made up this chant to mock the unimaginative methods of the German teacher, whose name was Marckwardt (*JJ* 194). For a while Joyce exchanged lessons with Marckwardt.

12. Probably H. J. Eyers, the other English teacher at Pola. Joyce discovered that he was a "lovely pianist" and had him over for musical evenings, but on one occasion had to turn him out of the apartment for making Nora cry. He described him as "a thoughtless young chap" (*Letters* II, 95).

only fair to take ourselves and our tents somewhere else. And so we had to leave, letting others have the honor of taking over—others with the same competitive spirit, willing to bark as we did, but—in all modesty—they did not appeal to the public as we did, lacking our esprit de corps.

The carnival—pardon me, the school—ended up in the hands of a German, a former hotel waitress, who was tired of her job and eager to advance herself. Improvising for the occasion, they made her director of the school and language teacher.

Joyce was one of her favorites. She flirted with him. She desired him. She desired his language. Poor Joyce! What a thing to happen to him!

The administration drew up a caricature of a contract with this little finch regarding Joyce. First they tossed him back and forth like a tennis ball. Then, with the skill of a magician, they made him vanish and grabbed him for themselves. They thought, if Joyce is so useful in luring insects for the finch, he might do the same or even better for us in Trieste. And so as soon as they had him in their hands, they seized him, packed him up like a salami, and sent him to Trieste by express freight.

After a while I joined him there.

In Trieste, life as usual: boring, lean, and stormy.

Few successes, many desires, and plenty of hunger. Everything was backwards, even the sense of the famous Tuscan proverb, "Give us a little fresh cheese and less Saint Francis."[13] We paraphrased this as, "They give us a lot of Saint Francis and little fresh cheese." By this we meant that we were given much work but little money. The more we worked, the harder we labored, the less we had in the cupboard. You wouldn't believe me if I told you how awful things were. But we met very interesting people. This at least kept us in good spirits. I have to admit that we used to laugh. Joyce laughed, too, and made us laugh.

Now I want to open a parenthesis—a rather long one, I know—but I must do so to entertain you and at the same time to let you see the constellation of little stars that were gathered around the major star.

I am giving you real life characters, as big as life, body and soul, physical appearance and personality.

How was the school in Trieste run? Who was there? For openers there was Beppino.[14]

13. The point of this proverb lies in Saint Francis of Assisi's devotion to poverty.
14. Real name Bertelli, a German and assistant to Artifoni.

Beppino was a champion boaster from my own town, a bungler, a botcher, a whisperer of tales, and a man on the way up. Having invested a few coins in the school, he began trying to grab everything. He elbowed and shoved other advisers aside, making himself director, head, all in all. He liked to say that he ruled with an iron fist, like Bismarck. As soon as he reached the Papal throne, this cunning and mean sponge started to milk the maximum effort out of his poor priests—I mean his employees. He wanted their hides. He wanted to see them squeezed like lemons. Oh, the stories I could tell you on that subject!

In the hall of the school, on the left wall at the corner, next to the *Stundenplan* (class schedules) and visible as soon as one came in, was a pencil sketch of a man, life size. He was a plain-faced, provincial-looking fellow, perhaps an agent from a farm or a gamekeeper, with a big beard. It was Benoit Malon, a famous French writer, socialist, and economist.[15] He was one of the Evangelists by whom Beppino used to swear.

But the portrait of the saint also had the very modest function of decorating a naked wall, or more likely of hiding where the plaster had fallen off. Beppino would introduce him to everybody, whether asked or not—as Mr. Berlicche.

"Mr. Berlicche," he used to say unctuously. Then, filled with well-practiced theatrical ardor, he would go on piously and obviously moved:

"This is the portrait of our sainted founder," as if to say, "This is the image of the Blessed Virgin of Val di Pompeii, such a miracle worker, you know, that you have only to look at her and she will grant your request."

When some blockhead came within his range by dropping in for information about the school prices and conditions, Beppino didn't want to lose him and so would think up a way of tricking him. Like a good hunter, he would begin by confusing him, taking him on a long detour and almost always bringing up the subject of the portrait.

"Look, Sir, this is our Mr. Berlicche."

And while the poor fellow turned around and ecstatically contemplated the miraculous image, the weasel behind him worked out a deal. Perched on his stool and leaning sharply forward, he quickly added and subtracted. Then he would make a receipt. Discrepancies in his favor were trifles and not to be worried about.

The other would turn around and say hesitantly, "Payment in advance, nicht wahr."

"Ja, jahwohl," the weasel would shamelessly answer immediately and

15. The prominence of this picture of Malon probably owed something to Artifoni, who was a socialist, as Joyce himself claimed to be at this time.

hand him the receipt with a ridiculously elegant gesture. The poor man would loosen his purse strings; the weasel would pocket the money, proud as a peacock. Then they would say goodbye with a great profusion of compliments.

"Danke, danke sehr."

"Bitte, bitte sehr." As soon as the simpleton was out the door, Beppino would rub his hands. Then he would say to himself with devilish glee:

"I just nailed his balls to the floor."

In his best Tuscan, of course.

As long as there were blockheads to dupe and jerks to nail, Beppino never tired of running from the portrait to his chair and from his chair to the portrait in order to stun the poor fools with his chatter. But on other occasions even he understood that the farce with the portrait would not work. Then he would get annoyed with those asking about it, even out of sincere interest, and would answer impolitely like the priest to the urchin.

You don't know the story of the priest and the urchin?

Well then, allow me to tell you. It is a nice story.

One day a priest was distributing communion to the faithful. Among those kneeling around the altar-rail was an urchin who had managed to slip in, only God knows how. First he watched the priest administer the Sacrament and the wafers disappear in the mouths of the faithful; then, seeing the priest walk back and forth, he gradually became arrogant. Finally, raising his voice he began to chant insistently and annoyingly, as children do, "What is that, what is that, what is that?"

The priest ignored him for a while. Then, angered, he turned suddenly toward the boy and, hitting him on his out-stretched hand, crossly said, "Crap!"

"Crap" is what Beppino used to answer when he had other fish to fry and somebody would ask him who that gentleman in the portrait was.

Just like the priest.

His friends, the initiated, knew this habit because, open as he was, he confided it to them in a moment of expansiveness, and they laughed out loud over it as they sat around their tables at the sidewalk cafe.

Beppino was one side of an equilateral triangle. First him. Then his wife. He was stocky and tall and had a black beard. She was a sententious, stringy runt.

She had a heavenly nickname: Cilestrina. Beppino and Cilestrina looked like a foot ruler and a yardstick when they went out for their evening stroll. She knew how to pronounce correctly "Mister J-o-y-c-e," "M-o-n-s-i-e-u-r," "F-r-a-ü-l-e-i-n," and how to pound the piano. She was a miser who would have skinned a flea to sell its pelt.

We were most afraid of her in the morning, when she would come into the school—I am not fooling, the director's wife—laden with stuff for her consort, scurrying around warbling and crowing, her flabby neck sticking out like a turtle's from the frills of her collar. She would trill lovingly when she came in, "Beppino, Beppino!"

This usually happened on Saturday, payday for us teachers, who would be standing in line like the *Hungry Ones* in a French picture at the Revoltella Museum. Payday was an important event and we shall talk again about it later.

"Beppino, Beppino," we would echo in different voices and in different languages from our dark room, which smelled like a chicken coop and had over the door the pompous inscription in capital letters, "Sala dei Signori Professori." And Beppino, who on Saturdays was always in a foul temper, would snort, without looking up from the mystical columns of his account book, "Uhm, Uhm," or at most he would say crossly, "Leave me alone, don't bother me." I think he was trying to develop a better method for nailing humanity. An important task! She, with her warbling and ogling, had him by the tail. But he had his moments, too; Cilestrina could not expect to have him always under her petticoats! And besides, dammit, it wasn't always wintertime when it is so nice to cuddle and keep warm together under the same pair of sheets.

"Beppino, Beppino."

"Uhm, Uhm," we kept saying in two distinct choirs, one answering the other.

"Beppino, Beppino, if you do not pay me, I won't have a cent." This insolent refrain, invented by God knows which hungry poet, toured the gang of teachers. They would pass it on from one to the other, chanting it dismally. He was there listening and sometimes he would swear behind our backs, but it was impossible to tell in which language.

As far as languages were concerned he was almost shameless. He spoke them all without knowing their fundamentals. To solve the most serious problems he had a monster of a sentence put together like a mosaic, with little pieces of words from every European language. This would make him understandable to everyone. No wonder he used to say that he spoke half the languages of the world.

"But French is my *pièce de résistance*," he always used to say. Maybe because of the portrait of Benoit Malon.

When he wasn't able to pay a bill, he would beat about the bush, calling on all his saints for help. He found philology especially useful for getting out of jams. He would start a very important discussion about cognates and similarities among languages with his teachers . . . and then conveniently forget to pay them. Harlequin used to be thrilled by the word, "eftsoons." Beppino was enraptured by the verb, "do not pay." He used to say that it was so beautiful when conjugated in the active form! But, in the passive form, it, too, was crap!

Finally, there was Fock—the third side of the triangle—who looked like a big hunting dog. He also was a Tuscan, mangy, full of fleas, and rigid. He was a real pain in the a—— (watch it, Francini) neck for everyone, teacher and students alike. In the classrooms people were yapping away in all the living languages; in the hall Fock was babbling away. Wasn't this a cage of lunatics? What else could you call it?

Joyce, skinny as an underdeveloped capon, cowardly, and in poor physical shape, was very much afraid of Fock. When he arrived in the morning still half asleep, if he saw Fock sitting complacently in the shadow of his kennel, Joyce would forget about drawing any money, even if completely broke, and would go blank regarding the lesson he had to teach. He would suddenly turn on his heel and slither down two sets of stairs so dark and slick they would frighten anyone. The students awaited Joyce, but it was Fock who would give the lesson instead. Joyce was the regular holder of the English chair, and Fock was his assistant.

The joke of Fock's job gave birth to the suspicion among the teachers that this dog had a very important and well-defined role in the agency, that of keeping troublesome creditors away with his growls. We communicated this suspicion to one another with knowing winks when our tongues had to be still.

Fock had enough to do just killing fleas, but the scummy villain wouldn't miss a word of our joking. He knew that we were being nasty, but he couldn't understand our language. Those strange sounds were unfamiliar to him—we saw to that—but still he must have known that we were mocking his associates and masters. And he was such a runny-nosed stool pigeon that he was capable of telling everything. So he would hang around and listen, staring at us with the hypnotic look that dogs have when they are trying to figure out what you really want of them.

First thing in the morning the trio would divide the day's work and get started: Cilestrina at the fish market, Beppino angling for souls like Saint Peter, and Fock punctually at school. Of the three Fock was most devoted to his work. He could say, "I earn my daily bread by the sweat of my brow." Punctually he was at school, spying. Man's best friend, indeed. The son-of-a-bitch would mark each teacher's absences and tardinesses. He was not a trained dog but rather an infallibly precise machine in the shape of a dog. His mark for tardiness had elaborate scrolls, like river courses on a map. Absences were indicated by small bars, stiff and elongated, like tiny Krupp cannons.

When entering the school Fock would do a little dance—one, two, three—and you could see clearly "cigar butts," as the witty Beppino called them, left by dogs in front of the door, the way they do at every school. Joyce, who couldn't see, would step on them and smash them, but the evidence would stick to the soles of his shoes. His blindness was a great help to this featherbrain.

Then next day Fock would fix matters with the cleaning woman when she came to clean the rooms.

So it went in Trieste before the war, when one made less money and laughed more. In Austria everyone laughed. Harlequin could pay the bills.

On Saturday morning we waited, jammed together in that dark, wretched rat hole (the "Sala dei Signori Professori"), for our extortion, I mean our salary, from Bismarck's hairy hand. We lined up as at a convent door for free soup. We had worked a whole week for this. The band of beggars waited for a sign from his Eminence so that they could enter one after the other to receive the holy alms from his hand.

The roll was called. Who was the first beggar? Do I really need to tell you?

Joyce would burst into the director's office, as straight and erect as a courting pigeon.

"Body of Christ," I would mock him, "you are not at the Bank of England's windows."

It didn't take long to figure out what he had coming, and there was no danger that it would break the bank. Joyce had eaten the egg a week earlier, before it had been laid.

A Maria Theresa's cartwheel, and it was ready.

Joyce would take it haughtily. He would turn it—first heads, then tails—in the palm of his thin, rigid hand and bring it up to his malicious eye; then with contempt he would put it in his pocket and sprint away into the unknown. After a while you would hear a great noise. It was Joyce kicking, in Irish fashion, the door of the first classroom he had bumped into. It was no use telling him that his students weren't there because that wasn't his class. Mulish as a boy, he would refuse to leave, insisting on giving an English lesson where there was supposed to be one in German.

This would make Beppino fly into a rage, but it amused Joyce and the students, who were always able to adapt themselves to funny situations.

Joyce would take out his cartwheel, stare with an evil eye at the first student he saw and ask:

"What is this?"

"It is money."

"Very much or very little?"

"Very much."

"Very money," Joyce would snap at the highpoint of the farce. "Is it my money?"[16]

"Yes, it is your money."

"It is your money, you ass!" And at this point an elegant and very learned discussion between teacher and students would take place on the etymology, meaning, and application of *money* in English and Italian.

One by one, everybody would pitch in.

God knows there were funny types in that tower of Babel.

It's too bad that I am in a hurry to get on, otherwise you would see many flagellants passing across the screen of my magic lantern. But I can't cheat you of the pleasure of an introduction to the number one French teacher, before telling you what happened to me, the last one of the troupe, when it was my turn.

French teacher No. 2, Mr. X—be careful not to mix up my characters —was an Epicurean type with whom Beppino used to share off-color adventures. Cilestrina, of course, didn't know. Therefore, he had to treat him with kid gloves and not upset him for fear of having his little altars uncovered. There were, nevertheless, tensions and even lively quarrels between the two of them over money. The French teacher wanted more and more and Beppino wanted to give less and less, so the French teacher would sharpen his tongue and begin sinking it into the flesh of his accomplice. As their French rose by half-steps, their friendship sank by octaves.

"Never mind," Beppino would say venomously, "better a scratch more from Cilestrina, better a horn more on her forehead than twenty crowns less in my pocket."

But then he would think it over:

"God knows the gossip this quarrel could start."

He didn't exactly like the idea of his gallant little adventures becoming common knowledge.

He would say, "No, it is not worth it," and then would surrender. They were like the two thieves from Pisa who fought with each other during the day and debauched together during the night.

But Frenchman No. 1 was the really interesting character. He was

16. Here the dialogue shifts from English to Italian, and the word used for "money" is "mona," which means "pudenda" in Venetian dialect.

a meek fellow; he looked like the blessed fool Joseph Labre, the saint of dirt.[17] Even his name was Joseph. He was not at all stupid, as all other Frenchmen are, when it came to calculation and diplomacy.

Taught by experience, when things smelled fishy on salary day he let the one behind him in line come forward. In this way he bought time to study the situation and adjust to it. He was acting just as we all do when the Bora blows and we shelter behind a corner waiting for the gusts to pass.

He would wait. And then he would calmly enter. How? Like Don Abbondio pretending to read his breviary.[18] Wiggling his bottom and humming softly the tune of a popular French song, "Il ne peut pas, il ne peut pas, il ne peut pas," he watched the soldier out of the corner of his eye. Beppino, hunched over, would study the maneuver holding his breath, praying to God that the moment soon would pass and pretending to be more and more involved in his paperwork.

All the while the other fellow wouldn't think of disturbing Monsieur le Directeur, who appeared very busy, for all the gold in the world. He was ready to apologize for coming in, except that that also would have been a disturbance. Finally, since no summons came, he would walk without stopping through the director's office and disappear, like Joyce, into the unknown.

Beppino, moved, would listen to the echo of those sweet words, "Il ne peut pas, il ne peut pas, il ne peut pas." But, as soon as the danger was over—that is, as soon as he felt safe from another attack—he would do as snails do and come out of his shell, antennae and all. He would restore and encourage himself with an impudent monologue. He would say to himself, "Can I be more generous than the king himself? If my professors are all *signori* what can I do? Why didn't that proud man come forward? His money was here waiting for him. Did he maybe expect me to deliver it personally to his home by car? Have you ever seen anything like it?"

No judge would have found him guilty.

Then I would come in to spoil his fun. Oh, with me Beppino's arrogance was of a different sort. He would flatter me with insults. He used to say with a mocking guffaw, "You came too late; the bank is closed."

"The bank is closed? The bank is broke!" I would shout, losing my temper.

17. Saint Labre (1748–83), known as "the beggar of Rome," spent years walking from holy place to holy place about Europe, finally settling in Rome where he slept in the Colosseum. He lived on alms and took no care of his body.

18. A character in the popular Italian novel *I promessi sposi* by A. Manzoni. In the scene referred to, Don Abbondio pretends to read his breviary while keeping his eye on two soldiers, hence the following reference to Beppino as "the soldier."

"Get out, you serpent's tongue!" He would confront me, raising his tight, knobby fists to my face. Though I simply wanted what was due me, all I received were threats.

But if he was arrogant, I had a tongue to match. I would say, "Ah, I see it is not only Fock who is assigned to keeping at bay those you owe. I see that you both take your turn at the job and that you compete with him in it!" Oh, what a Columbus I was in my discovery! But all the while I had to be careful and to retreat very slowly toward a corner, always keeping an eye on the brute. These were pleasantries such as are exchanged between equals from the same home town.

In these moments of total confusion, it wasn't unusual to see the secretary come running in and happily announce the visit of a bothersome creditor, for instance the gas man with his bill.

"Mr. Director, the gas man is here."

"Screw you and the gas man!" And then almost invariably the key of the safe had rusted in the lock, or had broken, or had been locked inside (it was Cilestrina's fault), or it had fallen through a hole in his pants, landing—what an accident!—in a rather inconvenient place in his shorts.

I have to admit that as a master of improvisation, Beppino couldn't be beaten. Then, playing his part to the hilt, he would swear, "To Hell with it!"

I never could understand if he meant the key or the gas man.

But if the gas man would not see reason and insisted on being paid or he would cut off the service, Beppino, who could easily smell an impasse, would come out as smooth as the leading man in a pantomime and say, half laughing, half serious, "You will have to come back another time; the key broke in the lock. I already have wired Vienna to send a repairman." Then he would go back to his room happy as could be, humming, "Di quella pira l'orrendo foco." [19]

He thought he could fool the world with such tricks. If they worked, good for him!

On Sundays, Beppino used to rest on his laurels. And on Mondays he was rested after his day off and was easier to get along with. He was even more agreeable if he had been able to trap some bird he had met in a bar. He would say with syrupy sweetness, "Mr. Joyce, this week you shall teach twelve additional hours. Twelve! (He would say it in English so Joyce could understand it better.) Aren't you glad?"

And he would start adjusting his *Stundenplan*—that thing on the wall that I had christened *Fahrplan* (train schedule), much to his anger. This checkerboard was covered with erasures and scribbles that revealed

19. "The sight of that pyre, those cruel flames"—*the* tenor aria in Verdi's *Il Trovatore*, sung by Manrico at the end of act 3.

numerous aborted maneuvers. God help us if it really had been a train schedule! In fact, with his Napoleonic stance, he looked rather like a general studying the map before a battle.

"Aren't you glad, Mr. Joyce?" he would say again.

Joyce, with psychological shrewdness, would answer in Italian with another question: "Got any Theresas? I haven't got a copper and haven't had a drop. Understand?"

❧

Beppino was like the triangular eye of the Almighty. He saw everything and attended to everything. He would open his arms as if to say, Take me, I give my heart.

To get more money he packed students into holes that were as slimy as cesspools and smelled like manure piles. He would have put them in the toilets. When in a friendly way I made him see that this did not consort with the school's reputation and that it was unsanitary besides, Beppino said, drawing out his favorite learned reference: "Shut up, you baboon. Socrates used to teach in the middle of the street."

"No, on the sidewalk, you bassoon," I would snap. "But if Socrates had owned even a hole like your school, Cilestrina—I mean Xanthippe— would not have needed to throw the chamber pot at him, whether it was empty or full doesn't really matter since it cracked the head of the poor old man anyway."

He would sally forth to capture students—Beppino, not Socrates— just as his teachers did to get their pittance from him. No hen could scratch for feed as he did. I don't know how he did it! He scratched them up from everywhere:[20] in the business district, where he lived (I think he was able to lasso even his janitor's wife, a mangy old woman who was deaf and hoarse and couldn't even read or write) at the waterfront—let me recommend those students to you; in the red light section—caught just in time; in the Jewish quarter—brought from hell to heaven, heaven of course being the school, though even Beppino couldn't have believed that; and . . . in the pissoirs. Oh, here things are getting out of hand!

In that perfumed Eden where every good man, as is well known, performs a very important and exasperating function, Beppino (I don't know how he did it!) negotiated, counterattacked, and made deals. He would bring it out—the business of the school, I mean—and get those good men so interested in it that they would forget their own

20. The specific streets mentioned in the list that follows in the text are Via Commerciale, Via della Pozzacchera, Via del Pozzo bianco, and Via delle Zudecche.

little business and—believe it or not—struck dumb, they would follow him, even with—my God, how can I say it—even with their flies open.

"No problem," Beppino would reassure them, "you can finish your business at my place, at the school. The school offers all the comforts."

And finally in the cafe Stella Polare. Does its name, "Pole Star," remind you of anything? It makes me think of the passage in the Gospels about Christmas Eve: "Et, ecce stella quam viderant in oriente antecedebat eos usque dum veniret supra ubi erat puer."[21]

It seems that at the Stella Beppino got into several fights, "dust ups," as we say today, and that punches flew back and forth like the fort of the Belle Alliance. Beppino said that he had given them all, but he was just playing the hero. It was in any case a wonderful method for advertising the school—persuasively.

And then one of the more cocky souls, to goad him, would ask: "Was it a pedagogical punch or a Florentine punch, Beppino?"

"A forbidden punch," he would answer, fiercely grinding his teeth and frothing at the mouth. Now was the time to stop, otherwise one would hear the sad story of the owner of the Stella—in the midst of the fight—crawling on his knees under the tables cleaning up the broken cups and glasses.

Beppino was as unmatchable in finding teachers as in finding students.

One day he brought into the school a book-binder friend of his, dug up God knows where, and introduced him to everybody as a professor who had been called on purpose from Zagreb to teach Croatian. He was a poor stick, who, when he appeared at the school to begin teaching, was as shy and frightened as a little turtledove. Beppino with all his impudence hadn't been able to give him a crumb of courage. That evening Joyce had to hold his sides to keep from bursting with laughter.

One day, and what a sad day it was, Beppino disappeared. It was said that he had emigrated to the New World. In any event, he took leave American style and nobody heard anything about him again.[22] Maybe he went to war to do his duty as a good Italian citizen. I forgot to tell you that he also was a corporal or a colonel in the cavalry. He used to say that he was a general, of course. But corporal or general, what difference does it make?

Jesus—I beg pardon, who?—yes, Jesus, weeping at the wickedness of

21. "And behold, the star that they had seen in the East went before them, until it came and stood over the place where the child was" (Matt. 2.9).

22. Omitting formal leave-taking is thought of as an American habit. Bertelli "had gone off with some of the school's money" (*Letters* II, 161, n. 2). Joyce, who was in Rome at the time of Bertelli's disappearance, wanted to know about it (*Letters* II, 161, 186).

Judas said the terrible words: "Melius erat ei si natus non fuisset homo ille."[23]

Well, Jesus would not have said those words for Beppino. If Beppino hadn't appeared in finished form like Pinocchio from Geppetto's hands, Jesus would have had to create him, along with Cilestrina, Fock, and all the rest. Joyce also agreed on that.

Screw Beppino! However, I shouldn't complain. If he hadn't summoned me and introduced me to that madhouse, which he directed so worthily, I wouldn't have had the good fortune to meet my friend Joyce.

Regarding Joyce I don't need to emphasize that he managed very well in all this hubbub.

He had accepted the situation well knowing that he had to make the best of it, especially in the school, where, if nothing else, he assisted Beppino in contributing to an irresistible hilarity.

Beppino had found the right man.

For him Joyce was always a Cambridge professor—remember that Beppino was an expert in geography—who came on purpose from the other side of the Atlantic to teach us poor devils that a chair has four legs and is a domestic animal belonging to the vertebrate species.

Now there is no need to offend anybody or to feel offended, but can you imagine a Cambridge professor leaving his country expressly to stuff the craws of a few derelicts with outrageous examples like these?

"Berlicche, Berlicche, what have I ever done to you or how have I offended you, that you use me in this way?"

"Mister Berlicche and Mister Joyce: a clown and a beggar."

"Wall-eye or cross-eye give the evil eye."

"A man without debts is repulsive, but one without money is even more repulsive."

"A husband usually is an ox with horns, and his wife without a brain. Together they make a four-legged animal."

"A stuffed roll is the Virgin Mary with child."

"The adulterous wife makes the husband sore."

"What is a pachyderm? That gentleman you see there with a nose like a trumpet and a great belly, that is a pachyderm."

And so on and so forth. All were very useful, very beautiful, very appropriate, and very instructive examples drawn from everyday life, as paraphrased by Joyce. For the more advanced students he had other vignettes, no less diverting, instructive, perspicacious, and expansive.

First vignette: "Mr. B. is an insatiable sponge. His teachers have had

23. "Good were it for that man if he had never been born" (Mark 14.21).

their brains soaked up. And their flesh? These crucified ones are hung on the pole, reduced to skin and bones. I offer myself to my students as an example of the giraffe species, thus teaching zoology objectively, according to the methods of my boss."

Second vignette: "That lady has nice little breasts. But her conscience is as large as a sewer. Her husband is happy because the gallants develop it for him."

Another vignette: "I also develop myself. You should go and do likewise. Suck up fourteen shots of absinthe on an empty stomach and you'll see. If this cure doesn't develop you, you are doomed. You can give up the idea of learning English by the method used here.

"My wife has learned Italian, just enough to run up debts with ease. I don't pay them. Will Berlicche pay them? I don't care. The creditors tell me to . . . be sensible.

"I'm not sensible. As long as a little money comes in, fine. But pay? Not me. I spit on their bills.[24]

"The tax collector is an idiot who is always annoying me. He has filled my desk with little sheets marked 'Warning,' 'Warning,' 'Warning.' I told him that if he didn't stop it, I would send him to be f . . . ound out by that swindler, his master. Today, the swindler is the government in Vienna. Tomorrow it could be the one in Rome. But whether in Vienna or Rome or London, to me governments are all the same, pirates.

"Regarding those little pieces of paper, I told him to go ahead and send them to me anyway. I can use them to scribble these and future caricatures on. Even my wife can use them for that little business that all mothers do for their children.

"Ireland is a great country. They call it the Emerald Isle. The Metropolitan Government, after so many centuries of having it by the throat, has reduced it to a specter. Now it is a briar patch. They sowed it with famine, syphilis, superstition, and alcoholism. Up sprouted Puritans, Jesuits, and bigots.

"Proverbially, our peasants are bred to be a kind of sleepwalker, whose sterile, froglike asceticism resembles that of fakirs. I think they are the only people who when they are hungry eat symbolically. You don't know what eating symbolically means? Let me explain it to you at once.

"The peasant's family, which is very large, is gathered around a rustic

24. In a book he had once lent Joyce, Dario de Tuoni found the following note addressed to Mrs. Joyce from a Trieste firm: "In your interest we invite you to pay up your account within 3 days; otherwise, we will be forced to turn the matter over to our attorney causing you additional expense and inconvenience" (*Ricordi di Joyce a Trieste* [Milan: Insegna del Pesce d'Oro, 1966], p. 18). Like his father, Joyce believed money was to be spent as one wished, which did not include paying bills or, as the following shows, taxes.

table as if it were an altar. Hanging from the ceiling, perpendicular with the middle of the table, is a herring that can feed every one of them. The head of the family arms himself with a potato. Now, he makes the sign of the cross—the 'big cross' as a Tuscan friend of mine says—high on the back of the herring, instead of rubbing the potato on the herring as any numbskull would do. This is the signal, and after him, one by one, the members of the family hieratically do the same. At the end they find themselves staring stonily at each other. The herring is doomed to mummify for posterity, unless it rots or the cat gets it first. This dish is called 'Herring Indicated.' The peasants are very fond of it and, as you see, eat it by the bellyful.

"Strictly speaking, Dubliners are my countrymen. But I don't like talking about my 'dear, dirty Dublin.' The Dubliner belongs to the race of the most vapid and inconsistent charlatans I have ever met in the island or on the continent. That's why the English Parliament has many of the biggest loud-mouths in the world.

"The Dubliner spends his time ceaselessly babbling in bars, pubs, and whorehouses, never tiring of the concoction which he is served and which always is made up of the same ingredients: whiskey and Home Rule. And in the evenings when he can't stand it any longer, swollen with poison like a toad, he feels his way out the door, and guided by an instinct for stability seeks out the sides of buildings, then makes his way home, rubbing his behind along all the walls and corners. He goes 'arsing along,' as we say in English. There you have the Dubliner.

"Ireland, however, is still the brain of the United Kingdom. The foresighted and ponderous English provide humanity's swollen belly with the perfect instrument of comfort: the Water Closet.[25] The Irish, doomed to express themselves in a language that is not their own, have stamped it with their genius and compete for glory with other civilized countries. This is called 'English Literature.'

"This morning—it is strange because it never happens to me—I didn't have a cent to my name. I went to the boss and I told him how it was. The key of the safe wasn't rusty, but he refused to give me an advance, saying I am a bottomless pit. I told him to drown himself in it and left.

"Jesus, what can a poor man do?

"My wife, if nothing else, knows how to produce children and how to blow soap bubbles.[26] Good, then we'll never starve. Children bring wealth, according to the Italian proverb. In fact, Giorgio's shoes are

25. This association of the English with water closets also appears in *Ulysses* (131).
26. Joyce wrote Stanislaus from Rome, "Nora has a talent for blowing soap-bubbles. While I was wading through a chapter of *Dorian Gray* a few days ago she and Giorgio were blowing bubbles on the floor out of a basin of suds. She can make them as big as a football" (*Letters* II, 152).

worn out. But my wife doesn't care and goes on blowing soap bubbles. Balls! We have George the First. If I don't watch out she is liable to stick me with a second heir to the dynasty.

"No, no, Nora, my girl, I have little appetite for that game. Therefore, as long as there are bars in Trieste, I think it is better for your husband to spend his nights out, dangling like an old rag.[27]

"Italian literature begins with Dante and ends with Dante. That's not a little. The whole spirit of the Renaissance is in Dante. I love Dante almost as much as I love the Bible. He is my spiritual nourishment. The rest is ballast. I don't like Italian literature because in the degenerated mentality of Italian writers only these four basic themes predominate: begging orphans and hungry people (when will Italians stop being hungry?), battlefields, animals, and patriotism. Italians have a strange way of showing their patriotism. They want to impose with their fists their intellectual supremacy over other people. Lorenzo the Magnificent, Leonardo, Titian, Michelangelo, Galileo—all good people, I admit. But still I haven't found an Italian yet who hasn't said to me, 'Shut up, you clown! The one immortal work for which Italians are responsible is the founding of the Roman Church.' I, too, say that the Roman Church is great . . . but it is great, great, great as a church and as a . . . Well, what would you say of a tart who appears to you with perfumes, songs, flowers, and music, mourning in black veils and in silken robes on a throne?

"Nevertheless, I don't like Rome. I am not talking of modern Rome, which is as insipid as the government residing in it. Ancient Rome seems like a cemetery to me. The odor of its exquisite panorama clings to the Royal Palace: mortuary flowers, ruins, heaps of bones, and skeletons. Curb your desire and find happiness, they say. The Italians pay dearly for the luxury of having such a panorama. The Rome of the popes appeals to me more because it reminds me of that pig of a pope, Alexander VI, lying in the arms of his daughter and mistress, Lucretia Borgia. Or of Julius II, who built his own tomb while he was still alive; of Leo X and Clement VII, two of the most indecent popes and great friends of Martin Luther. I can understand very well why Ibsen was uncomfortable in Rome.[28]

27. Joyce may have regarded spending his time in bars as a form of birth control; however, he was happy over the birth of his son Giorgio (July 27, 1905) and his daughter Lucia (July 26, 1907). When a third pregnancy resulted in miscarriage, he reported that he seemed to be the only one concerned at the loss (*JJ* 278).

28. This monologue echoes passages in Joyce's letters, where he expressed intense distaste for Rome and particularly for its mortuary atmosphere. In one letter to Stanislaus he said, "The neighbourhood of the Colisseum [sic] is like an old cemetery . . . ," and in another, "Rome reminds me of a man who lives by exhibiting to travellers his grandmother's corpse" (*Letters* II, 145, 165).

"I went to see Zacconi in *Ghosts* and *An Enemy of the People*. Compared with such an actor we who are not Italians should hide our faces. No other country has anything like it. The Italians have an enormous genius for the stage. Definitely they are the greatest actors in the theater of life. Zacconi extracted from Ibsen's drama more than was there. It would be curious to know what Ibsen himself would have thought of it. But I think that Zacconi puts a bit too much of himself into Oswald and Count Vassili. I shall go next to the puppet show, but never again to see *Ghosts* performed by Zacconi."[29]

✤

These are just a few of the fables that bloomed from Joyce's spirit and that I recall from our nearly twenty years of friendship.

But during the period I am speaking of, Joyce was almost at the end of his histrionic career at the school.

One day, modifying Mr. B.'s Hamlet-like question, "Who am I?", he asked himself seriously, "What kind of a joke is this and how long does it have to last?" And in no time he shook the dust of the place from his heels.

"Without proper formalities," you would say.

Not at all, just English style.

And so the merry band of cheaters was screwed.

"Why didn't you put some salt on his tail?" I said with naïve regret to one of them, who was having fits as though a Bird of Paradise had escaped.

"Or rather some silver," he added with great perception.

And he looked out of the window sadly, hoping, perhaps, to catch the sparrow again.[30]

Joyce had escaped from the dark, depressing cloud of the school to freedom, as from dusk to the morning light. His day was dawning. Now he had little desire to laugh but wanted to drink. He embraced the

29. The scene in *Ghosts* where Oswald goes mad was played with such force by Zacconi that Joyce "writhed in pain in his seat and made wild gestures." During another play in which Zacconi was performing Joyce called out, "Nobody back home has any idea there are artists like these" (*JJ* 275). Later in Paris Joyce continued this habit of expressing himself vocally during performances. Likewise, *Ghosts* continued to exert its strange hold over him (see Dr. Giedion-Welcker's recollection, p. 273 and note). "Count Vassily" probably refers to the central character in Turgenev's *A Poor Gentleman*. Joyce saw Zacconi in an Italian version of this play, *Il pane altrui* (*JJ* 275).

30. Joyce left the school in the summer of 1907 and thereafter taught English by private lessons. He had made a very favorable impression as a teacher, especially on several of his aristocratic students, who had praised him to the director, hence the concern over losing his services (*Letters* II, 94).

holy oil with passion. He knew by heart all the little holes in the wall around town and could locate them even by feel. The great problem came when he had to get out and find the bowel that would lead him from the blind gut of the old part of town to the main street. Then he would grope along with his hands, trying to chase the fog away from before his eyes, and, if he managed to find the main street, he would run down it until he reached the corner. Here he would prop himself against the wall and wait for some Samaritan to come and collect him.

Once in Rome when more muddled than usual, he received the charity of two crooks, who lightened his load by relieving him of his wallet and then accompanied him to the police station pretending to be patrol officers.

During his many reconnoiters around Trieste he had discovered among the various bartenders and tipplers a certain Sicilian tavern owner whom he had nicknamed "Storky."[31] He wanted me to meet him. His place was in Via Belvedere. He was a chubby little barrel, rosy as a doll's face, with two little elf's eyes in which all the alertness and craftiness of his race shone. He was all eyes when it came to checking on the crew camped among his vats. His nickname fit perfectly because he had a strange way of carrying his neck to one side and of standing balanced on one foot when he was listening to someone, just like a stork.

"It takes one to know one, Joyce," I told him. "Storky is a character but, admit it, you are one, too." And Joyce would laugh, his chin protruding like an old shrew's. He laughed because, although already drunk and glassy-eyed, he enjoyed stuffing poor Storky's head with extraordinary stories about the Emerald Isle. He would go on and on with a loquacity well oiled by wine. Storky, who was the only sober one among that unsteady herd, became stupefied. Without understanding a particle of what Joyce was saying, he would smile and say, "What things you know."

And as for me, who can't tolerate drunks, out of devotion to our

31. "Cicogno" in the original. Joyce had the habit of associating people, on the basis of some slight similarity, with animals and occasionally with vegetables. At various times he associated himself with the giraffe, the spider, and the grasshopper. The suggestion in an early draft of Gorman's biography that he was congenial with Dublin publicans called forth the following stiff note from Joyce: "*Davy Byrne*—I cannot find where the name of this publican occurs. Wherever he occurs he is a tiresome bore. [Joyce] did not know him or any other publican in Dublin however much he may have frequented their grimy houses. The only one to whom he ever spoke was the landlord of the "Ship" in Abbey Street and then only the exchange of cordialities. . . . In other words the 'over the counter' familiarity which seems to be implicated was non-existent" (Croessmann Collection, Carbondale). Joyce's delight in conversing with Davy Byrne's Triestine counterpart, "Cicogno," is an early illustration of the greater ease he felt in his relations with Europeans.

friendship I had to watch helplessly the spectacle of a good man reduced to nothing, nor could I neutralize matters by hiding him from the sight and mockery of the others. I had to accept the situation and smell Joyce's alcoholic breath, while in chorus with the other drunkards he roared a high-pitched, out of tune,

Ancora un litro di quel bon
Che no go la ciave del porton.[32]

But afterwards the problem was mine. How could I manage to get him home? I can assure you there was only one way; that is, to do as Simon of Cyrene did in helping Him carry the cross or, maybe even worse, load the dead body on my shoulders like Joseph of Arimathea and lower it in its grave.

In order to excuse my friend it is my duty to mention that these acts of desperate excess always occurred when his life was at its unhappiest. His artistic reversals had a disastrous effect on his animal spirits. His self-destruction was cold and premeditated. He would plunge recklessly when the world treated him badly.

I had great respect for the genius who was my friend, and it tormented me to observe the cynicism of a man consciously bent on suicide and darkness.

I knew better than anybody else.

He had climbed the first step to fame. It was the critical year of his life, the one when *Dubliners* was born, this jewel for which a Calvary had been reserved.

The manuscript was persecuted as soon as it entered the United Kingdom, and the English censors gave it no quarter. Preventive sequestration, banishment, confiscation, destruction of the plates after they already had been set up.[33] Anyone, even someone physically stronger than Joyce, would have lost his reason.

32. Roughly translated, "Of the good stuff let's have more / Because I've lost the key to my door." Francini gives the impression here of being more puritanical and dour than he apparently was in fact. Herbert Gorman writes, "There were evenings in the house on the Via Giovanni Boccaccio when Francini-Bruni would get into the infant Giorgio's carriage, suck at a milk bottle and cry, squeal and regurgitate like a baby while Joyce trundled him about the place. This would be at midnight. And after the clowning was over Joyce would sing Gregorian chants and the excitable Francini-Bruni, who had a high shrill laugh like a goat, would kiss the singer in an ecstasy of joy. Many a bottle of Triestine wine was emptied over the midnight table . . ." (*James Joyce* [New York: Farrar and Rinehart, 1939], p. 159).

33. English censors did not lay hands on the manuscript of *Dubliners*, but Irish and English publishers stalled for years over accepting the book as written. In 1912 printed sheets and presumably the plates of the book were destroyed by the printer John Falconer, an incident which inspired Joyce's broadside "Gas from a Burner" (*JJ* 346). *Dubliners* had no trouble from censors after it was published in 1914.

"Joyce, my friend," I would plead with him, "Joyce, don't be foolish. You should not give this satisfaction to your enemies. You brought your poor frail self here to this hospitable country where you have new friends who love you and respect you. Don't make a despicable wreck of it. You consciously darken your intelligence in a fury of alcoholism and madness. Stop this life of perdition. I know that what is happening is horrible, but it will pass. You are young. You have talent and time. You have a wife and children. This should be enough. Take courage."

Should I say that, moved by my words, Joyce, like the sheep-killing wolf, would cry and make resolutions and the next day would do the same as before, or worse? I'll not say it.

In those moments if you asked him, for example, about Ireland, you would have heard a man discoursing on the heartrending state of his land, all the while showering it with scorn, his moist eyes gazing at some point in the void. In an outburst of weeping he would speak of the tears cried from thousands of eyes by thousands of tormented souls over the course of the centuries, trying himself to drown those tears in a river of eloquence. Here was the sorrow of the laughing Pagliacci.

The war separated us for four years. Then I saw him again for several months, as you saw him yourself, just after the Armistice when he returned to Trieste to finish *Ulysses*. Triestine types must have offered him plenty of useful material, and Trieste thus has its baptism in this universal book written in the most universal language.[34] And then he left again.

So that you don't get the wrong idea, you should know that Joyce is a great gentleman, a born gentleman. He comes from a very noble family in the West of Ireland, a region that bears the name of his ancestors—the Joyce Country. He stinks of the gentleman a mile away, even when he is stinking drunk. He is proud of his origins, as you can see by the family portraits on the walls of his apartment. Excesses are one thing: true nature is another. "Spiritus quidem promptus caro autem infirma."[35]

Naturally, I don't expect you to reconstruct from these butcher's scraps the mentality, let alone the personality, of James Joyce. I have given you the small-change part of the man's life, my purpose being to speak to you less of the personage and more of the person. If you can trace the original features through the distortions of caricature, you

---

34. According to Ellmann the Triestines who probably contributed most substantially to *Ulysses* were Italo Svevo and Teodoro Mayer, publisher of the *Piccolo della Sera* (*JJ* 385). Joyce told Gorman that "there were two other major models for Bloom [besides Mr. Hunter in Dublin], one in Trieste, one in Zurich, the former Greek, the latter Hungarian" (note in the Gorman papers in the Croessmann Collection at Carbondale).

35. "The spirit is willing, but the flesh is weak" (Matt. 26:41).

essentially will have Joyce more or less as he appeared to those who were lucky enough to know him. On the other hand, it is not easy to reconstruct him in his entirety. The problem is like this: given the pieces for constructing a Christ, you must search among those scattered here and there and then assemble them one by one. But you find that they do not fit exactly. This piece would fit here if it were cut better, but it isn't. Never mind. Joyce put it there, and we shall put it there, too.

How can one discriminate? Joyce is all discordant. His head is a hive of discordant and disconnected ideas. All the same, there is a perfect order in it. If there is chaos, it is in his soul. You have to take him as he is. He is not to be imagined trivially as an undistinguished puppet of a man, the way one generally imagines men, ruled by the necessities of life, bodily needs, and the low tastes of the masses. Joyce is the inconceivable absurdity. He is an alloy composed of elements which, according to the laws of physics, should repel one another but which instead hold together through a miracle of molecular aggregation.

I would say in general that Joyce, constitutionally frail and hysterical, oscillates between the mud of the earth, to which he is bound by the law of gravity and in which he wallows, and a refined intellectuality that reaches the summits of asceticism. His is a seeking mind of the very first order in an unusually sensitive body. His morbid sensitivity is joined to a metaphysical sense of values so paradoxical with respect to the work of others that you find him accepting equally eagles and rabbits, the sun and the mud puddle. Where there is Ibsen and Dostoevsky, why not Verlaine? Even if they say too much and he says nothing. The Himalayas and Parnassus of thought on one hand, and the nullity of an ephemeral paradise on the other.[36]

He makes an idol of no one. I don't think Joyce idolizes even Ibsen, who for a long time sustained the young man's journey.

36. Joyce had read Dostoevsky, but this is the only indication that he had any special regard for the Russian novelist. He admired Verlaine's poems. Dario de Tuoni (*Ricordi di Joyce a Trieste*, pp. 60–61) recalled that during evening walks they used to take in Trieste Joyce "would often stop to recite [Verlaine's] 'Les sanglots longs / Des violons / De l'automne / Blessent mon cœur / D'une langueur / Monotone.' Or stopping where the shades grew darker, he would exclaim in a mysterious grieving tone: 'O triste, triste était mon âme / A cause, à cause d'une femme.' Or he would bend down his head under the weight of those desolate verses: 'Un grand sommeil noir / Tombe sur ma vie,' and then go on in a whispering, almost secret voice: 'Je suis un berceau / Qu'une main balance / Au creaux d'un caveau; / Silence, silence!' "

The first of these Verlaine passages comes from "Chanson d'automne" in *Poèmes saturniens*; the second from *Romances sans paroles*, VII; the last two from *Sagesse*, III, v. They are contained in *Œuvres complètes de Paul Verlaine* (Paris: Editions Messein, 1911), vol. 1. For Joyce's translation of "Chanson d'automne" see *JJ* (79, note); and for another instance of his reciting Verlaine, see below (p. 72).

In the pages of England's most intellectual magazine the sharp-toothed eighteen-year-old puppy hurled himself at a critic who had referred to Ibsen as a "dirty dog." This was the time of the play *When We Dead Awaken*, which had just been performed for the first time in England.[37]

Eighteen! I don't know if he would do the same now, at forty. Joyce is changeable, not through capriciousness but because the intellectual process works in him more rapidly and more intensely than in most people. Either he leans too far out toward the future or sticks too close to the past. When he really admires something he is not changeable, and he only admires completely the unchangeable: the mystery of Christ and the mute drama of the literature that surrounds it. Even here his attitude is determined by his acute sensibility. I can well imagine that his head was full of this mystery when he wrote *Ulysses* and that there in lies the allegorical point of this story of new martyrdom. Martyrs he gives us, but nothing of the messianic.

Joyce the writer is anything but the quintessence of a saint, anything but the quintessence of perfumed charity. He would be a complete enigma if he weren't a terrifying dialectician. He stretches language to express commonplace vices in a desolate and pitiless way that sends chills up the spine. Tongue ever turns to aching tooth.

It is not his fault that the material he works with appears dirty. Society is offended and that is natural since it is still so sunk in the mire as to feel scandalized at the putrefaction which Joyce reproaches it for.

Joyce is not irreligious. He is without religion. There is a difference. He doesn't even believe the bread he is eating. He is so consistent in his unbelief that his children have not been baptized. I, bonehead, without being asked never tired of telling him what I thought of this arrogance. And every time he would answer with the same argument: "Shut up, melon head!" Then the conversation could continue without difficulty.

In his house there is no religious practice, but on the other hand there is much talk of Christ and religion and much singing of liturgical chants. I can go even further. You had better not look for Joyce during the week before Easter because he is not available to anyone. On the morning of Palm Sunday, then during the four days that follow Wednesday of Holy Week, and especially during all the hours of those great symbolic rituals at the early morning service, Joyce is at church, entirely without prejudice and in complete control of himself, sitting in full view and close to the officiants so that he won't miss a single

37. Joyce's essay on Ibsen, published in the *Fortnightly Review* in 1900, focuses on *When We Dead Awaken*. In the essay he mentions a critic having called Ibsen "a muck-ferreting dog" (*CW* 48).

syllable of what is said, following the liturgy attentively in his book of the Holy Week services, and often joining in the singing of the choir.[38]

Joyce would not sacrifice a minute of this annual pleasure, not even for an intellectual kingdom.

Two years ago when he arrived here from Switzerland, among many interesting things in his briefcase he had the score of a liturgical piece with an exquisite motif that he had patiently copied from the original in the archives of an old Helvetian abbey. The motif was for the Easter Introit, "Vidi aquam egredientem de templo a latere dextro. . . ."[39] It was a wonderful example of a pure Gregorian chant, which he sang many times, accompanying himself on the piano. He sang it with an intense feeling made all the more striking by his nasal voice.

Joyce, born a Catholic in the most Catholic country in the world, was educated in a Jesuit boarding school.[40]

The Jesuits could be proud if such a student were restored to the Catholic faith. In the meantime Joyce remembers the Congregation of Saint Ignatius proudly.

Depending on the effect of their religious instruction, there are some who always move closer to the Supreme Good and others who move away. Joyce wandered away. But much of the instruction remained. This included first of all a lasting foundation of knowledge about church doctrine and liturgy—that is an enormous achievement— and secondly a Jesuitical casuistry of which Joyce can boast himself master. This means that he has the ability to confuse an opponent in a mesh of dialectical subtleties, make him skid on the pavement of the discussion, or lose him in a perverse labyrinth with an ambush around every corner.

This dialectic, which at times has the closely woven solidity of Saint Thomas Aquinas and at times the warm expansiveness of Saint Augustine, is a powerful weapon for a keen mind, and cannot be acquired at the desks of public schools.

---

38. Jacques Mercanton's recollection (pp. 214–15) shows Joyce still attending Easter services over twenty years later. The early morning service with the "great symbolic rituals" probably refers to the Holy Saturday service that Joyce attended with Mercanton, where the new fire, incense, paschal candle, and baptismal water are blessed.

39. "I saw water flowing from the right side of the temple. . . ." Stephen Dedalus sings this chant in the "Circe" chapter (*U* 431–32). As Weldon Thornton points out, after Willis E. McNelly, this piece is not the Introit for Paschaltide, but the Antiphon that is used with the Asperges during Paschaltide (i.e., from Easter Sunday to Whit Sunday)" (*Allusions in "Ulysses"* [Chapel Hill; University of North Carolina Press, 1968], p. 359).

40. Except for two years at a Christian Brothers' school, all of Joyce's education was under the Jesuits, first at Clongowes Wood, then at Belvedere, and finally at University College, Dublin.

Everything Joyce says or writes is full of this casuistry. He knows thoroughly what he is up to. He displays his full knowledge of a subject. He is familiar with the propounders of ideas and with their opponents, from the Irishman John Duns Scotus and the famous Erigena who lived in France at the time of Charles the Bald, on down.[41] Likewise he is familiar with all the great questions about religious issues and dogmas.

He considers Dante the master of the metaphysical world, the Minerva of Christian thought.

Two cardinal points dominate Joyce's star-studded sky—I don't know whether they can be described better as inaccessible mountains covered with snow or as central intelligences of the universe. They are the keys to the Incarnated Word: Saint John the Evangelist and Saint Thomas Aquinas, enraptured faith on the one hand and subtle reasoning on the other. It's not surprising that Joyce once suddenly uttered this unexpected aphorism: "The Roman Church is eternal; it cannot die and will not die." The corollary is that the Italian people, who created it, cannot die and will not die either. Joyce's affection for them stems from this notion.

Tell me if this soul isn't an enigma. I have been wondering about it for twenty years.

With whom is he to be compared? Is he to be called a Voltaireian? Not at all. An intellectual anarchist? This is such a trite phrase that it would disgust him.

I don't pretend to have all the right answers, but I feel that Joyce definitely is a negator.

Knowing the demands of his individualistic nature, I think his full knowledge that God condemns intellectual arrogance as the most irreparable of sins attracts him to it all the more, in a sort of Dionysian contradiction.

Ed ei s'ergea col petto e con la fronte
Come avesse l'Inferno in gran dispitto.[42]

Disdain, not defiance: Farinata, not Capaneo. Joyce is, in fact, the eternal contradictor.

---

41. Though they are often thought to have been born in Scotland, there is some reason to believe that Duns Scotus (c. 1266–1308) was born in Ireland and even more reason to believe that John Scotus Erigena (c. 800–c. 877) was.

42. "And he rose up to front me, face and breast, / As if of Hell he had a great disdain" (*Inferno*, canto 10, lines 35–36). This passage describes Farinata, whom Francini alludes to in the next sentence. Capaneo, also alluded to in that sentence, appears in canto 14 of the *Inferno*.

His attitude is as enigmatical toward politics as toward the Church. He told me one day, "My political faith can be expressed in a few words. Monarchies, constitutional or not, repel me. Republics, bourgeois or democratic, also repel me. Kings are clowns. Republics are worn out slippers that fit every foot. The Pope's temporal power is gone and good riddance. What is left? Do we want monarchy by divine right? Do you believe in the sun of the future?"[43]

I believe in Jesus, I mean the Man-God. Of course, Joyce doesn't; never mind, I still like him.

Through negation, derision, and sarcasm I come closer to Christ, and I am happy there. It doesn't matter if I blaspheme occasionally. It shouldn't be so, but it's a damned law of the Italian people to destroy idols and rebuild them again immediately afterwards in their hearts or on the sacred ground of immortal Rome. It is written on the terracotta vases of Montelupo. It's a commonplace that it has been like this for centuries.

Poor Saint Gennaro is so encrusted with the vituperation of his people that either out of distraction or fear his blood has solidified.[44] And no amount of lancing can make it flow again. The faithful invoke him and pray to him, but this screeching to Saint Gennaro is like pissing on the wall. He remains indifferent, cold. Even blasphemies slide off his back. Seriously, if it were true that a little blasphemy is all right and a great fat blasphemy even better, then the Neapolitans would receive all the miracles they ask for and Saint Gennaro would be spouting blood from every pore.

Joyce doesn't do it. He doesn't blaspheme because the Irish don't have our ambition in that exercise. He doesn't destroy and he doesn't rebuild. He does worse; he denies. He moves further and further even from Christ the Man. I feel sorry for him because I love him, because I would like to see him happy, and because happiness cannot be found in our talents, in the approval of the world, or in the masterpieces that we create. Happiness can be found only in the teachings of Jesus, over whose last words, "Eli, Eli, lamma sabactani,"[45] I have seen Joyce cry secret tears.

You are wise, Joyce, and you cannot laugh at the honorable intentions of a friend. You believe me because you know that I make sense. I pray that Jesus may give you the light of his faith, just as the rising

43. The phrase "sun of the future" refers to the Italian Socialist party and comes from the party's anthem.

44. Saint Gennaro, whose body is in Naples, is famous for the annual miracle in which his blood is supposed to liquefy.

45. "My God, my God, why hast thou forsaken me" (Mark 15.34).

sun striking the Prophet of Israel suddenly restored his power of speech. "Per viscera misericordiae Dei nostri in quibus visitavit nos oriens ex alto."[46]

TRANSLATED BY CAMILLA RUDOLPH ET AL.

Recollections of Joyce

By *Alessandro Francini Bruni*

WE MET IN POLA in 1904. Joyce had come from Ireland and I from Florence, both for the same purpose—to teach at the Berlitz School, he English and I Italian.

In Pola, as Gabriele d'Annunzio once said, the air was filled with the languages of Babel. For us the Babel outside simply was a continuation of the Babel inside. Nearly everyone knows about the Berlitz School. We taught practically all the languages of Europe: French, English, German, Spanish, Hungarian, Russian, Serbo-Croatian, and Slavic. We also had exceptional students, among whom the most illustrious, I recall, was Lord Horthy, the ex-regent of Hungary. There were a group of us, each teaching the language of his native country. We were all moderately friendly with each other, according to our inclinations. I was the director.

Because of certain affinities Joyce and I became friends, setting ourselves apart from our colleagues, who were a mixed lot. Our two families led a communal, bohemian life. Joyce's first child, Giorgio, was born in Pola, not exactly on a straw bed but certainly naked.[47]

"Do ut des,"[48] we used to say—Joyce made much more progress learning Italian from me than I in learning English from him. This was not due to laziness on my part. Joyce grabbed but did not give.

46. "Through the bowels of the mercy of our God, in which the orient from on high hath visited us" (from the Mass for the Dead, the Burial). Francini probably means to imply the line following the one he quotes: "Illuminare his, qui in tenebris et in umbra mortis sedent" ("To enlighten them that sit in darkness and in the shadow of death").
47. Giorgio was born in Trieste.
48. I give so that you may give."

Although he made sure of my *do* in Italian, I never got his *des* in English. Unable to be his student, I adapted myself to being his teacher, and what I lost in the exchange I recovered in authority. In fact, Joyce was not a beginner in the study of Italian. His progress up the scale of Italian phonetics had gone beyond the simple *do*. He had started studying Italian in Dublin. He could understand everything and read everything, though he had spent most of his time learning critical trifles and philological esoterica. He could quote Dante and Dino Campagni[49] from memory. But if he had to speak the language he got nowhere. His syntax was so garbled that he sounded like an escapee from a madhouse; however, he was an intelligent student and made progress. In one year he learned so well that I had to put the brakes on his linguistic enthusiasm to leave time for my own program and keep from being pushed too far into the dark labyrinth of linguistic curiosities and improprieties.

In the summer of 1905 we left Pola, he forced to go and I after him, expelled as an undesirable alien.[50] We drifted toward Trieste, where once again the Berlitz School rescued us. For six months we returned to living together. We shared a house half-and-half, in fact among three, since in the meantime Joyce's brother Stanislaus had arrived from Ireland. He stayed in Trieste and for twenty years was professor of English at the University. It was the most tormented period of our communal life. Joyce had begun to bend the elbow.

One day when he was drunker than usual, I said to him sharply, "My old Bacchus, have you gone mad?"

He answered meekly as an unweened calf, "No, I am developing myself."

He was glassy-eyed and thick tongued. That kind of development pleased me little and it pleased his brother even less, who showered him with invective enough to crush him. It was a comic scene, these Irishmen exchanging insults in Italian! Apparently they found English a less effective instrument than Italian for venting their emotions.

As long as the verbal blast continued, Joyce's tactic was to fold himself up completely and become silent and passive. That way he allowed

49. Apparently Dino Compagni (1260?–1324), a Florentine and contemporary of Dante. He wrote a few poems but is best known for his "Chronicle."

50. In a passage footnoted "Interview with A. Francini Bruni, 1954," Ellmann says, "The Austrians suddenly discovered an espionage ring in Pola, in which an Italian was prominently involved; in reprisal, they decided to expel all aliens from the city. Francini through influence was able to stay on for two weeks to settle his affairs, but Joyce had to leave at once" (*JJ* 201). This explanation of Joyce's departure conflicts with Francini's 1922 recollection. Seldom if ever silent about possible instances of persecution, Joyce said simply that he was "transferred" to Trieste (*Letters* II, 84). (Thomas Staley called this discrepancy to my attention.)

the storm to pass, and soon returned on his course toward—the bottle. Then little by little he crept out from under the incubus of rebuffs and launched into some discourse, his tongue oiled by a certain little wine from Lissa. Later on his exuberance was broken by periods of moderation, but that summer he reached the summit of his Bacchic indulgence. A liter of Opollo wine and later a flask of Tuscan had a place of honor on his work table.

In these circumstances he preserved a lucid subconscious, kept his imagination alive, and even planned the overall design of his works.

However ironically he may have treated it, Ireland was his agony. His spirit, particularly when he was depressed, would always return to Ireland. And if you were to ask him then what was on his mind, you would have heard a man discuss the torment of his country, showering it with mockery, while drowning his grimaces in a flow of unrestrainable tears.

One day we decided to go our own ways. Joyce went to live on Via Donato Bramante in the new district between St. Giusto and Montrizza in an apartment which he fitted out with custom-made furniture, constructed according to designs found in a Danish catalogue. This expenditure reflected not only his devotion to Ibsen but also a rise in his standard of living. Even after our separation we saw each other often, passing our free time together, usually at the Joyces'. He was as astute in his reasoning as he was amiable in his conversation. We discussed a variety of subjects—literature, art, and religion. We used to sing together. Religion and music were of equal interest to us. Born with a musical talent, Joyce had an inclination for liturgical chant. He had a tenor voice that seemed naturally suited to this kind of music. We frequently listened in astonishment as he sang parts in the traditional Gregorian style.

Joyce's interest in art was limited to Meštrović. He had an unbounded admiration for this Serbian sculptor, whom I believe he came to know in Rome. He had gathered various reproductions, cut out from here and there, assigning entirely subjective interpretations to their meanings and to the artist's intentions.[51]

Among Italian poets he preferred Prati, whose Ruello and Azzarellina

51. In his room Joyce kept three photographs of sculptures by Ivan Meštrović (1883–1962). "One represented a peasant woman, belly swollen, face contorted with labor pain, her sparse hair half covered by a wretched wig. Joyce's title for this was 'Dura Mater.' The second was a mother and child, the bony infant hanging from a withered breast, and under this he had written 'Pia Mater.' The third photograph was of an ugly old woman naked, and under it Joyce had had engraved the lines from Canto V of the Inferno: '*Elena vidi, per cui tanto reo / Tempo si volse . . .*' (Helen see, for whom so long / A time of ill revolved . . .)" (*JJ* 392).

had become mythic characters in his repertoire of universal poetry.[52] He set Azzarellina to music.

One year in honor of our suffering fatherlands we arranged to celebrate together the festival of Saint Patrick, the national saint of Ireland. My family and I celebrated the occasion with patient curiosity—the Joyce family almost with solemnity. The most serious part of the festivities was the preparation of the plum pudding, which, according to Irish tradition, required nine days to perfect. Joyce had to go from shop to shop searching for the ingredients. The entire family, including the writer himself, zealously joined in the preparation, disproving the proverb that "too many cooks spoil the broth." The pudding was exquisite. My family, of course, was invited; but in order not to appear simply as a freeloader and to give the impression of helping with this dish, I went each day at the same hour, like a doctor visiting a patient, to receive the tidings.

"How is the lump? Is it swelling? Has it begun to suppurate? Is a scab forming?" I would ask.

"Fine, fine," one or the other of the Joyces would answer from the top of the lighted stairway.

The ninth day found us nine devoted souls punctually at dinner on Saint Patrick's Day. The coincidence of the prophetic number nine was immediately noted, of course. The pudding, which was brought to the table on a large serving plate resembling the shield of Achilles, was of colossal proportions, sinuous and eroded, with cavities like the moon. One would have thought that it could never be eaten or that, as it had required nine days to create, so it would take at least nine to consume. This proved only an illusion—the saffron-colored planet disappeared in a flash.

In June 1906, I joined the staff of the *Piccolo*, while Joyce went his own way. Restless and discontented with his situation, he left the Berlitz School to devote his time to private teaching. Soon, however, he decided to leave Trieste for Padua and Rome.

In Padua Joyce, who already had a doctorate in letters from the University of Dublin, was awarded the diploma of Abilitazione, qualifying him to teach English in the Italian schools.[53] But he did not make

52. Giovanni Prati (1815–84) was a romantic poet whose patriotic verse was very popular in the nineteenth century. He does not seem a likely candidate for Joyce's admiration.

53. Francini's chronology is confused here. Joyce left for Rome in July of 1906, returning to Trieste in March of 1907. He quit the Berlitz School later that year. The trip to Padua was in the spring of 1912 to take an examination qualifying him to teach in the public schools. The two essays by Joyce that Louis Berrone discovered in 1975 in the files of the University of Padua were part of this examination. Berrone confirms Ellmann's statement that though Joyce's scores

use of his diploma. In Rome he became a bank clerk. It was a diversion for him to see the city, but the year was also one of hardship for his family. Feeling himself free and unrestrained, Joyce resumed his senseless wine drinking with the *vino de li castelli*. Because of his over-indulgence and loss of interest in his work he hastily returned to "his" Trieste, where he renewed his old acquaintances and pattern of life. Later he was invited to occupy the chair of English literature in the secondary school, Scuola Superiore di Commercio Revoltella, now a university. He remained there until the end of his stay in Trieste.

It was during these years that the *Piccolo della Sera* published a number of Joyce's articles, written in his usual densely packed and vigorous style. Though veiled in a steely coldness, they are intense pieces treating various burning issues related to his native Ireland. I recall well such titles as "The Last Fenian," "Home Rule Comes of Age," and "Ireland at the Bar."[54]

In August 1914 the war erupted, and ten months later I returned to Italy for the mobilization. Joyce, physically unsuited for soldiering, an English subject, and a friend of Prince Hohenlohe, whose sons were his former students, obtained a visa to enter Switzerland, although he was considered at that time an enemy alien. He chose to settle in Zurich and remained there until the end of the war, while his brother Stanislaus was confined to a concentration camp in Moravia. When Joyce left for Switzerland we separated with tears in our eyes and a heartfelt handshake.

Joyce's sojourn in Switzerland marked the beginning of his recognition as a writer. This favorable turn brought an improvement in his domestic and financial affairs. His acquaintances in Zurich, especially among wealthy Americans who were safe from the scourge of war, opened important doors of editors in England and America—doors which until then had been implacably closed to him.[55]

---

were high the Italian officials refused to recognize his B.A. diploma from Dublin and thus did not grant him the degree, as Francini says they did. (See *JJ* 331–33 and Louis Berrone, "Two Essays by James Joyce Unveiled," *Journal of Modern Literature*, 5 [February 1976]: 3–18.) Nevertheless, Joyce's friends in Trieste managed to get him a post at the Commercial High School (Scuola Superiore di Commercio Revoltella) in Trieste. He taught there in the mornings and gave private lessons in the afternoons. Dario de Tuoni describes how the cramped Joyce household was arranged to allow giving lessons there (*Ricordi di Joyce a Trieste*, pp. 9–12).

54. See Silvio Benco's recollection (pp. 52–54) for a discussion of these articles.

55. The only wealthy American Joyce knew in Zurich was Edith Rockefeller McCormick, who became his patroness for a year and a half and gave him a substantial monthly stipend. They were not close friends. It was the American poet, Ezra Pound, who was principally responsible for opening the doors of American and English publishers to Joyce.

After the war Joyce reappeared in Trieste, having returned to complete his *Ulysses*. In fact, some Triestines served as models for certain characters in his novel. Then we saw each other again and relived some of those hours that we had shared in the past. However, times had changed and Joyce was obviously no longer the same man. He seemed serious, almost conventional now.

Here the memoirs of my personal contact with Joyce end. He remained in Trieste until 1922,[56] the year in which we separated forever. He moved on to Paris and I returned to Florence to assume a newspaper position. For a while we heard of one another by way of friends and occasionally letters. But Joyce rarely wrote. Suffering from an eye ailment, he now required the services of a secretary.

It is difficult indeed to assess the personality of the Irish writer, even for me who observed him during his formative years. He had the temperament of an incoherent sophisticate, who was discriminative, destructive, and contradictory in all speculations concerning metaphysics, morality, esthetics. . . .[57]

It is not true, as the carelessly improvised biographies assert, that Joyce knew seventeen languages. That's a joke! He did not know even Irish, the language of his fathers. He spoke and wrote French and Italian, as well as English, with great skill, but his knowledge of other languages was limited.[58] Joyce used English with the precision of an expert craftsman. His stylistic innovations and way of treating his material have never been attempted by another writer.

English speakers may live in Italy as long as they like, but they will never be able to mask the hissing "s" which is typical of their language and of others. Joyce pronounced Italian in a way that would deceive others about his foreign origin. He knew Latin but not very well. I was convinced that he knew just enough about Ciceronian Latin to satisfy his general cultural needs. Never did I hear him claim to know Greek. It is possible that he learned it as an old man, as did Cato, though this does not seem likely. Most linguists are well aware that one lifetime is not enough to master the classical languages. On the other hand, it is possible not to know Homer's language and still to have a profound knowledge of Greek literature. So it was with Joyce. There is considerable difference between making this assertion and claiming that he

56. Actually, 1920.
57. Several pages of the original have been omitted here. They contain a nearly verbatim repeat of passages from Francini's earlier recollection, along with some critical commonplaces about Joyce's work.
58. Joyce was fairly accomplished in Danish and German, as well. In addition, he took lessons in Flemish, Spanish, and Russian and knew various other languages, including Latin and modern Greek. He took some lessons in Gaelic as a young man, but had only a limited knowledge of it.

knew so many living and dead languages. One cannot find in the history of European literature and language many examples of great linguistic achievement. Pico della Mirandolas and Cardinal Centofantis are rare.

In his judgments of Italian literature, Joyce was eccentric and paradoxical. His attitude was consistent but his knowledge of the literature itself was noticeably superficial. Italian literature interested him until the fifteenth century, but the world beyond these "pillars of Hercules" was unknown to him.[59]

One pleasing trait of Joyce was his genuine love for Italy, an obvious, luminous, and conscious love. His Catholic education and training was the real force that brought him irresistibly to our country. It is impossible to measure the increased admiration and respect for Italy that Joyce and his fame created wherever he lived, especially in those countries whose people and governments had previously looked upon Italy and her people with contempt. All the writers who have spoken of Joyce before and since his death have testified to his deep love for Italy. Even in Paris where his family settled, Joyce never forgot that his children were born in Italy. In family conversations, which had become polyglot through necessity, Joyce often initiated long discourses in Italian because he did not want the language forgotten. Although he allowed his guests to select their own language for conversation, there were two words that he never permitted to be translated—the names of his children. For Joyce they were always to be "Giorgio" and "Lucia." He used to say that the language of family affection could only be Italian. He understood Dante very well and could explicate him with the insight of a genius, not as the sterile and mummified commentators do. I saw him many times with tears in his eyes after such a reading.

Who could avoid noticing this eccentric during the years that he strolled the streets of Trieste? Agile and lean, his rigid legs like the poles of a compass, he went about with an abstracted look. In summer he wore a Panama hat of indescribable color and old shoes, in winter, a shabby overcoat with raised fur collar.

James Joyce was born a gentleman. He descended from a noble family in Western Ireland, a section which carries the name of his ancestors—the Joyce Country. He was proud of his birth and his family, as one could easily see from the many ancestral portraits that hung on a wall of his apartment.

What is left from all the turmoil? What became of the comfortable life that he had earned so laboriously? The family seems to have become

59. Joyce had read a number of works by the Italian novelist, playwright, and poet Gabriele d'Annunzio (1863–1938). For a while he considered d'Annunzio's *Il fuoco* "the highest achievement of the novel to date" (Stanislaus Joyce, *My Brother's Keeper*, ed. Richard Ellmann [New York: Viking Press, 1958], p. 147).

victims of a tragedy. The large and stately Paris apartment with its valuable library and its many manuscripts was abandoned, perhaps destroyed. Joyce died in Zurich—the alpha and omega of his cycle of glory. His wife and son Giorgio, thus separated from him, were crushed.

The tragedy of his daughter Lucia was even more distressing. A lovely girl with a promising intellect, wise and caustic like her father, she was later committed to a sanitarium in Paris and left there abandoned.[60]

Although we were poles apart in our religious beliefs, we were always friends. Joyce tenaciously held to his ideas, and I remained steadfast in my opposition to them.

Joyce had a personable and good-natured disposition. So far as his genius was concerned, one could say he was sovereign. In the more worldly and less significant matters, however, Joyce was naïve and almost childlike. A sort of hysterical man with a morbid hypersensitivity, he was insanely frightened by electrical storms. On occasion during such storms he would lose control of himself, becoming completely irresponsible and cowardly, like a child or a foolish woman. Overcome by terror, he would clap his hands over his ears, run and hide in a small darkened room or hurl himself into bed in order not to see or hear. Each time he would say that Italy was a country of cosmic revolutions and that he wanted to go away.[61] But he stayed.

TRANSLATED BY LIDO BOTTI

60. Joyce's daughter Lucia began to show serious signs of mental illness around 1930 and became progressively worse. When the Joyces fled to Zurich in 1940 they were forced to leave Lucia at a sanitarium on the south coast of Brittany, having failed in repeated efforts at arranging her transfer to Switzerland. A letter Francini wrote to Dario de Tuoni late in life may help explain the particular emphasis he places on the Joyce family's misfortunes. "Joyce," he said, "did not act well with me nor did his brother. . . . Both ended in a bad way—as always happens to those who do wrong" (quoted in *Ricordi di Joyce a Trieste*, p. 53). How Joyce mistreated Francini, if he did, remains a mystery.

61. Stanislaus admitted his brother's well-known fear of thunderstorms but insisted that Francini's account was exaggerated. "At most," Stanislaus said, "if I were standing at the window looking at the storm, my brother would say to me, with glittering eye and exasperated politeness: 'Will you be kind enough to close that window, like a good bloody fool?' And then to Francini in Italian: 'You know, my brother thinks that a thunderbolt knocks at the door before coming in'" (*My Brother's Keeper*, p. 19).

Silvio Benco

JOYCE'S ACCOMPLISHMENTS *during his first dozen years of exile were considerable, in spite of the hectic life described by Francini. Aside from becoming a popular and highly regarded teacher of English, he wrote nine articles for the* Piccolo della Sera *(the leading Triestine newspaper then), delivered a series of public lectures, learned considerable German and Danish, collaborated on translations of Synge's* Riders to the Sea *and Yeats's* Countess Cathleen, *dabbled in importing tweeds from Ireland, and, with the financial support of several Triestines, set up the first cinema in Dublin. More importantly, he published his first book,* Chamber Music; *wrote twelve chapters of his first novel,* Stephen Hero; *finished* Dubliners; *rewrote* Stephen Hero *as* A Portrait of the Artist as a Young Man; *completed his play,* Exiles; *and began* Ulysses.

The recollection of Silvio Benco (1874–1949), a respected novelist, journalist, and literary critic, shows something of the energetic and talented Joyce who accomplished these things. It also shows the public Joyce, "hurrying from house to house" through the city to give his English lessons. According to Benco the only Triestines Joyce spoke to about his literary work were the novelist Italo Svevo (whose real name was Ettore Schmitz) and Roberto Prezioso, editor of the Piccolo. *That he did not discuss it with other Triestines probably was owing to a conviction that the Irish subject matter of his work was too limited and localized to interest or be understood by non-Irish. Certainly he wished to discuss his work with someone and was upset at not being able to do so. While Stanislaus was still in Dublin Joyce regularly sent him chapters of* Stephen Hero *and* Dubliners' *stories, demanding immediate and detailed replies. "I expect you to write to me much oftener than you do," he told Stanislaus in a typical letter. "You know I have no one to talk to" (Letters II, 78). Stanislaus's arrival in Trieste did not fully solve the problem because of their frequent quarrels.*

In the meantime, however, Joyce met Prezioso and Svevo, who came to him as students. Svevo had written several novels as a young man, but they had not been successful and so he had entered the family marine paint business in Trieste. When Joyce heard of the novels he asked to see them. They so impressed him that he convinced Svevo to begin writing again. Svevo responded by encouraging Joyce to go on with Portrait, *which had been abandoned following a quarrel with Stanislaus. Later, when Joyce began writing* Ulysses, *he probed Svevo, who came from Jewish background, for material about Jews and discussed Bloom with him "from all angles."* [1]

Benco says that difficulty in finding an apartment caused Joyce's unhappiness with Trieste following the war. This was part of the problem. Joyce complained to Pound that he had to live in a flat with eleven other people and that as a result writing was almost impossible (Letters II, 467). But he also was bothered by the old problem of having no one to discuss his work with, Stanislaus and apparently Svevo no longer being suitably understanding or sympathetic. Joyce wrote to Frank Budgen, who had become his literary confidant in Zurich, that there was "not a soul to talk to about Bloom" in Trieste. He mentioned lending a chapter of Ulysses to several people, but added, ". . . they know as much about it as the parliamentary side of my arse. . . . O shite and onions!" (Letters I, 134). Benco was one of these people. But his account shows that in addition to lending him chapters of Ulysses, Joyce explained its Homeric basis and the various methods he used in preparing his material. All this suggests that Benco was being tried out as a possible replacement for Budgen. Whatever his feelings about the book, his devotion to his duties as newspaper editor made him unsuited for the nearly full-time job of literary confidant to Joyce. As the report of Benco's wife at the opening of the recollection shows, when Joyce moved to Paris he found sympathetic listeners and helpers in abundance.

In Paris Joyce continued to remember Benco fondly. He sent him a review copy of Ulysses, the only other Italian to receive one being Carlo Linati. He also sent him newspapers and greetings via Francini. As late as 1939, when Finnegans Wake was published, he thought of selecting Benco again as one of the two Italians to receive a review copy. Benco in turn wrote several sympathetic articles about Joyce, his recollection being one of them.

1. Stanislaus Joyce, Introduction to Italo Svevo's *As a Man Grows Older* (New York: New Directions, 1932), p. vii.

James Joyce
in Trieste

By Silvio Benco

"RATHER CHANGED, Joyce," says my wife who had just visited the writer in Paris. "He's getting younger, and has become altogether a man of the world. In his house, as always, music reigns: his daughter dances and has even performed in public; his young son is training his baritone voice; the whole family is always ready to pick up and follow the wanderings of a famous Polish singer whom Joyce admires.[2] And by way of contrast, the Triestine dialect is the family's customary language (the two children were born and raised in Trieste). They all speak our dialect, taking pleasure in preserving the harshness of the local accent. It's a strange thing, that luxurious Parisian apartment full of the speech of Trieste's slums. Unfortunately I had lost Joyce's address, and foreign celebrities are not widely known in Paris. In one of the larger bookshops, however, I found a man who knew the address. 'This is not one of the duties of my profession; it's just my own personal knowledge,' he insisted on informing me, pompously. So I was able to see Joyce in his new affluence and youthfulness; but also, alas, with his eyes so much worse that he cannot see to write and has to dictate everything. Seven times, since his years in Zurich until now, those eyes have been operated upon without any appreciable improvement; now he is about to undertake a decisive treatment from which they expect results. Meanwhile, at all hours and in every room, there are admirers and disciples of 'The Master,' young Englishmen, who read for him, take down his dictation and pound typewriters for him. Joyce's work literally pervades the whole house. That new work of his which will take seven years of his life, like *Ulysses*, and of which the first and some of the last parts are already published; the middle chapters are still in gestation.[3] He doesn't allow the state of his eyes to defeat him; he overcomes the bitterness of it bravely, and merely seems slightly distant and distrait in his ever-penetrating and sarcastic conversation. He recalls one by one the many

---

2. The "Polish singer" must have been the Cork-born, French-reared tenor, John Sullivan, whom Joyce did make trips outside of Paris to hear.

3. The completion of *Finnegans Wake* was to take sixteen years of Joyce's life. By 1930 much of the first part had been published, but only "Haveth Childers Everywhere" (*FW* 532–54) from toward the end.

Triestines to whom he taught English, he remembers certain streets of the city, his beloved streets of the Città Vecchia, with their wine-shops and cheap restaurants which probably don't exist any longer; he shows emotion at the name of Svevo, and is distressed that a man of such worth should have died so early.[4] He jumps from one subject to another, sandwiching in anecdotes in his favorite fable form. He is delighted by the first Japanese translation of one of his books—I don't remember which one.[5] The only thing, he says, which no longer interests him at all is politics. 'No one bothers with politics anyway,' he adds. 'It's no longer in style.' "

Now in place of my wife's recent impressions, I substitute myself with my more distant memories. I have to return almost to my youth: when people in Trieste began to talk of the newcomer who was a marvel at teaching English. Joyce, when he arrived in Trieste, was little over twenty, and Pola had been the first stop in a wedding-trip which was also a search for a means of making a living. A young Irishman, refined and moulded by the Jesuits until he had broken away from them, and an exceedingly young wife with a great love and courage behind her admiring eyes, cannot live on air. At Pola they found a young Florentine, Professor Alessandro Francini Bruni, and his young wife, hesitating before the same problem. The Berlitz School had called them, and for the moment saved all four of them. Joyce taught English, and Francini the official Tuscan, somewhat different from the Italian in which Joyce was beginning to express himself. "At that time he spoke a rather odd Italian," says Francini, "an Italian covered with wounds and scabs. It was, in fact, a dead language, come to join the Babel of living tongues." After a year, the two friends came to Trieste, still with the Berlitz School; but very soon the Commercial High School took Joyce from that humble chair, and then his fame began.

The fame of an English teacher, let it be understood. For he kept the poems which he sent from time to time to Dublin reviews a secret; nor did the Triestines have occasion to know the little book called *Chamber Music*. Joyce was already a name in his forsaken country; but in Trieste he never appeared as a writer, and perhaps he found pleasure in keeping everyone in ignorance. There was no need for

4. Svevo (b. 1861) was killed in an automobile accident in 1928.
5. In 1926 Joyce mentioned a visit from some Japanese about translating his work (*Letters* I, 242). According to John J. Slocum and Herbert Cahoon, the first of Joyce's books to be translated into Japanese was *Dubliners*, in 1931 (*A Bibliography of James Joyce, 1882–1941* [New Haven, Conn.: Yale University Press, 1953], p. 122). Joyce always took great interest and pleasure in having his books translated, but he became outraged when he discovered later on that the Japanese, who were not signatories to the Berne convention regarding copyright, were publishing his work without permission or payment of royalties.

*Joyce dancing. Drawing by Desmond Harmsworth
(courtesy of Humanities Research Center,
University of Texas, Austin)*

everyone to hunt down in him the already lived, if not yet relived, existence of Stephen Dedalus. Better to be the conscientious and successful teacher who accepted exile. Tall, thin, smooth-shaven (a member of the giraffe family, he used to say) he might have seemed (and without so much contradicting the facts) an overgrown schoolboy who had developed too rapidly. Except that no one would have taken James Joyce for an overgrown boy, so vivid was the impression of a mature, already decided life in his stiff, automaton-like bearing. He enjoyed spending his evenings drinking, says Francini; I know nothing about that, but he must have been still, secretly, something of a *révolté*. Those tumultuous emotions characteristic of the Irish, even when drowned in whiskey or wine, were not noticeable to us, who admired in his athletic gait the machine's perfect response to the exigencies of his peripatetic profession. He was always hastening from house to house to give their hour of English to all the Triestines. Energetic and punctual in his work, devoted to his wife, his children, and his house, he was remarkable for his sobriety. But within there was the poetic torment, the keen critical mind, the paradoxical *diablerie* of Joyce. His friend Francini was perhaps the only one to know it in the beginning, and after the war he recalled it in a delightful, but today rather rare, book with the ugly title: *Joyce intimo spogliato in piazza.*

But there was one moment at which Joyce the writer was almost discovered in Trieste. Roberto Prezioso, then editor of the *Piccolo*, one of the few who had come to know the Irishman well, asked me to go over the Italian of some articles on Ireland which Joyce had brought him. It is to this task that I owe my personal acquaintance with him. He wanted the revision to take place under his own eyes; I do not think it was from distrust so much as from a desire to learn. In fact, there was very little to change in the articles. The Italian was a bit hard and cautious, but lacked neither precision nor expressiveness. "Do you write in English and then translate?" I asked him. "No, I write directly in Italian." He had begun to study it three years before and our language has remained one of the most familiar among the eighteen ancient and modern tongues from which he gradually constructed his linguistic treasure. He knew ancient and modern Greek, Sanskrit, Arabic, all the major languages of Europe, and he was constantly making rare additions to this collection.[6]

My collaboration did not last long. The day we argued about a word and he was right, with his dictionary in his hand, it became clear to me that his manuscripts no longer needed my corrections. Moreover there

6. Joyce himself expressed astonishment at such exaggerations of his linguistic accomplishments. He mentioned another article, apparently also by Benco, crediting him with speaking "18 European and oriental languages" (*SL* 287).

were very few of them. Three in that year, 1907, and then a couple more at long intervals.[7]

At that time Joyce did not believe that politics were out of style. He had brought with him from Ireland a passionate interest in the subject: indeed he had the bitterness of disillusion, the intolerance of a persecuted man and the bravado of a sceptic ("Constitutional and unconstitutional monarchies make me sick," he once said to Francini. "Republics, aristocratic or democratic, make me sick. Can we want a monarchy through divine right? Do you believe in the sun of the future?"). Nevertheless, the evocation of his native country, guilty of having disillusioned him, never took place without causing him anguish. The first of those articles, "The Last of the Sinn Fein," spoke of a certain John O'Leary, who died in Dublin on St. Patrick's Day. It explained that in Sinn Fein there was a double struggle: the Irish nation against the English government; and also the "physical force" party against the moderate party. Now Sinn Fein was either dying or dead. Its psychological moment had passed. "In Ireland at the psychological moment the traitor always appears" (a remark which comes up again in *Ulysses*: "the Irish always betray their best men."[8])

The second of the articles in the *Piccolo della Sera* was entitled "Home Rule Comes of Age." It recalled the applause given to Gladstone, in 1886, when the aged statesman had declared that the English Liberal party would refuse to legislate for England until England had granted some measure of autonomy to Ireland. After more than seven years, Gladstone—"in the meantime having, with the aid of the Irish bishops, brought about the assassination of Parnell"—for the third time presented his plan to the House. Now, since twenty-one years had passed, Home Rule would have been of age. Instead Gladstone was dead, Irish parliamentarianism had failed, and everything was at a standstill. Gladstone had done more harm to Ireland than Disraeli had. He had, always with the aid of the bishops, swamped it.

A few months later, a third burst of pessimism: "Ireland at the Bar." Let us read that beginning as a clue to the ancient tribe from which the author springs:

7. Between 1907 and 1912 Joyce wrote a total of nine articles for the *Piccolo*. Five deal with Irish politics, two are travel pieces about Ireland, and two are on literary topics (one on George Bernard Shaw and one on Oscar Wilde). English translations of these articles appear in *The Critical Writings of James Joyce*. Joyce agreed with Francini and Benco about his skill as a journalist. "I may not be the Jesus Christ I once fondly imagined myself," he told Stanislaus, "but I think I must have a talent for journalism" (*JJ* 265).

8. This sentence does not appear in *Ulysses*, though betrayal is an important theme in the book. Benco may have been thinking of *A Portrait* (203), where Stephen speaks of Ireland's betrayal of her leaders.

Several months ago a sensational trial was held in Ireland. In the western province, in a desert place called Maamtrasma, a slaughter had been committed. Four or five farmers of the district belonging to the tribe of Joyce were arrested. The oldest of them . . . was particularly suspect to the police. Public opinion judged him innocent then, and now considers him a martyr. The old man and all the others accused knew no English. The Court had to have recourse to an interpreter. The examination carried on through him partook at times of the comic, at times of the tragic. On one side stood the over-formal interpreter, and on the other the patriarch of the poor tribe, who, unaccustomed to civil procedure, seemed stunned by all that judicial ceremony.

The figure of this old man, "relic of a civilization not ours, deaf and dumb before his judge," seemed to Joyce to symbolize Ireland at the bar of public opinion. "She does not succeed in making herself understood; she has no means of communicating with the public opinion of England and of other countries. The Irish are alleged cut-throats. The true sovereign of Ireland, the Pope, looks upon them as the English do."

Later they did manage to make themselves understood, but Joyce was not obliged to be a prophet.

He could not suffer in the same way over Trieste's own dogged effort towards national freedom. But precisely because he was not passionately and painfully involved, he could consider it with intelligent sympathy. His feeling for Italy was very strong; but his knowledge of Italian literature was incomplete. To Francini he confided these summary opinions: "Italian literature begins and ends with Dante. But that is a great deal. In Dante the whole spirit of the Renaissance is to be found. I love Dante almost as much as the Bible. The rest is ballast." He had instinctively found his point of affinity, and he was right; but his hasty judgment of the rest was only one of those opinions which one hears on any literature from superficial intellects. Nor did he like Rome. Only the Roman Church seemed great to him; but great with a sort of mixed grandeur, composed of good and evil—the idea which most foreigners draw from their hyper-romantic concept of the Renaissance papacy. Concerning Italy we have nothing to learn from Joyce.

He went often to the theatre, and considered the Italians the first actors and singers of the world; he used to read the dramatic criticism of Giovanni Pozza in the Corriere and found him clear and acute (later he also praised those of Renato Simoni). He showed an interest in several musicians of Trieste. But he did not talk of his own literary work except with Svevo, much older than he and already "an overlooked local writer," and Doctor Prezioso, to whom he had read in manuscript the stories which later made up the volume of Dubliners. He spoke of this book with much enthusiasm, and promised me a great surprise when it was published. *Dubliners* appeared just as the World War broke out. I did not read it at that time; I did not even know of its publication, for books could not get through to Trieste.

I had the feeling—so difficult to penetrate the cold exterior of the Nordic mind—that I had not made a favorable impression on Joyce. I knew that he had found much to laugh at in my youthful novels, though they were written in earnest. I did not hold that against him; but I feared that there had remained, instead of indifference, a sort of antipathy to their author. Later I was convinced that this was not true, and Joyce, who is fundamentally loyal, always treated me as a friend. He himself, perhaps, imagined that I had not seen the genius in him. In that case, he was wrong. Though I was far from guessing the tremendous equation between encyclopedia and life which the author of *Ulysses* carried about in his head.

With the declaration of war, James Joyce became a free prisoner in Trieste, a citizen of an enemy state in the hands of Austria. He had been obliged to cease teaching in the Commercial High School. Even his private lessons probably stopped. For some time he had been saying that he had taught everyone English, and would have to move to another city; but he was deeply attached to Trieste. At first the war must have completely upset him, given him the feeling of losing one's bearings which so many "intellectuals" experienced. One would meet him in the street walking, his lips tight together in a hard, horizontal line. He would bow and look at one fixedly, and avoided stopping or exchanging a few words. The official position of the Irishman at war with England was now that of a British citizen at war with Austria. It was not easy to accept and less easy to deny.

And the war: did he feel that great problem which weighed on every conscience? Had he already written, in the already begun *Ulysses*, the famous sentence: "History is a nightmare from which I am trying to awake"? [*U* 34].

After a short time, Joyce disappeared from the city. He had got permission to go to Switzerland. At Trieste with the Italian struggle coming ever closer, the imperial authorities were not eager to have the custody of citizens of enemy states. Joyce went to Zurich; and like the man he was, or as I judge him always to have been, rooted in his own intention, he held close to his artistic creations and paid attention to nothing else. Marvellous things were happening to him. The success of *Dubliners*, at a distance; the princely price paid in America for the manuscript, and even for the proof sheets, of *A Portrait of the Artist as a Young Man*; complete material ease for today and tomorrow; final in-

dependence earned by the work of the mind.[9] He was in good humor
(so says my friend Antonio Battara who was his companion in his Swiss
exile), and delightful hours were passed in reading his aphorisms and
paradoxes. He spent much time in bed, writing *Ulysses*; often he mixed
with the other Irish exiles, and helped them to found a company of
"Irish Players," which, having improvised a theatre, gave his comedy,
Exiles. Even the writer's wife sometimes acted—and acted very well. As
a diversion, he had occasional stormy scenes with the British consul.[10]
Perhaps one of them concerned that episode of *Ulysses* which, sent in
manuscript to England, was so incomprehensible to the censors as to be
judged a document in cipher; and only after some delay were they
persuaded that they had to do with a "type of literature as yet unknown."
Slight troubles. The most serious was the ocular illness from which
Joyce began to suffer seriously.

Some echoes of all this reached me in my place of exile, by way of
Zurich and Monaco newspapers. Joyce had decidedly become a famous
man. One day I received an unexpected visit from his brother, Stan Joyce.
I was stationed at Linz on the Danube and he in the neighboring camp
of Katzenau, and one free day he came to bring me his brother's greetings.
Thus I had more precise news of the fabulous growth of his fame; Stan
Joyce told me that the English had been struck by a sort of classic
conciseness in his brother's prose, and by a musical sentence-structure
new to their literature. Though not a literary man, he was intelligent
and the opposite of a snob; and the news he brought was precious to me.
On his second visit, he brought me *Dubliners*. And I made the acquaintance of the youthful Joyce: portrayer of living men, conscious
perfecter of his own style, neither less realistic nor less analytic than
the majority of prose writers of his generation, penetrating observer
and, more than dispassionate, capable of giving the proper perspective
to his own emotion.

On my return to Trieste in the spring of 1918, I found *Exiles* and a
little later *A Portrait of the Artist* came from Zurich. In the comedy
I at once recognized the Ibsenian inspiration (Ibsen, the great love of
Joyce's youth), but cruelly developed, somewhat in the manner of

9. *Dubliners* was far from the monetary success that Benco thought. It brought
Joyce no money at all during the Zurich years and little thereafter.

10. The name of the theatre company Joyce helped found was the English
Players, and it was composed of people from the English colony, though many of
the plays they performed were Irish. *Exiles* was a projected performance that
did not occur. The diversion with the British consul is an allusion to the court
struggles between Joyce and Henry Carr, which resulted in some harrassment
from the British consulate and almost sixty years later served as partial inspiration
for Tom Stoppard's comedy *Travesties*.

Strindberg, according to the natural law of the destruction of the soul when it is exposed to fire. Perhaps Strindberg would have ended with the bursting into flame; Joyce ironically viewed the complete destruction. In the *Portrait* I was struck by the precision and extreme lucidity of the draughtsmanship, the "resemblance" to its original revealed through the logic of its structure. It is too terse, too rigidly fresh and intellectually exact to be a favorite book with Italians.

One day in 1919 the author of *Ulysses* appeared suddenly and unexpectedly. I was then editing a newspaper in Trieste. He seemed to be showing signs of age, almost to be worn out, but that was not true. His tall and exceedingly thin figure was covered by one of those monastic habits with military belts which were being used as overcoats. It was too short for him and gave him rather strange proportions. After a few minutes he asked me to lower the lampshade, since the direct light hurt his eyes. And then we talked of his weakened sight, of Trieste, where he hoped to settle for good, of the chaotic times which had not, however, shaken his imperturbability, of the Danish language which he was studying, of the pronunciation of ancient and modern Greek, of Homer and of *Ulysses*.

That evening I got a general idea of the work, not sufficient however to give me even a vague conception of its real value. My measure of Joyce was still in the *Portrait of the Artist*: my expectations were naturally modelled on that criterion. But after a few more visits (no longer busy with his lessons, Joyce often came to my office), my curiosity increased until it was at its height. Then the magic talisman of *Ulysses* was revealed to me, the key to its secret, which all can now readily find in Stuart Gilbert's volume, that excellent commentary which, with the aid of the author himself, interprets every phase of James Joyce's novel.[11]

After that initiation, he wanted me to read what was already written of *Ulysses*. He brought me the numbers of *The Little Review* in which about a third of the work had appeared: the loud objections to its "obscenity" had forced the publication to cease. The following episodes were then simply typed, and five of them were still unfinished. He showed me the loose sheets on which he prepared the material of each episode, notes as to composition, quotations, references, ideas, essays in various styles. When the rough material was ready, he devoted himself to writing out the complete episode, and this he usually did in less than a month. Following this method, *Ulysses* had been begun in Trieste before the war, continued in Zurich, and now resumed in Trieste.

11. Gilbert's book *James Joyce's "Ulysses"* (1930; rpt., New York: Vintage Books, 1952), describes the Homeric parallels in *Ulysses*.

One might easily imagine that Joyce himself had experienced some of the life of Stephen Dedalus or Bloom. Many times during that last year of his life in Trieste, he offered to take me with him to one of those old inns of Città Vecchia which he loved so much, to spend the evening chatting, smoking, and drinking—as indeed poets and philosophers have always enjoyed doing. Though the temptation was strong, I was obliged to point out to him that the editor of a newspaper could not allow himself to desert his post in such troubled times. Joyce had a passion for white Chianti and Tuscan cooking, and he often liked to dine at Francini's and stay there until very late. Francini, an officer in the Army, had got himself assigned to an apartment on the fourth floor of the building in which I live. There Joyce went almost every week with his whole family, and generally some time after midnight, while reading in bed, I would hear the hushed conversation of the group as they descended the stairs, and Joyce's heavy step, for he did not trust his eyes in the candle's flickering light. One evening I accepted their offer to join them.

It was a very gay evening, although Nordic gaiety is not usually so demonstrative as that of our intimate Italian gatherings. But Francini saw to that. Joyce was accompanied by his wife, whose sleek blonde beauty is expressed in a motionless countenance of almost Greek regularity. They had with them their almost fully grown children; for there is no family more closely united than that one. Joyce said a world of good of Linati, with whom he had corresponded; and he praised the writers who were his friends, Wyndham Lewis, the poet Ezra Pound, and some others, urging me to read their books.[12] After dinner, pushing his chair back from the table, he began to sing—a habit since his earliest youth, when he thought he would devote himself to music and become one of the many famous Irish tenors. He sang church music. And seemed lost in his own singing. The author of *Ulysses*!

That was one of the last times I saw him. His Triestine days were drawing to a close. He was temporarily lodged at his brother's; everyone was uncomfortable, and it seemed as if there was not a single apartment in Trieste for James Joyce. Strange times indeed! He was annoyed at this, for it seemed to him that he could live happily only in Trieste. But one day he admitted his defeat, or else he felt obliged to follow the beckoning of Fate: and he went off to Paris.

12. Carlo Linati, the Italian writer, had translated Synge's *Playboy of the Western World* and Yeats's *The Countess Cathleen*. Joyce proposed that he translate *A Portrait of the Artist* and *Ulysses*. Ultimately, Linati translated *Exiles* and also wrote about Joyce's work. Wyndham Lewis, the English writer and painter, and Ezra Pound were both sympathetic toward Joyce's work at this time, though not later on. Pound in particular was instrumental in forwarding Joyce's work.

꒦꒦꒦꒦꒦꒦꒦꒦꒦꒦꒦꒦꒦꒦꒦꒦꒦꒦꒦꒦꒦꒦꒦꒦꒦꒦꒦꒦꒦

August Suter

*DURING JOYCE'S LAST YEAR in Trieste before the war, things
began going his way. Grant Richards, who eight years earlier had backed
out of publishing* Dubliners, *mysteriously backed in again and published
the book in 1914. The same year, Ezra Pound, having contacted Joyce
apparently at William Butler Yeats's instigation, helped get* A Portrait
of the Artist *accepted for serial publication in* The Egoist, *a London
periodical. His fortunes continued to improve during the four years
in Switzerland, where he arrived in the spring of 1915. Harriet Weaver,
who had become editor of* The Egoist, *joined Pound in taking from
his shoulders the burden of getting his work published. (*Portrait *appeared in book form at the end of 1916 and* Exiles *two years later.)
He also began to receive financial help from her and from other sources,
relieving him of having to teach. As a consequence, he was able to
devote nearly all of his energies while in Zurich to writing* Ulysses, *his
only significant diversion being the English Players.*

*Joyce made many friends in Zurich, by far the most important being
the self-educated English painter and ex-sailor, Frank Budgen, who
held a minor position with the British consulate. Through Budgen Joyce
met the Swiss sculptor August Suter (1887–1965) and Suter's brother
Paul, both of whom were long-time friends of Budgen. Paul Suter,
Budgen, and Joyce formed a convivial triumvirate. August remained
more or less apart, yet close enough to make some shrewd observations
about Joyce. The random notes that constitute his recollection bear on
some of Joyce's main concerns—music, literature, and above all his
own work.*

*One of Suter's observations, that Joyce habitually manipulated per-
sonal conversations to "model" scenes for* Ulysses, *sounds far-fetched.
Yet Budgen reported two bizarre instances of Joyce attempting more
or less the same thing. The first he learned of from Nora, who confided
to him one night as the three returned from a cafe that "Jim wanted
her to 'go with other men so that he would have something to write
about.'"*[1] *A veiled passage in Suter's recollections about Joyce*

1. Frank Budgen, *Myselves When Young* (London: Oxford University Press,
1970), p. 188.

"*playing with [Nora's] virtue,*" apparently alludes to this notion of having her cuckold him as Bloom is cuckolded by Molly. The second attempt at modeling material was Joyce's comic, largely epistolary romance with a Zurich woman, Marthe Fleischmann. This romance, as Budgen said, probably was meant to provide material for "Nausicaa," but it would have served equally well for Bloom's relationship with Martha Clifford.[2]

Though modeling was not involved, a visit to the Baroness St. Leger, mentioned by Suter, had the same purpose of producing material for Ulysses. The Baroness must have seemed a promising source, since she was known variously as Circe and the Siren and was reported to have her walls decorated with tapestries representing scenes from the Odyssey (JJ 469–70). A "trunk full" of erotic letters and pamphlets that she gave Joyce turned out to be useful in writing "Circe" (Letters I, 336). He often claimed that he had no imagination. "Chance furnishes me what I need," he told Jacques Mercanton and others.[3] It may have done so, but he often had a large hand in bringing that chance about.

The way Joyce kept Ulysses to the fore in conversations annoyed Suter;[4] the two remained friendly, however, on into the Paris years. One small but significant detail Suter recalls from those years is receiving on his fiftieth birthday a bouquet of flowers from Joyce. Such gestures by Joyce, who expected people to remember his anniversaries but who also remembered theirs, reflects a subtle change in his behavior toward his friends. He continued to make demands on them, as though they had nothing better to do than serve him or his art, but, as his career prospered, he began to give as well as receive.

2. Ibid.
3. See Mercanton's recollection, p. 213.
4. Budgen, *Myselves When Young*, p. 186.

Some Reminiscences of James Joyce

By *August Suter*

Zurich

MY FIRST MEETING WITH JOYCE took place in Budgen's room in the "Schipfe,"[5] over a glass of wine. My brother Paul was there too.

When Joyce saw me entering he called out: "That is Buck Mulligan!" I dislike comparisons of this kind, and in my reserve I noticed at once that, in the way a painter uses his models for his compositions, Joyce was assigning roles to the members of his company and that he imperceptibly brought on the conversation that he happened to need for his work. Later on I suggested this to Budgen, who had not realized it. Subsequent observations confirmed that this was Joyce's procedure in company.

One evening, in the Bahnhofbuffet of Zurich, a group of artists were sitting together, among whom there was one with a slightly inverted tendency whom Joyce had never seen before. Joyce suddenly produced a pair of white drawers (a doll's) from his pocket, put them over his hand, with two fingers sticking out, and walked them across the table towards this artist, with movements that were meant to be provocative. Women's drawers amused him, and he derived some pleasure from a scene in Zurich's streets when a well-dressed lady suddenly lost her drawers and found them gliding to the ground.[6]

One evening Joyce was in a public house in Niederdorf, frequented by working men. Some of the revellers scented something foreign about him and, enlivened by the wine, they kept (as you might put it) sniffing him. Joyce reacted sensibly enough, so that the event, which might easily have developed into a brawl, culminated in Joyce's being carried about the place in triumph, on the men's shoulders, with shoutmost shoviality [*FW* 6.19]—and Joyce, his head touching the ceiling, smiling maliciously. I wonder today if this was, for Joyce,

---

5. A row of old houses on the left bank of the Limmat River, which flows through the center of Zurich.

6. Joyce's preoccupation with women's drawers has been testified to by others as well. It is apparent in his letters and is shared by Leopold Bloom, of whom Molly recalls, "drawers drawers the whole blessed time till I promised to give him the pair off my doll to carry about in his waistcoat pocket" (*U* 746).

but one more game decided in his favour—or perhaps his first success?

In the Tonhalle, Zurich's concert hall, a performance of Bach's *Matthaus-Passion* was scheduled and I asked Joyce if he would like to attend. He declined: "Oh no, there you have texts from the gospels of Saint Matthew and Saint John mixed together, that's like lumping together Dostoevsky and Shakespeare." Saint John was for him the highest attainment of the Evangelists, and he was fond of quoting the opening: "In the beginning was the word."

I had met Budgen in 1910 in Paris; he was then a vegetarian, following the example of his painter friend Louis Sargent, and he came to appreciate drink only when coming across a Russian of the Czarist period in St. Ives in Cornwall. He was a self made man. Professor Fleiner, of Zurich University, once said he had never in his life met a self made man who was as intelligent, as knowledgeable and as cultivated. Budgen knows German and French literature as well as his own. Mrs. Joyce kept on good terms with Mrs. Fleiner in Zurich until her death.

In Ascona one day I had a call from Joyce who had much to tell me and announced his intention of taking a train to Locarno. He then walked to Ascona to tell me that a Quaker woman had put so much money at his disposal that he could now work in peace.[7] He wanted to see the isles of Brissago, owned by the Baroness St. Leger, who was then living with her seventh husband or friend, as the rumor went, on the island. The island is some 800 meters long and 200 to 300 meters wide and boasts of a rare vegetation as well as of a Romanesque chapel. The Baroness was then busy manufacturing dolls with a Japanese. Joyce got permission to visit the Baroness and in fact went there, no doubt to gather material for his book *Ulysses*.

On one of our walks, along the River Maggia,[8] there was a dry snake's skin, and in spite of his weak eyesight Joyce spotted it and said to me: "Look at this big preservative." On this walk he told me he would like to read something in German that was like Flaubert. I answered that I could imagine Flaubert only in French and recommended Gottfried Keller. "O no," said Joyce, "I don't like Keller's style of *derjenige dessen welcher*."[9] I suggested that he should read Goethe or Kleist and that I did not know of any German Flaubert.

7. This woman was Harriet Weaver, whose first gift of money to Joyce was made in February 1917. Later she gave him substantial quantities of stock. Though she led a rather austere life, she was not a Quaker. Her family were "staunch members of the Church of England, in its most evangelical form" (Jane Lidderdale and Mary Nicholson, *Dear Miss Weaver: Harriet Shaw Weaver 1876–1961* [New York: Viking Press, 1970], p. 23).

8. This river, which flows into Lake Maggiore, appears among the many included in the "Anna Livia Plurabelle" section of *Finnegans Wake* (199.15).

9. Joyce captures here an awkwardness in Gottfried Keller's (1819–90) use of relative and demonstrative pronouns. He later was impressed by Keller's

One evening, after closing time, we were walking across Walche-brucke when Joyce and Budgen were competing turning out doggerel, short syncopated lines, with the recurrent refrain "Stabou, tabou."[10] With this accompaniment we made our way to the British consulate and into Budgen's office where we drank the wine we had brought with us. Paul Suter was not equal to the strain and was sick on the carpet. Budgen enlisted all our help to clean the carpet by means of hot water. Paul Suter, leaning at the fire-place, said: "Toutes les eaux du monde ne suffiront pas pour nettoyer le consulat anglais."[11] This remark brought a lustre to Joyce's eyes and an inward smile appeared, and I wondered if Joyce, the Irishman, didn't love anything but the language of the English. Afterwards Budgen carried Joyce, a bit under the influence, home on his back, as he had done before.

Budgen had a knack of understanding a delicate situation and a per-ceptiveness and insight into the character of other nations that he loved. Joyce was ashamed of showing that he was capable of love; he hid his feelings. He loved Zurich, the Fendant wine that he drank there, and he used to say to Budgen later in Paris: "I am dining with Suter tonight and I hope there will be Fendant!"[12] (I was precautious enough to discover a supply of it in a Swiss restaurant in Paris.)

Paris

I settled in Paris in 1922 and consequently saw much of Joyce, spend-ing many evenings with him. He lived in Valery Larbaud's flat at the time. I noticed that his son was not working and looked bored. I suggested that Joyce should concern himself more about his son, but Joyce an-swered that he had so much work to do that he could not concern himself with his son.[13] Giorgio himself, during a visit in the Louvre, told me that he was going to write a book one day.

Joyce took me to the Church of Saint Sulpice and during Mass gave me a detailed account of everything that went on, in an objective and

suite of poems *Lebendig Begraben* when he heard it sung in a setting by the Swiss composer Othmar Schoeck (*Letters* I, 356). He translated a poem from the suite (Herbert Gorman, *James Joyce* [New York: Farrar and Rinehart, 1939], p. 345).

10. This song may well have been an elaboration of "Staboo Stabella," a bawdy piece attributed to Oliver St. John Gogarty and alluded to in *Ulysses* (392, 426-27).

11. "All the water of the earth will not be sufficient to clean the English consul-ate," apparently paraphrasing Lady Macbeth's "All the perfumes of Arabia will not sweeten this little hand."

12. Joyce's fondness for this wine became well known to all his friends. He alluded to it at length in *Finnegans Wake* (171.15-28).

13. If Joyce paid little attention to his son's career in 1922, that was not the case later on. When Giorgio decided to become a singer, Joyce exerted every possible effort to help him.

detached way. As we were driving to friends in a cab afterwards I asked him what he had retained from his Jesuit education. His answer was spontaneous: to arrange things so that they can be grasped and judged. Joyce lived in a side street close to the Gare Montparnasse, in the Rue de Rennes in some hotel. I visited him and asked about his work and the title of the book. "I can't tell you this—imagine a mountain which I am boring into from all sides without knowing what I am going to find." He often sighed: "I am at the end of English."

About 1922 Joyce lived in the Rue Jacob, and his wife had to leave in the afternoon so that he could work alone in his room.

One day I accompanied her along the Grands Boulevards where she liked to go to a shop where records could be listened to for little money and according to one's inclination. In the evening the three of us met in a small restaurant in the Rue Jacob, just across from their hotel, to have dinner. Joyce asked about our doings. I pointed out that Mrs. Joyce had become a Wagner enthusiast and had been sticking to Wagner records exclusively. Joyce's remark about Wagner was derogatory. Madame Joyce retorted with some excitement: "O, there are many obscenities in your book too!"[14] Joyce smiled calmly and wasn't angry, but she was!

In Zurich Joyce had introduced his wife to Greeks and Jews, models for Bloom, and apparently he would have liked, with a touch of curiosity, to see his wife discomposed. Mrs. Joyce realized that he was playing with her virtue, and refrained from thus serving as a model for her husband's books. She had more character and constancy than coquettishness.

Joyce liked singing and was a great connoisseur. He found that singing is generally bad in Paris and said that even in Toulouse and in Southern France there was a better appreciation of singing. He liked to sing himself, and one evening in our home, when the painter Gimmi and Mrs. Gimmi as well as Mrs. Joyce were also our guests, he went to the piano and sang Irish tunes surprisingly well and with expression in a light tenor voice.[15] Mrs. Joyce was proud and happy. He invited me to the opera and explained that his friend Sullivan, who would sing William Tell in Rossini's opera, was the only tenor capable of managing the highest parts of the original, while other tenors settled for a lower pitch. Sullivan was in fact extraordinary and reached the highest notes with ease.

Joyce asked me: "Whom would your wife (who was a singer)

14. "Oh, es gibt viele Schweinereien auch in Deinem Buche!" Later she made a similar remark to Ole Vinding (see p. 138).

15. Wilhelm Gimmi, the Swiss painter, later did three portraits of Joyce from memory.

recommend to teach Lucia singing?" I answered, "Maestro Cairati in Zurich, no doubt." Joyce continued: "And whom, in Paris, would Cairati recommend?" I answered: "My wife, no doubt." And so Lucia took singing lessons with her.

I was working on the monument of Spitteler, "Prometheus and his Soul," a motive from the epic poem *Prometheus and Epimetheus*.[16]

Joyce was watching attentively and then asked (he had finished *Ulysses*): "What kind of monument would you do for me?" I said I would think of Mr. Bloom. Joyce became very serious and said: *"Mais non!"* He would have preferred to consider Bloom a *création détachée*, but in my view it is impossible for an artist to get out of his skin—the leopard cannot change its spots—, a new one would grow after it.

During the Exposition Internationale of 1937 the Anthroposophic Society of Dornach brought its production of Goethe's *Faust* to Paris. Joyce and I went. After the "Prolog im Himmel" and the first act Joyce said to me: "Look at that, we've been here an hour and nothing has happened." I replied in the same vein: "I have read more than an hour in *Ulysses* and nothing has happened." Joyce smiled maliciously. But after the scene in the dungeon he was thrilled, the acting had been wonderful. He applauded enthusiastically and expressed his approval in Italian in a loud voice.—This is the opportunity to mention that he used to speak Italian to his children. His Italian was melodiously articulated and musical; it was, for him, the language of music.

I was working on Joyce's bust,[17] and he explained to me that he had just been working over a scene in which someone was pouring beer into a glass and that the noise—"glou glou" [*FW* 345.19]—was like that of sacramental wine upon the altar. The Holy Father himself, Joyce said, would have to smile. He was faithful to his sensations and associations—they were realities to him, and I did not get the impression that he wanted to parody or to ridicule; his sole intention was to present accurately the real effect of noises or similar phenomena, especially in the quietness of mental absorption.

Around that time I went to dinner with him to La Reine Pedauque, and he stated the evening's topic: "Someone is having people to dinner, and the *servante* knows everybody invited. But as she enters the room with the first dish there is one person sitting at the table whom she has never seen and whose arrival she has not noticed. What is the girl's reaction?" He seemed to set great store by systematically refuting all my answers, one by one, so that in the end it was he alone who could tell how the *servante* had to react.

During the first sitting for Joyce's bust he insisted on getting an

16. Carl Friedrich Georg Spitteler (1845–1924), a Swiss poet.
17. The bust was destroyed during the war.

easy-chair—an ordinary chair was not comfortable enough. Then, one day, he rang me up from his then flat in the Avenue Floquet to ask about the weather in Denfert-Rochereau. The weather, I told him, was sunny and bright and he said he would come out at once as there were clouds in his area. He had an immense fear of thunder and lightning. I calmed him by pointing out that I had a thick blanket and that he might always hide behind the folding screen in my study and cover his head with the blanket so that he would see and hear nothing.

Due to some misunderstanding he failed to find me in my study when he arrived and he left me a note: "I am sorry about missing your company,—but I am delighted at not being obliged to pose."

During this hot summer Joyce once enquired of a cool place in Switzerland. I suggested he go to Basel and to ask my brother there who was married to an Englishwoman and who would know Switzerland much better than I did. This is what Joyce did. Two weeks later I had a letter from my perplexed sister-in-law. They had been having tea in the Hotel Drei Könige in Basel and everything had gone smoothly— until Joyce, all at once, jumped up and left the room. She was aware, she wrote, that she wasn't Joyce's equal intellectually, but she couldn't think for the life of her how she might have offended Joyce or annoyed him. There had been thunder and lightning and Joyce had gone to hide under the coverlet. I was glad to set my in-law's mind at rest.

I was very much touched when Joyce sent me, for my 50th anniversary, a bunch of flowers, as to a primadonna—something that never happened to me before or since.

Joyce needed friends around him after the exertions of his work, especially arduous when his eyesight failed him. In his dissociation from seemingly all traditions he met the people, *from whom he was, at heart, so different*, with all the more courtesy and correctness. He was aware of the vanity of political controversies and discussions. I was impressed with Joyce's patience, the patience of a genius.

He expected to succeed—but did nothing, beyond his work, to bring about his success.[18]

During the war, in Ascona, I received a phone call saying that Joyce was back from France and would like to see me. I wrote to him that I would look him up on my return to Basel. The news of his death anticipated this, and so I had to take my leave of him at his funeral. Budgen was in London, and knowing about their friendship I threw a bunch of roses into the grave in Budgen's name.

TRANSLATED BY FRITZ SENN

18. As will be apparent in later recollections, Joyce did a great deal to promote the success of his books by encouraging reviews and studies of them.

Georges Borach

WHILE IT IS DOUBTFUL that Joyce consistently used conver-
sations to prepare or model material for Ulysses, *as Suter maintained,*
there is no doubt that he had a near passion for discussing the book.
Frank Budgen said of their conversations about Ulysses *that Joyce*
"was the Ancient Mariner, and I the Wedding Guest."[1] Another
acquaintance with whom Joyce discussed the book almost as intensely
was the Zurich businessman, Georges Borach (d. 1934). One of several
language students Joyce took on first arriving in Zurich, Borach
became a frequent companion, accompanying him on walks about the
city or along the lake shore and also attending the evenings at the
Pfauen restaurant, a favorite resort of Joyce. Unlike Suter, Borach
found these evenings delightful. Describing them some years later in a
letter to Herbert Gorman, he said:

> *Joyce often read aloud to his friends from his* Ulysses *manuscript.*
> *They would comfortably sit evenings in the restaurant "Pfauen,"*
> *drinking Fendant. . . . Many were the discussions at these gatherings.*
> *Full of wonder and admiration did the friends of Joyce follow his*
> *readings. War news, art, and music were discussed. . . . Wit and humour*
> *were ever present on these evenings at the "Pfauen," where the Irish*
> *temperament of Joyce held sway. He would, in his magnificent tenor,*
> *sing us Irish songs and often, as we trudged home, the tones would*
> *resound through the quiet, clear, snow-laden streets. In those days in*
> *this temperate, sober city, the so-called "Polizei-stunde" (closing hour*
> *for public houses) was eleven o'clock and often when our mood was at*
> *its best, we were obliged to take our leave.[2]*

In the same letter Borach pointed out that during their walks and at the
Pfauen, Joyce's conversation "revolved about his book." "Like Ecker-
mann with Goethe," he added, "I noted the talks. . . ." A selection
from those notes forms the substance of his recollection.

The friendship that developed in Zurich between the two men
continued after Joyce left. In 1930, on learning from a newspaper
account that Joyce's eyes had worsened, Borach wrote urging him to

1. Frank Budgen, *Myselves When Young* (London: Oxford University Press, 1970), p. 184.
2. This letter, written in English, is in the Croessmann Collection at Carbondale.

consult Professor Alfred Vogt and later made arrangements for his
meeting with the skilled Zurich surgeon. He also sent some suggestions
in connection with Joyce's campaign to forward the singing career
of John Sullivan. Never one to leave a willing hand idle, Joyce asked his
help in several other matters, and he complied.

Both in his active concern and in his letter to Gorman, Borach
displayed a loyal affection that increasingly characterized Joyce's
European friends. His death in an automobile accident profoundly moved
Joyce, who shortly after wrote Harriet Weaver:

> *...I had to conceal from my wife the facts about Borach as [in*
> *driving to Zurich] we had to pass over the place where he was killed*
> *a few days before. I told her in Zurich and then had difficulty in keeping*
> *her there as she found the place haunted by him. Every place we used*
> *to go he seemed to be there. The old parents are pitiable. The mother*
> *found a bundle of photographs of me locked away by him, taken at*
> *all ages from two on.[3] I often made the poor fellow laugh, thank good-*
> *ness, by pretending to be a little bit more sceptical, commonplace*
> *and uneducated than I really am. He was a very good son. . . . The*
> *strange thing is that his attitude to life, food, drink, flowers, animals,*
> *exercise, seemed to me often more catholic and sane than that of*
> *heathen people. I suspect he knew not too much about* Ulysses *and*
> *far less about W.I.P. ["Work in Progress"]. He just took them on the*
> *principle of my country right or wrong—as good a principle as the*
> *next in most cases. [Letters I, 339][4]*

The only other time in his letters that Joyce spoke with such affection
and in such detail about a person was following his father's death.

The conversations in Borach's recollection often bear on Ulysses
even though the book itself may not be mentioned. Thus in one of them
Joyce defined a major theme of the book when he said that "material
victory is the death of spiritual predominance," that successful states
become only "colonizers and merchants," and that "the Greeks of
antiquity, the most cultured nation," would have followed the same
pattern had they not been defeated. These remarks particularly illumi-
nate the "Nestor" section of Ulysses, *indicating a connection between*
the history lesson on the Greek defeat under Pyrrhus and the talk
later on in Mr. Deasy's office about money, merchants, and England
(U 24–25, 29–36). They also echo Professor McHugh in the "Aeolus"
section when he says, "I speak the tongue of a race the acme of whose
mentality is the maxim: time is money. Material domination. . . .
Lord! Where is the spirituality?" and goes on to mourn "the empire of

3. Harriet Weaver owned a similar bundle of photographs, Joyce apparently
having made copies of the originals for certain of his friends.

4. See also Carola Giedion-Welcker's account of Joyce's response to Borach's
death (below, p. 263).

the spirit . . . that went under with the Athenian fleets at Aegospotami" (U *133*).

Perhaps the most significant of the conversations is the long opening commentary on the Odyssey. One Joyce scholar, Nathan Halper, has noted that Joyce's letters often dwell on the number of hours that he spent on his books and on the technical problems in them, thus concealing their "humanistic, compassionate, and passionate" side and making them sound like "the barren, private, and pedantic puzzles that his enemies have always called them."⁵ *The same could be said with even more justice about the elaborate "schema" of* Ulysses *that Joyce drew up outlining the book's formal structure. However, his remarks to Borach about the* Odyssey *reveal the humanism, compassion, and passion in Joyce. At the same time they demonstrate more clearly than any of his other comments why he chose to base his epic on the* Odyssey.

Conversations with James Joyce

By Georges Borach

AT THAT TIME, during the war years, Joyce was working in Zurich on his *Ulysses*. People often sat with him of an evening in the Pfauen, drinking light gold Fendant, that strong Valois wine (*candide et effronté*, Colette calls it), and chatting about the events of the war, literature, music, and about the work in progress. Many of these talks I jotted down. Several may be put on record here.

Zurich, August 1, 1917

J.J. thinks:

"The most beautiful, all-embracing theme is that of the *Odyssey*. It is greater, more human than that of *Hamlet, Don Quixote*, Dante, *Faust*. The rejuvenation of old Faust has an unpleasant effect upon me. Dante tires one quickly; it is as if one were to look at the sun. The most beautiful, most human traits are contained in the *Odyssey*. I was twelve years old when we dealt with the Trojan War at school; only

5. "Mr. Joyce's Secretary" (review of Stuart Gilbert's edition of Joyce's *Letters*), *Nation*, 186 (Feb. 1, 1958): 104.

the *Odyssey* stuck in my memory. I want to be candid: at twelve I liked the mysticism in Ulysses. When I was writing *Dubliners*, I first wished to choose the title *Ulysses in Dublin*, but gave up the idea. In Rome, when I had finished about half of the *Portrait*, I realized that the Odyssey had to be the sequel, and I began to write *Ulysses*.[6]

"Why was I always returning to this theme? Now *al mezzo del' camin*[7] I find the subject of Odysseus the most human in world literature. Odysseus didn't want to go off to Troy; he knew that the official reason for the war, the dissemination of the culture of Hellas, was only a pretext for the Greek merchants, who were seeking new markets. When the recruiting officers arrived, he happened to be plowing. He pretended to be mad. Thereupon they place his little two-year-old son in the furrow. In front of the child he halts the plow. Observe the beauty of the motifs: the only man in Hellas who is against the war, and the father. Before Troy the heroes shed their lifeblood in vain. They wish to raise the siege. Odysseus opposes the idea. The stratagem of the wooden horse. After Troy there is no further talk of Achilles, Menelaus, Agamemnon. Only one man is not done with; his heroic career has hardly begun: Odysseus. Then the motif of wandering. Scylla and Charybdis—what a splendid parable! Odysseus is also a great musician; he wishes to and must listen; he has himself tied to the mast. The motif of the artist, who will lay down his life rather than renounce his interest. Then the delicious humor of Polyphemus. ' "Olus" [sic—tr.] is my name.'[8] On Naxos the fifty-year-old, perhaps bald-headed, with Ariadne, a girl who is hardly seventeen.[9] What a fine motif! And the return, how profoundly human! Don't forget the trait of generosity at the interview with Ajax in the nether world, and many other beautiful touches. I am almost afraid to treat such a theme; it's overwhelming."

6. In the fall of 1906, while in Rome, Joyce first got the idea for *Ulysses*. He originally planned it as a short story to be included in *Dubliners*, but four months later told Stanislaus, "*Ulysses* never got any forrader than the title" (*Letters* II, 209). He began writing the book in March 1914.

7. "*Nel mezzo del cammin*," from the opening of Dante's *Divine Comedy*. Dante speaks the line, which refers to his being in the middle of his life, i.e., thirty-five years old, the age Joyce was in 1917. The following year Joyce stretched facts in a letter to Marthe Fleischmann during his comic romance with her, telling her that he was thirty-five, and going on to identify himself with Dante at that age, as well as with Shakespeare (*Letters* II, 432).

8. The Greek, usually transliterated "outis" and translated "Noman," is what Ulysses says to Polyphemous when the giant asks his name. Through a fanciful etymology Joyce found this reply full of deep significance as well as an amusing pun (see Louis Gillet's recollection, p. 194).

9. It was of course Theseus, not Ulysses, who had the encounter with Ariadne. Joyce must have been referring to the elderly Ulysses' meeting with the young Nausicaa on the island of Phaïakia.

Zurich, November 15, 1917

J.J. explains:

"There are indeed hardly more than a dozen original themes in world literature. Then there is an enormous number of combinations of these themes. *Tristan und Isolde* is an example of an original theme. Richard Wagner kept on modifying it, often unconsciously, in *Lohengrin*, in *Tannhäuser*; and he thought he was treating something entirely new when he wrote *Parsifal*.

"In the last two hundred years we haven't had a great thinker. My judgment is bold, since Kant is included. All the great thinkers of recent centuries from Kant to Benedetto Croce have only cultivated the garden. The greatest thinker of all times, in my opinion, is Aristotle. Everything, in his work, is defined with wonderful clarity and simplicity. Later, volumes were written to define the same things."

Zurich, October 21, 1918

J.J. remarks:

"As an artist I attach no importance to political conformity. Consider: Renaissance Italy gave us the greatest artists. The Talmud says at one point, 'We Jews are like the olive: we give our best when we are being crushed, when we are collapsing under the burden of our foliage.' Material victory is the death of spiritual predominance. Today we see in the Greeks of antiquity the most cultured nation. Had the Greek state not perished, what would have become of the Greeks? Colonizers and merchants. As an artist I am against every state. Of course I must recognize it, since indeed in all my dealings I come into contact with its institutions. The state is concentric, man is eccentric. Thence arises an eternal struggle. The monk, the bachelor, and the anarchist are in the same category. Naturally I can't approve of the act of the revolutionary who tosses a bomb in a theater to destroy the king and his children. On the other hand, have those states behaved any better which drowned the world in a blood-bath?

"In my works there is a good deal of talk about religion. Many people think I am a spoiled priest. I profess no religion at all. Of the two religions, Protestantism and Catholicism, I prefer the latter. Both are false. The former is cold and colorless. The second-named is constantly associated with art; it is a 'beautiful lie'—something at least." [10]

10. In *Portrait* (244) Stephen puts the distinction a bit differently, describing the Catholic Church as "an absurdity which is logical and coherent" and the Protestant Church as one "which is illogical and incoherent."

Zurich, June 18, 1919

Sauntering up and down the promenades along the lake, J.J. says:
"I finished the Sirens chapter during the last few days. A big job.
I wrote this chapter with the technical resources of music. It is a fugue
with all musical notations: *piano, forte, rallentando*, and so on. A quintet
occurs in it, too, as in the *Meistersinger*, my favorite Wagner opera.
The barmaids have the upper parts of women and the lower of fish.
From in front you see bosom and head. But if you stand behind the bar,
you see filth, the empty bottles on the floor, the ugly shoes of the
women, and so on—only disgusting things. Since exploring them in this
chapter, I haven't cared for music any more. I, the great friend of music,
can no longer listen to it. I see through all the tricks and can't enjoy
it any more." [11]

To this notion I object, and, pointing to the magnificent, deep-blue
summer sky which overarches the city, observe that only music could
render this sky for me. Whereupon J.J. softly speaks Verlaine's immortal lines:

Le ciel est, par-dessus le toit,
  Si bleu, si calme!
Un arbre, par-dessus le toit,
  Berce sa palme. [12]

I, on the other hand, think of night strolls by the Lake of Zurich
and of those classically beautiful stanzas of J.J.'s:

The moon's greygolden meshes make
All night a veil,
The shorelamps in the sleeping lake
Laburnum tendrils trail.

The sly reeds whisper to the night
A name—her name—
And all my soul is a delight,
A swoon of shame. [13]

TRANSLATED BY JOSEPH PRESCOTT

11. Joyce also spoke of this experience to Harriet Weaver. "Since I wrote the
Sirens," he said, "I find it impossible to listen to music of any kind . . ." (*Letters*
I, 129). In his next letter to her he explained that the "Sirens" contained "all the
eight regular parts of a *fuga per canonem*," and added, ". . . I did not know in what
other way to describe the seductions of music beyond which Ulysses travels"
(*Letters* I, 129).
12. This is from *Sagesse*, III, vi. See *Œuvres complètes de Paul Verlaine* (Paris:
Editions Messein, 1911), 1:255.
13. This poem, titled "Alone," is from Joyce's small volume *Pomes Penyeach*
(1927). In his letter to Gorman, Borach said Joyce composed the poem during a
walk along the lake, hence the association here. Judging from Borach's and Dario
de Tuoni's recollections, evening walks turned Joyce's thoughts to poetry.

Nino Frank

*When Joyce arrived in Paris in 1920, he immediately set about working
on the two chapters that remained to complete* Ulysses. *At the same
time, partly through contacts arranged by Ezra Pound, who had urged
the Paris move, he became acquainted with a number of people in the
Parisian literary world. Among them were Sylvia Beach, the energetic
owner of the bookshop Shakespeare and Company, and Valery Larbaud,
the eminent French writer and translator of Samuel Butler. Miss Beach
became the publisher of* Ulysses *when it turned out that no regular
publisher would take the risk, and Larbaud became one of its most influential champions. The book appeared on Joyce's birthday, February 2,
1922.*

*Towards the end of that year, while vacationing in Nice, he began
"debolshevizing" the notes left over from* Ulysses, *in preparation for
his last work,* Finnegans Wake. *On March 10, 1923, he wrote the first
two pages of the book, and worked on it thereafter with varying degrees
of intensity for the next sixteen years. During these years he became
the director of a Joyce industry, gathering numerous people to help
in composing, publishing, promoting, and explicating his new book. At
the same time he arranged for and helped with translations of* Ulysses
*into German and French and of the "Anna Livia Plurabelle" section
of* Finnegans Wake *into German, French, and Italian.*

*Though Harriet Weaver had increased her gifts to Joyce so that he
could live comfortably during this period, his life was no less troubled
than it had been in Trieste. Apparently living by his precept that
"material victory is the death of spiritual predominance," he disposed
of his money at a rate to keep him in perpetual financial difficulty.
In addition, his "new work," as he persisted in calling* Finnegans Wake
*even after it was several years old, not only was attacked from all sides
in public, but also was disliked by many of his friends, including
Miss Weaver, whose attitude deeply upset him. Perhaps worst of all
were the physical collapse of his eyes and the mental collapse of his
daughter, both of which placed a terrific drain on his time, money, and
spirit.*

Finnegans Wake *was published in May 1939, though a copy had*

been prepared for him to receive three months earlier on his birthday.
In December of that year, war having been declared, the Joyces moved
away from Paris to the small village of Saint-Gérand-le-Puy. They
remained there a year and then left for Zurich, where Joyce died one
month later, on January 13, 1941.

Of all the people Joyce knew in Paris, the journalist and writer Nino
Frank (b. 1904) gives the fullest and most detailed account of his life
there. Frank was not one of Joyce's closest friends, but their relationship
was cordial and involved many meetings over the fourteen years they
knew each other. In his description of those meetings he portrays
Joyce with a vividness not often matched in other recollections of
the man.

The Shadow That Had Lost Its Man

By Nino Frank

1926

IT WAS A REMARKABLE TIME—far from "the" crisis, the time of troubles,
the wholesale death—and our lives would have been the poorer had we
not lived through it. It was the period of the Select (a Montparnasse
all-night cafe, where, among other things, the literary frenzies of Henry
Miller bloomed), the period of *Querschnitt* (a Berlin review concerned
with the avant garde and photography and perhaps with an inclination toward notable homosexuals), the period of F. Scott Fitzgerald
(who in *The Great Gatsby* painted a dramatic and delicate portrait of
the hero of those times)—it was withal an international time. Louis
Aragon was writing erotica, Diaghilev was staging his last ballets, Robert
Delaunay appeared to be as great a painter as Picasso.

It was an intensely poetic period, the atmosphere as steamy as a hothouse (it seems to me that it was always sunny, always summer,
whereas now the sky has turned strangely gray), and nothing more
was needed to aid the blossoming of such a rare flower as surrealism.

Does having been forty years younger really explain it all? With
time we have begun to tell each other that those were the last days
in which, despite unemployment, the illusion of peace remained, and

despite poverty, the pre-1914 sweetness of living lingered. Were we aware of it? By no means, we even would have sworn to the contrary. Our phonographs still played *The Rite of Spring*, but more often *Rhapsody in Blue*, which had just been released and seemed sad to us, whereas today we discover so much of the frivolously cheerful in it.

In those days every intellectual in the world lived for Paris. I found myself in charge of foreign arrangements for a journal founded in Rome by Massimo Bontempelli. The journal was to be published in French with the title *900*—the Italian way of saying "twentieth century." [1] Resolutely cosmopolitan, this publication meant to cultivate the current poetics, which were beginning to turn away from what had been called *le fantastique social* in favor of what was about to be named *le réalisme magique*. My task was to consist essentially of ensuring liaison with a board of editors on which we hoped to see Pierre MacOrlan, Georg Kayser, Ramon Gomez de la Serna, Ilya Ehrenburg—who was to join them later—and especially, for English and American letters, the Irishman James Joyce.

Ivan Goll, who in those days was participating in the fabulous collective adaptation of a few pages of what was still called "Work in Progress," gave me the idea of getting Joyce. He himself was in repeated contact with Joyce as a representative of the German publishing house Insel, which was considering publishing a translation of *Ulysses*.[2] I could have had no better sponsor—he was always tenacious, always smiling. But getting in touch with Joyce was by no means easy.

A literary cordon was stretched around him. Goll, a stubborn guide, arranged many a long consultation in Sylvia Beach's and Adrienne Monnier's twin bookstores in the Rue de l'Odéon.[3] I haven't forgotten the automatic but always springlike kindness of the first, or the ample, mocking gentleness of the second, and I might add that their good will was of great help to me.

Nevertheless, as in Kafka's *The Castle*, my efforts seemed destined never to succeed. I imagined (wrongly) that the resistance came from Joyce himself. The truth is that during this time that monumental

---

1. *900: Cahiers d'Italie et d'Europe.*
2. This contact probably had to do with Georg Goyert's German translation of *Ulysses*, which Joyce was helping with in 1926 and which the Rhein-Verlag (Switzerland) published the following year. The French poet Ivan Goll (1891–1950), whom Joyce had first met in Zurich, was the Paris representative of the Rhein-Verlag. The adaptation of "Work in Progress" that Goll participated in, along with six others, was the French translation of "Anna Livia Plurabelle," done mainly in 1930.
3. Adrienne Monnier owned the bookshop La Maison des Amis des Livres, across the street from Shakespeare and Company. Her shop was a center for French writers, as Miss Beach's was for English-speaking writers. The two women were close friends and collaborated in promoting Joyce's work.

egg, the French translation of *Ulysses*, was being hatched (to the first translator, Auguste Morel, who had worked alone, Stuart Gilbert and Valery Larbaud had been added, all working under the direction of the author himself), and routes of access to the great man were barred to prevent his losing any little scraps of his time.[4]

It was all the more irritating in that I knew my author very badly, having only skimmed through *Dubliners*, where I saw merely the tameness of a polished style, and through *A Portrait of the Artist*, where, while yawning, I had become rather lost. The inaccessibility of his writing led me to imagine at first that Joyce was a sort of Old Man of the Mountain. All that I had been told of his infirmities—a dozen operations on both eyes—heightened the image. Dare I admit that after a time I began to feel a sort of resentment toward someone who appeared me completely alien to our times? James Joyce was only forty-four in those days, twice as old as I . . . This is a relevant autobiographical detail: it accounts for my still being in revolt against intellectual coteries, whereas Joyce, after leading a poor and obscure existence for fifteen or twenty years, was reaching the point where it is a delight to have the advantage of these social comforts.

Nor was that all. When I saw James Joyce—and at first sight he appeared steeped in his greatness—I soon discovered that his reserve hid not haughtiness but a recoil from any new person or situation—a reaction inspired by a frantic desire for mental privacy. Thus, at the price of a slight misunderstanding, he allowed a line of skirmishers to protect him from literary and other worries. If this withdrawal from the outside world had become natural to Joyce, it particularly characterized this time of his life, when, like one entering a religious order, he was committing himself to the composition of what was to be *Finnegans Wake*.

One afternoon Ivan Goll succeeded at last in taking me to the mysterious Irishman's house in the Square Robiac. It seems to me that it was a sunny day and that the little drawing room where Joyce received us was flooded with sunlight. Upon entering I noted a piano, over which hung a large oval portrait in the style of Albert Besnard, showing an extraordinarily beautiful woman of the 1905 period—I was later to identify it as Mrs. James Joyce; this image floated in a sort of golden haze.

I had an impression of coldness, however, on stepping into this

4. The Oxford-educated Stuart Gilbert had retired as a judge for the British civil service in Burma and settled in Paris with his French wife. Having noted some errors in Morel's translation of *Ulysses*, he offered to look over the work and Joyce agreed. Larbaud, in turn, offered to supervise Gilbert. Ellmann describes the difficulties this collaboration entailed (*JJ* 613–14).

*James Joyce. Drawing by Ivan Opffer, 1924
(courtesy of Croessman Collection of James Joyce)*

apartment with its banal little rooms, its characterless furniture, and its light, blank walls. Aside from the piano and the portrait, I could never discover anything intimate about it, none of the warmth of a "home." Was it just that it was a furnished apartment of the moneyed-bourgeois type? I do not know, but I had the same impression of anonymity in the other lodgings where I saw Joyce later. It seemed that he was incapable of making a retreat truly his own (it was as if he were only passing through) and that his sole place of intimacy was within himself; whereas, one would have imagined a passionate sense of life radiating from him and surrounding him. Joyce did not seem at all bothered by this lack of a homelike atmosphere, and I thought of a verse by Jules Romains: ". . . l'air qu'on respire a comme un goût mental."[5]

Joyce was sitting there before us, mute and immobile in his chair, his gaze elsewhere, his gestures infrequent and somewhat weary. He seemed plunged in a well of thought where he could not be reached by the words we were obstinately dropping in. How many times I was to notice the thickness of the silence this man succeeded in establishing around himself! I believe that he was wearing one of those black ribless-corduroy jackets that he liked, over a vest of the Barbey d'Aurevilly type, and this elegance perfectly suited the period he had adopted as his own—the period twenty years before this century's birth. To be more precise, Joyce was ageless, for as I saw him that autumn day in 1926, so I was to see him fourteen years later, immutable, never growing old, frozen once and for all in the appearance he had given himself, as if for him—who had made himself the contemplator— the flow of time had ceased.

However, because of my preconception or the effect produced by his seemingly expressionless face, I persisted in looking on him as an old man. It was a long, narrow, and curiously concave face, dominated by the forehead and the boldness of the chin. The hollow was composed of eyes masked by opaque lenses, a fine and delicately bridged nose, and a little reddish moustache that molded itself to the line of his thin, tight lips. His complexion was pale and his facial skin translucent, revealing darker tints composed of a rich network of veins. It was this subterranean richness, in fact, which primarily characterized his face; despite his extreme thinness, despite a fragile body that did not seem built to withstand stress, this man scarcely gave the impression of physical weakness but rather of strength at once occult and curiously earthy. Perhaps because of his Musketeer moustache, I thought of the bony, tenacious frame of the Knight of the Mournful Countenance, the toughest literary hero known. I sensed then, without knowing it, the

5. "The air one breathes has a sort of mental flavor."

principle of Joyce's personality: he had roots in a place, he was the Irishman of Dublin, "Seventh City of Christendom."

The silence continued, deepened even, as our arguments lost their vigor. Joyce, who was not behaving at all like an Irishman but, instead, like an Englishman, did not waver, did not even stir except to uncross his long legs, only to retie them another way like some adolescent. Seized by the frantic feeling of a swimmer out of breath, I stood up first, certain that the cause of *900* was lost. We followed Joyce, who, groping vaguely and still not opening his mouth, led us toward the door. Then, as I was shaking his hand, he suddenly thawed out to tell me he accepted.

Although this last-minute victory left me exalted, I confess that afterwards I did little to further our ties with such a laconic patron. James Joyce's editorial contribution to *900* was very limited: aside from a fragment of the French translation of *Ulysses*—the first version, which only Auguste Morel signed—he had me publish a short story by Robert McAlmon, a juicy story about fags, translated, as I discovered when I met him twenty years later, by the composer Guy Bernard. McAlmon delighted Joyce in those days; he was one of the pillars of the Select, the other being Hemingway, but Joyce had less esteem for the future author of *A Farewell to Arms*, perhaps because the latter was still a friend of Gertrude Stein's. I had a drink with the dark-haired and amusing McAlmon, who was already drunk and practically sprawled on the bar. I also had one with Hemingway, a young boar not yet with beard. Was it then (for *900*) or a little later (for *Bifur*) that Joyce had me ask Hemingway for a story? I have a letter from Hemingway, sent from Spain, offering instead of the short story he had promised me, a chapter of the novel he is writing, which, he says, takes place in Italy at the time of the rout from Caporetto . . .[6]

Actually, I do not believe that the doctrines and people of *900* interested Joyce in the least. As I said, the journal exalted *réalisme magique*, a literary slogan of the times—as a matter of fact, the phrase, used for the first time in *900* by its director Massimo Bontempelli, was

6. The McAlmon story published in *900* may have been "Miss Knight," which Joyce admired. Joyce often discussed his own work with McAlmon, went drinking with him, and depended on him for various favors, including regular loans of money. McAlmon's recollection, *Being Geniuses Together* (1938; rev. with supplementary chapters by Kay Boyle, London: Michael Joseph, 1970), contains numerous passages about Joyce. If Joyce at one time had less esteem for Hemingway than for McAlmon, it probably was not because of the former's association with Gertrude Stein, to whom Joyce paid little attention. Aside from recommending Hemingway's work to Frank, Joyce read his manuscripts, something he apparently did for no one else. See Ole Vinding's recollection (p. 148 and n) regarding Joyce's admiration of Hemingway. The Hemingway novel Frank refers to is, of course, *A Farewell to Arms* (1929).

my invention. Nothing was more foreign to Joyce than theories, especially hazy ones. I seem to remember taking Bontempelli, once when he was in Paris, to see Joyce; I was to do the same for Ilya Ehrenburg, who was equally curious to meet him. In dueling parlance, these were *rencontres sans resultat*; Joyce contented himself with addressing perfectly interchangeable remarks to them, and his visitors left shrugging their shoulders. A year later the journal *900* was suppressed after having been denounced to the Fascist government by professional agitators—foremost among them was the Germano-Tuscan who still signed his name Kurt Suckert; the "mala" of his later signature, Curzio Malaparte, was already beginning to appear. When I attempted to explain the affair to Joyce, he told me distinctly that he was utterly indifferent to political and social questions— and for the moment the matter was closed.

I well remember one of the last visits I paid him during this early period of our relations. We were in the same little drawing-room and again it was bright and sunny. Joyce questioned me about Dante's *Paradise* and Vico's *Principles*,[7] and suddenly, to my horror, I experienced the same mental agony I had felt during exams in school—it had been only three years since I had graduated. But it was not to inform himself that Joyce asked me about these authors; he knew a great deal more than I and was simply yielding to the need to talk of subjects dear to his heart. Later Dante's importance was to recede, and only Vico's philosophy, with its "turn" and "return," would remain part of the inspiration of *Finnegans Wake*.

The fact remains that on that day I was reliving my student nightmares, and I had but one idea, a trivial one—to slip away. The four steps necessary to reach the door seemed interminable. Yet this must have been the occasion that I was struck by the youthful and at the same time uncertain character of Joyce's gait. He had the look of a blind man, but, if I may say so, a blind adolescent.

Up to this time we had never spoken anything but French.

1929

Long afterward we fell into speaking Italian together. Nothing more was needed to bring me much closer to Joyce and to discover that he was a totally different person from the one I had imagined. He must have felt the same way, for, a short while later, he unhesitatingly allowed himself to become part of another literary enterprise that I was involved

7. The Italian philosopher-historian Giambattista Vico's *Scienza nuova* (1725) provided the basis for *Finnegans Wake*. The title *Principles* does not appear in lists of Vico's works.

with, although he was usually very suspicious about this kind of adventure.

The Italian episode was introduced by Italo Svevo, who made a trip to Paris with his wife in 1928, concerned that the translation of his *Confessions of Zeno* was behind schedule. This masterpiece, recommended by Joyce and Valery Larbaud to Benjamin Crémieux, was stalled by a somewhat lukewarm reaction on the part of the publishers. In fact, it was not to appear until after Svevo's death, and then only in an abridged version titled *Zeno*.

In 1928, after the publication in Italy of his third novel (the first two had appeared thirty and twenty-three years before), Italo Svevo, then over sixty, was "discovered."[8] His position was similar to that of Proust fifteen years earlier in France, not that their works had anything at all in common, but Svevo, whose real name was Ettore Schmitz—the pseudonym was supposed to indicate his double origin, both Italian and Swiss-German—was a rich manufacturer and "wrote poorly". . . Where did Joyce meet Svevo? In Trieste, where Joyce had long resided at the time when the city was still part of the Austro-Hungarian Empire. The Irishman, who was teaching English at the Berlitz School, had had the Italo-Swabian as a pupil; today, critics add that he was to borrow some of Leopold Bloom's substance from Italo Svevo.

I had gone to interview Svevo for the *Nouvelles Littéraires*. In a little hotel near the Rue de Rivoli, I had found a man both worried and amused by his sudden celebrity. Why did the subsequent little article so delight Joyce? He alluded to it in his letters, and when I later asked his permission to publish a portrait of him in a newspaper that asked me for it, he consented on condition it be "as good as the one on Svevo."[9] In any event, a few days later I returned to pick up the Svevos at their hotel. Perfectly Adriatic, Svevo had the Venetian Jew's mischievous good nature and sharp subtlety, which are among civilization's finest virtues. With a large, ponderously wagging head and a voice full of the tone of nonsense, he was somehow infused with an air of the old-fashioned. I see us—him, his excellent wife, and me—leaving their hotel, they are bickering, dawdling, walking in opposite directions under the arcades—like the Italian fishermen under other arcades in Chioggia—and I am trying very hard to make this childish and touching elderly couple move along . . . The problem was that James Joyce was waiting

8. *La coscienza di Zeno* (*The Confessions of Zeno*) was published in 1923; the earlier novels, *Una vita* (*A Life*) and *Senilità* (*As a Man Grows Older*), were published in 1892 and 1898, respectively.

9. Joyce was so impressed with Frank's portrait of Svevo that he asked *transition* to reprint it in homage to the Triestine writer, following his death in 1928 (*Letters* I, 270). Frank's sketch of Joyce was published in the French paper *Intransigeant*, February 6, 1930.

for us to lunch in a gourmet restaurant near the Gare Montparnasse, and I was greatly excited at the invitation my little article had won me.

Was Larbaud one of the party? He is mentioned in Svevo's biography as being there. I myself remember Benjamin Crémieux, with his sad, myopic gaze, his damp handshake, his somewhat Assyrian beard, his voice that sang, but badly.[10] And again it was a sunny morning, undoubtedly a fine day for sailing. From the start we spoke Italian, and in Joyce's and Svevo's mouths the language quickly turned into the Trieste dialect, which I understood. But Crémieux, accustomed to the pedantic Tuscan idiom and slowed besides by his way of speaking, was a little lost. Although a descendant of the papal Jews of Avignon, he was the foreigner, doubly so, since the conversation came around to Apulia, where I was born, and Svevo and Joyce teased me, following the custom that those from the upper Adriatic have of baiting those from the lower: we three formed an exclusive country of our own. I am afraid our loud voices and laughter in the narrow room of this gathering-place for gastronomes caused something of a scandal. Actually, we no longer felt that we were in Paris but instead were by the "infinitely briny" sea sung by d'Annunzio, and the Irishman was not the least fervent of the three of us. Poor Crémieux tried to follow us, and, in an attempt to join in our harmony, he ordered sea urchins, which he swallowed enthusiastically before our somewhat disgusted eyes, for this echinoderm is disdained along the Adriatic. As a humble witness, I had the feeling all of a sudden that two races were face to face: the men of genius, joined by an enigmatic kinship, and the man of letters, isolated, although he and Svevo belonged to that supposedly tenacious brotherhood of the Israelites.

Under the aegis of Svevo I was involved in another, much less intimate, episode. The Pen Club honored him with a dinner at the Closerie des Lilas—Ehrenburg and [Isaak] Babel were also to be honored —and the vanity of these official dinners is well known. The only exceptional thing about this banquet-with-speeches was that Joyce had agreed to go because of his friendship for Svevo, who was walking on air. Both of them had insisted on inviting me. This time the man of letters remained in the background, but from the looks we exchanged— Joyce's vague and Svevo's laughing—I saw that our complicity was confirmed.

It may seem trivial that to discover Joyce as he really was, in all his simplicity and vivaciousness, we needed only to change languages. Even after this discovery, I myself did not fully comprehend the

10. The French writer and critic Benjamin Crémieux (1888–1944) did much to forward Svevo's recognition in France. Like Joyce's close friend Paul Léon, Crémieux died in a Nazi concentration camp.

importance in Joyce's life of his sojourn in Trieste, the attachment he felt for everything Italian. His fidelity to Vico, however, should have opened my eyes.

Later, when I became better acquainted with his family life, I was to find that the members of his household almost always spoke in that language, and even in the Trieste dialect. His wife addressed him as "Jim," but what followed was the lisping speech of those who dwelt in the shadow of San Giusto.[11] The two children, Giorgio and Lucia, were born there, and it was there they had learned to talk. One can see that this city of exile was like a second Dublin for Joyce: he found in it a certain mixture of drollness and deep melancholy, an irredentism, and that northern-port fog that soaks into one's very soul.

Before leaving these recollections of the good Italo Svevo, let me say a word for lovers of bibliographical oddities. After his death, friends of mine in Florence who were publishing the review *Solaria* asked me to collect some foreign articles in homage to him for a special issue. I obtained one from Joyce of ten or so lines, which he dictated to me, weighing each word carefully, as was his custom.[12]

On this occasion he told me that while in Trieste he and a friend had made an Italian translation of *Riders to the Sea*, and that he had sought in vain to have it published. I saw from the way he spoke of it that he was still deeply disappointed by his lack of success. I eagerly undertook the necessary inquiries (Joyce's collaborator was an old Triestine lawyer named Nicolo Vidacovitch, who fortunately was still alive) and *Solaria* snapped up the translation hungrily. Thus it was that the only Italian text bearing James Joyce's signature was published.[13] I remember the delight of the author of *Ulysses* when I brought him the issues containing the piece, which has become today one of the obsessions of American thesis-writers.

I noticed that following our luncheon Joyce kept in touch with me. Soon after it he had Sylvia Beach propose that I, along with other writers, sign a protest against the pirated edition of *Ulysses* that had just appeared in America;[14] later he sent me the special number of *transition* (with a vaguely mocking title) in which his "twelve apostles" wrote

11. A cathedral in Trieste.
12. This homage is reprinted in *CW* 256–57.
13. Frank apparently has overlooked the nine articles that Joyce wrote for the *Piccolo della Sera*, while in Trieste. The translation of *Riders to the Sea* appeared in *Solaria*, 4, nos. 9–10 (Sept.-Oct. 1929); 3–16.
14. In July 1926 Samuel Roth began printing, without authorization, a slightly expurgated version of *Ulysses* in his magazine *Two Worlds Monthly*. Joyce started legal proceedings that eventually halted the piracy, but in the meantime drew up an "International Protest" against Roth and circulated it in Europe and England, eventually gathering 167 signatures. It was released to the press on Joyce's birthday, February 2, 1927.

about "Work in Progress," which Eugene Jolas' journal was publishing in portions.[15] Then, with a kindness that began to bewilder me, he summoned me to ask if I cared to have an author's copy of the imposing first edition of *Ulysses* in French, which Adrienne Monnier was getting ready to publish.

Of course, I accepted eagerly. But, looking back, I find this act of Joyce's extremely revealing: not content with showing his friendship for such a young puppy as I by giving me a splendid gift, he had to go so far as to ask permission. There was in this request a sort of humility that attests his genius better than ever so many poses. On the other hand, need I describe the apprehension and promptness with which, having received my copy of the book, I set myself to deciphering it, assisted by the reader's guide that Stuart Gilbert had fortunately just published in the *Nouvelle Revue Française*![16] I felt more and more in the shoes of an ill-prepared student with an exam to take, and I dreaded the fatal day when I was certain that I would have to give the author a report on my reading in order to receive a place in the army of followers.

Along came a new episode that in the drollest way allowed me to pass my exam, although not quite in the way I had supposed. History has recorded the solemn side; there was another—truer—view.

One morning an immense bus was parked in front of La Maison des Amis des Livres in the Rue de l'Odéon: it was June 24, 1929. I can give the date with such precision because the vehicle was waiting to carry some people to the Chevreuse Valley to celebrate the twenty-fifth anniversary of Leopold Bloom's day in Dublin.[17] I owed my invitation to this family party to my friendship with Joyce—that and the fact that my birthday was three days after the date of the odyssey in *Ulysses*, a date that had great significance for the author.

At the risk of seeming to harp on the subject, I must say that it was

15. Apparently, *Our Exagmination round His Factification for Incamination of Work in Progress*, which was published in 1929 by Shakespeare and Company. Most of the twelve essays had appeared previously in *transition*.

16. As a result of almost daily consultation with Joyce about the French translation of *Ulysses*, Gilbert decided to write a study of the book. Joyce encouraged and helped him with the project. A French translation of part of the resulting book appeared in the *Nouvelle Revue*.

17. Ellmann (*JJ* 628–29) and Joyce (*Letters* I, 282–83) give further accounts of the festive afternoon. The date was not June 24, which Frank mistakes for Bloomsday, but June 27. The celebration honored the publication of the French *Ulysses*, as well as the twenty-fifth anniversary of Bloomsday, hence Adrienne Monnier's part in organizing it. Joyce, who always tried to convince Miss Weaver of his quiet sobriety, told her that he wasn't looking forward to the celebration and "would much prefer a glass of milk and a bath bun" (*Letters* I, 281). However, he obviously had a delightful time.

another bright and sunny day. Many impressive personages showed up: the tall, white-haired Edouard Dujardin, who, as the father of the stream of consciousness, had been revived by Joyce, as Svevo had; Paul Valéry, with his smoke-yellowed moustache and June-bug manner; Léon-Paul Fargue, who, if I am not mistaken, had just entered a bearded phase; and Jules Romains, who was still wobbling between eroticism and good will, although morally he had already put on considerable weight.[18] Then James Joyce, slow, distant, laconic, accompanied by his family.

Adrienne Monnier was beside herself with pleasure and urged the great men to sing in chorus so we would depart as they do in musical comedies. I must confess that because I have little taste for such cere- monies I shrank in my seat. I shall not give an extended account of the luncheon in a Vaux-de-Cernay inn, surrounded by greenery—it seems to me it was a cheerful meal with very few speeches, some of Fargue's turn-of-the-century comic songs, and the presentation of the first copies of *Ulysses* in French. A menu covered with autographs from this banquet was displayed at the 1937 Exhibition, just as everything ends up in exhibitions. Actually, I have forgotten the specific details of that party, at least up to the point when a few of us woke up from the euphoria in which the party had sunk and suddenly recognized one another as kindred spirits.

We were few: there were two Irishmen, quite as laconic as Joyce who were instructors at the Ecole Normale—Thomas McGreevy, stocky and gloomy, who has become today an important art critic and curator of some Dublin museum or other; and a blond bean-pole with glasses, who turned out to be gravely truculent, like a Synge character, and whose name was Samuel Beckett.[19] Beyond them I recall only Philippe Soupault, myself, and, to my surprise, Joyce—Joyce himself.

Were we the youngest, then? I don't know, but we were suddenly the wildest. The torpid gaze of the other guests rested on us, at first complacently, then with consternation, as we romped around engaging in all sorts of absurd antics. And Joyce, who was called back to the table, if not back to order, obstinately joined in with his awkward gait;

18. Joyce's insistence that he owed the interior monologue to Dujardin's novel *Les Lauriers sont coupés* (1887) brought the almost forgotten French writer into prominence and the Joyce circle. Of the three other French writers mentioned, only the poet Fargue (1878–1947), a lover of word play, witty story teller, and mine of gossip, was at all close to Joyce. He assisted in the translations of *Ulysses* that were read during Larbaud's *séance* on the book and also in the translation of "Anna Livia Plurabelle."

19. McGreevy and the now well-known writer Beckett assisted Joyce at various times with his work, and each wrote an essay included in *Our Exagmination*. Mc- Greevy became director of the National Gallery of Ireland.

one might have thought him the smallest and clumsiest of a bunch of kids, trying to ape the older ones.

I have a feeling that we were hurried onto the bus for the return trip. Our jokes were becoming stupid. On the interminable ride it was we, the silent ones on the way out, who now were singing (with voices no doubt a bit vinous), and Joyce mingled his with ours. Then someone asked to stop at a pub long enough to answer the call of nature. How did we contrive it? In the twinkling of an eye there were five of us, including Joyce, lined up at the bar drinking white wine, all seized by the incomprehensible joy that comes from who knows where and that will never be forgotten.

The faces in the bus expressed annoyance. We tried our trick two or three times more, thanks to the complicity of our driver, who came in to drink with us. The others tried in vain to detain Joyce, and Nora, to whom this was an old story, didn't budge but withdrew into an attitude of queenly indifference; I would almost swear that on her face was the ghost of a smile.

The curious local inhabitants were hardly surprised by this cheerfulness on the Route de Robinson, though they may have been surprised not to find a bride inside our vehicle. Once back in my seat, I turned around and saw the disgusted eyes and austere lips of Jean Paulhan, undoubtedly a water-drinker. I think he even scolded me in convoluted phrases to which I replied with a particularly foolish grin.

The last straw was when, at the Porte d'Orléans, Samuel Beckett suddenly became enraged because the bus refused to stop, although this time he really needed to relieve himself. We had to slow down and let him get off, which he did with great dignity. We watched him stride off, stiff as a poker, until he was lost in the crowd. I was observing Joyce in front of me; the man, as he now appeared to me, no longer had the least connection with the pompous writer I had originally fancied him.

His coolness, his reserve, were only to protect his way of life. Actually, his constant youthfulness—one might have thought he had become fixed in Stephen Dedalus' adolescence at the Martello Tower— was the heart of a personality at once of the air and of the earth and cemented by something Tolstoyan, a personality I could not help but associate with certain Synge heroes, a personality that Joyce himself evoked the rare times he happened to speak to me of the fabulous being his father seems to have been. This old man, ruddy and hoary, dignified and truculent, stubborn as a mule and witty as the devil, would soon dominate his son's life again, this time from a portrait painted by an Irishman and hung on the drawing-room wall. Joyce attached at least as much importance to this painting as to the portrait of Mrs. Svevo, named Anna Livia, who, as we know, was to lend her golden hair to Anna Livia Plurabelle and to the waters of the Liffey.[20]

Now that the paths of friendship had been smoothed, I had no trouble some time later obtaining Joyce's consent to serve on a board of directors for the review *Bifur*, which Georges Ribemont-Dessaignes was preparing to launch.

This time, appointed especially to cover British letters (William Carlos Williams, with whom I maintained a brisk correspondence, took charge of the Americans), Joyce carried out his responsibilities assiduously. I mean that he accorded me frequent interviews; however, they often digressed into commentary on "Work in Progress." The problem was that because of his poor vision Joyce did not keep up with what was being published. I noticed, however, that despite his insular loyalty and his disdain regarding political questions, he had little interest in English writers and wanted me to publish instead an Irishman such as Lord Dunsany, or Australians and South Africans, as if he were attracted in directions where irredentism was an issue. When I once spoke to him about T. S. Eliot, he grimaced.[21] The same thing happened when, learning that D. H. Lawrence was in Paris, I hurried to consult Joyce.

"That man writes really too poorly," he said. "Ask his friend Aldous Huxley for something instead; at least he dresses decently."[22]

I might add that of Joyce's works, we printed some proofs from "Work in Progress," corrected in the Proustian manner, as well as a translation of the little collection *Pomes Penyeach*, which Sylvia Beach

20. See *JJ*, plate XVI, for a photograph that illustrates the dominating presence of John Joyce's portrait. Joyce had commissioned the portrait from the Irish painter Patrick Tuohy in 1923. Mrs. Svevo's name was Livia Veneziani.

21. This grimace at the mention of Eliot is surprising. When they first met in 1920, Joyce was reserved and gave no sign that he even had read the poet's work, except for remarking once, "I was at the Jardin des Plantes today and paid my respects to your friend the hippopotamus" (*JJ* 509). In his notebook, however, he wrote, "T. S. Eliot ends idea of poetry for ladies," which sounds like high praise, and according to Arthur Power he spoke admiringly of Eliot's work, particularly *The Waste Land* (*Conversations with Joyce* [London: Millington, 1974] pp. 75, 100–1).

22. Probably annoyed that Lawrence's work kept being linked with his as pornography, Joyce once had Stuart Gilbert read him a few pages of *Lady Chatterley's Lover* and read a few more himself. He found the prose "lush," the English "sloppy," and the pornography imitation. Commenting on a plan for an expensive French edition of the book, he said, ". . . I cannot understand how they can expect any sensible person to pay hundreds of francs for such a production when the genuine article much more effectively done can be had in any back shop in Paris for one tenth of the money" (*Letters* I, 294). (Lawrence, on the other hand, objected to *Ulysses* on the grounds that it was real pornography).

had just published and which was apparently the only part of Joyce's works that Nora knew and appreciated.[23]

Joyce was continually drawing back, but my curiosity, inspired from now on by his method and by something apparently diabolical in the things that he said, gained me some insights.

Coming after *A Portrait of the Artist*, *Ulysses* (which I had just read) attested to the extraordinary skill of a perfect linguistic technician, to whom no venture in the domain of expression seemed forbidden. This undoubtedly produced in Joyce a sort of *toedium artis* that led him joyfully to abandon the prey for the shadow and to attempt the impossible: giving an idiom to the night, thus to the ineffable, by dynamiting the language. This attempt reminded me of the faint suggestion of Don Quixote that I had seen in Joyce earlier.

We were living in a time still favorable to battles with chimeras, a golden age that preceded the time of crisis when the windmills would set out irresistibly to counterattack. And for fifteen years Joyce was to give himself up entirely to the composition of this book—nocturnal, magical, powerfully rhythmical—which now stands in history as a gigantic megalith around which the exegete crawls in dismay . . .

Joyce kept himself constantly in practice as a polyglot by daily skimming through the four or five most important European newspapers, among others the *Osservatore Romano*, the Vatican organ, which this confirmed enemy of God held dear (he was perfectly delighted to find a long, respectful review of his work in it one day);[24] and the *Neue Zürcher Zeitung*, undoubtedly because of the importance Zurich had for him as the fourth city of his life. This was another point in common between us, since Zurich is one of the cities I call home. We often talked about it and he assured me that the Hotel Dolder, which overlooks the city, was the most beautiful hotel in the world. It was in Zurich that Joyce died . . .

Joyce put on thick lenses for reading. He showed me the typewriter with enormous characters that had been procured for him in order to help him with his work. He liked to read passages aloud with his admirably expressive voice; the BBC still has a recording of him reading a fragment of *Finnegans Wake*, made during a stay in England the summer of his marriage.[25] During this rare visit to England Joyce

23. Auguste Morel's translation of seven poems from *Pomes Penyeach* appeared in the September 1929 issue of *Bifur*. Joyce's wife also knew and apparently appreciated the poems in *Chamber Music*.

24. This review, which Joyce referred to constantly, appeared in the *Osservatore Romano*, no. 245 (October 20, 1937), p. 3. It is partially reproduced in the *James Joyce Quarterly*, 9 (Summer 1972): 460.

25. Joyce and Nora were formally married in London on July 4, 1931.

renewed his ties with Dublin, where his work was beginning to be respected, and afterwards he became less laconic concerning his homeland.

Heat and frost were continually coming and going in the atmosphere around him. During this period I detected in the household a childlike cheerfulness alternating with that "mental" air which had struck me at the outset. Cheerfulness predominated at the little receptions Joyce loved to give, particularly on his birthday, which fell on Candlemas. There I saw Mrs. Joyce, a beauty faithful to her portrait, barely powdered by the years, patient, gentle, and infinitely distant, the only one of the household who occasionally made use of English; then their two children, Lucia, apprentice dancer, lovely and elusive, who resembled her father but had her mother's eyes, and Giorgio, who studied singing and readily chaffed Joyce with typically Triestine good humor. One year the queen of the evening was an American, who had the beauty and open smile of certain Henry James heroines; Giorgio Joyce was going to marry her a short time later, but their union was not to be a happy one.[26]

Americans in general were very well received. I remember Caresse and Harry Crosby, a millionaire couple who were poets—their suicide soon after in New York was one of the first episodes of the crisis or one of the last of the *nouveau mal du siècle*.[27] We drank those Rhine or Alsatian white wines that Joyce, like many Irishmen, was fond of. Stuart Gilbert, former judge in Burma and new translator of *Ulysses*, told slightly risque stories with the mocking tone of an Anatole France canon who had had Dickens do his make-up. Then came the somewhat solemn moment when, in compliance with tradition, Joyce sang—his voice was fragile but of an extreme purity—after which it was the turn of the better-endowed Giorgio, and sometimes the baritone [sic] Sullivan, the writer's idol. Joyce recruited his friends to go and applaud the singer each time he performed at the Opera.

In the course of one of these soirees I came upon a strapping fellow with a brick-red face and green eyes. He was the heaviest drinker of all and had an air of a tough boxer and a brutal laugh that did not harmonize at all with the tone of the party; however, the Joyces were attentive to him, and he inspired me with a lively enough curiosity that several

26. The American was Helen Kastor Fleischman, whom Giorgio married on December 10, 1930. Giorgio was living apart from her in 1939, by which time she had had several mental collapses. The following year she returned to the United States, where she was instiutionalized for some time before finally recovering.

27. Harry Crosby was a suicide (December 10, 1929), but not his wife. In August 1929 the Crosbys' Black Sun Press published *Tales Told of Shem and Shaun*, containing three fragments of *Finnegans Wake*.

days later we met for a drink. It was Liam O'Flaherty, a book of whose had just appeared in French—it was a fairly crude book and did not seem to have the least affinity with Joyce's cerebral universe.[28] As we were talking about Joyce, Liam O'Flaherty gave me the key to their relationship with an abrupt burst of laughter: "Joyce?" he barked. "He's the playboy of the western world." There was not the least hint of sarcasm in his definition, for to any true Irishman Synge's hero is no figure of fun but a sort of ideal.

Interlude

One summer's end, finding myself near where Joyce was vacationing at Saint-Jean-Cap-Ferrat, I went to pay him a visit. In the little deserted port we chatted a long while, near boats whose colors appeared drab to us compared with the Adriatic boats that were present in our memories. That particular year this part of the coast was as literary as could be: André Maurois, in a room near mine at the Cap; Jean Giraudoux in a nearby villa; Paul Morand, who came from Villefranche in his white boat. This high society met on the hotel's little beach. The day Joyce surprised us by appearing there, we had all that was needed to improvise a Pen Club conference. My knowledge of Joyce suggested that this would be enough to make him flee. He did.

Why had we stopped seeing each other regularly? Doubtless because *Bifur* had suspended publication. Actually, I was approaching a long illness during which I had to lead a somewhat retired life from Paris. And Joyce himself? . . .

In this period when I no longer had occasion to see him, I had two singular encounters, which my imagination tends to connect, as if a drama-like relationship could be established between them.

On the Champs Elysées one morning, about 1933, I ran into Lucia. I had never seen her so pretty, so gay, so strangely tranquil. We exchanged a few joking words, then I watched her move off with a lithe, startlingly light step . . . She was on the threshold of madness.

One afternoon three of four years later, at exactly the same place, the sidewalk in front of an ugly bank building—as if time had stopped and I saw the second figure in a chase—a familiar silhouette appeared; to be precise, I first caught sight of one of those white canes the blind were beginning to carry, but this one was being wielded like a switch. It was James Joyce, all alone, whistling under his breath, the brim of his felt hat turned up, as he liked it, looking even more jaunty,

28. O'Flaherty (b. 1896) is an Irish writer whose best-known work is *The Informer*.

more youthful than usual, in short, giving no sign of that which his cane proclaimed.

He gave me his new address, we promised to see each other some time, and, as I spoke of his daughter, he informed me, his eyes suddenly averted, that she was staying in a sanitarium. All at once I discovered that his face had become still thinner and appeared more concave, sharper, more stubborn, with a colder pallor. He left me, brandishing his white cane, and I seemed to behold the weightless walk of Oedipus.

1938

The apartment on the Rue Edmond-Valentin (Joyce remained faithful to the Gros-Caillou quarter) was of the same substantial and anonymous sort as the one on the Square Robiac, less cramped, however, and including in particular a vast drawing room, where Mrs. Joyce's portrait occupied the place of honor. Perhaps they had hoped to have more frequent get-togethers of the kind Joyce liked, such as the Square Robiac gatherings, which sometimes succeeded in fixing the fleeting happiness that I have tried to describe. But the children were no longer around—Giorgio was married, Lucia in the hands of psychiatrists—and the parents found themselves alone in an apartment that had become immense and silent.

I detected something new in this apartment: the absence of sunshine, of abundant light. Does my memory deceive me? It seems to me that I always saw it plunged in semiobscurity or invaded by ever-darkening air. Nevertheless, there Joyce was to achieve the summit of his freedom and to surrender himself most completely to the beloved demons of eternal youth. But I anticipate. I want to record the impression which surprised me most after these years of separation; it was primarily an impression of a brand-new solitude, of a kind of destitution, replacing the former animation and numerous friendships.

We were at dinner in a luxurious Champs-Elysées restaurant re-nowned for its bar, which movie moguls and near-moguls had made an annex to their head office. Joyce sat in his regular seat, turning his back to the public as was his custom, and ordered bisque, which he loved, and some Rhine wine. I remember this dinner where I chattered without stopping, agonized by the gentle silence of Mrs. Joyce, who was always a little abstracted, and by her husband's weary mono-syllables. The latter had brought a copy of the new edition of *Ulysses* in French, which had just come out; he intended it for the maitre d'hotel, who regularly served him. But it turned out that the man was absent, so I offered to get the package to him the next day. I delivered it in person, as curious as could be. The amiable fellow seemed flattered by the gift, praised Mr. Joyce, who "was a refined gourmet," then confessed to me that he lacked the time to read . . . Where had the 1926 prestige gone?

What I saw later confirmed this impression of solitude. I was told that among the disciples there had been disagreement, jealousy, even estrangement—but perhaps they would not have gone so far as to be unfaithful if we had not finally entered into the great prolegomena to the crisis, into the flatulencies of politics, into the hazy and suffocating air which led up to that long and perilous period. Joyce's intimate circle had shrunk: apart from Samuel Beckett, apart from Eugene Jolas and his wife—who had become the writer's good angels and who remained with him to the end—apart from poor Paul Léon, who was designated to help Joyce with business matters (but it was Joyce who demonstrated the firmness and rigor of the "businessman," the other replying with timid, meandering buffooneries), everyone else had disappeared. And Joyce was scarcely bothered by the situation, it seemed to me: his eyes were feeling better, Lucia's treatment was going to cure her, Giorgio would soon give him a grandson. One was struck by the will to live revealed in his remarks, by a sort of somber and tenacious levity.

What was happening?

The explanation of his isolation, as well as of his cheerful vision of the future, lay with "Work in Progress," which had not yet received the title *Finnegans Wake*. Penetrating year by year more deeply into this work, advancing with slow, groping pace in his mine tunnels, perceiving ever more clearly that he no longer knew exactly where he was going, Joyce was giving the slip to a distinguished intellectual world, which had at first found the experiment amusing (thus the praise and glosses) but had dropped out as soon as the game proved to consist of an obscure, stubborn, and interminable undermining. To abandon the prey altogether and chase the shadow is not to be done in six months; "Work in Progress"—in progress already for over twelve years—was taking shape as an Operation Penelope, an Operation Sea Serpent. In the name of *Ulysses*, a work of sure merit, people shook their heads at the great man inexorably leaping into the unknown. By ridding himself of the dead weights with which life had loaded him, he sought to attain the utmost velocity of thought, a velocity of lightninglike immobility—the tragic *surplace* of bicycle racers and perhaps the measure of the eternal.

Joyce no longer read anything but works of geography or science that might feed the private lexicon he was fabricating. Speaking of books, a brief digression: among the works which comprised his library at his death, a popular Italian edition of Petrarch's poems was found, and, since the copy was well thumbed, it was concluded that the Italian was one of the Irishman's favorite poets. I have even seen the volume exposed under glass, and I believe that it is now to be found in a museum. I am afraid that I must give the lie to Joyce's exegetes. He knew nothing, or next to nothing, about Petrarch. Once we were speaking of "Anna Livia Plurabelle" and the allusions to rivers in it. When I reminded him of the "song," "Chiare fresche e dolci acque . . . ," he asked me to procure Petrarch's poems for him. I borrowed the book from my friend Michel Arnaud, who did read Petrarch assiduously. In fact, Joyce found nothing in it that he could use and put the copy aside, where it remained, for it sometimes happens that I am forgetful— a habit that Michel Arnaud has never forgiven me, even though he has become immortal through the agency of his book.

Actually, all conversation with Joyce henceforth bore upon his labor. It was incessant labor but left him a few moments nearly every day for an often somewhat demonic gaiety. One day, after an afternoon spent in churning and grinding words, he took a taxi to the Bois to get a little fresh air, and when he paid the driver he called him a "cauliflower."[29] The fellow's reaction may be imagined. The strangest of all, added Joyce in telling the story, was that the taxi driver had the flattened ears of a boxer, so the evocation of that vegetable was not at all gratuitous.

Another time, when I was questioning him stupidly about when he would complete his book and what he was planning to write afterwards, he said gravely, "It would be funny if I wrote a little commonplace novel like Paul Bourget's . . .[30] They would be tripped up, wouldn't they?" "They" meant not his readers but the fanatics who were forging a Joyce according to their own fancy.

My most poignant memory of Joyce's dizzying levity dates from one of his birthday parties—Candlemas 1938, if I am not mistaken. The party was at Giorgio's house, near the Trocadero—Giorgio's wife seemed as laughing and affable as ever but with a new, undefinable aggressiveness in her tone, especially in her way of addressing her father-in-law. The very next year she was to return to America in order that she too might undergo psychiatric treatment.

As it happened, I had obtained permission from Jean Masson and Paul Gibson for her young husband to be interviewed and to give a brief singing recital on Radio Luxembourg. My memory of that broadcast is very blurred: Joyce accompanied his son (I can see him arriving

29. A pun on "chauffeur." In French "cauliflower" = "chou-fleur."
30. Bourget (1852–1935) was a popular French writer of society romances, psychological studies, and didactic fiction. The term "monologue intérieur," which Valery Larbaud used to describe the method in Ulysses, came from Bourget's Cosmopolis (1893).

at the Rue Bayard and receiving a solemn welcome) and agreed to
participate, although it was to be a laconic participation—let us specify
for biographers that this happened long after the little Candlemas
party and that unfortunately no trace of the program remains since the
broadcast was "live." To return, the announcement of this project
was joyfully received by everyone at Giorgio's house.

We sang, we laughed, Joyce blew out the candles on his birthday
cake, we also drank a lot. Someone put an inviting dance tune on the
record player, and suddenly, while I was confessing my ignorance
of the most elementary steps, Joyce took me by the arms and compelled
me to whirl about with him.[31] In vain the others and I tried to stop him;
he was enjoying the joke. Prudence bade me fall in with him, since
both of us were unsteady on our legs; he dragged me along with a child's
joyful giddiness—and I will never forget the agonizing sensation of
trying to hold up this man, fragile as a statuette, while all present looked
on in consternation. Fortunately the step was only a *bourrée* style
applied to the waltz. In any case the party was soon brought to an end.
Another time I will tell the story of how that same night Beckett and
I, both of us drunk and accompanying each other, barely escaped a
falling out on the corner of Boulevard Pasteur and Rue de Vaugirard,
where we carried on one of those illogical conversations in which
both parties talk at once.

I associate Beckett with another image of Joyce that I remember from
those days—the scene is a hospital, the Hôpital Cochin, to be precise.

Sam Beckett, the beloved disciple, quarreled with a drunken tramp
one night on the Boulevard St-Michel, and, as one thing led to another,
the fellow slipped a knife in his back. Joyce asked me to go with him
to see the wounded man—who by the way got well very quickly.
We found him in a state of concentrated fury: although he had refused
to file a complaint, the tramp was being kept in jail; on top of that,
Beckett had been interrogated and was going to have to testify in police
court.

The room where he was lying, his glasses sparkling, his lips tight-
pressed, a wry smile on his face, was intensely gray and crowded, and
one could catch the looks of the bedridden bluntly fixed on us. I guessed
that although Joyce saw nothing, he was perfectly aware of what
surrounded us and relished the atmosphere. His eyes raised to the
indefinite light of the window, he sat placidly facing Beckett, as the
two of them marinated in intolerable silences; from time to time, they
exchanged a few words, a short laugh.

31. When elevated by drink Joyce characteristically turned to dancing, often
solo. See Vinding's recollection (pp. 150–51) and Carola Giedion-Welcker's
(pp. 273–74) for a description of this habit.

James Joyce and Robert McAlmon.
Drawing by Paul-Emile Bécat, 1921
(courtesy of Princeton University Library)

I have never felt so close to Ireland, to its sentimental isolation, to the very air of *Ulysses*, as I did that day, sitting between those two brothers, in their shape and their keenness like twin knifeblades. The elder and the younger were united by a profound bond, to find the explanation of which one need go no further than Swift or simply any post card showing a Dublin pub, some shops, and the passers-by.

Joyce confirmed my feeling when, having had enough of silences, we left. As we were returning to the Rue Edmond Valentin he openly made fun of his young friend's misadventure.

"He is truly Irish," he told me. "He doesn't hold it against the tramp at all, but do you know what he's mad about? The knife made a hole in his overcoat. He wants the judge to make it up to him and buy him another one." [32]

It was some time later that I received an unexpected proposition from Joyce: he asked me to try to transpose into Italian, with his help, a fragment of his current book. While I protested at the difficulty of the proposal (therein mistaking the extent of his part in our collaboration) he insisted:

"We must begin work before it's too late. For the moment there is still one person in the world, myself, who can understand what I have written. I can't guarantee that in two or three years I will still be able to."

Thus I was led to spend two afternoons a week for a good three months with Joyce. The fragment of *Finnegans Wake* that we did was the very one—the scrubwoman's dialogue in "Anna Livia Plurabelle" —which ten or so French writers, along with Joyce himself, had taken six months to make a French adaptation of several years before. Joyce and I were very proud to have beaten the numerous French team by an ample margin. It is true that we benefited from the indirect assistance that their successful version afforded me and from the fact that Joyce himself—to whom the French language always remained somewhat foreign, although he knew it to perfection—felt the same delight in playing games with Italian as he did with English. Thus I can say without any false modesty that Joyce is responsible for at least three-quarters of the Italian text; for the most part I served as guinea pig and fellow-worker.

A dozen lines an afternoon, such was our harvest. We worked in Joyce's room, a characterless place that I have no recollection of, usually with him stretched out on the divan in his dressing gown. Already fairly dim, the room, as I mentioned, seemed to darken gradually as we advanced in our labor, especially as Joyce's words, always meditated at length and falling like verdicts, became more infrequent, more

32. In reporting Beckett's stabbing to Giorgio (*Letters* III, 411), Joyce did not treat the episode as a joke but gave a solemnly technical account of the wound.

circumspect, more distant. I read and interpreted the text on my own, after which Joyce explained it to me word by word, revealing to me its various meanings, dragging me after him into the complex mythology of his Dublin. Then began the slow tennis of approximations; we tossed short phrases to each other like slow-motion balls through a rarefied atmosphere. In the end our procedure resembled incantation.

I left there with migraine headaches—and the feeling that I had found out the secret of Joyce's perpetual escape. Two things struck me: first, that the rhythm, the harmony, the density and consonance of the words were more important to him than the meaning, and that, for example, having written one thing, Joyce scarcely hesitated to put down something completely different in Italian, as long as the poetic or metrical result was equivalent.[33] On the other hand, with each elucidation he furnished me, this is what I noticed: whatever the phrase or word, the key remained his birthplace, be it an occurrence of his Dublin life, a recollection, or a legend. I know very well that Dublin is the deliberate setting of all that Joyce wrote, but there was something fatal about this obsession . . . Thus, between one moment and the next, I passed from a revival of my former prejudices regarding him, caused by his playing the juggler, to an emotion inspired by his indestructible bond with the land that was the source and sustenance of his artistic personality.

This attempt at an Italian translation must have been one of Joyce's last great pleasures, if I am to believe the little book Louis Gillet dedicated to his friend. According to that book Joyce claimed this version was the best introduction to the reading and understanding of the original.[34] Actually, it is perhaps richer harmonically, if I may say so, than the French. The Italian language is better suited than the others, even than English I sometimes think, to the at once colloquial and epic style that, along with a deliberate break from a certain Cartesianism, was sought by the writer. And, the work completed, I apologized to Joyce. I had opposed him continually on the principle that Italian was, in my opinion, too monumental, too set, to be broken down into an interminable pun.

I had the thing typed in well-spaced characters so Joyce could read it, and afterwards he never tired of exhibiting it just about everywhere.

33. Frank told Ellmann about protesting one Italian phrase because it failed to capture the rhythm of the original. Joyce replied, "I like the new rhythm" (*JJ* 713–14). As Ellmann (*JJ* 645–46) and Philippe Soupault (see his recollection, pp. 114–15) show, Joyce's method in translating "Anna Livia Plurabelle" into French closely resembled that described by Frank. But while in some instances he disregarded his original meaning or rhythm, in others he was very concerned about them.

34. See Gillet's recollection (p. 193).

On his next birthday, Candlemas 1939, at the Jolases' in Neuilly (in the villa where de Gaulle elected to live after the Liberation, I was told, and where the night we were there a strange Louisiana dinner had been prepared for the guests) he solemnly demanded that I give a reading of it. I believe this entertainment was as painful for my listeners as for myself, since they scarcely understood Italian and I have neither expressive gestures nor a melodious voice. But Joyce applauded enthusiastically and would not stop until I began again *da capo*. I remember George Pelorson-Belmont's eyes, by nature worn out, becoming doubly so. At the time he was a teacher in the school for English and American girls directed by Mrs. Jolas.

That evening remains memorable because of another event, which I find described in an article written several days later for *Candide*:

> During the sixteen years its brooding has lasted, "Work in Progress" has kept this provisional title. It has just been baptized at last, on the occasion of its completion and in the course of a party given for the illustrious writer by his friends. That evening a table was prepared showing Dublin, the birthplace of the author and the subject of his book, symbolically wedded to Paris, the habitual residence of James Joyce: the Liffey, the river that runs through Eire's capital and the night in "Work in Progress," was running between a little Arc de Triomphe and a little Moulin de la Galette. At dessert there appeared another superb edifice which represented James Joyce's books with their titles. Only one was missing . . . "*Finnegans Wake*," pronounced James Joyce. And so *Finnegans Wake* made its solemn entry into the world.

The man lived on the tightrope of his nerves, in permanent vertigo above the chasm of his work. Yet he had his hours of relaxation. On the Champs-Elysées there was an Alsatian restaurant where the wines were to his taste, and he used to invite us there—the Jolases, the Léons, the Becketts, sometimes the Gilberts. I remember some heroi-comic things that happened to me there—Joyce and the others were unaware of them, but the author of *Ulysses* would have relished them highly. One evening I had accepted the Joycean invitation in a peculiar state owing to the fact that, lacking money, I had been fasting for forty-eight hours.

Once the company's orders were taken—it was a large party—the dishes were not long in arriving, all but mine, a simple steak with French fries. Frustrated and with the customary low spirits of the famished, I kept mum, waiting for someone to take notice, but the Joyces saw nothing, and the others had eyes only for the Joyces. Finally the good Paul Léon observed my empty place; everyone exclaimed, and my steak soon arrived. In my agitation I failed to notice, as I was adding pepper, that the pepper-shaker's top was loose, and I emptied the contents in my plate. Repressing my coughs and hiccoughs, I was obliged to feed on this fiery dish. The result was that since the white wine flowed, I returned home, two or three hours later, once again on all fours.

Although Joyce preferred to question and to listen quietly rather than to talk himself, I recall some scraps of conversation about the Vatican (the life of the pontifical microcosm never ceased to intrigue him), about d'Annunzio (whom he knew little about but for whom he felt a special esteem),[35] about Switzerland (he adored the air in Zurich, where the specialist who treated his eyes lived), about surrealism (which left him cold: the path along which Breton led his followers went from the subconscious to the conscious, whereas Joyce traveled the other way), about his departure from the Austro-Hungarian Empire in 1914 after several days of captivity. Sometimes we talked about the cinema; James Joyce was interested in the cinema and asked me to take him two or three times.

How can I forget these occasions, painful for me because his poor vision compelled us to sit in the first row? They allowed me to discover his esteem for "grand drama," where, as they say, there is something to sink your teeth into, and for a film of Jean Choux's about Paris, where Harry Baur's well-measured tremolos triumphed. I also remember another time when, with a young admirer who had come from Ireland to see him, we went to a local theater in the outer boulevards: they were showing some western or other inspired by Fenimore Cooper, and it seems to me someone had assured Joyce that he would find in it some plays on words to please him. Such was not the case, and, to refresh ourselves after our fruitless undertaking, we followed Lord Carlow to the Ritz where tea awaited us.[36] This was the occasion of yet another of those "conversations" based on brief remarks and interminable silences, such as the one I spoke of in connection with the visit to Beckett. I had leisure to observe its oddity since my modest command of English reduced me to silence.

As regards pastimes, I recall another anecdote. Having seen an operetta entitled *Trois valses*, Joyce had taken a fancy to the star of the show, her voice, and the songs she sang. One afternoon, to please him, I brought him the record of Yvonne Printemps singing one of these songs, and that day there was no question of our working on the job "in progress." We had to sit in front of a phonograph for hours to decipher the words, which were, of course, silly:

35. See p. 45, note 59.
36. George Lionel Seymour, Viscount Carlow (1907–44). In 1937, his Corvinus Press published two fragments of *Finnegans Wake* under the title *Storiella as She Is Syung.*

Je ne suis pas ce que l'on pense,
Je ne suis pas ce que l'on dit:
Au cinéma, pour qu'on vous lance,
D'être soi-même, c'est interdit. . . .[37]

I have rarely seen Joyce so delighted. Afterwards he sang the song at every opportunity, and during the party at the Jolases' he made me sing it along with him. I certainly had to be a jack-of-all-trades!

Another episode. The Pen Club was inaugurating its center on the Rue Pierre-Charron and Joyce, having promised to attend the ceremony, asked me to accompany him. It was a fairly pompous reception, which the President of the Republic—Albert Lebrun—was to honor with his presence. Hence we noticed as we entered the brilliantly lighted room an emotional atmosphere reigning among the notables there, Jules Romains, Benjamin Crémieux, and company. They hastened to welcome my companion respectfully, and then, as an excited hubbub already announced the arrival of the republican sovereign, we were pushed into a corner.

The crowd of writers, some of them heavily bearded and all dressed to the teeth, formed a double line: Joyce found himself, by chance, next to Adrienne Monnier. She had just been decorated and bore on her bosom, which was imposing, a very beautiful red ribbon. Has the worthy and apparently weepy character of Albert Lebrun been forgotten? In compliance with custom, he went through this ceremony vacant-eyed, coming to a stop every four or five paces in order to seize and shake one of the hands that happened to be at the right height. This he did with Adrienne Monnier, doubtless impressed by the red of her ribbon. As he was preparing to cover another four paces toward other hands, Jules Romains, who was leading him, detained him in front of James Joyce and named the illustrious writer for him. Long handshake. What happened in the presidential head at that moment? Chance had stowed me between Adrienne Monnier and Joyce; it is possible that the chief of state suddenly took pity on the poor devil installed like a hyphen between the glory of Ireland and this high-placed Legion of Honor; in any event he held out his hand. I was so flabbergasted that I hurried to catch it, while babbling who knows what civilities.

The babbling was too much. It must have alerted Joyce, who, despite

37. "I am not what they think. / I am not what they say: / To be launched in the movies/ Yourself you can't play. . . ." In 1938, during a stay in Zurich, Joyce sent Stuart Gilbert a two-line picture post card: "Je ne suis pas *où* que l'on pense / Je ne suis pas où que l'on dit" (*Letters* III, 416). That is, "I am not *where* they think," etc. The picture on the card is of the Alkoholfreies Kurhaus (Temperance Sanitarium) in Zurich.

his poor vision, understood what had happened and could hardly stifle his hilarity. As I was in the same state, although completely shaken, we made off.

"He probably took you for Sylvia Beach," whispered Joyce on the stairway, at last free to indulge his mocking spirit.

In front of the door was a large body of police, since the president was still inside. Highly imprudently I pointed them out to my companion with the slang expression, "Twenty-two, there's the cops," and Joyce, who failed to distinguish their proximity, asked me with inopportune insistence if I knew the origin of the expression. Outraged, one of the guardians of the peace approached and challenged us threateningly. Fortunately, a passing taxi was free and we took it—otherwise, five minutes after the signal honor of a presidential handshake, we would have suffered the indignity of arrest for insulting the forces of law and order.

This was one of the last times I saw Joyce laugh whole-heartedly. It was even one of the last times I saw him at all, our enterprise having been completed. Moreover, the following event had taken place.

Having made the acquaintance of an Italian writer, Ettore Settanni, who did not lack talent, Joyce had given him our attempt at translation to read. Settanni was enraptured, but added immediately that it might be improved here and there. Joyce then summoned me to explain the affair and to introduce me to the young Italian. Naturally, I raised no objections whatever but refused to participate in any mending of the text myself. Instead I invited the new collaborator to identify the changes that he thought necessary.

Settanni promptly cited two or three changes, which we easily showed him to be unsuitable because they failed to capture the meaning of the original. He then discovered that the text did not consist of simple quests for sounds or verbal fancies but was supposed to express an idea. Let me say in his defense that he was no more familiar with the English original than with the English language as a whole. Appearing now less keen on the undertaking, he carried off a copy of our text, and we heard no more from him.

That is, Joyce didn't. I myself saw Settanni again, but he said nothing more about this famous translation. Instead, he told me the story of his life and explained that as a result of his militant antifascism he had taken refuge in Paris, where he was nearly dying of hunger because his part time job in an Italian bookstore earned him a pittance. Although he struck me as a dubious character, I helped him publish his book—on the questionable joys of Capri—by finding him a translator, but she did not receive a single penny for her work. Settanni had made off with all the money, having decided in spite of his supposed antifascism that the momentous events under way since Munich required his presence in Italy.

And the translation of *Finnegans Wake*? After Munich, as we know, the times became more and more momentous. Let us anticipate. We were right in the midst of that "phony war" when Settanni informed Joyce from Italy that through his efforts the text had been published in the journal *Prospettive*, the editor of which was Curzio Malaparte, another well-known "anti-Fascist." A dozen slight modifications, most of them absurd, had been made in our text—I mention only a particular sentence in which, by means of puns, Joyce inserted the names of four counties of Ireland: Derry, Cork, Dublin, and Galway; the newcomer had changed the words and spoiled the puns. Furthermore, the text was presented as the work of James Joyce and Settanni himself, my name having completely disappeared; the Italian wrote that I "would understand."[38]

His reasons were doubly good: for more than ten years I had been a literary *fuoriuscito*,[39] and it happened that I owed my exile to the hate of that very Malaparte—it dated from his "ultra" days. (To finish with Settanni, I will add that these reasons no longer existed around 1955, when he republished the text, still omitting my name. He was later forced to rectify the error.)[40] Yet Joyce seemed somewhat troubled the day he informed me of the intrigue and gave me a copy of the journal; he found the proceeding unfortunate and asked me to point out the corrections that had been made in our text. They, too, displeased him; however, I could easily see that he was delighted by this publication as well as by the articles of homage which accompanied it. Egoism? Vanity? Not at all; something else that is extremely poignant.

Harnessed to an inhuman task, this man had been leading an hallucinatory and raw-nerved life for a long time. By a supreme effort during the years 1938 and 1939 he had finally completed *Finnegans Wake*. This was an event of the utmost importance for himself, but not for the so-called civilized world, which at that time was otherwise occupied. The book completed—it was a volume of ordinary size and weight, considering the fifteen or so years of labor it took—Joyce prolonged his exaltation by correcting the proofs, by planning for a cover. And his

38. Settanni explained the problems in a letter to Joyce, who in turn explained to Frank (*Letters* III, 468–69). The text was published in the 15 February 1940 issue of *Prospettive*.

39. One exiled from Italy for political reasons.

40. The 1955 publication Frank mentions is apparently *James Joyce e la prima versione italiana del Finnegan's* [sic] *Wake* (Venice: Cavallino, 1955). In this small volume Settanni includes a brief reminiscence, according to which not only he but also Benjamin Crémieux worked with Joyce on the translation.

blindness persisted regarding Europe, which was cracking and falling apart. On the day when he held the first copies in his hands, the continent was crossing the threshold of night; from then on all was lost in the inane noise of the first cannonades.

The last stage of Joyce's life was therefore to be the time when the arrow shot from his bow disappeared into a derisive void. When the self relaxes after such a long effort, it no longer offers any resistance to the forces of destruction. The avidness with which James Joyce sought some attention for his work was without any doubt the cry of a life in danger. I was informed that, his daughter still mentally unbalanced, his daughter-in-law in turn had had to be hospitalized. It was as if around the old hero—I have mentioned Oedipus as well as Don Quixote: doesn't *Finnegans Wake* seem to be man's answer to the sphinx?— some obscure vengeance of the gods was falling.

The strangest memory I have of the truly nocturnal night we were then living in is that of my last meeting with Joyce. He had lent me one of the very rare copies of the book; afterwards this copy was to circulate among other readers who were certainly better decoders than I, above all Louis Gillet. I passed several very long evenings spelling out, or rather singing to myself, this interminable rebus that harmonized so well with the darkness enveloping us. I divined in a confused way the great mass of a sublime work; a megalith, I have said, like those at Carnac or Easter Island. Though lacking a meaning clear to me, it impresses me because it bears witness to the heights man's art may aspire to.

At the beginning of the war James Joyce had left his apartment and elected to live in a large hotel on the Boulevard Raspail. My wife and I went to pick him up there one evening; we had not seen each other for some months, during which time many things had happened, above all the beginning of the end of several worlds. That evening the great sunny days were forgotten and even the somber gloom of the afternoons on the Rue Edmond-Valentin; we were immersed in the blackout, that cloying and insidious darkness where words died out like embers. Such was the caricature that the times provided in opposition to the miraculous night of H.C.E.—of Here Comes Everybody—the Oedipean underworld of *Finnegans Wake*.

What shall I say about that evening permeated, on the whole, with a black humor, an evening that Leopold Bloom might have participated in? It is stamped on my memory like a permanent picture. Joyce scarcely liked to go out into a night he now felt to be his enemy, so we decided to dine at his hotel, even though the invitation came from me. For this reason I did not concern myself with restocking my wallet, which was often empty in those days. But when we arrived at the hotel, we found the Joyces ready to go out. They had changed their minds; and, since I had previously suggested a certain restaurant on the Rue du Cherche-Midi where the cuisine was exquisite but truly expensive, my consternation may be imagined.

The dinner's end remains a nightmare memory. Nora was entirely her gentle, affable, silent self, more distant than ever. She and Joyce sat side by side, like judges, he plunged in a stolid silence that was intensified by the need to speak French, since my wife did not understand Italian. Above all he was lost in a hostile night that was no longer his. Facing them, we said whatever came into our heads, while at the same time exchanging anguished looks and scraping out our pockets and handbag under the table, one eye on the formidable check. I was too engrossed in our own plight to ask myself what Joyce was hiding behind his pale and expressionless face, slightly bent toward the shoulder, while with the diaphanous fingers of one hand he stroked his cheek in a habitual gesture like that in *A Portrait of the Artist*. In a deep shadow that drowned everything, he was hiding the death agony of an intense flame.

The check was almost entirely paid by one of those miracles that Bloom knew so well how to accept; we put the Joyces in a taxi and left them on some hare-brained pretext. How could I know, when at last we were free to loose the interminable laugh that kept up during the long return on foot, that I had just shaken Joyce's hand for the last time?

He wrote to me from Saint-Gérand-le-Puy, where he had taken refuge, fortunately a few weeks before the exodus. An amusing detail is that he now wrote in French, undoubtedly finding Italian dangerous or condemnable. Friends who had seen him assured me that he was well, that he did not worry too much about the fate of *Finnegans Wake*. He knew how to deceive people.

Then, in January 1941, one of the coldest months we have ever had, two lines in a newspaper announced his death at the age of fifty-two[sic]. The picture of his death-mask preserves for us today his young, thin, sharp smile and that deep, extraordinary pallor. I was able to publish two articles about him in the "collaborating" press in Paris; it was necessary to remind the German censors that he was Irish before they let pass these homages to an English writer.

1945

Shortly after the Liberation I met Samuel Beckett; he was preparing to leave Paris for a few weeks and urged me to visit Lucia Joyce in Ivry.[41]

41. Maria Jolas says, ". . . When Joyce had to leave Lucia alone . . . Beckett took over his role. He was the one to go to see her regularly, he was the one who

Her mother and brother were still unable to leave Switzerland; Lucia remained hospitalized in the sanitarium where Antonin Artaud was to die three years later. So I went on an afternoon of bright and youthful sunlight, and in a vast fallow garden found the beautiful girl of days gone by, her features slightly heavier, locks of gray hair falling over restless blue eyes.

She received me in a friendly way, without seeming to recognize me, and scarcely reacted when I alluded to her father's death. We were speaking French and our conversation was almost mundane: she asked about the fashions and, pointing to a nearby apartment building, assured me that her uncle lived there and that he would soon come to get her. Little by little she became excited, and a nurse came over to ask me to end my visit. As I made ready to leave, Lucia addressed me abruptly in Italian, speaking quickly and looking at me for the first time:

"They say he is underground. Do you believe that? You don't know him, you don't realize how sly he is! He's only pretending to be underground; actually he's here, believe me, well hidden and watching you all the time!"[42]

I moved away.

The rest—all the rest—is silence.

TRANSLATED BY JANE CARSON

---

constantly felt that she was his responsibility until the war was over and, in fact, as long as there was nobody else close to Joyce to take that responsibility. Even today [1973] I hear rather frequently from Lucia, and she very often says, 'Mr. Beckett sent me this, or Mr. Beckett sent me that.' In other words, he does not forget her" ("Interview with Carola Giedion-Welcker and Maria Jolas," ed. Richard M. Kain, *James Joyce Quarterly*, 11 [Winter 1974]: 109).

42. Lucia Joyce remains institutionalized, now (1978) in England.

Philippe Soupault

EZRA POUND PROBABLY ENCOURAGED Joyce to settle in Paris
because in the twenties it presented an ideal climate for literary experiment. The same conditions that allowed the publication and sympathetic
reception of Ulysses and "Work in Progress" there also fostered the
Surrealist movement in literature. The French writer Philippe Soupault
(b. 1897), along with André Breton, founded this movement, the
beginning of which traditionally is dated from the appearance in 1920
of Les champs magnétique, composed by the two men in a fortnight
of automatic writing. The aims and methods of the movement were
antithetical to Joyce's; however, these theoretical differences did not
interfere in his relations with Soupault, whom he met shortly after
arriving in Paris. At the time Soupault was translating William Blake's
"Jerusalem," a project that must have interested Joyce, who admired
Blake and had given a public lecture on him in Trieste. Later Joyce came
to know and like some of Soupault's verse, though there is no evidence
that he read Les champs magnétique (JJ 715).

In spite of having a busy career as poet and novelist, Soupault, like
Larbaud and others, became involved in the Joyce industry. He helped
with the earliest French translations of Ulysses and with the French
translation of "Anna Livia Plurabelle." He also delivered a lecture about
the latter translation as part of a program at Adrienne Monnier's and
during the thirties lectured in the United States on Joyce. There
were, he discovered, not only literary projects with which Joyce
sought assistance but also a seemingly endless series of small tasks. "You
go to see him," Soupault said; "he asks which way you will be going
when you leave. You say, 'To the Etoile,' and before you know it
he has you doing an errand for him at the Bastille" (JJ 712). Some of
these errands involved considerably more than simply traveling to the
opposite side of Paris from one's direction. Missing his son, daughter-in-
law, and grandson, who then lived in New York, and learning that
Soupault was about to leave for the United States, Joyce asked him to
call on Giorgio, tell him that his father was unwell, and suggest therefore
that perhaps Giorgio and family should return to Paris (JJ 696).[1]

1. Many others besides Soupault found themselves leaving Joyce's flat with

The movement that Soupault helped found became a major force in the literary world of Paris. It also became something of a headache to Joyce. A number of circumstances, including superficial resemblances between "Work in Progress" and Surrealist productions, led to a widespread assumption that he had joined the movement. From this assumption grew much of the criticism and misunderstanding that he attempted to combat through the publication of Our Exagmination.[2] *A typical instance was the Boston University professor whom he reported as having said that a recently published fragment of "Work in Progress" "was just turned off unconsciously in an idle half-hour" (Letters I, 254). His friend Stuart Gilbert specifically warned against the tendency to "confuse the work of James Joyce with that of the harumscarum school of the* surréaliste *group . . . whose particular* trouvaille *was a sort of automatic writing, no revision being allowed."[3] Nevertheless, the confusion persisted.*

Though Soupault broke with the Surrealists, his part in founding the movement allowed him to speak with special authority on those features of Joyce's work that distinguished it from theirs. Moreover, his lectures in the United States provided an opportunity for emphasizing those features in the country where they seemed least recognized. Not one to miss such an opportunity, Joyce discussed the lectures with

---

errands to perform. In his recollection of a visit in 1930, Carlo Linati gives an amusing account of Joycean requests ("Ricordi su Joyce," *Prospettive* [Feb. 15, 1940], p. 16). Joyce began immediately by urging the reluctant Linati to translate *Ulysses* into Italian. As he did with Nino Frank over the translation of "Anna Livia Plurabelle," Joyce persisted, giving up only when Linati argued that no Italian publisher would risk such a project. After a moment's silence Joyce said, "Do you know Francesco Soave?"

"The priest? The moralistic writer?" asked Linati.

"Yes, him. When I was in school in Dublin, they made me read *Racconti morali* [*Moral Tales*] by Father Soave in order to learn Italian. I would like to re-read that book."

"He made me promise," said Linati, "that as soon as I returned to Milan I would send him the *Moral Tales* of Francesco Soave." As Linati was about to leave Joyce added a further request, this time for a list of the leading tenors and baritones at La Scala. Linati was astonished that Joyce could be interested in "such stuff" as Soave's book, but it and the list of La Scala singers were probably meant to fuel some future passage of "Work in Progress."

2. Joyce admitted that he had guided the writers of the essays included in *Our Exagmination* (*Letters* I, 283). Dougald McMillan's excellent account of these essays summarizes their chief points, each of which tacitly stresses some trait of "Work in Progress" that distinguishes it from Surrealist writings. McMillan also points out the prominence of Surrealist work in *transition*, explains the effect of this circumstance on the criticism of "Work in Progress," and identifies several allusions in *Finnegans Wake* to surrealism (*Transition: The History of a Literary Era, 1927–1938* [New York: George Braziller, 1976]; see especially pp. 79–89, 184–201, 204, 210, 211, and 214).

3. Stuart Gilbert, *James Joyce's "Ulysses"* (1930; rpt. New York: Vintage Books, 1955), p. 31.

Soupault before the latter left for the United States. "And I listened with attention," says Soupault. "It is probable," he adds, "that I was influenced by our conversations." [4] *It is equally probable that his recollection was influenced by them. To a greater degree than any of the other recollections, it focuses on Joyce the writer, making clear that his work was anything but the product of a fortnight's, let alone a half hour's, automatic or unconscious writing. Though the particular confusion that existed at the time of Soupault's lectures probably has passed, his insistence on Joyce's total commitment as a writer and his observations about the consequences of that commitment for readers remain as valid today as they were then.*

James Joyce

By Philippe Soupault

NO ONE TO MY KNOWLEDGE has subjugated his life to his work more completely than James Joyce did. Not without suffering, which I have witnessed, he accepted that perpetual slavery, a slavery of body and spirit. I see him again, during one of the days I spent with him, tortured by a word, almost rebelliously constructing a framework, questioning his characters, extracting a vision from some music, throwing himself exhaustedly on a couch, the better to hear that phrase which was about to be born, about to burst into light. Then for an hour or more a deep silence, broken by laughs. At the end of the day he sought in vain to escape, jumped into a taxi, visited a friend, had a section of a dictionary read to him, and, when night had fallen, returned home after many "stops." He allowed himself one compensation, the theatre . . . Around him there were private or public, economic or social storms. He witnessed them, amazed to see the bloody, turbulent, or corrupt world, as one of us "witnesses" a concert. His distraction is comparable only to that legendary kind of certain scholars. People who met him in passing, without observing him and without his noticing them, spoke only of his distraction, sometimes calling it egotism. But he was the most affectionate, the most sensitive of friends, and the one who had the greatest impact on me of all those that I have had.

I speak with some authority because I had the privilege of knowing him during several phases of his life. When I met him in 1918 [sic], he was

4. Letter to me, July 2, 1976.

writing *Ulysses*. He was famous among only a few, but he neither doubted nor marveled at his genius. He already had given himself over to that kind of daily hell, the creation of the Joycean world.

What strikes one about this phenomenon, one of the purest, in the scientific sense, that the history of literature offers, is its unity. The first work of Joyce announces and prepares for the blossoming. That which is to be perfected in *Ulysses* is already foreshadowed in *Dubliners*. In those fifteen stories the reader, the author, and the central character become one. The writer refuses to lie. He rejects everything that we pejoratively call "literary." All poses, all tricks, all ambivalences are rejected—the most complete good faith is kept.

As soon as Joyce felt compelled to write, he gave himself over to it entirely. All of his actions, all of his reading, his studies, his joys, his pains were dedicated to his work. He was the exact opposite of a dilettante.

That way of life, scrupulously led and without a day's lapse, that alone would deserve to be commented on at length. As far as I know, it is unique.

That life dictates the reader's attitude. It demands that in order to approach the work an effort be made. It restores to reading a different sense and a dignity that most contemporary novels had caused it to lose.

But the most important point about that way of life, which lasted almost forty years, was that it resulted in the creation of a body of work representing one of the highest summits of literature. That achievement, as has already been said, began with *Dubliners*, was followed by *Portrait*, rose to a peak with *Ulysses*, and concluded with *Finnegans Wake*, which appeared a few months before Joyce's death. It should be pointed out that in the margin of his work, so to speak, Joyce wrote a collection of poems, *Chamber Music*, a play, *Exiles*, and a little book of songs, *Pomes Penyeach*.

Each step, each book, marks a rise, which people have dared call an improvement. It is this improvement that I have referred to as a blossoming.

Consequently, it needs to be remembered that since he is no longer independent of the writer but an associate the reader should read *Dubliners* before *Portrait*, then go on to *Ulysses*, and end with *Finnegans Wake*. Let us repeat, Joyce has created a world, and this world is accessible to us only if we can humbly obey the writer's wishes.

Of equal necessity with that obedience is a knowledge of Joyce's life. It is, moreover, a life of great simplicity. But it is little known. The many biographies already published are generally accurate. They always lack an element that, for want of a more exact word, must be called poetry. James Joyce was a poet, a great poet, who knew

what poetry meant and who lived by it and for it. The whole first part of
of his life is told by himself, with an intensity that borders on despair,
in his youthful book *A Portrait* and later in the first part of *Ulysses*.
He has depicted himself under the name of Stephen Dedalus. Everything
that went into his formation, the whole background, the whole
nature of his future life, is fixed with a precision and carefulness that
makes all later accounts vain. When Joyce stopped writing his biography
it was because he thought that he no longer pertained to his work. One
knows that after he left Ireland he came to Paris to study medicine,
that he passed through Zurich and went to settle in Trieste, where
he taught English in the Berlitz School.[5] The Trieste period, which pre-
dates 1914, is without doubt the most important of all his life. He
completed *Portrait*, but it was also at this time that he became aware
of the grandeur and importance of his life's work; it was at this period
that he detached himself definitively from our world in order to con-
ceive the Joycean universe.

I have found Joyce's tracks in the unrecognized city *par excellence*,
this city that the vicinity of Venice obscures so unjustly. (And wasn't
it only to find evidences of Joyce that I myself went there?) On the
edge of Austria and across from Italy, Trieste, where Stendahl
meditated and Fouché died ignominiously, is the most beautiful, the
most European crossroads in all Europe. Joyce lived there ten years in
a poverty that bordered on destitution. I have visited the building
where he began writing *Ulysses*; I have walked through the streets
that he frequented; I have retraced his daily route; above all, I have
listened to the stories, the sounds, the cries, the language (one of the most
varied, one of the richest, one of most "composite" in the world) that
Joyce listened to with a passionate attention.

Others more learned than I will be able to describe the influence
that the Triestine language, and above all the life and the richness
of that language, had on Joyce's thought. In my opinion it was
considerable. Trieste also provided Joyce with a necessary detachment:
he felt himself far removed from Ireland, still distinguishing images
and echoes of Dublin, but seeing, feeling, and hearing better from
afar that city where he had loved and suffered and where he was to set all
of his work. Distance gives harmonies to love and confers a supernatural appearance on it.

It would be useful to retrace those years step by step. We can know
as yet only a few episodes. One of them that I am going to recount
seems to me especially important and will demonstrate one of Joyce's
powers—influence.

5. Soupault confuses Joyce's 1902 trip to Paris, ostensibly to study medicine,
with his 1904 trip, the beginning of his exile.

*James Joyce. Drawing by Constantin Brancusi
(courtesy of Fred B. Dennis)*

Isolated and unknown, the young Irishman, serving as part-time professor, was visited one day by a forty-year-old Triestine named Schmitz, who wished to take lessons. He was a timid and unusual man, a merry dreamer, an inveterate humorist. He was attracted by his young professor, whom he taught about Trieste, without making much progress in English. During their conversations they both confessed that they were writers. Joyce read the works of his student and immediately saw their remarkable value. With that enthusiasm and that relentlessness with which he protected and defended his friends (they were not numerous), he set about seeing that justice was done to the man we now know as Italo Svevo, whose two works, *Zeno* and *Senilità*, are the most original and the most influential that Italian literature produced in a quarter century.

In spite of the exiled Irishman's concentration, the fecund suffering his memory inflicted on him, what I remember above all is the revelation of his influence. People have called attention to the prestige, to the legend which surrounded his life as soon as his name appeared in print. I know that for my part I was less sensitive to the éclat of genius, though bathed in humanity, than to that power which allowed him to transform things and that marvelous address which allowed him to reach the essential in one try.

When he came to stay in Paris, having left Trieste after a brief sojourn in Zurich—another crossroads—he already possessed certainty. On my first meeting with him I sensed it immediately. When I knew that I was going to see him, I naïvely thought of comparing him. At that time I was living among writers. Literature and its illusions impressed me very little. I saw a vibrant man, paying little attention to the impression he made, a man of intimidating simplicity. Very casually but tenaciously, he learned Paris. As in Trieste, he had chosen to live in one of those buildings which are, he said, "symbolic." Thus he mixed with the crowd and went to small cafes. He listened to the talk. I know that people in his neighborhood thought of him as a phantom. Already at that time his very bad eyesight prevented him from going out alone and barely permitted him to live alone. But he certainly knew how to hear! He claimed to judge people by their voices. I was able to follow his surprising method and to admire his memory. The importance he attached to language and the role he attributed to it are well known. Perhaps people have been overeager to celebrate his virtuosity with language in order to define and even to limit his achievement. Without doubt the author of *Finnegans Wake* was an extraordinary virtuoso, but he meant to utilize, to dominate, and not be dominated.

He was just as interested in people. He chose Dubliners as his example, but he was aiming at mankind. No one has illustrated better than he that road leading from the particular to the general. Thus in *Ulysses* he limited his view to the single day of one individual. Going beyond the realm of experience, the author has used a wide variety of "methods" to recreate that human universe only a small part of which we suspect in our waking state.

Observing gestures and what might be called their harmonics, reading facial expressions, provoking reactions, made up only a small part of Joyce's daily work. He compared and above all contrasted the recently or distantly remembered living and dead, who compose the "profound now," then fade away; he replaced in their atmosphere imagined beings who mix with the crowd; he followed their footsteps . . . Can one limit the work of Joyce the observer, endowed with a memory of irritating certitude? His work enables us to measure both his imagination, which bordered on hallucination, and his power to relive and make others relive.

Can one say that Joyce worked? He "lived" his books. I have observed him many times during his leisure, or so-called leisure. Together we often went to the theatre, which, like all good Irishmen, he loved. It was the theatre as theatre that he loved. I mean that he was attracted less by the play than by the atmosphere, the footlights and spotlights, the spectators, the kind of solemnity in a theatre. He preferred opera. When he had decided to go, he was happy as a child. He chose a companion, refused to dine (I prepare myself for a sacrament, he told me, explaining this abstinence), and after the performance he had supper at a restaurant, where he had arranged to have his favorite white wines. At the theatre, seated in the first row—presumably because of his very bad eyesight—he carefully watched the action and listened closely to the performers. Only children are as passionately attentive as Joyce was. He was always the first to applaud and to shout "encore" after the great arias. One evening at the Paris Opera he was responsible for two repetitions of the great aria in *William Tell*. The singer, it is true, was Irish and one of his childhood friends.[6] He liked everything, even the crudest vaudeville. Obviously what he sought on these occasions was that atmosphere which remains one of the fascinations of the theatre. He also took a singular pleasure in contact with the crowd.

It was doubtless this same pleasure that he sought in bringing together his friends to celebrate special occasions. He gathered us to celebrate his birthday, his name-day, and the anniversary of his marriage, as

6. Doubtless the tenor John Sullivan, whose performance in *William Tell* particularly impressed Joyce. The two were not childhood friends, but met for the first time in late 1929 (*JJ* 632–33).

well as Candlemas,[7] Twelfth Night, Christmas, the dates on which his various books were published . . . Usually we dined late. There were candles on the table, many white wines, an excellent dinner, a cake with small candles. After dinner one or another of the guests sang, then Joyce himself took his turn at the piano and, according to his mood, either hummed or sang the words of some Irish songs, usually always the same ones. That lasted at least a good hour. Then his son, who hoped to be a professional singer, took his turn. Léon-Paul Fargue, when he didn't arrive too late, skillfully delivered some argot songs of the 1890s or his inventions of the previous month. There were sometimes scenes because, in the Irish tradition, people drank exuberantly. It wouldn't do to try leaving the party before its finish, that is to say around three or four o'clock in the morning. There were, however, some precipitous departures following "words." Most of the time Joyce was gay; sometimes, very rarely, he was somber. On the latter occasions, he had to make a strange effort to pull himself out of that torpor, which in some ways resembled the sulky unhappiness of a child.

When, as was often the case, I was not in a mood for the slightly monotonous nature of these parties, I wondered what possible happiness Joyce could be looking for and finding in them. I know that he loved his friends, even if a bit tyrannically. I know that he could have and wanted to have only a few people and that he avoided ceremonious receptions and what was called society. But I was wrong to argue. In these little gatherings the author of *Ulysses* only wanted to regain contact. Every creative artist has an inhuman side, and it pains him to feel himself on the outside, removed from other beings and daily life. By jogging him out of himself, by drawing him to them, Joyce's comrades forced him to their level. That is why he demanded sincerity from them and banished respect, ceremony, snobbery.

As I recall these memories, I recognize once more that Joyce suffered much from his vocation of writing. What sensitive person would bear, without a pang, that ceaseless tension, those daily sacrifices, and that unremitting toil? Toward himself Joyce had a brutality, a hardness that sometimes went beyond understanding. At the time when he and I translated, or rather when he translated with my assistance, a fragment of *Finnegans Wake*, the "Anna Livia Plurabelle" episode, I had occasion to see and hear him work.[8] These translating sessions lasted three hours. They were exhausting and Joyce was never satisfied with his successes. Yet, I have never met a man who was such a sure,

7. Joyce's birthday and Candlemas are the same day, February 2.
8. By the time it was published in 1931, six others, including Soupault, had been involved in this translation. Ellmann gives a detailed description of the undertaking (*JJ* 645–46).

such a faithful translator. He had to treat words like objects, stretch
them out, cut them up, examine them under a microscope. He pursued
his object obsessively and never yielded. It was not a matter of conscience or a mania, but the application of a pitiless method. It concerned
a "matter" so moving, so rich, so new, so fleeting that he could never
relax, not for a second. And I am convinced that because of his fellow
translators, Joyce restrained himself, taking pity on them. When he
worked alone, he was even more intransigent. He let himself be drawn
down by that torrent of ideas, plans, memories, comparisons, images,
sounds, descriptions, smells . . . At the center of this vortex, he
retained his detachment and critical sense, fearing the cowardice that
makes one accept the approximate, the almost. When I want to describe
his state while he worked, I cannot escape the cliché, body and soul.
Before my eyes I see Joyce, his index finger raised, saying "no,"
refusing a word, a sentence, criticizing, rejecting, questioning a whole
fragment, destroying pages on the point of being finished . . .

To examine James Joyce's work and his method, it is not necessary
to have had direct contact with him as I did. It is necessary and it is
sufficient to read his books. *Ulysses* is perhaps the best example.
Each chapter, where not one false note, not one error, not one thing
to regret is discernible, forms so definitive an ensemble that even an
inattentive or uncertain reader cannot escape a spell that he is completely
incapable of explaining or of throwing off. Joyce exacts from his reader
an effort which cannot be dispersed. He first imposes on him his tone,
his color, his style. The imagination is never allowed free rein.
From the first word, he who dares to begin reading is as though seized,
and, cost what it may, he must submit himself to the will of the author.
It is a test of strength. Therefore it is not surprising that so many
people, out of fear, are content to declare: "I don't understand," and
to add: "It is too hard for me . . ."

On the first time through the book, even reading with great care,
one cannot grasp its richness. Thus in order to gain only a superficial
knowledge of it, one is forced to traverse an immense countryside.

Joyce's attitude toward his critics was remarkable. He was not
indifferent. He was often amused by the attacks and immensely delighted
by the efforts of some people to explain him, especially when they
were farthest from his aim. But the attacks, the mockeries, the
misunderstandings, the praises, did not touch him and taught him
nothing.[9] This was not due to pride or to a stratagem, but to his having

9. This description fits Joyce's response to the attacks on *Ulysses* but not those
on *Finnegans Wake*. The critics of *Finnegans Wake* probably taught him nothing
and certainly did not alter his aims; however, they did "touch" and concern him.
On one occasion he denounced them with a bitterness that he usually reserved

decided once and for all that it was impossible for him to retrace his steps. And in spite of that pride, he often had a disconcerting humility. At the end of his life testimonies of admiration, fervent homages, were lavished upon him. He received them with a great gracefulness, but he did nothing to instigate them. He could have orchestrated his publicity, had he wished to do so, for he knew how to be shrewd and very clever. He was often asked to visit the United States, the first country to salute Joyce's true greatness. He refused. Having had occasion to speak about him many times in all the major cities of America, I can imagine what a reception they would have reserved for him and what a triumph they would have organized. He knew it, too, but he always held off, despite the pleas of Irishmen, who are numerous in the United States and who would have greeted him with the enthusiasm they alone are capable of.

More strange was his refusal to return to Ireland. Can one say that he loved Ireland or that he didn't love it? All his work has Dublin and its environs for a setting.

Thus, each day, and each hour of the day, he thought of Ireland; he lived and relived his memories; thousands of times he mentally traversed the streets and squares of the city, the pathways of the surrounding area; he looked at every house, he conversed with the inhabitants; he described, painted (and with what minute detail) the hours and the colors. Since his departure in 1904, he never wanted to retrace his steps. At the urging of an Irish friend, I one day asked him the reason for his refusal. In reply, he only looked at me and with his elongated hand stirred, like a blind man, the pages he was writing at that time. Have I mistranslated his response in thinking that to complete his work it was necessary for him to avoid comparing the reality and the evocation, to avoid disturbing his image of Dublin by an inevitable disappointment? [10]

It never can be sufficiently emphasized that Joyce lived in exile voluntarily, lived in exile in order to complete his work. It would have been sweet and exalting, especially for an Irishman, to be received in Dublin, to take his revenge thirty years later on those who mocked the

---

for his relatives and fellow countrymen, saying that their "indignant hostility" reflected only "the personal rancours of disappointed artists who have wasted their talents or perhaps even their genius" (*Letters* I, 258). The attacks on *Finnegans Wake* convinced him that he had to defend the book, and he did so, indirectly as usual, through *Our Exagmination*.

10. To others he indicated that he feared placing himself in Irish hands. He wrote Constantine Curran, who had urged him to visit Ireland, "I am trying to finish my wip ['Work in Progress'] . . . and I am not taking any chances with my fellow-countrymen if I can possibly help it until that is done, at least" (*Letters* I, 395).

poor student going into exile. His work was not finished. That was enough to silence his desire.

Many people, in my presence, came to him bearing news of Ireland. He remembered one and all and laughed in speaking of old So-and-So, of Pat, or of Mother X, the one who had such a strange nose . . . He laughed, he laughed, but one sensed in the childlike laugh a kind of pain, a regret, and doubtless a sense of remorse.

In order to complete his work he had adopted Paris as his refuge, cherishing the city with a singular and touching love. He knew only its atmosphere, because his bad eyes and his work prevented long walks or casual strolls. But he "breathed" Paris and discovered a reason to love it at each stage of his exile. Perhaps one could say that he knew and loved Paris like a song and God knows that he loved songs. He found there a rhythm which helped him to live and to work. Indeed, he was not blind to the danger of his relentlessness.

Paris helped him to complete *Ulysses* and to write *Finnegans Wake*. To my knowledge, never has any work of that type been attempted and completed. *Ulysses* seemed already a superhuman attempt. When people are able to study and read Joyce's final work with the care it deserves, they will be convinced of its special greatness. Let us not conceal that for today's reader, the difficulty of reading it is very great. People could facilitate their reading of *Ulysses* with the help of commentaries. A book would be necessary to help a willing reader who wanted to tackle *Finnegans Wake*. It is only with time that people will be able to read this great book, if not comfortably, at least with relative simplicity. It is years ahead of the time when it was written. It is the privilege of certain geniuses to be far in advance of the attitudes and the intelligence of their contemporaries, and it has its price . . .

James Joyce was aware of that advance. He did not say, as Stendahl did, that he would be understood "later on," but believed that he would only acquire readers slowly and wanted to exact from them an effort matching his own. He did not scorn his readers, never tried to flatter their taste for the easy. Nor did he write for the "happy few," because he did not consider that his books were reserved for an elite. He ceaselessly enriched his art, imposing on everything he wrote a rigor and a precision that excluded uncertainty and misinterpretation. Joyce had a horror of misunderstandings and approximations. For him, and consequently for his readers, there is no middle way.

Having indicated Joyce's attitude, I would like to be able to suggest a way of approaching his last work. But the issue is no longer one of advice, of commentaries, or explications. The role a single reading plays for some people, the influence that it can have, is well known. The whole problem of literature and its consequences is posed by Joyce's last work. It is obvious that one does not try to resolve it in a few lines or even to define it in a few phrases. It is important, however, to indicate the bases of it. The story is the simplest device that we know, the most primitive. To tell the truth, it is a *pis aller*. What Joyce proposed for himself and imposed on himself was to engross the whole mind and not just to set up a few signposts for the imagination. The result is not comparable to the power of music, which invades the mind and carries it along irresistibly. The mind, it is properly said, abandons itself in the musical current. Joyce's art imperiously demands the attention that poetry worthy of the name always should obtain. The mass, the weight, the volume of poetry cannot be measured. The efforts necessary to discover new methods are made too rarely. In this respect, Joyce's effort stands alone or nearly so. It is because of that effort, even more than because of his success, that we must proclaim him a genius.

TRANSLATED BY CARLETON W. CARROLL

Adolf Hoffmeister

THE DISTINGUISHED CZECH artist and writer Adolf Hoffmeister (1902–73) often visited Paris during the twenties and thirties and knew many of the writers then living there, including Joyce's friend Philippe Soupault. However, his two recollections of Joyce, written shortly after the meetings they describe, are the only record of their acquaintance.

The recollections show an unusual Marxist perspective on Joyce. (Hoffmeister's loyalty to the Communist party was sufficient to gain him appointment as Czech ambassador to France from 1948 to 1951, but not to save him from losing favor at the fall of Alexander Dubček and remaining persona non grata *in Czechoslovakia from then until his death.) In general Marxists attacked Joyce, the most famous instance being Karl Radek's address to the Congress of Soviet Writers in 1934.[1] Hoffmeister's recollections, however, show a total sympathy with Joyce's work. Joyce would have found this sympathy especially satisfying since he thought, on somewhat whimsical grounds, that the Marxist criticism of his work was ill founded. "I don't know why they attack me," he said to Eugene Jolas. "Nobody in any of my books is worth more than a thousand pounds" (JJ 3). He also would have appreciated Hoffmeister's indignation at the fate of* Ulysses *in the United States, however strong the flavor of Marxist rhetoric in that indignation.*

Apparently the purpose of the meeting described in Hoffmeister's first recollection was to draw Joyce, who often resisted being sketched, painted, or photographed, but usually relented in the end. The drawings were to be caricatures, a form that particularly appealed to Joyce during his later years. He not only insisted that César Abin's portrait of him be a caricature[2] but also, as Hoffmeister's account reveals,

---

1. Partially reprinted in *James Joyce: The Critical Heritage*, ed. Robert H. Deming (2 vols.; New York: Barnes and Noble, 1970), 2: 624–26. Following this speech Hoffmeister published a caricature of Radek holding Joyce's severed head, an ironic memorial of the occasion in that several years later Radek himself was executed.

2. See Eugene Jolas, "My Friend James Joyce," *Partisan Review*, 8 (March–April 1941): 86.

greatly admired the caricatures of George Grosz. This taste is reflected in Finnegans Wake *where people, historical events, legends, songs, popular sayings, and texts of various kinds all are caricatured.*

Delight at Hoffmeister's bringing him a copy of the Czech translation of Ulysses *no doubt had much to do with Joyce's unusual talkativeness about his work during the meeting described in the second recollection. It is the only recorded occasion of his discussing at such length the relationship among his books. He touched on this subject in a letter to H. L. Mencken in 1915, remarking that* Ulysses *was to be "a continuation of* A Portrait of the Artist *and also of* Dubliners" *(Letters I, 83). His conversation with Hoffmeister shows that, in spite of their great differences from each other, he still saw these three books, along with* Finnegans Wake, *as a "seamless whole," though in a play on their contrasting subjects he often said that his last two books were as different as day and night.*[3]

This second meeting with Hoffmeister also is the only recorded occasion of Joyce talking at length about number, though he had a special interest in numerical correspondences, numerical symmetry, and other features of number, as did Dante. Previously in "Grace" and Ulysses *he had used the tripartite structure that appears throughout the* Divine Comedy. Ulysses, *for example, has three parts, the first and last being composed of three chapters each, the middle part of twelve chapters being divisible by three. There are also three main characters, Bloom, Stephen, and Molly. Numbers play an even more important part in* Finnegans Wake, *where they appear on almost every page, but three no longer predominates. Other numbers do, among them four and twelve, as in the four old men and twelve pub customers, hence Joyce's emphasis on those numbers in his talk with Hoffmeister. In suggesting to Hoffmeister that four and twelve have a greater significance in life than the three emphasized in the* Divine Comedy *Joyce seemed to be indicating that in this one respect, at least,* Finnegans Wake *surpassed Dante's poem. Though the mature Joyce usually spoke deprecatingly of his work, he was not above harboring exalted notions of it in private.*

Normally when Joyce discussed his work he spoke simply and clearly, so the occasional obscurity of his remarks in these two recollections probably is owing to faulty reporting by Hoffmeister, whose prose is frequently awkward and unclear in the original.

3. Louis Gillet, *Claybook for James Joyce,* trans. Georges Markow-Totevy (London: Abelard-Schuman, 1958), p. 63.

James Joyce

By *Adolf Hoffmeister*

IN THE CULTURAL CIRCLES OF PARIS, Joyce is talked about everywhere, thoroughly and as a matter of course. Like the Bible, *Ulysses* belongs among those books that no one ever really reads through properly but whose beauty and wisdom everyone thinks it modish and necessary to refer to. Joyce filled the city with realism, which joined the eroticism of its daily life. The French will always return, in one form or another, to that logic called "realism." The epic minuteness with which the day of June 16, 1904, is depicted only enchanted people all the more in that time of the Freudian mania. In cafe and salon conversation Joyce's name crops up from the subconscious, like a Freudian slip. He fascinated or bewitched the public by his microscopic truthfulness. There is no reality that he failed to see or to reveal. It is a question whether he alone had the courage to say what up to then no one else had said about people, or whether he alone first succeeded in doing what others had failed at. That one day is so faithfully described that it approaches absolute truth. Truth in art is crushing, overwhelming, disrupting. A normal, ordinary man, a writer, even a poet, who is decent or motivated by a more-or-less petty ideal can never tell the truth. He would need the profound skepticism of this admirable cynic, this tall man, whom humanity hates precisely because of his too-exact truth, with the result that his spirit has been scorched at the stake, amidst the heap of his confiscated books, in that country of the starriest flag, the biggest statue of liberty, and the greatest judicial murders.[4]

The world is afraid of Joyce. But that fear does not come from any real offense that he gives, so that if a millstone were hung about his neck to sink him in the depths of the ocean, it would fit him like a dress collar. What the Pharisees and narrow-minded fear is opening their eyes. For them the luxury of their households is a preparation for eternal bliss, because in general no one gives a thought to what he is doing. People are not bad, but in their daily round of working, sleeping, eating, and digesting, they are afraid to think about the significance

4. Announcements of *Ulysses* said that five hundred copies had been seized and burned by the customs authorities in New York, but James F. Spoerri questions the accuracy of the claim (*A Bibliography of James Joyce, 1882–1941*, ed. John J. Slocum and Herbert Cahoon [New Haven, Conn.: Yale University Press, 1953], p. 27).

of words and of their own actions. They remain happy by overlooking tiny riddles, avoiding mysteries, dodging talk that disturbs them. They would go mad or get a stomach ache from laughing if they realized what they do or saw themselves on the toilet, in bed with their mistresses, in a shop buying carrots, and in all such activities where, being alone, they lose the pathos of life. Joyce could see simultaneously the surface and the disintegrating thought processes of the whole bourgeois society. *Ulysses* is not psychoanalysis; it is a perfect, too truthful novel.

The question, What is pornography? has been thrown like a lasso over the neck of this faun. Some people claimed that certain chapters in *Ulysses* are swinish. Joyce did not play the insulted artist, but returned the question with another one, asking, Aren't certain chapters of life itself swinish? Among the hidebound professors representing the critical artillery in some half-cultured countries, he found few poets sincere enough to accept such a simple explanation of art without excuses. Art does not need to be explained artfully. It is useless to debate the content of a great work with those philanthropic hens who enjoy laying decorated Easter eggs and those censors who are the henpecked of officialdom. We do not read the Bible for amusement, and if some snobs read *Ulysses* for onanistic pleasure, they should be forced to read a hundred pages in addition to the few lines they found to excite their demented sexuality and their depressed spirits, or should one say their depressed sexuality and their demented spirits? But worse is the confusion of the cultivated but narrow-minded intellectual about this thick volume of truth.

For if you are asked whether Joyce's work is pure, you will answer, not enough. Whether it is licentious, not enough. Whether it is scientific, not enough. Whether it is entertaining, not enough. Whether it is comprehensible, not enough. And clear, not enough. And what of Joyce's style? Just haphazard, changeable, varied, very free. What about his language? Difficult to say, because beneath a conglomeration made up of countless echoes from all the continents, runs the basic note of English, an English that one does not speak but perhaps only thinks.

Translators are guaranteed the fate of martyrs. *A Portrait of the Artist* is difficult to translate, as is any piece of dense writing, but to translate *Ulysses* requires the ability of a scientist who can walk the high wire or can balance a flaming torch on his nose while juggling a dozen plates. The whole art will consist of avoiding destruction here, of not turning this great novel into a heap of broken plates. The real test of skill certainly will be the last chapter. There are, I think, forty-two pages of one breathless thought, without periods or commas, without capitals or logically placed dashes. It is the waking dream of a woman before going to sleep. Women whom you ask deny that they are capable of such volatile and sensual thoughts. Perhaps it is so, or perhaps they are only ashamed to confess their secrets; but it would certainly be better to believe Joyce rather than these women.

When a protest appeared in *The Humanist* against Samuel Roth, the self-appointed barbarian of American publishers, who edited Joyce's work as he himself saw fit and delivered an emasculated *Ulysses* as fodder to the cultural void of Protestant America, the world was amazed by the names of those who signed the protest: Wells, Pirandello, Paul Valéry, Einstein, Galsworthy, Mann, John Dos Passos, and hundreds of others.[5] The immortals were fighting in behalf of this infernal book, and the judge could only repeat the memorable words that have now become an anecdote in the history of culture: "If only he would not use foreign words."[6] The persecution of his work veiled it in a secrecy that served as publicity.

Translation after translation enlarged the dominion of his glory. The resounding celebration that accompanied publication of the French translation of *Ulysses* was the signal for his official assumption among the geniuses. But what can one say about a man who, for an occasion when the greatest and most widely known poets of proud France were to make speeches celebrating him, rented a bus, loaded it with all of his mortal friends as well as with the immortal Academicians, and after dinner at Leopold's outside Paris made this whole magnificent society completely drunk; then, standing up in the returning bus, sang duets with the youngest, totally indifferent to being consecrated a great poet of the century?[7]

One can find in the encyclopedias of any country that Joyce was born in 1882 to a good Catholic family in Dublin, that he was taught by the Jesuits, and later studied philosophy, mathematics, medicine, languages, singing. He founded the first Dublin cinema; he taught languages in Zurich, started a theatre company there, and moved in 1920 to Paris, where he leads an eccentric and unique life, like all those who could not live in the United States or the United Kingdom of Great Britain and Ireland—Lewisohn, Hemingway, Jolas, Josephson, Maugham, O'Neill, and others. I saw him often on Montparnasse; he used to dine at Surcouf's. He would take a taxi here and there, or

5. See above, p. 83, note 14.
6. I have not been able to locate the source of this remark.
7. See Nino Frank's recollection, pp. 84–86, for a description of this celebration. As Frank points out, it was Adrienne Monnier, not Joyce, who rented the bus and invited the guests.

he would wander aimlessly along the boulevards or about the Mont-parnasse station, alone, in the clouds, and shy, a tall, slender, impressive man. He has the reddish complexion of an Irishman.

I asked where he lived. His address is a riddle, 2 Square Robiac. The squares are blind streets, cul-de-sacs, such as one finds along the interminable Rue de Grenelle. No one knows them nor their names. The policemen do not, nor the postmen. They are real harbors of anonymity. I rang the bell of a new house that was as quiet and solemn as a sanitarium.

"Does Mr. James Joyce live here, please?"

"Yes, I will announce you at once."

Later I spent several hours trying to make an exact record of our conversation, which was not supposed to be an interview. He refused on principle to give interviews. He did not receive even the famous Lefèvre.[8]

Joyce speaks a clipped, precise English: "I am very glad that you came. Sit down, but I won't 'sit.' "

"Thank you. I don't need you to."

"You know, someone painted me. He used to come here as to the office. After the eightieth time I myself had to announce that the picture was finished."[9]

"I don't think it is."

"No, neither do I. *Portrait of the Artist* is a truer picture."

"But it is not recent."

"No, it is from much earlier years. Before Gibraltar.[10] Let's speak a little French now." (Joyce's French is the best that I have heard from the mouth of an Englishman.)

"You were in Gibraltar?"

"As a language teacher. Then in Trieste, in Zurich, etc."

"But you have definitely settled in Paris?"

"Yes, but I am no longer a language teacher. But you are from a strange country that goes by many names and has many languages. What nationality are you?"

"Czech."

"Then you speak German. Let's speak it a little. I enjoy remembering

8. Frédéric Lefèvre (1889–1949) interviewed most of the important contemporary writers in France, publishing the results in the *Nouvelles Littéraires* in a series headed "Une heure avec . . .".

9. This picture apparently was the one done by the Irish painter Patrick Tuohy, who did the famous portrait of Joyce's father. Tuohy began Joyce's portrait in 1924, but did not finish it until 1927.

10. Joyce made Gibraltar the birthplace of Molly Bloom but was never there himself.

*James Joyce. Drawing by Augustus John
(courtesy of Sir Caspar John)*

and speaking the languages I know, but I don't have any opportunity here. I am sorry, but I don't know Czech."

"You write only in English?"

"Actually yes, but I am thinking of a beautiful book where each occasion, each situation, and each word will choose its own language.[11] In all the languages and dialects of the world there is only one word that exactly designates a given thing. I have already tried it in *Ulysses*, although there it gives the impression of being a jumble of quotations and a superfluous stuffing of foreign words."

"If you write that way few people can read you."

"What is that to me? In the work I am writing now I use eighteen languages. The English-Parisian of the Americans is a language that no one understands any longer. My new work, coming out in *transition*, does not yet have a title. For the present it is called 'Work in Progress.' "

I glance around the room. On the piano stands a vase with several Greek flags.

"Are you looking at those flags? There are a lot of them, aren't there? *Ulysses* has a Greek theme; therefore, they are Greek flags. Each new edition of *Ulysses* is a new flag in the vase. At present there are nine. Likewise, my room is blue, and I have requested that wherever *Ulysses* is published it have a blue cover. I am sorry to say it has not earned me much. You will notice that my glasses have thick lenses, with violet glass in the left one. I have spent the whole year being operated on. I was bandaged and kept in the dark. My sight is miserable. There are days when I scarcely see. I will write something in your book, but do not watch me. I write with my nose in the book."

"I don't collect autographs, Mr. Joyce, and would not want to trouble you."

"No, no, I will do it gladly. Show me what you have drawn. Caricature amuses me. Do you know George Grosz? An excellent fellow. His girls, gentlemen, ministerial cattle, and the profiles of the governing class are captured convincingly. I would like to see his latest things. Have you finished your drawing?"

"Thank you, long ago."

"But I cannot let you go now."

"Why not?"

"It is pouring outside as though from a watering can. I will lend you an umbrella. Someone left it here, probably because it is not very good. You need not return it. We will meet again sometime for dinner."

I started down the stairs.

"Hallo! Do you speak Russian?"

"Sorry, I do not know it."

11. This book apparently is *Finnegans Wake*.

Up to now we had used German, Italian, Greek, Spanish, Latin, and again English words. Joyce obviously enjoyed this game.

Afterwards I saw him several more times. He is tall, and his reserved, aristocratic behavior striking. He has red hair that stands up somewhat. His profile looks as though sharply carved in wood. His nose has an unusual shape, indicating a well-developed sense of smell. His mouth is closed in a narrow, straight line. His goatee and mustache are rather thin, also sprinkled with red. He has long legs and arms. He looks like a quiet, indulgent, somewhat dreamy Bernard Shaw. He wore a white flannel coat with the colored insignia of a university on its left pocket, the sort of soft, immaculate blazer worn by cricket or eight teams. But he cleans his fountain pen on the left elbow, where a series of lines converge into one large blot.[12] He has an astonishing memory and yet nothing around him seems to concern him. He is the kind of man who goes to a restaurant in order to read the newspaper. He tells the waiter, Bring me what you like. One would swear that nothing interested him on the street. But suddenly he stops, for example, by some workers laying asphalt and watches them long and attentively. With similar attentiveness he watches a dog urinating against the corner of the Institute. Then he goes slowly on and never promises anything to anybody. He has a wife and a son who is well known for his beautiful girl friends. Joyce loves music very much.

Someone could rise and ask, Is Joyce modern?

That is difficult to say. He is unique.

TRANSLATED BY NORMA RUDINSKY

Portrait of Joyce

By Adolph Hoffmeister

DURING AUGUST of 1930, Joyce was in and out of Paris.[13] His apartment had the emptiness of vacation time, and the doorbell resounded with crazy loudness in rooms lacking draperies and rugs. In my mind's

---

12. A picture of Joyce wearing this sartorial curiosity, though without the inky stains showing, can be seen in *Letters* III, following p. 224.

13. The Joyces had just returned from six weeks in England and Wales. In a letter to Miss Weaver from Etretat on September 6, 1930, Joyce alludes to Hoffmeister's visit: "Paris was a furnace so we left after 4 days but I had time to arrange for the 2nd Czech edition of *U* and the first of A.L.P." (*Letters* III, 201).

eye I saw us acting in a highly solemn and ceremonious event. I with dress coat, high collar, beard, and top hat; Joyce with white robe and laurel wreath. As in a newsreel, we glide slowly and gracefully between marble columns; with stately gesture I hand him the first copy of the Czech translation of *Ulysses*.[14] Music is playing, the trumpets are trumpeting . . . In reality, we sat down where we could in the tidied apartment, the draped furniture making it look like moving day in a museum. Joyce caressed the four volumes of his translated work. We were surrounded by emptiness.

"It is cobalt blue, isn't it?" he said.

"Yes."

He referred to the color of the binding. Nothing in the world is bluer than that color.

"It is strange, Mr. Hoffmeister, but every event this summer seems to me especially important."

Joyce takes me by the hand, pulls me to himself, and looks into my eyes.

"Today is the first time I have seen you, in spite of our having met many times."

"I am very glad that your sight is so much improved. There was considerable news about it in Prague, even in the daily papers."

"I went to an excellent doctor who performed a difficult operation on my eye. In September I will return to Zurich to see him again. I am grateful to him for saving my eyesight and also my life. He is Professor Alfred Vogt of Zurich . . .[15] I can see. I can see."

Joyce sees, distinguishes things, but unfortunately not so well that he can walk confidently through the room without bumping into the table or the corners of furniture. His handwriting is illegible and smudged, but life returned with his eyesight, and with life has come new resolution and courage. His eye trouble had made it impossible for him to go for walks. Previously, one would not have been surprised to encounter him in any of the city's quarters in the least expected places—at a children's performance at the Palais Royal, in a factory cafeteria having lunch, in a small cafe in the suburbs, at a style show of a great fashion house. He would wander through the city, refreshing his

14. This translation, by Ladislav Vymětal in collaboration with Olga Fastrová, was published in Prague in 1930. Several years earlier Joyce had learned with great interest of a reference to *Ulysses* made by Masaryk, the President of Czechoslovakia (*Letters* III, 181). It was, in fact, Masaryk who encouraged the translation and provided the copy of *Ulysses* from which the translation was made. It appeared in an edition of four volumes, the first being a translation of *A Portrait of the Artist* done by Staša Jilovská.

15. At the urging of several Zurich friends Joyce consulted this brilliant surgeon in the spring of 1930. Vogt operated on the left eye in May and by June, after various complications, Joyce's sight had improved.

steps with wine. He would wander without goal, direction, or sense of time. For such walks sight is essential. It was feared that he had lost his sight forever. But the Swiss specialist gave him great hope and a small part of his sight.

"I hoped I would be allowed to finish my last work, 'Work in Progress.' Now I can. But I never finish any of my works; I always want to rewrite them completely. From *Dubliners* on, everything is always 'work in progress,' though it does not bear that title. *Ulysses* is the most finished. The fragments of "Work in Progress" that have come out at different times have changed and still are changing constantly. "Anna Livia Plurabelle" in the 1925 edition in *Le Navire d'Argent* differs substantially from the last version, which appeared in the Faber and Faber collection, *Criterion Miscellany*. In between there is the version printed in *transition* number 8.[16] My work is a whole and cannot be divided by book titles. *Ulysses* is, of course, one day of a life, but it could just as well be one second. Time is a scale marked with beginnings and endings."

"I think Marcel Brion in his excellent article about the concept of time in your work started from the hypothesis that the difference between God and man is possibly only a question of time."[17]

"Yes, he compared me with Marcel Proust. In Proust time is the center; it is the *ding an sich*. This Mr. Brion found the principle of relativity in my work. Only he reads my work with as much difficulty as he does Einstein's. Number is an enigma that God deciphers. Along with Beckett, a small, red-haired Irishman and my great friend, I have discovered the importance of numbers in life and history. Dante was obsessed by the number three. He divided his poem into three parts, each with thirty-three cantos, written in terza rima. And why always the arrangement of four—four legs of a table, four legs of a horse, four seasons of the year, four provinces of Ireland? Why are there twelve tables of the law, twelve Apostles, twelve months, and twelve Napoleon's marshals?[18] Why was the Armistice of the Great War trumpeted forth

16. The *Navire d'Argent* version of "ALP" appeared in October 1925, the *transition* 8 version in November 1927, and the Faber and Faber version in June 1930.

17. Brion's article, "The Idea of Time in the Work of James Joyce," appears in *Our Exagmination round His Factification for Incamination of Work in Progress* (1929; rpt., London: Faber and Faber, 1961), pp. 25-33.

18. Joyce also discussed the significance of numbers with Padraic Colum, confirming Colum's speculation that the four old men in *Finnegans Wake* were the four Evangelists and the Four Masters, who compiled the annals of Ireland. Joyce added that they also were the four provinces of Ireland "or the four ingredients in a salad." "Twelve is the public number," he said. "Twelve hours of the day, twelve men on a jury" (*Our Friend James Joyce* [New York: Doubleday and Co., 1958], p. 124).

on the eleventh minute of the eleventh hour of the eleventh day of the eleventh month? Number as the measure of time is uncertain. The significance of the same number varies, depending on where it occurs and what it refers to. To create something in a segment of time one must employ all of the senses: if one is omitted or is described with the help of the others, the result is labored and lacks the proportions of reality. The detailed description of a completed act can require such a long time and so much space that motion, endlessly slowed down, will equal stasis, although measured by eternity there is no difference between the two. The life of Bloom and Stephen is not the life of real people; it is not based completely on living Dubliners. However, it is tied in with human life and therefore it is measurable by time—by the hours, in other words by the events, of June 16, 1904. Certainly it took all of Bloom's life, his whole life, to give birth to one day of his life, but though *Ulysses* is 735 pages long, it would have been just as possible to devote a whole library of books to describing a single minute of Bloom's life. "Work in Progress" gives the first view into the kneading trough of creation. In the beginning was chaos. But chaos is also at the end. The reader participates in the beginning or the end of the world as it occurs. Everyone is anyone and every instant is any instant. The fall of the angels is mixed with the Battle of Waterloo, and H.C.E. is more changeable than history can provide names for."

Joyce was in a talkative mood.

"You know," he said, "the admirable Mr. Valery Larbaud praised *Ulysses* exaggeratedly by a beautiful metaphor, likening it to the stars of the sky, whose beauty is increased, when we study them for a long time, by the discovery of innumerable new stars.[19] What was the reaction to the Czech edition of *Ulysses* on the issue of its morality?"

"It was privately printed," I replied. "It was not picked up by the shrill reporters and unreliable papers. But I think one has to attribute the success of the book—it sold out in spite of a very large printing— partly to the effect of 'pornobibliophilia,' which seduced people into reading such a difficult book."

"The reaction of the Anglo-American public to the book is totally out of proportion and corresponds neither to the real interest nor to the indignation of the readers. Along with the realistic form and rhythmic linking of action that gave the book general significance or made it a

19. This passage appears in Larbaud's influential article on Joyce in the *Nouvelle Revue Française* of April 1922. See *James Joyce: The Critical Heritage*, 1:259–60, where the passage reads, "As we arrive at this conclusion [that the parts of the book form an organic whole] all sorts of coincidences, analogies, and correspondences between these different parts come to light; just as, in looking fixedly at the sky at night, we find that the number of stars appears to increase."

universal symbol, there were a few passages written in slightly unconventional language about things and thoughts habitually passed over in silence. In *Ulysses* the nakedness of animal human nature is shown, quite truthfully and moderately, it seems to me. But to the Irish censor's office these passages qualified as 'anything calculated to excite sexual passion.' Obscenity occurs in the pages of life, too, and if a book is to be complete it cannot cower silently away from those things which are thought or done but which are not supposed to be written about. No book has been able to, beginning with the Bible. No book. Some Frenchman wrote about Swift, with whom I have been compared and whose influence I do not deny, that he is capable '*d'une sérénité dans l'indécence.*' "[20]

"Can you tell me what is the similarity or the difference between *Ulysses* and 'Work in Progress'?"

"I believe that there is no difference. My work, from *Dubliners* on, goes in a straight line of development. It is almost indivisible, only the scale of expressiveness and writing technique rises somewhat steeply. After all, I was only twenty years old when I wrote *Dubliners*, and between *Ulysses* and 'Work in Progress' there is a difference of six years of painstaking work. I finished *Ulysses* in 1921, and the first fragment of 'Work in Progress' was published in *transition* six years later.[21] The difference, then, comes from development and from that alone. My whole work is always *in progress.*"

"I know that Czech readers will exclaim with Mr. H. G. Wells: 'This is a great work but I don't understand it.' "[22]

"I don't think that the difficulties in reading it are so insurmountable. Certainly any intelligent reader can read and understand it, if he returns to the text again and again. He is setting out on an adventure with words. On the contrary, 'Work in Progress' can satisfy more readers than any other book because it gives them the opportunity to use their own ideas in the reading. Some readers will be interested in the exploration of words, the play of technique, the philological experiment in each poetic unit. Each word has the charm of a living thing and each living thing is plastic.

20. Hoffmeister cites Emile Pons, *Jonathan Swift: Les années de jeunesse*, as the source of this quote.
21. The first fragment of "Work in Progress" to be published appeared in the *transatlantic review*, April 1924. "Opening pages of 'Work in Progress' " appeared in *transition*, no. 1, April 1927.
22. Hoffmeister is perhaps quoting from a personal conversation with Wells. Wells, who had written a highly favorable and influential review of *A Portrait of the Artist*, met Joyce in 1928 and offered further assistance. After looking over the published fragments of "Work in Progress" that Joyce sent him, Wells retracted his offer on the grounds that the work was "vast riddles" (*Letters* I, 274–75).

"In the first story in *Dubliners*, I wrote that the word 'paralysis' filled me with horror and fear, as though it designated something evil and sinful. I loved this word and would whisper it to myself in the evening at the open window. I have been accused of making up some words influenced by the conception of a universe that I never have seen. Perhaps my weak sight is to blame, so that my mind takes refuge in pictures evoked by words, and certainly it is a result of a Catholic education and an Irish origin."

"Your nationality is very visible in your work."

"Each of my books is a book about Dublin. Dublin is a city of scarcely three hundred thousand population, but it has become the universal city of my work. *Dubliners* was my last look at that city. Then I looked at the people around me. *Portrait* was the picture of my spiritual self. *Ulysses* transformed individual impressions and emotions to give them general significance. 'Work in Progress' has a significance completely above reality; transcending humans, things, senses, and entering the realm of complete abstraction. Anna and Humphrey are at the same time the city and its founder, the river and the mountain, as well as both sexual organs; there is not even a chronological ordering of the action. It is a simultaneous action, represented by the novel's circular construction, as Elliot Paul has pointed out very accurately.[23] Wherever the book begins it also ends."

"Do you think your book will be treated by critics or only by commentators?"

"So far, as many excellent explicators as miserable critics have written of my work. The article by Rebecca West in the *Bookman* in New York certainly caused a great storm.[24] I am very curious about how *Ulysses* was received and what will be said of 'Anna Livia Plurabelle' in your country."

"I have not seen any Czech criticism of *Ulysses* yet. I think that is only because our critics have not had the courage to read it."

"It seems to me that it is a sign of great courage to want to translate even a fragment of 'Work in Progress.' And for the translator it is something more than a great responsibility. I cannot decide about giving permission to publish a translation, particularly because it would not be really a translation but a new Czech poem. The difficulties you will encounter are tremendous. *Ulysses* was certainly a test

23. Joyce is referring to Paul's essay, "Mr. Joyce's Treatment of Plot," included in *Our Exagmination*.
24. "The Strange Case of James Joyce," *Bookman*, September 1928, pp. 9–23; partially reprinted in *James Joyce: The Critical Heritage*, 2:430–36. This article provoked a reply from William Carlos Williams, which was included in *Our Exagmination*. And his article in turn generated a response from Miss West ("Letter from Europe," *Bookman*, September 1929, pp. 664–68).

James Joyce. Drawing by Adolf Hoffmeister
(courtesy of Lilly Hoffmeister)

and a difficult work for translators, but it is nothing compared to 'Anna Livia.' "

"I would like to know your final decision. I would like to leave today bearing your permission to translate the book."

"I know, but let's leave it for now. We will speak about it later. At six o'clock some candidates for the French translation will be coming here. Translaturi me salutant.

"Would you please open the shutters a little? It is quiet on the street now, and the sun is no longer glaring. As you see, I am here only briefly. Perhaps I will go to Etretat for the weekend and then in a few days leave Paris again."

Joyce is sitting back in a deep armchair, tall, thin, in clothes that contrast with the white dust covers. His hair is beginning to turn gray. His expression is disdainful and his lips are tight together. His wife Nora apologizes for the disarranged apartment. The riddle of his personality is reflected in his life.

Paris has become quiet. We are not talking.

The room is blue, the color of blue eyes.

"Cobalt."

Joyce enjoys pronouncing words, their tone illustrating the course of his thought.

"Cobalt."

Without any connection and without direction, the isolated words fall one after the other into the room, into the echoing silence. Into the quiet of the shrouded, lifeless apartment.

The quiet is total and all-encompassing. The furniture is covered, and everything not imprisoned in the cupboards is standing in its place and sleeping. To speak in such a silence requires the courage to hear one's own voice, because the words fly around the room like disturbed pigeons that change into bats, and after they are spoken their images continue hovering soundlessly over the white dust sheets on which poisoned bread had been set out for mice. I did not dare to speak first. I expected Joyce to break the silence, but I did not expect to hear the words, without introduction, in clear Czech and with a perfect accent.

"České Budějovice."[25]

I was startled.

"Živnostenská Banka."

"Have you learned Czech since our last meeting?"

"Oh, no, I have only discovered a few interesting stems in your language and mine. However, I am well acquainted with the rhythm of your language."

"Have you been in Prague?"

25. The Czech name for the famous beer-making town Budweis.

"No, but my brother-in-law was a Czech. My sister Eileen met him in Trieste.[26] His name was Frantisek Schaurek; he was a cashier at the branch of the Živnostenská Bank there. At that time we lived together with my brother Stanny, a language teacher. Schaurek was Czech; his family probably still live in Prague (in the Zizkov quarter). He knew Czech, German, and Italian perfectly. During the war they moved to the Schaureks' in Prague. Frantisek Schaurek later shot himself, and my sister now lives in Dublin. Would you be so kind as to have a copy of the Czech translation sent to her? I doubt that she has read the English original, but perhaps she will be able to catch the meaning of the sentences in Czech."

"I did not expect to find any connection between you and Prague."

"It is only a family connection; I don't like to speak about it."

In Western Ireland there is a section called Joyce's Country. The Joyces go back to an old noble family from there. Joyce's father was a typical magnificent Irishman, of indefinite employment. They had an old house in Dublin where they lived a heedless life on the crest and in the trough of the waves of success and privation. Days of feast were succeeded by weeks of famine. A sense of money and the future is not part of the Irish character. The Joyce family was large. There were some thirteen or fifteen children. The majority are still living.[27] Two sisters are nuns, one at the Loretto in Dublin, the other in a mission in China or somewhere in the Far East. The father was tall, with blue eyes, and had a wonderful voice. The mother loved her son Jim. Whenever she felt miserable she asked Jim to play the piano for her. German critics attacked Joyce for composing and playing on the piano in a room adjacent to the one where his mother lay dying. Joyce's sister affirms that he was playing at his mother's request.[28]

The whole family was very musical. When Joyce returned from a concert they sat down in a circle, and Jim talked at length about the piece and the performance, analyzing it movement by movement and bar by bar. He had a penchant for nocturnal discussions in which even the most trivial matters were probed deeply. These discussions did not always concern music. He used to go to antique shops, bringing home statues, artifacts, art objects, and he could talk about them all night. His voice, as the voice of a poet, was respected as well as feared. His family was not happy that he was a writer and liked even less what he wrote. Dublin, which he celebrated many times in works where the

26. Joyce had brought his sister to Trieste in 1910 to provide some companionship for his wife. She married Schaurek in 1915, with Joyce as best man.

27. There were ten children in the Joyce family. None are now living.

28. Joyce was accompanying himself as he sang Yeats's lyric, "Who Goes with Fergus." This incident is recalled in Stephen Dedalus' memory of his dying mother (*U* 9).

atmosphere and moral perspective is unmistakably Irish, cast him out for having scandalized a few narrow minds. After the publication of *Dubliners* Joyce left Ireland, apparently forever.[29] He even goes to England rarely and almost incognito. Society is "horrified," and in Ireland his name is anathema.

We agreed on the translation. One year later "Anna Livia Plurabelle" was published in Czech.[30] The principal credit for this translation belongs to Dr. Vladimir Prochaska. We worked on it more than six months, and the book is barely over thirty pages long altogether.

TRANSLATED BY NORMA RUDINSKY

29. *Dubliners* appeared in 1914. Joyce's last visit to Ireland was in 1912, when he attempted but failed to get the book published.
30. This translation was published in Prague in 1932.

Ole Vinding

*DURING A VACATION TRIP to Denmark in the late summer of
1936, Joyce took his usual precautions against interviewers. But the
Danish writer and journalist Ole Vinding (b. 1906) learned from
an obliging clerk at the Tourist Hotel in Copenhagen that the Joyces
were staying there. Through a ruse he managed to meet them and to
spend parts of three days guiding them around the city and environs, all
the while keeping detailed notes. He arranged these notes in a narrative
and sent a typescript copy to Joyce with a request for permission
to publish it. The response was a one word telegram, "No." Vinding
abided by this terse injunction until after Joyce's death. Then he
published two short accounts and later on the longer one that is
translated here. Several brief passages from the short accounts and from
Vinding's original typescript have been silently incorporated in this
translation.*[1]

*Joyce always enjoyed visiting and exploring new places, but he had
been especially attracted to Denmark ever since his early admiration
for Ibsen. That admiration led him to study Danish, to read other
Scandinavian writers, and even, as Francini reported, to order Danish-
style furniture for his Trieste apartment. His fascination with Hamlet
provided another connection with Denmark, which he jokingly referred
to as "the land of Hamlet" (Letters I, 373). In spite of the purely
fanciful relationship between the play and its Danish setting, he visited
Elsinor and sent post cards from there to various of his friends. A notion
that he expressed to Vinding about having Viking blood in his veins
seems equally fanciful, though he may really have believed it. By
themselves, these spiritual and real or imagined ancestral links with
Denmark would have made his trip a special event, but it also gave him
an opportunity to practice his Danish and to discuss the possibility of a
Danish translation of* Ulysses. *In addition he liked to visit places
connected with his work, and Denmark had close connections with*

---

1. The earlier accounts are "Et Interview med Joyce," *Forum* (Copenhagen),
no. 1 (February 1941), pp. 21–22; and "James Joyce," *Perspectiv*, no. 8 (Summer
1959), pp. 14–16. Copies of the typescript are in the Joyce collections of the Universities of Cornell, London, SUNY/Buffalo, and Yale. A translation of the typescript, with several pages missing, is at SUNY/Buffalo.

Finnegans Wake, *where a main theme has to do with the Viking invasion of Ireland.*

Vinding's account shows clearly Joyce's deep interest in the country and also his characteristic fluctuations from mood to mood. At times he asks endless and precise questions, a habit noted later on by Jacques Mercanton and Dr. Carola Giedion-Welcker. At other times he sinks into nearly total silence, and at times speaks openly about himself, describing his behavior at parties, explaining the reasons for his well-known habit of eating out, and, in one striking passage, revealing the hold that Finnegans Wake *had over him. That revelation gives a poignant interior perspective on the intense commitment to his work stressed by Soupault and makes it easier to understand his laboring at the book with seldom flagging intensity for nearly seventeen years. An episode from 1924 gives a good illustration of the book's hold on him almost from the start. That year his doctor forbade him to do any writing, but he found the drawing power of typescripts and manuscripts too great while they were in his room, so he bundled them up and deposited them with Sylvia Beach at Shakespeare and Company. Even that was not enough to break the book's spell. He told Miss Weaver that he constantly had to "resist the temptation to go down to Miss Beach's shop and get out, at least, the typescript."[2] For Joyce even vacation time did not mean cessation of work. As he told Vinding, "I am always writing."*

In most accounts, Nora Joyce appears, if at all, only as a hazy figure in the background, serving tea, talking about hats, or being puzzled by her husband's work. Vinding, however, often focuses on her, revealing that, like Molly Bloom, she responded intensely to natural beauty, though she indulged her husband's whims with a passivity foreign to Molly. He also shows Joyce, unlike the uxorious Bloom, harshly rejecting his wife's wishes or simply displaying indifference toward her. Such behavior on Joyce's part was no doubt common enough and helps account for several times when she parted from him to live briefly in a hotel. Her attitude toward his work must have troubled him. Vinding recalls her saying of Ulysses, *"Das Buch ist ein Schwein,"[3] a remark she made to others as well. And he clearly was not an easy man to live with. Nevertheless, their relationship had a closeness belied by what Vinding saw of them in Copenhagen. They remained together almost constantly, even to the point of one taking a room in the hospital when the other was there. Moreover, Joyce's*

2. This letter, written on June 4, 1924, is in the Harriet Weaver Collection at the British Museum.

3. Letter to me from Ole Vinding, October 17, 1973.

admiration for her was great. Few fathers have been more attached to their children than he was to his, yet he once remarked of his wife that personally she was "probably worth both of her children rolled together and multiplied by three" (Letters I, 366).

According to Vinding the Copenhagen trip disappointed the Joyces. He says that they found the food and service in the restaurants bad, not surprisingly since they were used to dining in the most expensive Parisian restaurants, and that Joyce himself was depressed at his inability to understand spoken Danish after twenty years of studying it. Ellmann, however, says,

> *Joyce's stay in Copenhagen contented him. He liked the postmen with their red coats, the pillarboxes, the fur-helmeted guards. . . . He and Nora were delighted with a performance of Délibes' Coppélia at the opera, and thought it as a spectacle the best they had ever seen. . . . So after a crowded three weeks Joyce left with the intention, not to be realized, of renting a house in Copenhagen the following spring. [JJ 709]*

This discrepancy provides another instance in Joyce biography where "the unfacts, did we possess them, are too imprecisely few to warrant our certitude" (FW 57.16–17).

James Joyce
in Copenhagen

By Ole Vinding

JAMES JOYCE WAS THE KIND OF PERSON WHO, aging early, remains youthful long after youth has passed. Thus the years play with us, compensating somewhat for past injustices. He had a student's body, long-limbed and skinny. He also had the long nape of a student but carried his head in the up-tilted way of the blind. His movements were boyish, his hands and feet very small, like those of a doll. But his face was aged and his sight that of a very old man. He saw the world, literally and tragically, only with half or quarter of an eye. His glasses had one lens of window-glass and one like a magnifying glass, the window-glass for the blind eye, the magnifying glass for the half-eye.

He behaved with a carefree gaiety; yet something about that gaiety made one doubt that he ever enjoyed himself. One always had the feeling that he was perhaps not really paying attention to his surroundings. His work seemed to be gnawing at him inwardly.

Joyce originally planned to stay three weeks in Copenhagen, but he could not last that long.[4] After the first day his enthusiasm gradually decreased. The language, the food, everything was wrong.

An old dream had failed to come true. For sixteen years he had been longing to come to Denmark[5] and had become convinced that he had Danish blood in his veins—Viking blood. Nothing less would do, but how much of it is left today even in the natives? Did his realization that it was a minimum contribute to his dissatisfaction with his stay?

He had begun to learn Danish when he was eighteen years old, and now in his fifty-fourth year he had to speak it.

That was in September 1936.

Since he would not permit journalists near him, I assumed an incognito, presenting myself as the painter Ole Vinkaer. I kept most of the letters from my real name, and I did dabble a little in painting, and I love wine,[6] so the truth wasn't stretched too much. My idea was to offer to show Joyce the town and the area around it, to write down everything he said, and then, when his stay was over, to ask him for permission to publish the conversations.

The ruse worked better than I expected, and for three days I accompanied Joyce and his wife Nora like a shadow, but by the fourth day I had had enough; in spite of my admiration for him, I found him exhausting. He sucked energy from his surroundings and was untiring in spite of his frailty and obvious physical weakness. His knowledge was broad, his questioning constant and of inquisitorial precision. Everything appeared to interest him, buttermilk, the soft "d" in the word "gud," the difference between "a" and "o"—for instance in the sentence, "Toget holdt i taagen"[7]—the folk type in Denmark, Icelandic sweaters, and so on.

4. Joyce departed for Copenhagen on 18 August, and on 13 September wrote to Budgen, "Just back from Denmark . . ." (*JJ* 703, and *Letters* III, 388). Even allowing for several days' layover on the way to and from Denmark, he would have had a full three weeks there.
5. Actually for longer than that. In 1906 he wrote his brother from Rome, "I wish I could go to Denmark." At the time he was taking his first lessons in Danish and also reading Ferrero's *Young Europe*, where he found Stockholm, Abo, and Copenhagen identified as "the finest cities in Europe" (*Letters* II, 201). In 1927 he told Michael Healy, "I would like to go to Denmark but it's a long, long way to Copenhagen and the fare's right dear" (*Letters* I, 257). Eight years later he wrote to Giorgio, "I yearn to go to Denmark because the Danes massacred so many of my ancestors," but a plan to make the trip then fell through, to his great disappointment (*Letters* III, 359, and I, 373).
6. Vinkaer means "wine lover" in Danish.
7. "gud" = "god"; "Toget holdt i taagen" = "The train stood in the fog."

I was far from able to satisfy his endless curiosity. Constantly restless, his small body performed miracles of endurance. He wanted to go everywhere, on foot, by tramway, as quickly as possible, as far as possible. He seldom used a car, partly because he wanted to see other people than his wife and me and partly because he was thrifty.[8]

Mrs. Nora Joyce followed, patiently as a cow, without the slightest activity, as if her endurance depended upon her passivity. It was a long-standing arrangement and it had its cold fronts. She must have heard his stories thousands of times; his impulses never surprised her, and she ignored his periods of grumpiness. In this latter mood he answered everything with a "hm" and turned his head away just like the camel in Kipling's story "How the Camel Got Its Hump." Occasionally she desired something for herself, for instance an Icelandic sweater, but she always was denied immediately. He bought it for himself, period! He had become accustomed to everything turning on him, and she passively indulged this habit. He was like a spoiled boy with his quiet, eternally permissive mother.

We started our conversation in English, but it did not last more than five minutes before he suddenly said in clear Danish:

"Take me out and show me the city, Mr. Vinkaer!" My surprise over his ability pleased him, and he explained:

"I taught myself Danish in order to read Ibsen in his own language, so all I can speak is Ibsen language, which is no longer spoken in his own country.[9] I have not been able to master the Norwegian spoken today, but with my Danish I have read both Ibsen and Gunnar Heiberg.[10] Now I hope I can get enough practice while here to be able to speak fluently, really fluently. I have often wished to be able to do that, but I have never been able to find travel companions. Now I have made the jump, and today I sent my son a wire in verse about my arrival. I rewrote an old Irish immigration song, called 'I Go Down to Philadelphia in the Morning' [sic—in English], which he, as a singer, is fond of, and I put something about Copenhagen and Denmark into it as homage to Denmark.[11] Ireland was originally Danish, and cities like Dublin and Cork owe their origin to Danish Vikings. No doubt I, also, have Danish blood in my veins! But I can't figure out if the Danes are a dark or a light people. What do you think?"

8. One quality that Joyce never had, cultivated, or admired was thrift.

9. As a result of the Norwegian nationalist movement early in the century, the essentially Danish language in which Ibsen wrote had been replaced by a native one.

10. Heiberg (1857–1929) was a Norwegian dramatist, author of *Aunt Ulrikke* (1884), *King Midas* (1890), *The Balcony* (1894), and *The Tragedy of Love* (1904).

11. This wire apparently has not survived. The Percy French song "Off to Philadelphia in the Morning" is alluded to a number of times in *Finnegans Wake*.

"That we are primarily light."

"In Ireland we speak about 'dovegalls' and 'fingalls.' The former were the dark, they were the Danes; the latter, the light, were the Norwegians. I don't seem to see many light people here in town; would that be because there are so many foreign tourists? I can't see the national type."

"Yes, but it is Sunday today and good weather, Mr. Joyce, so the people are out of town."

"Good, it is perhaps also because it is Sunday that I saw only two ships in the harbor? That seems to me hardly enough for a sea-faring nation!" He chuckled.

On our first trip we went down to Gammel Strand and through the Bibliotheksgarden. To get an impression of the places, Joyce constantly shaded his seeing eye with his hand.

"So this is the old part of town? I wouldn't mind living here," he said. "My plan is to get a furnished apartment and stay here for a while."

In front of one shop hung some Icelandic sweaters that delighted the author of *Ulysses*. He bought one for himself. His wife also wanted one but he refused decisively: "No, and certainly not for George, whose elegant American wife has always been scornful of our simple, 'primitive' taste. But I shall have mine to write in during the winter. Must one wear a shirt underneath it?"

After the purchase was wrapped Joyce said, "I'm not much interested in souvenirs but I have a five-year-old grandson, and he certainly must have a toy as a reminder of H. C. Andersen. He is Denmark's greatest writer; there's no one like him in the world. No one will ever manage to tell stories for children as well as he did. He is unique."

A little later: "Do you often have thunderstorms here in Copenhagen and Denmark?"

"The summer has been cool this year and thunderstorms have been rare."

"Thank god! I am horrified by thunderstorms. I panic just at the mere thought of them. You must not even tell me stories about thunderstorms if you have any. I think everything is nice here now. The air is wonderful, it is peaceful. I also believe Danish food will suit me very well, at least the bread is wonderful and the butter and the milk; that is already a lot. And the beer! I remember the name: Carlsberg. Hmmm, that doesn't sound particularly Danish, does it?"

Of course, during these conversations I had to avoid revealing any special interest in literature or Joyce's work so that the idea of an interview would not occur to him. As far as possible I just answered his questions. The second day of their stay I left the couple alone but met them again on Tuesday at 3:30 at the Tourist Hotel where they were staying. Mrs. Joyce was in the same dress as on the first day, but Joyce had changed his thin, gray-striped suit and his even thinner chevrau-shoes for a suit of dark flannel and a pair of more sturdy walking shoes. He kept a worn-out raincoat over his shoulders.

"Today we are going out to Frederiksberg!" he declared in Danish, almost without an accent.

In the garden of the Garden Society he stated that he didn't care for flowers but only grass and trees. Nevertheless, he was enthusiastic about the pretty beds in the little fairy-tale garden, which glowed in rich autumn colors.

It began to rain and Joyce complained to his wife that she had not brought along an umbrella, to which she remarked that she found umbrellas comical. This led him to tell of a friend in Paris, a young nobleman from Cambodia, whose title gave him the right to carry no less than six umbrellas, one above the other, and whose father, the old nobleman, had the right to seven.[12] "Umbrellas are not so comical," he said, "but very distinguished implements, Nora."[13]

Mrs. Joyce did not listen at all but commented excitedly on the changing light. She could not recall having seen a more beautiful effect any place outside Denmark. This led the conversation to the art of painting, "my" area, and Joyce carried it on to his daughter:

"She is a painter herself and has just illustrated a medieval poem by the monk Gregorius, which Geoffrey Chaucer translated. It is called 'ABC' because it has as many verses as there are letters in the alphabet, each verse beginning with its own letter.[14] I hope to receive a copy of the book soon. My friend Louis Gillet has written a charming foreword to it. When it comes I will show it to you."

This same French friend once said about Joyce: "He stands outside time—like a man cleaning his nails!"[15] He must have felt as I did that Joyce really was never aware of his surroundings, or had only one will: a will that centered on Joyce and apparently reduced the world around

12. In a letter to Lucia, Joyce reminded her of Prince Norindett Norodum Doum Doum, who was "entitled to hoist seven umbrellas over his bald head because he is of kingly race" (*Letters* I, 382). This prince, whose name Herbert Gorman gives as Norrindett-Norrodun, accompanied Joyce on several trips outside Paris to hear John Sullivan sing. He also had a royal cousin in Paris who had changed his name to René-Ulysse in honor of Joyce's book and who "used to send his visiting card under his new style to his adopted literary father [i.e. Joyce] on the first day of every Annamite year" (Herbert Gorman, *James Joyce* [New York: Farrar and Rinehart, 1939], p. 326).

13. Bloom also had trouble getting Molly to carry an umbrella (*U* 687).

14. See below, p. 165.

15. This echoes Stephen Dedalus' remark, "The artist, like the God of the creation, remains within or behind or beyond or above his handiwork, invisible, refined out of existence, indifferent, paring his fingernails" (*P* 215).

him to something just to be used, something that served as nourishment, for example, but was not interesting in itself.

Now enjoying the conversation, Joyce continued, "I know nothing of the mania for collecting. I have a couple of pictures by the Irish painter Yeats, and a perfect likeness of Georg Brandes, drawn by your countryman Ivan Opffer. He drew me also, but I don't like it nearly as well."

I could insert here that Georg Brandes became very angry over Opffer's drawing and that the drawing of Joyce was perfect, but neither of the two famous men apparently wanted to be perceived in Opffer's way. However, at the time I did not say anything for fear of making "Mr. Vinkaer" appear too knowledgeable about famous men; furthermore, it was impossible to stop Joyce.

"Do you know Augustus John?" he asked. "He is England's greatest living painter, a Derain if you will. I have a funny story about Augustus John!" he said.

"It is much too long, Jim," interrupted Mrs. Joyce, but he waved her aside impatiently.

"I'll be brief, Nora!"

He turned toward me: "John wanted to paint or draw me and had made an appointment with me in Paris. While he was working we were surprised by a press photographer. That is the only time in my life I gave in to the press. I did it only so as not to offend John. We were photographed and the picture appeared in the newspapers.[16] A short time thereafter I was phoned by a Mr. Nelson, whose accent wasn't English at all. He turned out to be a Norwegian named Nilsson. We spoke Norwegian together so it was probably true. He said he was a friend of Augustus John and asked if I would come to dinner at his hotel. I went because I didn't want to deny a friend of Augustus John. My host offered me champagne and expensive cigars in vain. I prefer to smoke the cheap 'Voltiguer,' and I never drink champagne, especially at a light lunch, not so much because I am temperate or virtuous as simply because I can't stand it. My moderation saved me. The hotel porter arrived at my place a few days later and asked if I weren't a school friend of Mr. Nelson. I denied that, but he did not believe me, and it now became clear that my friendly host was a hotel rat. He not only had borrowed from the hotel owner, the porter, and even the chamber maid, but also had stolen towels, bed clothes, and soap and had disappeared with all bills unpaid. He had left only two suitcases. They proved to be full of— potatoes! Isn't that funny?" Joyce laughed and continued, "But it is still funnier than an honest man never can cheat his hotel of even a centime!"

16. This picture can be seen in *Letters* III, following p. 224.

James Joyce. Drawing by Ivan Opffer, 1922
(courtesy of Croessman Collection of James Joyce)

"Mr. Nelson apparently took advantage of your name. Does that happen often?"

"You mean blackmail?"

"No, not that alone, but also regarding political questions, for example."

"It has been tried, both by the right and the left, but without success. I don't want anything to do with politics."

"The example of Gide in France, though, shows that it can be difficult for a famous author to stand outside."

"Yes, unfortunately, but I have succeeded. By the way, I have a funny story about Gide. He has dallied with communism, of course, and one day a young man by the name of Armand Petitjean came to him. Let me add here that at the age of sixteen this M. Petitjean started writing a big volume about my book 'Work in Progress,' long before it was finished. Well, this enthusiastic admirer of mine went to Gide to ask him what they should do with me if communism won. Gide thought it over for some time and then answered: 'We'll let him be!' "

Joyce chuckled, "Then I could feel relieved, if I ever had been worried. By the way, I love two of Gide's books: *La symphonie pastorale*, which is a masterpiece, and *Les caves du Vatican*, which is funny."

We walked up Frederiksberg hill; as soon as the rain stopped, Joyce wanted to go to the zoo.

"You said Sunday that you weren't welcome in Dublin. Is that for political reasons?"

"No, it's because of my books."

"*Dubliners?*"

"Among others."

"Do you ever miss Ireland?"

"I didn't live there very long, but every day I get papers and other news from home. I am not sure I would care to go back. *Ulysses* is coming out this month in England; let us see how the Irish take it.[17] Furthermore, I am afraid to go back to Ireland. You see, when one is almost blind and can't see whom one is talking to, then one becomes suspicious. Recently an Irish friend asked me to join the Irish Academy, but they are just out after my name so I am not interested.[18] The day they become interested in my work that will be another matter. But let us change the subject!"

"What is wrong with your eyesight?"

17. This edition of *Ulysses* by John Lane/The Bodley Head appeared on October 3, 1936, marking the end to a long series of negotiations and delays over the book's publication in England.

18. The friend was William Butler Yeats. For the invitation see *Letters* III, 258–59, and for Joyce's reply see *Letters* I, 325.

"I've had green starling, gray starling, and all kinds of starlings.[19] A very complicated case but I think it was originally caused by some kind of rheumatism in the eye."

"Your endurance is admirable; the poor eyesight must have delayed your work considerably."

"Yes, of course, and I can manage to read only what I need for my books, but of course I have read everything about Denmark I could get my hands on, even the text on the tramway tickets. And how sad it is to discover that after many years of trying I still can't understand what people say around here. I can make myself understandable when I speak slowly, but I can't understand what others say. I have read Danish since I was nineteen and have taken lessons everywhere I found Danes, in Danish churches, or homes for seamen, or in private homes. One man I studied with is still around; he was something in a large department store, but I can't remember his name. (Joyce's Danish teacher proved to be Mr. Max, owner of "Interior" in the Kanneworff Building.) To read Danish, to understand it, has been a passion with me. I was seventeen when Ibsen's last drama *When We Dead Awaken* was published. I was still in school but immediately wrote a long article about it and sent it to the most prestigious journal in England, the *Fortnightly Review*, which to my surprise accepted it.[20] I was even more surprised when, one day while sitting in the swing in the garden, I was brought a letter from Ibsen. It wasn't written with his own hand but by his translator William Archer, but still! The master thanked me and I threw myself into Danish."

"Did you have further contacts with Ibsen?"

"For his birthday I wrote him a letter which must have made him fall under the table with laughter—it was in Swedish! My Swedish![21] But the article was my literary debut—I started at the top!"

"Do you still admire him as much now as you did then?"

"Yes, he towers head and shoulders above everyone else, even Shakespeare. Ibsen will not become dated; he will renew himself for every generation because his problems always will be seen from a new side as time goes on. He has been called a feminist in *Hedda Gabler*, but he is no more a feminist than I am an archbishop.

"He is the greatest dramatist I know. No one can construct a piece as he can. There is not an extraneous word in his work. It was wonderful to see what Lugné-Poë did as Old Ekdal in *The Wild Duck*, with

19. In Danish the terms for "glaucoma" and "cataract" are "*grøn stær*" and "*gra stær*." "*Stær*" also means "starling."
20. Joyce's article on *When We Dead Awaken*, "Ibsen's New Drama" (*CW* 48–67), appeared on April 1, 1900.
21. This letter (*Letters* I, 51–52) would have been written in Danish.

Ludmilla Piteoff, a little fifty-year-old woman with ten or fifteen children, playing Hedvig. I am sorry that I never have seen *Little Eyolf*. The first act is a pure wonder. By the way, are there any famous actors in Denmark?"

"The most famous abroad is Mr. Poul Reumert."

"Yes, I saw him play Tartuffe in Paris and perform in another piece, *Galgemanden* I believe it was called.[22] That's a scary play."

"Do you like the plays of O'Neill?"

"I have seen only a few of them."

We reached the zoo, and Joyce declared that he didn't care much for the animals; only cats and goats appealed to him. But in front of the cage of the Siberian tiger he remarked comically:

"That is a terrible, restless animal, and look how petty his face is. The lion is much more majestic!"

The goats entertained him highly with their pranks; through association with the pictures of antelopes in Hemingway's *Green Hills of Africa*, Joyce said:

"We were together with Hemingway just before he left for Africa; he promised us a living lion, but fortunately we escaped that. We would rather have his book. He writes well, he writes as he is, we like him. He is large and wonderful and robust like a buffalo, athletic, created to live the life that he describes and that he could not describe without his physique, but such giants as he are bashful. Beneath the surface, Hemingway is more intensely 'Hemingway' than has been assumed."[23]

On Thursday the joy over Denmark had decreased. Joyce and his wife were disappointed over the food, which was served in too large quantities to appear esthetic, and they felt the service was the worst of any place in Europe.

It surprised Joyce that we, who have good fish, good milk, good butter and bread, could not come up with anything but an unappetizing mish-mash. The language gave him trouble and irritated him more and more. He was grumpy and turned his head like Kipling's camel and said "hm" to almost everything. However, he had not yet completely given up the plans about coming again and living in a furnished apartment.

In a landau we drove that day past the Hermitage, which he did not care for, and on to Lyngby to see a working farm, which interested him greatly. In the Frilandsmuseum, he signed the guest book and looked

22. *The Gallows Man* by the Finno-Swedish writer Runar Schildt (1888–1925).
23. In *Green Hills of Africa* (New York: Charles Scribner's Sons, 1935), p. 71, Hemingway mentions his evening with the Joyces prior to leaving for Africa. Hemingway also admired Joyce, referring to him with near reverence in *Islands in the Stream*. For other expressions of Joyce's regard for Hemingway's work, see Arthur Power, *Conversations with James Joyce* (London: Millington, 1974), p. 107.

around absent-mindedly while talking all the time about Italy:[24]

"For many years we lived in Trieste, where both my children were born. At home we speak mostly in Italian."

"What do you think about d'Annunzio?"

"Magnificent."[25]

"And about Italy, now?"

"I love it, now as ever! Not to love it because of Mussolini would be as absurd as hating England because of Henry the Eighth."

"Is the edition of *Ulysses* which is now coming out in England just a new printing?"

"No, the first printing in England. The real first printing came in Paris. I wonder how it is going; the publisher must take all the risk. I insist that every little line must be included. I've done the same at Martin's Publishing Company.[26] If they do not obey that rule, everything is off. Tonight I shall look at the galleys."

After that the conversation switched to language and the art of singing. He did not care for Stravinsky or for contemporary music in general.

Mrs. Joyce wanted a cup of tea but was categorically denied. Joyce had had buttermilk in Lyngby and was satisfied with that.

The following Saturday was our last meeting. He finally spoke about his new work:

"I haven't lived a normal life since 1922, when I began 'Work in Progress.' It demands an enormous amount of concentration. I want to describe the night itself. *Ulysses* is related to this book as the day is to the night. Otherwise there is no connection between the two books. *Ulysses* did not require the same amount of concentration. Since 1922 my book has become more real to me than reality, and everything has led to it; all other things have been insurmountable difficulties, even the smallest realities such as, for instance, to shave in the morning. There are, so to say, no individual people in the book—it is as in a dream, the style gliding and unreal as is the way in dreams. If one were to speak of a person in the book, it would have to be of an old man, but even his relationship to reality is doubtful. Now I will soon be through with it; about one-fourth remains to be written, but that will go faster now. The book has already had a strange fate, a fate which I would say corresponds to the nature of the book. Fragments of it have appeared in *transition*, an

24. The Hermitage is an old hunting castle, now a tourist attraction. The Frilandsmuseum is an open-air museum of old buildings from various parts of Denmark.
25. In the typescript this reads, "He *was* a magnificent poet."
26. Joyce had heard that Mrs. Kastor Hansen was going to translate the book. According to Tom Kristensen, who accompanied him to Martin's, he walked up to Mrs. Kastor Hansen and said, "I am James Joyce. I understand that you are to translate *Ulysses*, and I have come from Paris to tell you not to alter a single word" (*JJ* 705). Mrs. Kastor Hansen turned out to be too busy to undertake the job. Martin's finally published a translation of *Ulysses* in 1949.

English journal published in Paris, and in *La Nouvelle Revue Française*. The small piece[27] which appeared in the latter took three months to translate, and I even had five helpers for it. That was hard work. If *Ulysses* should be published by Martin's, which has asked first and therefore has priority, they must have more than one man for the job, but I am a little worried. The representative for the publisher told me that Jack London was the most popular author in Denmark. I haven't anything against him, but I dare say we are rather different!"

"Is 'Work in Progress' constantly going forward?"

"Yes, still in progress, but slowly because of my sight."

"Are you writing while you are here?"

"I am always writing."

He smiled, "It pleases me very much."

"Why is the new, unfinished book so intensely commented on already?"

"Yes, you may well ask that question. It is a mystery to me, too.[28] My book has been judged and conclusions drawn from it long before I have finished with it or drawn any conclusions myself."

"You write rather slowly, don't you?"

"Yes, extremely slowly."

"You must be rich in order to allow yourself that?"

"Rich? Me?" He laughed. "Why in the world do you believe that?"

"Because you take your time and because you must know in advance that your work is written for a minority—without any guarantee or support from the snobs."

"Yes, I was aware of that from the beginning, but it went along anyway. Yes, you are probably right, it was probably something of a miracle that it could be done. It is strange that doesn't even occur to one at the time. One works and will finish what one has set out to do."

"Where did you write *Ulysses*?"

"In Trieste, Zurich, and Paris."

We sat down for a glass of buttermilk at "Josty," and Joyce wanted to tell about the hell he always raised at parties. He said he had invented his own dance and Mrs. Joyce remarked dryly: "If you can call flinging your legs over your neck and kicking the furniture to pieces 'to dance'!"

"Well, Nora, I *do* dance! I know the rules of dancing and request that the floor be cleared—that's the least I can do. I once went to a New

27. The French version of "Anna Livia Plurabelle."
28. Joyce could hardly have been mystified at the many articles on *Finnegans Wake* since he personally encouraged and directed a number of them, but he preferred to keep his part in this critical activity to himself.

Year's party with some friends and won first prize for my costume of a beggar, a real *clochard*. I dressed up in a diplomat's coat that was old and way too short; underneath I wore a blue shirt and, naturally, I wore yellow gloves. In this getup, I was introduced to a very solemn young man. He greeted me somewhat ceremoniously, but I was in the middle of a dance, so I cut a little caper and answer hastily, '*Enchanté*,' whereupon I forgot the new acquaintance, whose name I didn't even catch. That was M. Armand Petitjean, my energetic commentator! He was the oldest at the party, age-old. The hostess wasn't particularly happy with my behavior and the next day called on the old-young man to hear what impression I had made on him. He answered laconically: 'Yes, as usual, Mr. Joyce had more interest in the expression than in the impression!' "

He laughed, enjoying the memories of those times when he let himself go.

"After I have worked all day, the thought of eating at home becomes unbearable. I want to see people, I want to get away from the work and loaf with a 'Voltiguer'! For the same reason I abhor literature after dinner; I must escape my work. I eat out, smoke my 'Voltiguer,' look at people and what else? Why in the world should I take a position on deep literary and philosophical questions? Why should I decide if this or that author is great or small? I become a convinced materialist, and only in that way can the night be separated from the day; the exertion of the work is forgotten for a time. One is free. It is wonderful to let go, to chat away without reservations and say all the stupid things one wants to!"

He sat for a while and then added:

"There is also the other miracle that I still can see at all. Six years ago I was completely blind,[29] but a Swiss surgeon has brought back a little of my sight in the left eye, just enough so I can see to write when I put an extra magnifying glass on. It is not known if the other can be saved by an operation; the operation is considered very risky."

"Can't you dictate?"

"No, impossible."

"Is it the style of your books which makes it impossible?"

"I can only write alone, more and more alone. It has developed that way, like my style, which has developed and changed so that what I write simply cannot be expressed in any other way than like dream talk. With day-time talk such as I used in my youth, I would not achieve anything."

29. More accurately, he was in danger of being completely blind. The Swiss surgeon referred to later in the sentence is Alfred Vogt.

And this fourth meeting became the last. When he had left I sent him a telegram asking permission to publish what I had written in my notebook while he was here, and received a refusal. To the regret of my editor I obeyed and turned a deaf ear to his eternal quote from the megalomaniac Lord Northcliffe, "Everything counts, nothing matters!"

TRANSLATED BY HELGE IRGENS-MOLLER

Jan Parandowski

JAN PARANDOWSKI (b. 1895) is a distinguished Polish novelist whose best-known book outside his own country is The Olympic Discus. *His recollection of Joyce is based on a single encounter during and after the PEN meeting in Paris in 1937. For the meeting Joyce had written a paper defending authorial rights, a subject he took such a militant interest in that he was willing to make this rare public appearance in its behalf. To his disgust, however, a turmoil of recriminations broke out between Fascists and anti-Fascists, almost completely overshadowing his paper. He left the meeting immediately after it was delivered, accompanied by Parandowski.*

In his recollection Parandowski deals briefly with the meeting itself, and then goes on to give a remarkably detailed account of his conversation with Joyce after they left. That account includes the most substantial record of Joyce's comments on Ulysses *in the years following its publication. During that period he usually spoke only briefly and reluctantly about the book, always preferring to talk about* Finnegans Wake. *But Parandowski's love of Homer led to a warm discussion of the* Odyssey, *reawakening Joyce's old interest in it and leading him to think back nearly twenty years to the ideas and aspirations he had had while writing* Ulysses.

Some of his remarks to Parandowski about Ulysses *echo things he had said in the past about the place of the human body in the book's design and his intention of giving a minutely accurate picture of Dublin. One indicates more clearly than ever before his sense of identity with Dante as he worked on the book. Others reveal that he had felt great excitement at the time he was writing it, believed that he was producing a work of similar importance to Homer's, and was convinced, in retrospect at least, that Homer's spirit had guided him. Previously he had seldom even hinted at having such feelings and grandiose thoughts about* Ulysses, *but habitually spoke of it with humorous deprecation or weary exasperation. Perhaps now that the book had appeared in England and thus was fully launched, he felt that he could risk the dangers of hubris.*

His reasons for choosing the Odyssey *as the basis for his book have been discussed frequently, beginning with T. S. Eliot's famous essay,*

"Ulysses, *Order and Myth.*" [1] *He himself indicated to Frank Budgen and Georges Borach that among his reasons was an admiration for the hero and the themes in the* Odyssey. *From Parandowski we learn that he also admired the structure or "way the fable unfolds" in the* Odyssey. *The fable unfolds in a complex way. One part of an episode is given here and another there; the incidents often are retold, sometimes with significant variations; and the chronology is mixed, with much jumping back and forth in time as well as in space. While these structural traits characterize* Ulysses, *they are even more prominent in* Finnegans Wake, *suggesting that Homer's work provided a model for the latter as well as for the former.*

Toward the end of his meeting with Parandowski, Joyce finally brought the conversation around to Finnegans Wake, *questioning the book and its future. Occasionally criticism from Miss Weaver or some other source to which he was particularly sensitive would move him to defend the book, as he did in saying to her, "Either the end of [the "Anna Livia Plurabelle" chapter] is something or I am an imbecile in my judgment of language" (Letters I, 249). In spite of such defenses, which usually were carefully limited, he had doubts about the book. Some of them will appear later in Mercanton's and Gillet's recollections, but those recorded by Parandowski are the most poignant and extensive.*

Meeting with Joyce

By Jan Parandowski

NOT MANY NATIONS HAVE ENJOYED the privilege of a translation of Joyce's *Ulysses*. But whenever a translation of this remarkable work has appeared, it has been an exciting and controversial event. I lived through such a time in the fall of 1946, toward the end of my sojourn in Sweden. The translation was published [in Stockholm] by Bonnier, who also publish *BLM*, one of the outstanding periodicals, or rather magazines, worthy of the name "literary." The editorial board of Bonnier asked me if I would be willing to write a few pages on *Ulysses* or Joyce. It was at that time that I recalled my only meeting with this remarkable Irishman and our conversation, which was as striking as any that I have ever had with a contemporary writer—a recollection

1. *Dial*, 75 (Nov. 1923): 480–83; reprinted in *James Joyce: Two Decades of Criticism*, ed. Seon Givens (New York: Vanguard Press, 1948), pp. 198–202.

somewhat obscured by time, like an old photograph, and for that reason all the more intriguing. I wrote up our conversation in French, which was translated into Swedish by Marika Stiernstedt, a distinguished writer whose name is well known in Poland both as an author and as a great friend of Polish literature. Today, while putting my papers in order, I discovered the record of our conversation. I thought that, although a translator of *Ulysses* will not soon be found among us, Polish readers, who generally are well acquainted with Joyce's short stories and *A Portrait of the Artist as a Young Man*, know enough about the man himself that I might share with them my recollections.[2]

It was in 1937—in Paris. Joyce came to a plenary meeting of the PEN Congress, being held in the Jouvet Theatre. On the stage were the president's table and a lectern. As Joyce mounted the stairs to the stage, he wavered at every step and would have fallen had someone not helped him at the last moment.

"He is nearly blind," someone near me whispered.

Joyce used our congress as an opportunity to denounce the censors' attacks on *Ulysses*. Since he himself could not read his report, he gave it, if I am not mistaken, to one of the Irish delegates, and, taking a seat at the corner of the president's table, accompanied the reading of the report with a rhythmic tapping of his fingers on the red cloth. The fortunes of his book were being recounted.

An edition of a thousand numbered copies was published in Paris by Shakespeare and Company (this name struck me as a bit of pretentious symbolism). In the fall of the same year an edition of two thousand was published in London by a company with, it seems to me, an equally peculiar name—the Egoist Press. Five hundred copies from this edition were sent to America where the New York postal authorities burned all except a single copy, kept for the Post Office archives. The same fate met the third edition—five hundred numbered copies—which was burnt by order of the customs authorities. The "Nausicaa" episode had thoroughly incensed the guardians of morality. But Joyce reserved most of his outrage for the "abridged" version of the book, which had been published without his permission and for which he received not a cent.[3]

The American delegation listened with embarassment, while Marinetti was exuberant, though a bit earlier he had sat there ill-humored when the distinguished historian Guglielmo Ferrero spoke of the burning

2. A Polish translation of *Ulysses* was published in 1969. The Polish reception of Joyce is discussed in the *James Joyce Quarterly*, 9 (Fall 1971): 93–98, 99–116.

3. The published version of this speech (*CW* 274–75) differs somewhat from Parandowski's recollection of it. The "abridged" edition of *Ulysses* was that pirated by Samuel Roth in 1926–27.

of his books by the Fascists.[4] When his paper had been read, Joyce picked it up, put it in his pocket, and left the stage, groping his way into the darkened auditorium. Since I was sitting on the aisle in the second row, I hurried to give him my hand and direct him to a vacant seat. However, he whispered that he wanted to leave and leaned on my arm. I asked if he had someone there with him. He waved his hand toward . . the door and quickened his steps with the élan of a boy who was about to skip school. We passed through the door and out to the street, where he turned to me abruptly:

"I can tell from your accent that you are not French. What are you? I can't figure it out." He spoke these last words with a kind of nervous impatience, but when I satisfied his curiosity by giving my name and identifying my country, he received the information with complete indifference. He asked with some concern, however, if I didn't wish to return to the meeting. Naturally, I preferred his unexpected company. We walked along silently for several minutes. In my wish to break this silence, I could find nothing better than to ask this nearly blind man if he had noticed that on the stage had been some of the scenery for Giraudoux's *Electra*, which was currently playing there.

"No, and I will tell you right now, Giraudoux interests me very little."

"And yet he is a master of French prose."

"It's too bad that he doesn't write in verse. He would have been able to unmask himself more easily. Giraudoux belongs to the school of poets whose day has passed, the so-called rhetoricians, and waits in vain for his Du Bellay and his Ronsard to come to life again. Never have I come upon a writer who was such a brilliant bore."

4. Filippo Tommaso Marinetti, who founded the "Futurist" movement in Italy, was an enthusiastic supporter of Mussolini. Ferrero, an outspoken anti-Fascist, had fled Italy and taken refuge in Switzerland. Joyce's anger at this eruption of politics into the meeting surfaced a few days later when Nancy Cunard made the mistake of sending him a questionnaire asking his opinions on the Spanish Civil War: "He telephoned to say, 'I am James Joyce. I have received your questionnaire.' 'Are you going to answer it?' she asked. 'No! I won't answer it because it is politics. Now politics are getting into everything. The other night I agreed to let myself be taken to one of the dinners of the P.E.N. Club. The charter of the P.E.N. states that politics shall never be discussed there. But what happened? One person made a speech, referring to one angle of politics, someone else brought up a conflicting argument, a third read a paper on more politics. I wanted the P.E.N. to take an interest in the pirating of *Ulysses* in the United States, but this was brushed aside. It was politics all the way.' He concluded by saying he was sending her the script of his remarks at the P.E.N. meeting and commanded, 'Print that, Miss Cunard!'" (*JJ* 717).

Joyce had reason to feel a special sympathy for Ferrero, whose *Young Europe* he had read with admiration thirty years earlier, finding in it the inspiration for "The Two Gallants" as well as interesting discussions of the Irish, Jews, and other subjects that concerned him. He even identified himself, half jokingly, with Ferrero (see *Letters* II, 133, 159, 212). But all this apparently was forgotten in the face of his aversion to politics and his concern over the rights of authors.

Clearly, the creator of *Ulysses* could not admire the creator of *Elpenor*.[5] However, both of us happened to be already thinking of Homer, and immediately we began discussing the *Odyssey*. When I told him that I read it almost every day, he responded with an appreciative murmur and then said quickly:

"You, too, certainly have noticed that I have leaned extravagantly on this work?"

Before I could reply, Joyce led me into a little restaurant, which, unfortunately, I would be unable to locate now.

"They serve a more or less true Orvieto[6] here," he said.

He must have gone there often because a wicker-covered bottle along with a plate of crackers appeared immediately on the table. Joyce raised the small glass to his impaired eyes, which glittered light blue through the thick lenses of his glasses. We talked a while about the city of Orvieto, its cathedral, its quiet as though woven of the sound of church bells.

"Certain of the rocks there give a bell sound if you strike them."

"You have noticed this," he said happily, as though I'd flattered him.

We stayed on the topic of Italy for a long time. He spoke affectionately of it. He had spent some of his happiest years there. I got the impression that his wife was Italian and their children had Italian names. In the midst of his rambling reminiscences, he shifted from French to Italian, the latter language sounding more natural in the mouth of this elderly tenor. He became silent, then returned to French and the *Odyssey*. His erudition amazed me. He knew not only the chief works on philology, archeology, and history, but also the minor treatises that contained something out of the ordinary. But best of all, he knew the *Odyssey* itself. He expounded upon many facets and features of the work, including the smallest details, fragments to which the glow of genius adhered, as a tiny rainbow does to morning dew. He derived extraordinary meanings from otherwise commonplace words. I listened to him in blissful delight.

"It is strange that you have retained such appreciation for a book that has provided a springboard for your own work," I said.

"Why?"

"Because usually after finishing a long work one has become surfeited

5. But Giraudoux apparently admired Joyce. He sent him a copy of *Elpenor*, a Homeric parody published in 1919, inscribing it: "*A* James Joyce *moi qui depuis si longtemps voulais offrir un hommage, en hommage*, Jean Giraudoux" (Thomas E. Connolly, *The Personal Library of James Joyce: A Descriptive Bibliography*, University of Buffalo Studies, Vol. 22, no. 1 [Buffalo, N.Y.: University of Buffalo Press, 1955]). In 1940 Giraudoux helped Joyce in his struggle to escape France (see below, p. 275).

6. An Italian white wine.

with it and feels perhaps distaste or aversion for the sources that have provided material for it."

"Possibly, but that didn't happen with me. I worked on *Ulysses* eight [sic] years; however, it is essentially the product of my whole life."

He ordered a second bottle of wine and, when it appeared on the table, became lively and talkative.

"You say that you read *Ulysses* in French. It is not a bad translation, I myself supervised it, but only the English original is really authentic."

"As always."

"But even more so in this instance. Ah, how wonderful that was to get up early in the morning, around five o'clock, and enter the misty regions of my emerging epic, as Dante once entered his *selva oscura selva selvaggia*.[7] Words crackled in my head and a multitude of images crowded around, like those shades at the entrance to the Underworld when Ulysses stood there awaiting the spirit of Tiresias. I wrote the greater part of the book during the war. There was fighting on all fronts, empires fell, kings went into exile, the old order was collapsing with a crash; and I had, as I sat down to work, the conviction that in the midst of all these ruins I was building something for the most distant future."

He spoke these haughty words quietly and naturally as if referring to a banal, self-evident truth.

"Yes. I created the epic of our era, and the spirit of Homer was always beside me, to sustain and encourage me. I believe that this was the first time he did such a thing, since he could hardly have been concerned with all those feeble imitations that every second generation feels duty-bound to produce. Poets allow themselves to be drawn to epic poetry as if to the scaffold—out of bravado, devotion, or cowardice."

Joyce lifted his glass close to his eyes and held it there awhile, as if to observe the golden flecks playing in the miraculous juice of the Umbrian earth.

"Much is said about my debt to Homer. It is simple. I took from the *Odyssey* the general outline, the 'plan' in the architectural sense, or maybe more exactly, the way the fable unfolds, and I followed it faithfully, down to the tiniest detail."

"That is exactly what astonishes me the most."

"Astonishes?" Joyce exclaimed. "Then perhaps I completely misunderstood when I heard you say that you revere the *Odyssey*. Its construction is incomparable, and one must be a German ass to detect

7. "Dark, wild forest"—from the opening of the *Divine Comedy*. If Joyce got up at five to write *Ulysses*, that contradicted his usual practice, which was to go to bed late and rise late.

in it the work of several authors. It is a unique work, at once fairy tale and cosmos. Such a thing cannot be done a second time; therefore, I took Homer's work and placed in its framework my nice little people, with their bodies and souls. Their bodies—*Ulysses* is more an epic of the body than of the human spirit."

"That is perhaps all too apparent."

He waved me off impatiently.

"Always the same complaint; for too long were the stars studied and man's insides neglected. An eclipse of the sun could be predicted many centuries before anyone knew which way the blood circulated in our bodies."

Then in support of his argument, he quoted a long passage out of Saint Augustine. Unfortunately, I can neither remember this quotation nor find it in Augustine's writings. At the time I expressed mild surprise that he should have read such an author.

"You will understand when I tell you that I was raised by Jesuits. And so far as the human body is concerned, I studied medicine in Paris.[8] In my heart Paris is the second city after Dublin. Dublin! I transformed it into a whole world of adventure in my *Ulysses*. My book wanders through my city as Homer's did through the Mediterranean, from bed to bed, through streets, offices, cafes, restaurants, bordellos, and like his book, mine has its dead and its sorceresses."

A charming smile appeared on his thin, straight lips.

"I believe that on the basis of my book it will be possible to reconstruct Dublin a thousand years from now just as it was at the beginning of the twentieth century."[9]

I was astonished at this, since *Ulysses* gives no exact description either of the streets or the buildings; those which Leopold Bloom encounters along his way are hardly even named.

"Then you depend upon the commentators," I said, "on those patient scholars, to reconstruct Dublin on the basis of your book, just as Troy is being reconstructed today, and just as fantastically."

But he was no longer listening to me. After a while he suddenly told me to recite a Polish poem. Surprised, I could come up with nothing for a minute.

"Well," he said impatiently, "you must know something by heart."

Either because he wanted to encourage me or because he felt the need to enter into a foreign rhythm, he himself began to recite. It was a page from Flaubert's "Herodias"—the dance of Salome. His delivery of

---

8. In 1902 Joyce attended a few medical classes, first in Dublin and then in Paris.

9. This echoes his remark to Budgen: "I want to give a picture of Dublin so complete that if the city one day suddenly disappeared from the earth it could be reconstructed out of my book" (*The Making of Ulysses*, p. 67).

the passage sounded splendid; he recited it vigorously with his full voice and broke it off shortly and sharply, the way Flaubert always concludes his long, swollen sentences.

I asked him whether he experienced the same effect that I did when reading the last sentence of "Herodias," which describes the school children carrying the head of John the Baptist, "Et comme elle était très lourde, ils la portaient alternativement."[10] "Admirable," he exclaimed. Then he repeated the sentence. And the way he did it! In his harsh rhythm there really was all the pain of carrying a heavy burden.

Finally I reached into my memory. I recited several of the *Crimean Sonnets*, a fragment from *Pan Tadeusz*, and several verses from *King Spirit*.[11] He rested his high forehead on the palms of his hands, leaning his ear in my direction and listening intently. When I stopped he remained silent for a while; then he asked me about the meaning of certain of the expressions that had stuck in his memory. He repeated them several times, trying to pronounce them accurately.

"What a mystery human speech is! So many varieties! What divine harmony amidst dissonances. Perhaps you have heard that I am writing something . . ."

" 'Work in Progress.' "

"Yes. It doesn't have a title yet. The few fragments which I have published have been enough to convince many critics that I have finally lost my mind, which by the way they have been predicting faithfully for many years. And perhaps it is madness to grind up words in order to extract their substance, or to graft one onto another, to create crossbreeds and unknown variants, to open up unsuspected possibilities for these words, to marry sounds which were not usually joined before, although they were meant for one another, to allow water to speak like water, birds to chirp in the words of birds, to liberate all sounds of rustling, breaking, arguing, shouting, cracking, whistling, creaking, gurgling—from their servile, contemptible role and to attach them to the feelers of expressions which grope for definitions of the undefined. I took literally Gautier's dictum, 'The inexpressible does not exist.' With this hash of sounds I am building the great myth of everyday life."

After a while he added, "Perhaps it will end in failure, be a wreck or 'catastrophe' such as Virginia Woolf believed *Ulysses* was; and perhaps

10. "And because it was very heavy, they took turns carrying it." This same sentence provided Joyce with one of the "boners" that he had a penchant for collecting. He said "*Alternativement* is wrong since there are *three* bearers" (*JJ* 506).

11. *King Spirit* and *Pan Tadeusz* are nationalistic epic poems, the former by Juliusz Slowacki (1809–41), the latter by Adam Mickiewiez (1798–1855), who also wrote the *Crimean Sonnets*, a sonnet sequence.

in the years to come this work of mine will remain solitary and abandoned, like a temple without believers."[12]

He did not finish his distant reflections. And I could not come up with anything that would prompt him to continue. I knew several fragments of "Work in Progress" which Louis Gillet had shown to me and had claimed to be very interesting. Up to this moment, however, up to this memorable conversation, I had almost decided that this work was the product of a madman, although I am always very cautious about making such judgments in literature. All that I could recall of the work was an astonishing mumble, as though coming from the tower of Babel, where the words entwined themselves in some kind of fantastic linguistic sodomy. I saddened at the though of the exhausting, obstinate toil that Joyce put into his book, which had no other chance than to be regarded by both his contemporaries and posterity as a genial caprice. And in fact, with the death of its creator, *Finnegans Wake*, as it is now called, lost the only reader capable of enjoying it in the clear light of comprehension and not just in the fog of conjecture.

What writer has not been tempted to confuse the harmony of language, to mix up its laws, to liberate it from boundaries imposed upon it by timid and ignorant ancestors? Must the three persons of the pronoun and the three degrees of an adjective suffice? Can inflexible parts of speech never enjoy inflection? The Futurists have been breaking their heads on this issue; others are content to reject punctuation, which once was also a great innovation. In *Ulysses* there are thirty well-packed pages without punctuation. But the polyglot Joyce, with his great passion for sounds that were meant to unify heaven and earth in innumerable variations among races and peoples, surrendered to more powerful temptations. For years on end he dwelt amidst rocks and reefs, like a shipwrecked man, but illumined by the wisdom of time because he was a great poet. His last work seems to me a wrecked ship, incapable of delivering its cargo to anyone. This gigantic charade contradicts divine and human laws of language—language as a means of communication between people who are locked up in their thoughts and dreams.

Such, more or less, was the burden of my silence, from which I could not rouse myself. Joyce was whistling thoughtfully some sort of tune that I did not recognize. I asked, "What is that you are whistling?"

"Oh, it's one of those old, old ballads from the music hall; it ends: 'Isn't it the truth I've told you,/Lots of fun at Finnegan's wake.'"

He repeated the last verse again. I didn't know at the time that it

12. Virginia Woolf, who was both attracted and repelled by *Ulysses*, called it "a misfire," "diffuse," "pretentious," and "underbred" (*A Writer's Diary* [New York: Harcourt Brace and Co., 1953], pp. 46–49, 349).

contained more or less the hidden source and the very title of his curious work.

Joyce appeared exhausted. He paid, we left, and I called a taxi for him. He held out his hand to me and said:

"If you should wish to record our conversation (I always reckon with such a possibility), please do not publish it while I am alive. It would be indiscreet. After my death it won't do any harm; it will become part of the scholarship business, which will probably never let me out of its grip. Goodbye."

I never saw him again . . . I kept my word, and, in now writing down this recollection of that distant meeting, it seems to me that I am adding a small contribution to a gigantic commentary which is growing up around the man and his work.

TRANSLATED BY WILLARD POTTS

Louis Gillet

IN THE BATTLE to get his work accepted by the English-speaking world, Joyce placed special faith in the "long-range guns" of French criticism, particularly Valery Larbaud's. By the thirties, when illness forced Larbaud out of the battle, another influential French critic appeared to take his place as champion of Joyce's work. This was Louis Gillet (1876–1943), literary critic for the intensely proper Revue des Deux Mondes, curator of the Abbaye de Chaalis, member of the French Academy, and son-in-law of the wealthy René Doumic, who was director of the Revue and secretary of the Academy.

In 1925 Gillet had written an unfavorable article about Ulysses in the Revue, but subsequent study of the book won him over. He decided to write about it again, expressing his new view, and also to treat Finnegans Wake. Before dealing with the latter he wanted to discuss it with Joyce, so a meeting was arranged in early 1931. Gillet was apprehensive because of his 1925 essay, but when they met Joyce exhibited no resentment. In his recollection Gillet attributes this amiable behavior to "Anglo-Saxon politeness," according to which "an author ignores criticism." Certainly Joyce cultivated politeness, often using it to fend people off. But in fact he had considered the 1925 article a success. He wrote Miss Weaver at the time it appeared, "As regards the article in the R. de D. M., I have been planning that for three years. I tried first the Revue de Paris, then the Revue de France. It does not matter as the R. de D. M. is even better. The tone of the article does not matter much" (Letters I, 232). The Revue des Deux Mondes was "even better" because its strong association with the French Catholic aristocracy made it "something like Lambeth Palace and Buckingham idem rolled into one" (Letters I, 301). An article appearing in it, even an unsympathetic one, gave his work a kind of imprimatur that he thought helped its acceptance and that apparently gave him considerable private satisfaction as well.

Naturally, Gillet's new attitude and his promise of further articles pleased Joyce, who immediately reported the good news to Miss Weaver: "[Gillet] told me that he had now read my book [Ulysses] several times and was preparing another article about it and

*also one about my present book. He seemed to be astonished by the lack
of hostility shown by me when we met and invited me to dinner. He
has also written me several letters and sent me copies of his books
dedicated to me . . ." (Letters I, 301; see also Gillet's letter to Joyce,
Letters III, 210–11). When the first of Gillet's promised articles appeared,
Joyce found it "certainly a most remarkable document, full of good
will and common sense (Letters I, 309). Probably at his instigation it
was translated and published in* transition, *to help it penetrate the armor
of the English-speaking world. Gillet's efforts did not stop with that
article but went on to include several lectures about Joyce and later a
long, sympathetic essay on* Finnegans Wake. *Meanwhile, the relations
between the two men developed into a close friendship.*

*Ellmann says of Joyce, "He surrounded himself with people who were
mostly not known: some were waiters, tailors, fruitsellers, hotel porters,
concierges, bank clerks, and this assemblage was as inevitable for
Joyce's temperament as marquises and marchionesses were for Proust's
(JJ 5). It is true that in his life as in his work Joyce took an extraordinary interest in people "mostly not known." But along with frequenting
expensive restaurants, where tailors, concierges, or bank clerks must
have been rare, Joyce appreciated having friends with the sort of social
position and connections that Gillet had. He seldom failed to mention
these connections when informing non-French acquaintances of his
new advocate. "People in Paris gasp at the hold I seem to have got there,"
he told Budgen, adding that Gillet's father-in-law was "perpetual
secretary of the French Academy, director of the most artistocratic-
catholic-reactionary review in France, and a man who has the disposal
of milliards not millions" (Letters I, 337).*

*Gillet's position made no detectable difference in his personal relations
with Joyce. The two confided in each other as friends, often discussing
and sharing each other's concern over their children's problems.
Joyce's anguish over Lucia produced moods of intense depression
vividly expressed in letters to Harriet Weaver. At the conclusion of one
he remarked, "Perhaps I shall survive and perhaps the raving madness
I write will survive and perhaps it is very funny. One thing is sure,
however.* Je suis bien triste." *And in another, "I feel like an animal which
has received four thunderous mallet strokes on the top of his skull"
(Letters I, 362, 366). He also gave expression to his despair in conversations with Gillet, who responded with sympathy and encouragement.
"I would like to hear from you," he wrote Joyce, "and be sure that you
don't give way to despair which is your temptation and secret malady.
Don't give yourself up to the Devil . . . ! Try to make some effort to shake
off your demons."*[1]

1. Introduction to *Claybook for James Joyce* (London: Abelard-Schuman,

Besides attempting to cheer his friend, Gillet participated in a project designed to help Lucia. She had begun drawing small illuminated letters or "lettrines," the publication of which Joyce hoped would bring her some happiness and promise. Seeking an outside opinion, he sent them to Gillet, who praised them. This praise so pleased Joyce that he copied it out and sent it to Budgen (Letters I, 319). Gillet also suggested that the lettrines be used to illustrate A Chaucer ABC, *the translation of a prayer by Guillaume Deguilleville, who had been a monk at the Abbaye de Chaalis. When it was decided to go ahead with this project, Gillet agreed to write a preface. After many delays and difficulties the book appeared in July 1936 on Lucia's twenty-ninth birthday.[2] No matter what his social position or power as a critic had been, Gillet's active sympathy for Lucia would have bound Joyce to him in friendship.*

Gillet's two recollections, the first written two days after Joyce's death, the second and much longer one written several months later, record both the personal and the professional side of their relationship. Joyce once told him, "Don't make a hero of me. I'm only a simple middle-class man" (JJ 5). Gillet doesn't make a hero of him. He sketches Joyce's youth with a semi-amused detachment reminiscent of A Portrait *and recalls the mature Joyce with sympathy but not reverence. Over fifteen years after the recollections had been published, Joyce's long-time friend Stuart Gilbert called them "one of the best appreciations of the man and his work that have so far appeared" (Letters I, 231n).*

Farewell to Joyce

By Louis Gillet

DEAR JOYCE! ... He wrote to me only a few days ago. From Switzerland, where he had found refuge in the midst of the big brawl, he waved to me, wishing me kindly "the best of all possible Christmases." This meant: "I am becalmed. Here I am in port." The port! He was there undoubtedly, but to embark therefrom on quite another journey.

I saw him for the last time in a small village of Central France,

---

1958), p. 19. This Introduction, by Georges Markow-Totevy, contains a good discussion of the relations between Joyce and Gillet.

2. See especially *Letters* III, 266, 385, for Joyce's feelings about the importance of this book.

half-Berry- and half-Bourbonnais-like, called Saint-Gérand-le-Puy. How he had run aground there is quite a long story. Neither the charming author of *Ondine* nor the author of *Le grand Meaulnes* could ever have dreamed of anything more strange than the presence of this aerial being deep in a French village—it was Trilby, it was Puck captive in a stable, among cow- and swine-herds. The simple folk, full of consideration, did not suspect at all the quality of the extraordinary guest they had among them: a prince of the mind, an artist of world-wide renown, a man whose books were famous from Moscow to New York and from Berlin to Tokyo, and who had received among the heaps of telegrams for his fiftieth birthday one from Prague, addressed "to the first of all living poets."

That day I found him agitated by a deadly anxiety; he was all impatience to flee elsewhere. He was restless. During our meal he could not sit down and circled around the table, stopping at last, exhausted by torment, to take only a draught of wine. He dreamed of going to Switzerland where he had spent a few happy years during the last war, believing that there he would rediscover his youth. He was irritated by the delays and the formalities. He was Irish, but a British citizen, and in order to admit him Switzerland required a guaranty of one hundred thousand francs (in gold, of course). He was fluttering like a sylph, like a furious bee limed by the crepe of its wings. One would fancy he had received an order, a summons from fate commanding him to leave; he was longing to get away and fly to this rendevous with his best years, to the country where once his genius had hatched. Once there, he said to himself, all would be rest, deliverance. What he took for a call of happiness, was a flap of wings from the beyond, the shiver, the anxiety of death. Death gave him an enigmatic sign from there, inviting him to this last journey, the only one made today without passport.

Marvellous Joyce! Not long since a friend showed me on the heights of Dublin, in a shabby and triangular square decorated by a puny linden tree, the shanty where he was born sixty years ago. A sad cradle, conveying a recent downfall, a shameful distress, the most lugubrious of all miseries. Was it from there that he departed one day in his childhood, or rather one night, with his tearful mother, expelled by the landlord and pulling a cart with old clothes, while his father, callous (and perhaps slightly tipsy), sang at the top of his voice and rapped out roulades to the stars? [3]

This wandering household, the flight in Egypt with a mother in despair and a bragging father screening his retreat with fanfares, seems

3. These night removals to avoid paying overdue rent did not occur until later. Joyce was born in a "modest and comfortable" house in the Dublin suburb of Rathmines (*JJ* 23).

to me an image, a symbol of the whole life of the artist who has just died—there he is already in all his entirety. Thus was announced to him the adventure of existence. Thirty-five years of wilful exile, of nomadic sojourns at Venice,[4] Rome, Trieste, Zurich, and finally at Paris where he settled almost twenty years ago: settled is not the word, for he continued wandering between Passy and the Gros-Caillou, Montparnasse and Grenelle, not counting the escapades, the eclipses, the letters which without warning showed him to be in London, Folkestone, Basel, Copenhagen. His page in my address-book is filled with numerous erasures. I never saw him in the same lodging for more than six months. I have known him to have three apartments on his hands simultaneously, one of which was a very expensive flat in Kensington Gardens where he never set foot,[5] while his furniture, in the superfluity of choice, remained in a furniture warehouse. He was something of a meteor, a will-o'-the-wisp. He burdened the ground with no more than his shadow which he could fold up as an Arab folds up his carpets and his tent from bivouac to bivouac.

I never met his unparalleled father who was certainly the person he admired most in the world. He owed him two things: a way of flouting life and unyielding pride, an incapacity for bending his knee and capitulating. This simple man, tramp and drunkard, was a sort of lord. It was from him that the great writer had inherited the haughty air, the prodigious faith in himself, the refusal of all compromise and concession which are the features of his work. I can still see his long, delicate and aristocratic silhouette, surmounted by a strange cylindrical head, whose bony face with its enormous forehead in the shape of a tower seemed to have been cut out in the zinc of stovepipes, like certain surrealistic sculptures: I had never seen in anybody else more haughtiness, a demeanor more courteous and at the same time more aloof. Only in him did I see this concave and crescent-shaped profile, with the double protuberance of skull and chin, taciturn and imperious, sharp and stubborn, similar to what we see in the bust of Philip the Second.

From his father he had also inherited another trait, an exquisite tenor voice, the gift for music and vocalizing. All Ireland is melomaniac. And the name of Joyce is an old French word which reminds us of M. de Joyeuse. The musical climate of Dublin is similar to that of Naples. The ambition of the artist had been to become an opera singer

4. Joyce did not live in Venice; however, for a while early in World War I he used Venice as an address for mail coming from England.
5. In 1931 Joyce and his wife thought of moving from Paris to London, partly to establish residence in England for their formal marriage there in 1931. They took a long-term lease on a flat in Kensington Gardens and lived there during the summer of 1931. Neither of them liked the place, so they returned to Paris, leaving Miss Weaver the problem of subletting it.

(his son Giorgio possesses a splendid voice also). He could not stand modern music and except for *Die Meistersinger* and some arias from *The Flying Dutchman* he had a dislike for Wagner; the Tetralogy[6] irritated him. "Operetta music," he used to say. On the other hand, he doted upon singing, adoring Rossini, Meyerbeer, Verdi, *La Gazza ladra*, *William Tell*, *Muette*, *La Juive*, *L'Africaine*. He knew how many high-C's there were in all the scores. He took the train for Lyons, Brussels, Milan, any time that one of his favorite operas was performed there. He was mad about *bel canto*, as people were at the time of la Malibran and Rubini. Often in the evening, or rather about two o'clock in the morning, whenever he felt in the mood, he sat at the piano and started to shed his treasury of Irish melodies. We remained suspended on the doleful and nostalgic cadences; we could have spent all night listening to the nightingale.

At the age of about twenty, when living in the Hôtel Corneille in the Latin Quarter, he began suffering from serious dental disturbances. The poisoning of the jaws was carried to the eyes. For twenty years, the great poet was half-blind; the left eye was lost and in the other remained only a flap of retina. Reading and writing was a torture. The wretched man retained a gleam of light thanks only to twenty operations—each time a very cruel martyrdom.[7] I still see him, in order to decipher a text, placing the paper sideways and bringing it into the narrow angle where a ray of his ruined sight still subsisted. To wend his way in the street, he went along tapping the iron point of his white cane on the pavement, with a gesture groping and self-assertive. In fact, this unusual walker was not of this world. He was a stranger, a phantom whose shadow only was among us and who wandered with sureness in the universe of his thoughts and memories.

Does the reader know Kipling's short story "The Finest Story in the World"? It is about a small town clerk, a vulgar bank employee, in whom revives in flashes the soul of his fathers—the Vikings. The ancestral memory breaks free at times from his numbed consciousness, like gas-pockets wheezing in a burning fire-log. This story is similar to Joyce's. In college, at twelve, a question by his teacher "Who is your favorite hero?" brought forth the answer "Ulysses." "But Ulysses is not a hero," objected the astounded good priest. The child remained obstinate, and he did well—he had found the idea of his life.

6. The *Ring of the Nibelung* cycle, consisting of four operas: *Das Rheingold*, *Die Walküre*, *Siegfried*, and *Götterdämmerung*.

7. The exact number seems to have been ten operations. For a detailed discussion of Joyce's eye problems see J. B. Lyons, *James Joyce and Medicine* (Dublin: Dolmen Press, 1973), pp. 185–210. Gillet appears mistaken about the left eye, which Joyce referred to as "the good one" (*Letters* III, 281). He was "luminous to larbourd only" (*FW* 178.28).

Irish literature is the literature of an island of navigators: to the world it made a present of a big theme, the theme of quest, voyage, discovery, adventure. It was the Quest of the Holy Grail, the voyage of Saint Patrick, of Saint Brendan which was no other (four centuries before Columbus) than a route to the New World; later, with Dean Swift, it was *Gulliver's Travels*. I have told of Joyce's existence and wandering life. It was natural that life should appear to him as an odyssey. An extraordinary odyssey which never left the circle of Dublin's streets; the poet's whole story is but that of a single book, a single dream. While the exile wandered from town to town, on the shores of the Tiber or the Adriatic, on the quays of the Seine or the banks of a Swiss lake, he was—like Ulysses—a dreamer in search of Ithaca, and living only in his fatherland.

At the time of his youth, there arose in Ireland a curious literary movement, a national revival. Joyce parted violently from it. No one has been less of a prophet in his own country than he. All his books have been proscribed, spurned, banished; no modern writer has been denounced as more heretic or scandalous, has burned in more autos-da-fé. His entire work is but a challenge to the conventions of his own people. He repudiated all local narrow-mindedness; he did not care for the glory of a provincial celebrity. To his isle he gave however the significance of a myth of humankind, of a jewel, of a grain of radium in universal poetry.

There is no work more intellectual, more disengaged from the worry about contemporary matters, more estranged from Time and Space, more foreign to politics, war, the torments of a wretched Europe; none more preoccupied with the great interests of life, love, desire, death, childhood, fatherhood, the mystery of Eternal Return. Amidst his majestic thought, what a tenderness! Just listen to these few lines:

> Lead, kindly fowl! They always did: ask the ages. What bird has done yesterday man may do next year, be it fly, be it moult, be it hatch, be it agreement in the nest. [*FW* 112.9-11]

I would like to quote also the magic incantation which ends his last book and which starts with this movement: *Soft morning, City!* [*FW* 619.20]. It was dawn, the end of darkness, a greeting at the threshold of mystery and eternal day. No one has written thus since the prose of Shakespeare. Farewell, miraculous poet! ... Farewell, Joyce! ... Farewell, Ariel! ...

January 15, 1941

TRANSLATED BY GEORGES MARKOW-TOTEVY

The Living Joyce

By Louis Gillet

LAST CHRISTMAS I was supposed to visit the Red Cross in Geneva, and I wrote to him: "See you again soon." The trip, however, was made without me; I could leave only a month later; Joyce had died on the 13th of January.

The following Sunday I arrived in Zurich. It was evening, a dismal evening of thaw, rain, and glazed frost. On the wooded hill in back of the city, I had no trouble in finding the villa of Doctor Giedion.[8] I was received as a friend and the writer's son Giorgio gave me an account of his father's last moments. Friday night Joyce was awakened by a fierce pain. He was taken to a clinic. The X-ray revealed a stomach ulcer. Curiously enough, no one had ever suspected this. It was not the first time that such an attack had assailed Joyce, but it had been believed that the gnawing pains were of nervous origin and seemed to present no danger. Joyce ate obviously without appetite, he always toyed with his food as if searching for something, and would then push back his plate with a disgusted look: he could put up with almost no food. We knew him to be frail; nobody was alarmed. He enjoyed entertaining his friends at restaurants, finding nothing too expensive and too refined for them; he was a regular customer of the Trianon and Fouquet's where the luxury pleased him as a relaxation after his daily work, but at all these places he barely picked at his food, merely nibbling from his plate some leaves of salad or a piece of cake. He seemed to live on air. His overly delicate system could not endure our food, a most select meal was still too coarse for him. After the first mouthful he would light a cigarette, he had finished his dinner. We did not suspect him to be sick.

On Saturday morning Joyce underwent an emergency operation. He could not meet the challenge and died during the night, at 2:00 A.M. He was 59 years old.

Giorgio opened a door. On a cushion in the parlour, pale against the black velvet, lay the head of his father. I had a shock: I had not believed I would see him again. A sculptor, M. Paul Speck, had taken a casting. The imprint of the left ear lobe had blurred in the plaster. The face lived. His eyelids were closed, but this was not the pose of sleep. Under

8. Siegfried Giedion and his wife Dr. Carola Giedion-Welcker, whose recollection appears later, were old friends of the Joyces.

the short moustache which gave him a pout of disdain, a strange smile played on the edge of his lips. I had never seen him without his sombre myopic lenses which seemed to be part of his person. Now the mask appeared bare, abruptly confessing its truth. At the moment of death, a relaxation takes place, the face seems washed as if a hand had wiped the wrinkles of life from it. This occasionally imparts a spark of youth to the dead, whence the medieval belief that they all have in heaven the common and perfect age of thirty-three.

But here the dead preserved an attitude of combat. It was indeed the prominent forehead, the slender cheeks and sharply-etched bones, the determined chin, the long phiz—that is the word—of a Don Quixote just lifting his vizor. I still saw defiance in it. This was not the look of someone vanquished, of someone defunct—as termed by the beautiful language in which the Church embalms its dead, *defunctos*, those that have resigned, relieved themselves from existence—there was never so much haughtiness, so much inflexibility, never a look of pride more abrupt! It was the No! of the unsubdued, the refusal of a rebellious angel. On his emaciated features he seemed to bear a double expression of *Noli me tangere* and *Non serviam*; that of fierce modesty and of revolt. Defeat and death reduced nothing of his insolence. The closed eyelids seemed to veil the face, simplifying its contour, suppressing the glare of its glance, sealing the visage into its secret as if by a slab. All that Pigalle displays in his masterpiece in Strasbourg on the intrepid countenance of the hero braving Hell and defying the terrors of the grave, was summed up in this cut-off head.

Yet the mask's lower part stood in contrast with the upper part— as in the mountains where some earth on the slopes is overhung by a bare rock. Joyce was smiling—a smile mischievous and somewhat waggish, the gaiety of an escaped prisoner, of a mystifier who had just played a hoax. This smile seemed to say: "Good evening! The farce is over, I am out of the trap. Where I am, you will never catch me. You will never know if I made fun of you. Hands off! Your politics, your fights, your tragedies, your playthings, just as you like, much good may they do you. I slip away, unseen, unknown. Disentangle it yourselves, my friends!" It was a smile from beyond all there is, from beyond the grave, the smile of a survivor certain to have come through the venture without loss and, as they say, to have found salvation.

This visage of prince and street-urchin, with its domineering forehead and its ironic mouth, was indeed extraordinary. It had the aware look of someone who knows, of someone who has gone through a great panic—of a soldier saying of death after his first battle: "Pooh! if that's all there is to it!" [9]

9. For a picture of Joyce's death mask see *Letters* III, between pp. 480 and 481.

I recalled the wonderful legend about the Germanics' apostle Saint Oran, disciple of Columbanus. They were celebrating his funeral. At the end of the service he rose in his coffin and began disclosing the news from the next world:

—Hell is not, he let slip, Hell is not what they told us to believe in.

—Some dirt, shouted Columbanus, throw some dirt and shut his mouth. Silence at the sacrilege which returns whence no one returns.

In spite of myself, I thought of another recollection. I remembered that summer day when not long ago I visited the great Yeats in Dublin. Outside around the blind Apollo, the garden was blazing in the sun. A group of young women clustered about him like grape vines suspended on the marble of an ancient Terminal; at his feet, the most beautiful was leaning in a caressing attitude on the knee of the old man. The poet was speaking of Joyce, such as he had known him of old, age eighteen, student of Christ's College,[10] at the time of Queen Victoria's Jubilee, the good days of the Boer war and Irish Revival. The example of the Transvaal was then turning everyone's head, stirring up the hopes of the Irish Republic. In Dublin a National Theatre was founded, for thus all movements of this kind begin. That was the theatre whose birth, rise, and fall are related by George Moore in his best book, the charming chronicle entitled *Ave, Salve, Vale*. There would be however a postponement; the achievement would come only twenty years later, after a war and many martyrs. Even then Joyce did not conceal his disdain for a timorous enterprise that blossomed in the drawing-room of a society woman; this chauvinism around the fireplace and five o'clock tea provoked his sarcasm.[11] In matters of revolution, he had in view something far more radical. This student of Christ's was meditating nothing less than an attack on our saintly mother, the Catholic Church. He was dreaming of a petard that would blow up the whole shop. His gods were Ibsen, Giordano Bruno, Julian the Apostate. He was quite a "bad lot" with a poor reputation already:

—"He was the pillar of all taverns, a wencher, spending his time inveighing against the parish priests. He spoke highly of himself as the house-breaker of religion, the arch-heresiarch, the Antichrist. After him the priests are done for! Pretty tricks they would see! One would remember him in the world for more than two thousand years."[12]

This bragging makes one smile. It reminds me of Dedalus entering the

10. Joyce was a student of University College, Dublin.

11. The "society woman" could be either Lady Augusta Gregory, who helped found the Abbey Theatre, or Annie E. Horniman, who was its principal backer. Joyce expressed his scorn for the movement in "The Day of the Rabblement" (*CW* 68–72) and in "The Holy Office" (*The Portable James Joyce*, pp. 657–60).

12. The context suggests that Gillet is quoting Yeats's recollection of the young Joyce.

musico of Bella Cohen while singing the Introit of Easter.[13] Youth will have its fling. When Joyce sows his wild oats and is up to all sorts of tricks in a way disapproved by good taste, however, that is not a waste of time; he is completing his picture of the world, he is working for the future. He jumps greedily upon any possible pleasure, out of bravado, out of disgust, and particularly in order to fight a cerebral excess. He is all eagerness to know his body, to know the happiness of coachmen and sailors, to affront the intellect by pulling it down into the mud. This attitude is not immune to romanticism. It is mainly a method for systematic breakdown, a discipline of disorder (see Rimbaud). Let us not be duped by these impudent boastings.

I have seen on a beach, in a section of Dublin's suburbs south from the river, the old watchtower changed since into a customs house, where the young man took up his residence during this period of his life. One can see similar towers, called Saracen, on the coasts of Sicily. It is quite a tumble-down ruin, one league from town, lonely on the sandy beach and facing the sea.[14] The view is beautiful; on the gulf's north end one catches sight of the entrancing ridge of the point of Howth. This is the setting for the first chapter of *Ulysses* (the dialogue with Mulligan) and then for the farcical adventure which further on constitutes the episode of "Nausicaa." The boy who would take up such a hermitage certainly had in mind something quite other than women. He was not a vulgar individual. This choice of solitude, this face-to-face with the sea, indicates a certain aloofness, a certain asceticism, love for inner life and contemplation. If he used to go out to lose and forget his self, he also knew where to rediscover it.

As for the atheism of the young man, it is a misfortune; God forbid that we should take offence! If one ever lived in countries where the clergy is king, as in Ireland, where it makes the sun rise and set, the jacobinism of Joyce seems natural. Oppression engenders revolt. One should admit, moreover, that in this presumptuous duel the rash young man showed himself more discerning than his friends of the Irish Revival. The question of Home Rule might be a tiny detail in the total of world affairs; on the literary level it is of no more consequence than the Félibridge and the Museo Arlaten. But to declare war on Heaven meant stepping out of local intrigues; it meant giving to this enterprise a titanic character and placing oneself on a level with the universe.

13. See p. 36, n. 38. Stephen sings the chant while making his way along the street to Bella Cohen's (*U* 431–32).

14. The Martello tower at Sandycove, where Joyce lived for a week in 1904 with Oliver St. John Gogarty, is still in good repair. It was not used as a customs house. Gillet also is in error later on in identifying the beach at Sandycove as the setting for "Nausicaa." That chapter is set at Sandymount Strand, on the south edge of Dublin.

These words seem quite big for a merry ne'er-do-well emancipating himself; but I doubt that they were actually bigger than the boy's thoughts. He placed himself at once among the descendants of the greatest master of his race, the immortal Dean Swift. Swift's superiority when dealing with dogmas is due to the fact that he belonged to the clergy; it is as theologian that he maltreats theology. This renders his criticism far more corrosive than the witty satires of his Irish colleagues; G. B. Shaw and Oscar Wilde are but amateurs in this genre. The most erudite dialectic delivered with an air of folly creates the humour of the Dean and confers on it, when we laugh, its high seriousness. Perhaps Joyce has never written a line against religion, or even more precisely, on religious matters (I do not take into account the doubtful joke when Bloom, half-drunk during a tavern Sabbath, hears a thunderous voice rumbling and reverberating the anagram GOOD–DOOG [*U* 600]). But to apply to all things the system of *Gulliver* and *The Tale of a Tub*, to dislocate the forms of logic and reasoning, to demolish the edifice of our representations upon which our conventions rest—our ideas of order, consequence, continuation, conformity, even of space and time—to dissolve at last the language itself and the words by which we designate all things, this was to shake the columns of the universe and make the Temple quiver to its base, it was to substitute a new creation, the world of consciousness and dream for the reality of things and gods. Is this just a smashing of everything, a general upheaval? It is quite another thing. As an act of liberation and enfranchisement it is far more than a vague charter of independence for the Republic of Eire: a prodigious *Walpurgis Nacht*, an immense *Götterdämmerung*.

We do not know, I repeat, whether during his salad days Joyce had a clear idea of this extraordinary venture. But he was brim-full of self. He knew that he would achieve something great. He had the head of a Lucifer! Frankly, he must have been unbearable. It was not easy in Dublin, with two pounds a week, to be prince of all youth and to play in Merrion Square a role similar to young Barrès' on the *boulevard*; he was a great actor on a provincial stage. This boy of excessive pride simply grated on the nerves of most people. Few creatures more proud and more impertinent than the young extravagant; add the boasting, the air of braggart and flabbergaster, the Irish glibness, what one calls gab, blarney, and you have something hardly bearable. At a distance of forty years, the impatience of Yeats still bears witness to it. The students of *Joyceana* have found in his notebooks, next to some impious songs, some lines where the idols of the day are given a trying moment. This young fop had a bump of irreverence. Here is one of his remarks: "Contrary to Saul, son of Cis, who left searching for his father's donkeys and found a kingdom, Tolstoy left the kingdom of his father in the lurch in order to bring back a herd of dunces." [15]

When you think what the glory of this patriarch was at that time, the self-confidence and lashing tone of this aphorism make you shudder. To dare this blasphemy at the age of seventeen! Joyce was right however. Who will deny it? Who can still bear the preachy-prattle of *What Is Art* or *Big Crime*? What a pity to see the great artist of *War and Peace* sink to the rank of sermonizer and give in to sociology and unction.

As for Joyce, the artist, he never faltered. In the worst difficulties and the strictest misery, being hard up and burdened with a family, still nothing could make him compromise with himself. He has never written a mercenary line, never a commonplace word upon profane matters, upon the interests of secular life, the things that impassion the vulgar, never an article of polemics, a gesture of propaganda, a "paper" for the press.[16] He never traded his soul. Stoically, he condemned himself to mean and thankless tasks, to humble jobs of bookkeeping or tutoring, adding up numbers in a bank or giving English lessons to clods rather than bargain away his pen and his mind. He had the courage to starve for twenty years, to suffer from the delays and rebuffs of editors, the hardships, the anguish of the morrow, the tribulations of the poor, the dreary loneliness of exile, not weakening or yielding or ever hurrying, not condescending to complain, not hastening or delaying by a day his astonishing work. Sick, his sight lost, without shelter, wandering from town to town, he spent eight years writing in darkness his inordinate book, and he answered misfortune, the snubs and strokes of fate, the indifference of the public, the persecutions by his own people, by throwing at their heads his colossal masterpiece. Famous at last, he had all the gazettes wrangling for his copy; the Americans were ready to spread the golden carpet for him. Wilfully he shut himself up in his most abstract work and retired into a monumental silence of seventeen years. During his life—that just ended in one of the most tormented ages of history and after two wars—he never made an allusion to all that tears us apart, never said a word on the problems which throw races, peoples, classes, continents against each other. While the battle was raging at its full in 1916, he chose an ordinary day of twenty-four hours, taken at random from the most everyday pattern of a secondary town—

15. Gorman quotes from Joyce's notebook, "Unlike Saul, the son of Kish, Tolstoy seems to have come out to find a kingdom and to have found his father's asses" (*James Joyce* [New York: Farrar and Rinehart, 1939], p. 136).

16. Not quite true considering the articles Joyce wrote for the *Piccolo della Sera* in Trieste.

June 16, 1904—a day that is not set apart for any famous crime, gossip-item, event or discovery, but only for an ordinary funeral and birth, and he made it the subject of his global restitution, his miraculous chronicle.—Dear Péguy, you who grew angry to be living during such dull days that would leave no memory, you who were all eagerness to note down this precious "historical inscription!"—The clatter of the world, kings, leaders, all magnitude, force, glories, all our scale of values, Joyce greeted with a definite *No*. Once and for all he judged them and turned them out; he ignored them, unruffled, like a Spinoza or a hermit of the desert; he wronged them by refusing to know anything at all, occupied solely by the most common matters, the simplest and most ordinary actions which constitute the dense fabric of life.[17] And later on, in his second poem, letting his mind float to a world of images, as the stevedore of Bassora snoring in the gutter and dreaming that he is king, he imagined a Nocturne, this immense *Thousand-and-Second Night* where all creation, all myths, histories, centuries, the Caesars and Alexanders, the Cyruses, Cambyses and Napoleons, like flotsam of a shipwreck or the debris of day on the waves of darkness, roll in the confused thoughts of a sleeping drunkard—tale of an idiot, or dream of a boozer, it is phantasmagoria without beginning or end where every-thing repeats itself, where nothing happens, where no event changes the fundamental notes and the elementary functions of eating and drinking, kissing and sleeping. Joyce spent forty years constructing these two immense books, this double epic of Day and Night, of a dream with open eyes and closed eyes. The second remains an enigma which will long embarrass man and which has not yet disclosed its last word. In a complete bestowal of himself, he has buried in this book his days and nights, his thoughts and strength, indifferent to all the rest, criticisms, honours, fortune and exile, granting no memory to what was not a reflection of his inner world, a stranger to the passions and follies of men, their ambitions, covetousness, to money, intrigue, vanity and fear, despising fortuitous matters, inaccessible to all that could distract and divert him from his work, alone master of himself and an empire of ideas and words; in short, a marvelously noble being, a heroic example of the artist's sacrifice to the Absolute of Art.

My relations with Joyce began in the winter of 1931. I used to see Sylvia Beach every so often, the Rue de l'Odéon being not too far from

17. " 'Tis as human a little story as paper could well carry . . ." (*FW* 115.37). ". . . The most purely human being that ever was called man, loving all up and down the whole creation . . ." (*FW* 431.11-12). [Gillet's note]

my home in the Rue Bonaparte. There was however a greater distance between the chronicler of the *Revue des Deux Mondes* and the young literary school. This sprightly woman enjoyed bringing them closer. When I browsed in her book shop, she amused herself by trying to convert me. A lady is always an amiable servant of Parnassus: she is clever, tactful—in one word—a woman. Moreover Miss Beach knew how to talk; soon we became good friends. I already regretted my first move and was willing to learn. On thinking it over I began discerning the greatness of the phenomenon *Ulysses*. I did not know Joyce, I wished to meet him but was afraid I had offended him. Miss Beach recognized my inclinations and arranged an interview.

Joyce received me with exquisite courtesy and a somewhat ceremonious dignity. He made no allusion to my unfortunate article. That is Anglo-Saxon politeness, a rule of the game; an author ignores criticism. He neither thanks for a benevolent article nor, in the opposite case, does he condescend to protest if his book displeases.[18] Opinions are free. In my whole life, I received but one note of thanks from an English writer: Conrad, who was Polish. The ways of the press are entirely different from what they are in the French manner, i.e. a publicity affair of concern only to publishers. Furthermore, author copies are unknown: Kipling used to get six only because he was Kipling; and paid out of his own pocket for those that he gave to his friends. The latter, as a rule, do not expect this gift—they buy as they please. In England, you will not find the exchange of dedications, widespread in our country, which confuse so oddly the habits of advertising with those of friendship. Instead, they have recourse to a system of private editions printed by subscription and signed by the author, as with numbered etchings, but without any mingling of sentiment and comradeship.

Joyce, at the time I met him, had been working for almost ten years on his extraordinary and profoundly mysterious book which had as yet no other name than "Work in Progress" ("Work in Pregross," as he says somewhere, in a droll pun containing the French word *grossesse*—pregnancy).[19]

Perplexed, we were witnessing this stupendous birth. At long intervals, a few pieces had begun to appear from 1925 on in Adrienne Monnier's *Le Navire d'Argent*:[20] for instance, the overture or prologue in Phoenix Park, with the museum keeper's farcical tale of the battle of Waterloo, and the finale of the first part, the dialogue of two washerwomen telling about the myth of Anna Livia (The Liffey). These samples

18. In fact, Joyce often thanked those who wrote of his work.
19. "The word in pregross" (*FW* 284.22).
20. Only one fragment of "Work in Progress" (*FW* 196–215) appeared in *Le Navire d'Argent*.

baffled, we have to admit, the most faithful friends of *Ulysses*; they bore
no resemblance to anything known. It was Hebrew or Arabic, a real
headache. Léon-Paul Fargue was himself discouraged and used to tell
me dejectedly about these unintelligible pages. We wondered if the
author had not lost his mind. Meanwhile, a new review baptized *transition*
(after the example of Princesse de Bassiano's miscellany[21]) was founded
in order to rally the intellectual *avant-garde* of English youth under
the banners of the commanding general Eugene Jolas. It considered itself
honoured to publish fragments of "Work in Progress" as soon as they
were ready. Like the first instalments of a serial novel, the issues containing the original publication of these strange pieces, appearing
successively but in a capricious order, are in keen demand by bibliophiles.
I have seen at Roquebrune, in the hands of Mme Bussy (sister of Lytton
Strachey), the first copy of *transition*, a little notebook in 12mo, quite
thick and with a navy-blue cover; soon however the imposing format
octavo of the *Edinburgh Review* was adopted. Now and then, in a
solemn fashion, decorative and clandestine, de luxe editions printed by
American or Dutch presses on moiré rice-paper were put on sale
for booklovers; besides these there were popular editions at one shilling
of pieces like "Anna Livia" or "The Mookse and the Gripes," published
by Faber and Faber.

Joyce was willing to explain to me the scheme of his book. He spoke
in a most simple tone, without any sort of pretention. He gave me the
clue to his work. He explained the mystery of his immense H.C.E., this
unrivalled hero, thick-textured, of boundless embodiments, whose
master-key character lends itself to all kinds of metamorphoses and is
up to every role, like a kind of universal Fregoli. He spoke of the
language he had used in order to give to vocabulary the elasticity of sleep,
multiplying the meaning of words, playing with glisterings and iri-
descences, making of the sentence a rainbow where each drop is a prism
assuming a thousand colours. This language cost him infinite pains.
He was kind enough to analyse for me the washing scene on the river
bank, into which he had inserted cunningly, more or less disguised,
six hundred names of rivers, making a show of the world's aquatic theatre,
of fountains in full play, of the ballet of all universal nymphs. He also
explained to me in detail the phrase of *Irrawaddyng* [*FW* 214.09],
and then an unpublished one he had just composed, the delightful phrase
on a girl's sleep (*It is dormition* [*FW* 561.28]), as beautiful as
the poem "Dormeuse" by Valéry: *Dormeuse, amas doré d'ombres et
d'abandons . . .*[22]

21. Princesse de Bassiano (Marguerite Caetani) published *Commerce* (1924–32),
which printed the first fragments of *Ulysses* translated into French.
22. "Sleeper, golden mass of shadows and surrenders . . . ," from the second

This text belongs to the third part. Thus I learned that the author was working on separate portions of his book; he tackled it from all angles, a little here, a little there. He did not write it all in one breath, beginning at the first line, but worked on the fragment that suited him at the moment, leaving blank spaces. It would be curious to establish the chronology of the book. The second part, it seems to me, was written last; and the most recent passage appears to be the burlesque story of the tailor and the hunch-backed ship's captain. What facilitated the system was the fact that Joyce possessed an unerring memory. He knew his book by heart. In his mind the text was written in an indelible way. I believe that he even used to do most of his corrections by memory. Nevertheless, I would have been pleased to see his manuscripts. We shall really understand Joyce's thought only on the day when we can have it in its first state, before all the retouches with which he complicated it—after the fashion of Mallarmé who, being congratulated for a clear speech, answered, "Yes, I will have to add a few shadows." Our conversation, which was nothing more than a monologue, lasted for almost an hour. It was all very technical, without any farrago and sentimental verbiage. I noticed that the author explained his intentions in a most reasonable way and abstained from braggadocio, from all quackery. He knew that he was taking up a challenge, the venture of a dare-devil. If he was risking perhaps the impossible, he was doing it, at least, with full lucidity. He was following his demon, his prodigious verbal genius, his astonishing instinct which made him discover the method of inward language, interior murmur. He was aiming deliberately for extreme consequences, like the heroic discoverers of new elements who first leaped forward into the void. "Am I mad?" he said at the end. It was not an affected remark.

This lesson was not renewed. Joyce never went to the trouble of referring again to an explanation of his scrawl. I was instructed once and for all. I had in hand the thread of Ariadne. I learned the rest from quite a curious pamphlet just published by Miss Beach, and from the collective commentary, entitled jokingly *Our Exagmination*, etc. . . .[23] Joyce graciously gave me a copy of "Anna Livia" and I used its cover to jot down some notes from this interview. When leaving him, I noticed in the hall a picture representing the customs house in Dublin along the quays of the Liffey. It is an elegant monument from the century of

verse of "La dormeuse" ("The Sleeping Girl"), *The Collected Works of Paul Valéry*, ed. Jackson Matthews, vol. 1 (Princeton, N.J.: Princeton University Press, 1971), p. 138.

23. *Our Exagmination round His Factification for Incamination of Work in Progress*, a collection of commentaries on "Work in Progress" was published in 1929 by Sylvia Beach's Shakespeare and Company (rpt., London: Faber and Faber, 1961).

Louis XVI, of a type similar to the toll-houses by Ledoux, around Paris. Some bearded masks of springs and rivers decorate the rustically carved windows and animate the façade of this small water tower. One of these mythological heads is that of a smiling girl, her hair down and mingled with herbs: I doubt that the sculptor had attached a precise meaning to her—this beautiful face of a naiad was nothing else than the smile of the water world, a drop that oozes from the rock and remains suspended like a pearl.

—Look, it is the Liffey, said Joyce. Here is Anna Livia.

The picture was almost the only adornment of these lodgings, quite cheerless and half-stripped. So, he was always thinking about his native land! There his treasures were stored, there his heart had remained. I was moved by these simple words, as if the author had just disclosed his soul to me. I was also surprised: I did not expect to find *Ulysses'* author having anything in common with a master of stone-work or being indebted to him. A strange enchantment! I remembered the legend about the old Emperor enamoured of a dead girl, adoring her and refusing to be separated from her body. To break the spell, the girl's ring was thrown into a pond. Charlemagne fell madly in love with the pond and, in order never to be separated from it, he built there Aix-la-Chapelle. In the same way, on the place of his love, the artist built his book, his city of nostalgia and dreams. In his dialogue with the entrancing nymph, smiling like a water lily on the water surface, he becomes himself the hero of the adventure. He brings in all his ideas, his prodigious memory equal in volume to the mass of human memory,[24] his gift for languages, his fantasy. He is the Man, H.C.E., *Everybody*, Earwicker, the Male, all men,—and she, the river, Anna, the fleeting, the brilliant, the wave, the Woman, the Eternal Feminine.

The article in which I surrendered to Joyce appeared in August. I saw him again in the autumn. From that time on, our contact became more frequent. It rapidly acquired a confidential and an almost intimate character. One should not expect to find here an account of our meetings. Sometimes we met at my house with Paul Valéry or with Léon-Paul Fargue and John Sullivan. The great tenor was in capital form and he used to sing for us his big roles of Siegfried and Tannhäuser. Put into the mood about midnight, Joyce would try his hand at the keyboard and with his silken fingers, like a delicate ripple on the waves, would begin to caress the keys. He had a rather feeble but delightful voice, with a penetrating quality of tone, a touching flexibility: "Quite a musical genius in a small way and the owner of an exceedingly niced ear, with tenorist

24. "What a wonderful memory you have too" (*FW* 295.15–16). "The learning betrayed at almost every line's end" (*FW* 120.24). [Gillet's note]

voice to match" [*FW* 48.20–21]. It was a marvel to hear him. All his mocking, musical, ironic and melancholy race seemed to float on his lips; ballads were linked to ballads, songs to songs, romances followed laments. Those who have not heard Joyce in his Irish songs do not know what was most secret within him, his source or underground level of folklore, the chivalrous modesty of his slender strophes of *Chamber Music*, a tiny collection, a booklet which gives the diapason of his soul and which was the basis of his future work, as *Vita nuova* contains the germ of Dante's.

At other times the gathering took place at the home of his son Giorgio. The young man had married a beautiful American girl and had a boy who was a splendid lively youngster. Joyce was proud of this family: it was an aspect of existence where his life took up root again and regained its security. He was excessively fond of the child. Joyce emphasized family affection to an extreme degree. This terrible nay-sayer was a family man; in the chaos of the universe, as in the Deluge, his family was for him a sheet-anchor, the sacred Ark. He was attached to rites, dates, anniversaries, to a secret calendar to which he ascribed a superstitious importance. For his mind so daring and so free from all dogmas, this intimate religion was a liturgy that he never could forsake; it was the religion of the Lares, the Penates. For nothing in the world would he miss celebrating Candlemas, date of his birth, or July 4, date of his father's birth. These were his happiest days. He had decided that the latter (July 4) would be the great day when his new book would come to light and would be given to the public. The editor objected that this choice was against all sense—one does not publish a book on the eve of the vacation season, one risks missing all publicity. Joyce answered coldly that his publicity was already made: his name was enough. "At least," added the editor, "what will be the title of the work? Sometimes a book is published anonymously but never was a book published without a title."

Joyce retorted that the title was a secret between his wife and himself. He had imparted it to her alone, as a precaution, in the event he died before the printing of the book. Nobody would know anything until the day when the final copy would be ready for titling. Joyce remained intractable; no one could make him change his mind. The book did not appear however in July 1938. The publication was delayed until February 2 of the next year.

Till the last instant the poet was correcting by telegram, sending his ultimate "repentances." The first copy, still wet from the press and bound in haste, arrived finally by plane at four o'clock in the afternoon. The poet did me the kindness of having it brought to me immediately by the faithful Paul Léon. It was like the arrival of Desaix at Marengo. Joyce was content; he thought that this date would bring him luck.

I remember also another Candlemas eve at Giorgio's, a few years earlier; it was the day of the poet's fifty-second birthday. A cake with fifty-two candles was brought in. Joyce took his time, then blew them all out at one go. *Out, out, brief candle!*

Frequently we used to receive a telephone call, inviting us to a restaurant that evening or the following day. We met invariably at the same Montparnasse place, well known to gourmets and men of letters. Pierre Benoit could be seen there on his stops between Saint-Céré and Les Landes or Martinique and Beirut. Paul Bourget and Henry Bordeaux came to have lunch on Thursdays and to talk *tête-à-tête* about Académie matters before the weekly session. Joyce was a man of habit: "I am so dumb," he used to say, "that in ten years I have not discovered another restaurant." However, when he migrated later on to the Rue Galilée, he took his station at Fouquet's; he kept this new custom, even after he came to lodge again on the left bank, at Champs de Mars. He always occupied the same table, and at the table, the same seat. The menu was also determined once and for all: marenne oysters, chicken, flap mushrooms or asparagus, cup of fruit or ice-cream. He himself did not touch anything, smoked or ordered the same muscatel, emptying three or four carafes of it nervously until half past eleven or twelve, at which time his night's work was to begin.

I have few recollections of our dinner conversation, for most of the time Joyce said not a word and confined himself to listen absent-mindedly to our gossip. In an undertone he would give some news about his daughter Lucia whose ill-health tormented him and was his poignant worry (this young girl, full of talent, who danced, painted ravishingly, suffered from a mental illness); then he would relapse into silence, into a sort of absence, pursuing his reverie which I was far from trying to disturb.

But besides these parties with our wives, he and I used to get together at regular intervals, almost each month, half-way between our homes, in a café at the Invalides on the corner of the Rue Fabert and Rue Saint-Dominique. The place was almost deserted. Here and there two or three couples, with a constrained air of scant fortune, whispered in low voices; in the corners, retired old gentlemen played at dominoes or became absorbed in their newspapers. It was winter, at dusk, around five o'clock in the evening, and outside, behind the clouded windows, the quincunxes of the Esplande were shivering like acquarium plants. Joyce used to arrive punctually, sit down, sigh, order some lime-blossom or vervain tea, never coffee or liquor (only at dinner did he allow himself some wine; and then, he preferred the least full-bodied, such as certain white wines from Lausanne and Neuchâtel; he could endure a little champagne, but not the burgundy, which made him sick). These hours were a halt in his day. He used to get up late, around eleven o'clock (having stayed up long into the night), worked after lunch and allowed himself, before his nocturnal session, a respite at the end of the afternoon. During this time of relaxation, he liked to talk, confided readily. Then he would pull himself together, get up, seize his cane (the white cane of the blind), and on my arm make his way towards the Rue Las-Cases, to the house of his friend Paul Léon who used to take care of his affairs. I would always accompany him to the door.

My recollection of my friend's confidences go back to these hours of conversation in the small café. These were quite different talks from those with Rodin whom I used to see in the low pubs around the Hôtel Biron, and even more from those with Barrès who indulged invariably in a rather long soliloquy while walking from Porte Maillot to the Chamber of Deputies. I never took notes of these conversations with Joyce and it would be difficult to restore their character. It was always the same amalgam of private news and remarks upon his work, domestic worries alternating with the problems of craft. I believe Joyce liked me because I had children and he could speak to me about his own. I had my preoccupations, I shared his. I was not indifferent. These matters were the usual basis of his thoughts. Who could have recognized in this anxious father, tormented by pity for the distress of a daughter, the famous banterer, the cynic and satirical author of *Ulysses*? This image of the sick child, delight and torture of her father, was like the picture of a first communicant slipped out from the secret pocket of Bixion's wallet. Besides, I do not recall, during all these years, that Joyce ever said anything on current events, uttered the name of Poincaré, Roosevelt, Franco, Baldwin, de Valera, Stalin, made an allusion to Geneva or Locarno, Abyssinia, Spain, China, Japan, and the Negus or the Mikado, the Stavisky and Prince affair, Violette Nozières; to armament or disarmament, petroleum, the stock exchange, the races at Auteuil, Gorgoulow, the murders of Doumer, Dollfuss, King Alexander; to the Rhineland, Austria, Morocco, the Congo or the Gerolstein, or to anything else that encumbered the headlines of the newspapers—it was as if all this did not exist for him. I do not know if he was ever curious enough to go over a gazette. He was constructing his myth. All the realities did not equal the power of his dream. That is why I lack a trail or a guide mark in order to date these recollections. I take my bearings blindly. Almost all of them refer to the same subject: the life of the artist and the relation of his strange poem with his strange fatherland.

Joyce spoke little about Ireland. He had left the country very early, first at nineteen to spend one year in Paris, then forever at twenty-seven, swearing to himself not to return.[25] He kept his word and never in thirty-two years did he set foot there again. But never in thirty-two years did he spend a day without thinking of his native isle. *Irrland, Errorland* [*FW* 171.06 and 62.25], he writes with sarcasm. What kind of rancour made him so bitter, what was the reason for the estrangement, what grudge did he bear against his mother country? This we do not know and it would be difficult to explain. One can hardly imagine the degree of bitterness and spite that ill-feelings sometimes acquire in the provinces—or what amounts to the same thing—in small capitals. The day when Joyce embarked in Dublin, they were burning his first book. And which book! The charming collection *Dubliners*, jewel-case of short stories as perfect as those of Chekov or Mérimée! Bearing off from the harbour, he could see the smoke of this bonfire float over the city.[26]

A few years later, shortly after the armistice, he wanted his children to meet their grandfather; he sent them to Ireland with Mrs. Joyce. It was in the thick of the civil war—the days of the Vendée and the Terror. The Irish took the opportunity to be up to their old tricks; they sniped at one another in streets, in villages, at hedge corners. Gangs of rebels would attack trains and give battle, firing over the seats, from one corner of the car to the other, at passengers whose looks they did not like, slaughtering Tommies and all those who seemed suspect, as in a game of cops and robbers. These were the pleasures of the trip. Mrs. Joyce had just time to lie flat with her tots under the bench, while above her the mad ones had it out among themselves with guns, the republicans doing her the favour of driving out the tyrant.

I went to Ireland shortly after the revolt. Half of Dublin was down in ruin. Sackville Street ripped open, losing its bowels, was much more stricken than Madrid's quarters of Moncloa and Carabanchel which I saw after their ten months of siege. The opponents had gone at it whole hog. My old friend Gerald Campbell, representative of *The Times*, who had seen a war (I first met him at Verdun), told me horrors about the civil war that made one's hair stand on end. On the eve of my arrival, they found in Phoenix Park a severed head, with tongue and

25. In December 1902, when he was nearly twenty-one, Joyce went to Paris, ostensibly to study medicine. He spent about three and a half months there. His last visit to Dublin was in the summer of 1912, when he was thirty.

26. This hyperbole reflects Joyce's constant claim that *Dubliners* had been burnt. George Roberts, who was supposed to publish it, said it had been pulped (*JJ* 346).

teeth pulled out. The governor was then Earl of Athlone, brother-in-law of King George V, an old neighbour of ours at the front in Flanders. In Dublin Castle one lived in a state of alert and everybody at table, Princess Alice, sister of the King of England, included, had a loaded Browning next to his plate—it was part of the place setting.

For such pleasantries, which Irish citizens deem excellent sport, Joyce barely hid his disgust. Out of a kind of constraint, he preferred not to talk about them. In fact, he judged all these matters of Republic and Irish Constitution as not too serious; he considered them child's play. The only freedom worthy of a man had nothing to do with the political state—it was of the freedom of soul that he was jealous. The latter seemed to him much better off in the large unity of the *Commonwealth* than in the limits of an intolerant and annoying fatherland. Like Saint Paul who always claimed the title of *civis romanus*, Joyce kept, while living abroad, his British passport. This condition most closely resembled universal citizenship. As for the Gaelic language, in his view it was foolishness to try to revive it. What could one do with a dead language and with a poor patois spoken by no more than a few thousand peasants? One might as well undertake a masterpiece in the dialect of the Bambara or the Botocudo.

But Joyce could not forget the great memory of Parnell. The figure of this tribune and powerful agitator, today three-quarters forgotten, was the first to impress his young years. He had been the hero of his childhood. Joyce used to hear about his exploits as about those of Napoleon; both had been giants who made England shudder. They had awakened the world, had caused a fever in Europe, had troubled the rest of the great countries and agitated those buried alive, Ireland or Poland. When Parnell died, victim of intrigues and pharisaism, Joyce was ten—one never gets over one's first impressions. The memory of this martyr had dominated the writer's youth as his monument in Phoenix Park, rivalling Wellington's, reigns today over hills and woods.[27] Whenever Joyce spoke of Parnell, he did so with a smile. But I do not doubt that in his intimate thoughts, he dreamed of this landscape where the future would erect perhaps a monument to him, the poet. For lack of stone and bronze he was constructing by himself, at least in the memory of men, a monument that would not perish.

In the meantime, nothing interested him more than the news from his fatherland. What news? That of his own people. I mean, his rivals, brothers in poetry. He spoke tirelessly of Padraic Colum, Sean O'Casey, and especially of the beloved J. M. Synge, author of *Deirdre of the*

27. Parnell's monument is not in Phoenix Park but at the end of O'Connell Street in the center of Dublin. Aside from referring to Parnell constantly in his work, Joyce wrote an article about him for the *Piccolo della Sera* (*CW* 223-28).

Sorrows and *The Playboy of the Western World*, a charming figure which long ago, in his youth, he had met in Vaugirard. Many times I heard him recite with admiration the marvellous poem of Yeats: *My impetuous heart, be still! be still! . . . ,*[28] these eight or ten verses that he held to be the world's best, or the majestic tercet, as noble as a chorus by Sophocles, which ends his drama *Countess Cathleen:*

> *The years like great black oxen tread the world,*
> *And God the herdsman goads them on behind*
> *And I am broken by their passing feet.*

These verses came to his lips like an ever-present echoing of a previous existence. They were his world, his fatherland. He never stopped corresponding with a lot of faithful friends and former college comrades who constituted his secret party, as if he were a pretender in exile keeping in touch with his agents in his old kingdom. I have seen some of these devout friends of his, who secretly collected exceedingly rare brochures, untraceable off-prints of Joyce's first writings.[29] He was grateful for their worship; their piety was sweet to him and consoled many a bitterness.

At the time I had the opportunity of going to Ireland again; it was the end of May, during the Jubilee holidays. I could not help telling Joyce about my trip and I shall never forget the tone of his voice when he said: "Don't miss going to Howth. You will see the rhododendrons."

What was there in this word 'see'? Was it the exile or the blind man that spoke? I did not fail to go on the short outing that Joyce had recommended. I had done so once before, with Roger Chauviré, on a winter day and during a terrible storm; I had a baleful memory. Now it was June. The castle of Howth is a pleasant white mansion on top of a green hillock, covered by woods and meadows and advancing into the sea like a sort of uncouth and pastoral Posillipo. The isthmus which connects this cape to the coast has a cut at one place—the cliff appears bluff; there is a small ravine, a shady and screened gorge, moist with sea breath and warmed by the summer sun, a sort of hothouse in the open air. The vegetation in this bowl is of extraordinary luxuriance and vigour. It is an abyss of greenness, a kind of secret Eden, a Paradise of flowers. The sunbeams glide on the oblique shadows cast by the ridge and light up everywhere with glimmers and incandescences, with vermilions and crimsons, the flaming cups of rhododendrons which glitter like torches on candelabrum branches, sinking the rest in half-light—it is

28. Apparently "Be you still, be you still, trembling heart" from Yeats's poem "To His Heart."
29. The principal one of these friends was Constantine Curran, whom Joyce arranged for Gillet to meet during the latter's trip to Ireland in the spring of 1937.

the enchantment of the Latomies in Syracuse, or the terraces of Cintra. One could imagine the houris of the Klingsor garden displaying in this dale, as in an alcove, their secret and savage roses and giving in this desert a mysterious wedding feast. Feast of love, bouquet of delights, voluptuousness of the Orient, so unexpected in the climate of this Ultima Thule! I was inebriated by this epithalamium. What recollections from his youth had the poet left there? What images of his past were resting in this grave of flowers? He would not see again with his mortal eyes this garden of his adolescence, he carried its magic only in his memory. By making this pilgrimage I could almost imagine him opening to me, like a Fingal's Cave, a scented corner of his heart.[30]

Parallel with this stood the figure of his father. From the little I know, one suspects him of having been a superior *déclassé*, a country squire on the rocks, idler, drunkard, braggart, gambler, glib tongued, unfit for steady effort or work, in short, an impossible creature, real scourge of the family, but gifted with the vitality of a cat and a kind of genius. This simple man was a grand fellow, merry and maleficent, disorderly with an air of innocence, capable of all mischief, but always ready with a joke; one could not be vexed with him. This boozer, head over heels in debt, and obviously banished by good society, was consoled for all things only if he could shine, jug in hand, among his admiring cronies, dazzling them with his verve. He always found a way to snub bad luck with chaffing.

Elsewhere I have told how on a beautiful night, he led his family in search of shelter, while out of bravado he launched serenades to the stars. The anecdote of this rascal singing as he guided forward the march of a sobbing wife and a frightened youngster, has something that reminds one of *Fioretti* or *La légende des trois compagnons*. I have always thought that this heroicomic individual played a leading part in the imagination of Joyce; he was one of those magnificent failures having in them abundant material for poetic creation, one of those originals from whom the artist can reprint at will a hundred copies. He was for Joyce what we imagine John Shakespeare to have been for the great Will. I presume Joyce made from this model the types of Bloom and Earwicker in turn. It was he, with his imposing and jovial figure, who had filled his childhood; he had been God, the executioner, king of the house where he spread misery and sometimes storms of joy. The child

30. Whatever personal significance Howth might have had for Joyce, the most passionate episode in the courtship of Bloom and Molly occurred there. It also plays an important part in *Finnegans Wake*. Gillet's trip there illustrates Joyce's hold over him. Constantine Curran reported that he and a friend tried to persuade Gillet that Glendalough would be a better place to visit, but Gillet was not to be deterred from following Joyce's advice to see Howth (*James Joyce Remembered* [New York: Oxford University Press, 1968], pp. 91–92).

had admired him, had suffered from him. As time passed, he had for this old *enfant terrible* stores of indulgence, as Rabelais for his Panurge or Shakespeare for his Falstaff. The roguish old man died in the last few years, I believe around 1936, at the age of about seventy-five.[31] He was still alive at the time of my last trip to Ireland. Joyce gave me some letters for his friends, but did not ask me to see him nor did he entrust to me any message for him. From this tiny fact anyone may draw whatever conclusion he desires. Father and son had not met for more than twenty-five years. Without writing to one another, neither being a great letter-writer, they always found a way to correspond and exchange news about themselves. Above all, they felt bound by a common complicity and a connivance of nature which dispensed with formulas and further explanations. They understood each other by hints, even without words. The father followed from the corner of his eye, attentive but pretending to be unconcerned, the splendid and resounding career which the author of *Ulysses* made in the world. Without having read a single line of his works, he derived some glory from them. The old Fenian knew that his lad was playing in the world the part that he himself played obscurely but not without talent in his humble corner. *The Fenn, the Fenn, the kinn* (king) *of all Fenns* [FW 376.32–33]. Undoubtedly, it is to his extraordinary father that this brilliant line of Joyce applies. Perhaps the two were the only ones to be in on the secret of the comedy. Naturally, when someone spoke of his boy, the old man feigned a perfect indifference. One day they showed him Joyce's portrait (not the fine drawing by Augustus John or the study painted by J. E. Blanche), the one arranged by somebody in a cubist fashion— two simple vertical lines overshot on one side by the edges of a conk and a chin, and on the other by a rainbow representing the back of the head. "Ah! it's James," said the old man, "he is quite changed since I last saw him."[32]

Another anecdote will help us judge of this silent understanding between father and son which I am trying to define. It was before Joyce's departure and hegira to Trieste. He was married, but something was amiss in this marriage—had the young man forgotten to consult his father? Had he been satisfied with a secret marriage? The old

31. John Joyce died December 29, 1931, at the age of eighty-two. A letter Joyce wrote to Harriet Weaver shortly after his father's death confirms Gillet's speculation about the influence of the father on the son's work. "Hundreds of pages and scores of characters in my books came from him," he said (*Letters* I, 312).

32. Joyce also told this story to Harriet Weaver (*Letters* I, 312) and others. The "portrait" was Brancusi's impression of Joyce, which is reprinted as the frontispiece to Ellmann's biography. In addition to the impression, Brancusi made several more conventional sketches of Joyce.

James Joyce. Drawing by Otto Christensen

Bohemian was a stickler for the regard due him; no one more formal and touchy than a tramp. In short, he sulked. He declared that he would not recognize this union and would never meet the young bride. The estrangement lasted for one or two years. Finally, one day while the two men were taking a walk in the country, they stopped to refresh themselves in a village inn. There was a piano in the corner of the room. The old man sat down and, without saying a word, started on a cavatina, the baritone's aria in the third act of *La Traviata*. Then, when they were leaving the place he said without further explanation: "Did you recognize the aria I just played?"—"Yes, it belongs to Armand's [sic] father in Verdi's opera."—Nothing more was said. Thus Joyce learned that there was peace between them.[33]

This peculiar rapport with his father would appear, the more one thinks it over, as the central factor in Joyce's life, the basis, the axis of his work. Curious indeed! In this life the principal experience, the decisive and characteristic adventure was not at all, as for others, a romantic episode—the woman had almost no part in it. She was completely dethroned from her role of Beatrice. She existed as a pure physical necessity, for play, pleasure, recreation, procreation, as a device, or an accessory that one could not dispense with, for nature had invented nothing better by which to reproduce—she was confined almost to the condition of feminine understudy of man, a she-animal for caprice and fecundation. Nothing more remote from sentimentalism or insipid gallantry. Joyce seemed to revive the morose views of ancient theology, which granted to Eve's daughters a walk-on part, the small roles, that of figurante or maid, in the drama of nature. *Ancilla Domini*. And this stern thought has been attacked as cynical and libertine! And people have reproached Joyce about his complacent lewdness! With as much truth, one would condemn the manuals of confessors which deal with concupiscence and sins of the flesh. As a matter of fact, for Joyce love appeared to be an exclusively male function, a virile abstract affection which had nothing to do with a trifling affair and was placed entirely outside the domain of the senses: a current going from man to man, without passing through the intermediary of maternal entrails, a type of genealogy similar to the imposing introduction of Saint Matthew, *Isaac autem genuit Joseph*, etc., or to some aristocratic announcements where ladies' names are not included. One should say that the problem

33. The great baritone aria in which Alfredo's father seeks reconciliation with his son, recalling Alfredo's happy childhood in Provence by the sea ("Di Provenza il mar"), comes at the end of act 2 of *La Traviata*. Since Joyce was not married prior to his departure from Dublin, the reconciliation event Gillet describes would have to have occurred during one of his return trips. Joyce's arrangement that his formal marriage in 1931 take place on John Joyce's birthday sounds like a gesture of atonement on his own part.

of paternity, the relation between father and son, or vice versa, between son and father, this connection at one time ascending and at another descending, but entirely extra-sexual, completely non-voluptuous, is the essence of the Joycean problem. This explains in *Ulysses* (in the third chapter of the "Telemachiad") the long meditation on *Hamlet* by Stephen and Mulligan.[34] This episode is the clue to the book. Joyce maintained that the true hero in *Hamlet*, the main character, the one that dominates everything, was not Hamlet but the Ghost: not the living but the Other, not the mortal but the immortal. It was his apparition that set the whole drama in motion; it was he who led and delayed, controlled and hastened the action (in the sublime scene of the Third Act). And his weakling child appeared only as a ghost of the Ghost, whose gestures it repeated meekly on earth. (One can never emphasize enough that this miraculous play was the real source for Joyce's work, with its very conception of the "interior language"—*I have something inside of me talking to myself*—and even more, with its scenes of humour and madness that led to the monumental folly of *Finnegans Wake*.)

Relation so intellectual, affiliation so free from all physiological ties, union partaking so little of the flesh that Ulysses-Bloom recognizes at first sight Dedalus-Telemachus as the son of his soul—this is the entire meaning of their odyssey. During one whole day they advance towards each other, unaware that their destinies are bound together in the stars by secret affinities. And this occurs outside the sphere of blood and race (at least biological race), by a sort of election or spiritual attraction, a phenomenon comparable with the adoptive system in the families of the Caesars. It is a kind of salic law carried on from male to male, without the intervention of women. The mother does not count. Stephen Dedalus denies his; it is a weakness that he abjures. "Woman, what have I to do with thee?" A passage of imposing grandeur, where the hero sacrifices blood affections, immolates his humanity. Bloom-Stephen are the male couple, the binomial Father-Son, above all accident and alloy, all impurity—united as a proposition to an axiom, as the Procession of the Divine Beings. The basic problem in *Finnegans Wake* is always the same: how the One doubles and triples in sleep, how the Being multiplies and passes from the Simple to the Many, how the father begets his sons Shaun and Shem, who at the same time are derived and yet detached from him, resemble him and differ from him, prolong his life and deny it: the eternal mystery of Creation, Genesis, Paternity.[35]

In this enigma of the generation and transmission of all being, lies

34. Stephen's "meditation" on *Hamlet* occurs in chap. 9 (*U* 184–218).
35. "The family umbroglia" (imbroglio and umbrella) (*FW* 284.04). [Gillet's note]

for him the essence of everything, the very depth of existence and destiny. He sees in it a drama comparable in spirit with the old Christian dogma of original sin.

This natural pessimism increased in him even after the birth of his children, whom he adored. Their minor illnesses, their coughs, the slightest of fevers that children are subject to, maddened him. From an early date he had to recognize with terror the alarming signs of a nervous disturbance in his daughter. How could an innocent creature, a beauty so young and naïve, carry unknowingly in its body the germs that would destroy it? Joyce did not drink—I never saw him take anything other than lime-blossom tea, or at table, some very light wine. However, he had behind him centuries of alcoholism. His father, the old joker, had left him this heritage. But Joyce accused himself alone, held himself alone responsible; it was again he and not his charming wife, too disconcerted to protest, that he considered guilty. It was his fault; he was the father.[36] For everything that went wrong, for everything that turned out bad for his beloved daughter and son, he was the cause through all the abnormality that his genius possessed. That thought crucified him.

During his last years, it gave him no peace. The image of his suffering daughter tortured him. This was almost the only topic of our conversation. Sometimes I fancied hearing the complaint of King Lear carrying Cordelia in his arms. "Stabat mater" was written. The Middle Ages have multiplied the group of the *Pietà*. Few artists except Shakespeare and Balzac knew how to depict the Passion of the Father. Joyce did not write this passion; he lived it.

Sometimes he would escape from this nightmare. At such moments he liked to remember his happy days and spoke preferably of Trieste. His thoughts lingered on this topic with delight. There for a few short years he had enjoyed some moments of respite; fate had spared him some time. This pretty, good-natured Austrian city, half-Slavic and half-Italian (Edmund Gosse termed this "life in Germany"), with the gaiety of the Midi, the medley of languages, the animation of a harbour, and an already exotic, oriental flavour (as Veronese's Venice), had given him an extreme pleasure: there no classical monuments, no Roman mementos as in Split or Ancona. But there was the rock of Ithaca, and on the sea, the sail of Ulysses.

Joyce adored Italy. We know how much he owed to Vico. He had

36. Bloom also considers the father responsible for weaknesses in the child. He thinks, "if it's healthy it's from the mother. If not the man" (*U* 96).

learned Italian at twelve, for the love of it, from a reverend Jesuit father who had no suspicion that he was bringing up a future disciple of Giordano Bruno and Campanella, of Ariosto and Pulci. Trieste was the birth place of his children. He had retained the habit of speaking to them in the language of the country—they were for him always Giorgio and Lucia. He also had a taste for a certain Italian style, half-serious and half-amusing, closer to Machiavelli's than to Petrarch's or Metastasio's, far from the baroque turgidity of a d'Annunzio.[37] He used to quote with delight a cue from the dramatic poem in prose by Ettore Morelli, entitled "Glauco": *Preferisco il vino col sapore delle stelle* ("I prefer wine when tasted under the stars").

Moreover, he had discovered much to his surprise that his own prose, and even his verses, could be translated into Italian much better than into any other language. He greatly admired the Italian version of Yeats' beautiful poem which I mentioned above, done by a friend of his in verse; he considered it superior even to the original text.[38] The last time that I saw him at the Hôtel du Commerce, in the village Saint-Gérand-le-Puy where he had run aground God knows by what mishaps, he was solely occupied by a new translation of the first pages of "Anna Livia" just published in Rome or Milan, in a de luxe magazine of futuristic tendencies entitled *Paradossi*.[39] The fact is that this version is an outstanding *tour de force*. If it is ever completed, I cannot too strongly advise the beginners to read *Finnegans Wake* in the Italian text.

It was in Trieste that Joyce was fortunate enough to discover a brother, or at least a half-brother, in the person of a writer who had published nothing as yet and who was the most remarkable of his Italian contemporaries—I mean, Italo Svevo. He was a Croatian Jew, son of a wealthy family of shipbuilders. I think his real name was Schmitz.—The firm first put out canned sardines. One of the partners invented a red lead paint which happened to be excellent not only for the tin cans but also for the preservation of ship hulls.—This millionaire was a timid man, without self-confidence; his mother directed the business and was boss of the company. He liked only literature, but a literature of a miniaturist, so humble, so matter-of-fact, so devoid of events that it did not seem to have human traits. The two young writers would exchange ideas and projects. Their views corresponded. This was the period when Joyce began writing *Ulysses*. The idea of making Ulysses a Jew, and

37. Nevertheless, Joyce at one time admired d'Annunzio's work (see p. 45, note 59, and Constantine Curran's *James Joyce Remembered*, pp. 105–15).

38. Apparently the reference is to Carlo Linati's translation of *The Countess Cathleen*.

39. See Nino Frank's account of this translation, pp. 96–97, 101–2, which appeared in the February 15, 1940, issue of *Prospettive*.

a Jew from Central Europe, could not have come to his mind without help, for Jews were not numerous in Dublin. Probably in Trieste, in the society of his new friend, the thought came to him to make Leopold Virag *alias* Bloom, his hero and to identify in his person the vagabond petty Greek king and the Wandering Jew. All this was confirmed later by the theories of Victor Bérard and his curious research on the Phoenicians and the *Odyssey*.[40] Joyce had succeeded in convincing himself, God forgive me, that Ulysses was a Semitic type. I have related elsewhere his strange etymology for the name of Homer's hero (Odysseus-Outis Zeus). So that, when Ulysses in the cave of Polyphemus says to the Cyclops that his name is *Nobody* (Outis), it is Zeus renouncing himself. And if we accept a Semitic element in all this, I leave it to others to guess the consequences. Joyce claimed to perceive here the sacrifice of Calvary! We have to admit, it was quite far-fetched; he was going to the bother of an exegesis for a nursery tale as simple as the fable of the Ogre and Tom Thumb.

There was also an excellent opera-house in Trieste. The best companies, the best singers stopped there on their way to Vienna, coming from Milan and Venice or going in the opposite direction; it was a halt on the route between Hofopernhaus, Monte Carlo, La Scala and La Fenice. Life was spent in music. It was a windfall to Joyce. He fancied being again in Dublin, for Dublin is also a melomaniac city. Joyce's father sang, Joyce sang, his daughter danced, his son has a magnificent voice, the whole family is musical. For Joyce, if there was no song there was no joy. We know that he studied opera singing, and quite extensively. I have said before, his greatest regret was not being Chaliapin. I was mistaken; I should have said Sullivan. The unforgettable Arnold, the unrivalled Florestan, this first tenor of the world since Jean de Reszké, was an intimate friend of the poet—Joyce envied him his triumphs. In *Ulysses* he does not fail to indicate this Irish passion for songs and singers by a peculiar allusion. When Bloom enters the newspaper office (or if you prefer, Aeolus' cave), the journalists stare at him.[41]—"Don't you think his face is like Our Saviour, Red Murray whispered . . .

—Or like Mario . . ." Mario, Count of Candia, was a famous tenor, performer of Donizetti, darling of the dilettanti in the good days of

40. In 1907 Joyce met Svevo, who no doubt contributed significantly to the novel. The previous year he had thought of writing a short story called "Ulysses," to be based on a Dublin Jew named Hunter (see p. 33, note 34). Around 1917 he learned of Bérard's *The Phoenicians and the Odyssey* (1903). Subsequently he often mentioned the book, giving great importance to its confirmation of a historical basis for his merging a Jewish theme with the Greek in *Ulysses*. Contrary to Gillet's assertion, Svevo had published his first two novels when Joyce met him, but they had gone unnoticed.
41. Actually, they are staring at Braydon (*U* 117).

the Second Empire. Now, Mario had died in 1883, after being retired from the theatre for more than fifteen years, and Joyce's novel takes place in June 1904. Dubliners therefore had not heard him for more than forty years, but they still remembered him. This curtain-call, as they say in theatrical slang, speaks volumes about the character of the Dublin public.

I shall not mention again the tastes of my friend, his determined preference for vocalized singing, his dislike for Wagner and instrumental music. In the eighteenth century he would have been deliberately on the side of Jean-Jacques, against Gluck and French music; he would have been a Puccinist. Like Stendhal, he was for the Italians. He was not susceptible to erudite music: fugue, counter-point, structure in the German fashion found him indifferent. I never heard him say a word about Bach, Beethoven, Schumann; the abuse of development, the insistence on and repetition of formulas, the exploitation of themes to the utmost by these great masters, annoyed him. He made an exception for Strauss, the author of *Der Rosenkavalier*, who under his amazing symphonic virtuosity and the veils of his orchestration barely succeeds in masking and disguising his Viennese roguery, gaiety, banter, and his Italian singing style.

"I don't like music," he used to say, "I like singing." These are two quite different things which are often wrongly confused, especially in modern music. Moreover, Joyce did not enjoy just any kind of singing. He set little value on feminine voices. Neither the soprano, nor the mezzo, nor the contralto found any favour in his hard-to-please ears; he always detected in them something imperfect, as if an impure expression of nature gave itself away even in this most immaterial form. He was not a dupe of the angelic side of women. His sense of hearing, like that of the blind, gained in acuteness all that was denied to his sense of sight; it became more exacting and more uncompromising. Like the Greeks, in everything he awarded the prize to the *kouros* rather than to the *koré*, to the ephebus rather than to the girl. Here again one can find a classical pessimist, a determined misogynist. Among the voices of men, it was not to the basso, the lyric bass or baritone, that he assigned the palm; for him the tenor existed exclusively, the tenor who was able to sing the highest notes without effort, the tenor of the type of Escalaïs or Tamburini. Only this voice touched him and appeared enviable to him. I do not doubt than *in petto*, though he said nothing about it, he did not condemn the times when such voices were considered so beautiful that one did not hesitate to obtain them by a crime and that he deemed it very natural to make castrates, like those who gave glory to the Sistine Chapel.

To a man for whom a piano tune took the place of speech and who, as we have seen, came to an agreement with his father by several measures of a ritornelle from *La Traviata*, music was a language and perhaps even something more. It was an atmosphere, a condition of thought, an *aura* beyond all words, which nevertheless was to be found in the words, grouping them, guiding them, giving them breath of life. For Joyce, a sentence was not severable from its melodic qualities, for they alone gave existence to it. Attention has been drawn many times to this fact and the remark has become trite: Joyce's art is primarily musical. It was for Joyce that the divine rule of Verlaine's *Art poétique* appears to have been dictated: *De la musique avant toute chose* . . .

One might draw the wrong conclusion on first reading certain passages, which startle by what seems to be an excess of realism, certain scenes from which Céline himself would have shrunk. One must recognize that these crudities are like the discords of a predominantly lyrical composition. An editor suggested that the author publish in America an expurgated text of *Ulysses*, which would be easier to sell. Joyce would not hear of it. He valued nothing more than the unity of his work. Everything, down to the last detail, had been weighed and ordered with minute calculation. "My book has a beginning, a middle and an end; which one do you want to cut off?" he retorted to the editor. It would take too long to study what Joyce's composition, style and art of writing owe to music. E. R. Curtius has studied it with a great deal of subtlety and a little injustice; he reproached the author for having confused the techniques of two different arts (this censure, if it is indeed one, he could have applied to all Symbolists). I doubt, however, that he would have made it had he heard Joyce read the passage that he criticizes. Joyce was a consummate reader (a common talent with English poets, Edith Sitwell for instance). There is a recording by him of the famous chapter of "Anna Livia" and this reading enraptures with its variety of movements, its suppleness of intonations, its chain of rhymes. I have played the record before people who did not know a word of English and it gave them as much pleasure as the performance of a song.[42]

Musical matters came up most frequently in conversation with Joyce. On this topic, as on everything else, he had his own opinions. For instance, can one guess which language seemed to him most fitted for singing? Not German, of course, for its excess of consonants; not Italian either, for its excess of vowels; and English even less. Contrary to all expectations, the musical language *par excellence* for him was French,

42. The Ernst Roberts Curtius study is *James Joyce und sein Ulysses* (1929). Joyce's reading from "Anna Livia Plurabelle" (*FW* 213.11–216.5) is included in the Folkways album, "Meeting of the Joyce Society" (FL 9594; 1951).

because of the softness of intervals and the quantity of silent syllables that gave to it something airy and diaphanous, which Claude Debussy felt so well, something *soluble dans l'air* as the delightful Lélian says. By the way, do you know that in his youth Joyce had tried to translate into verse some of the *Poèmes saturniens?*

Les sanglots longs
Des violons
De l'automne . . .[43]

One is well pleased to find Verlaine among the good genii of the poet of *Chamber Music.*

After the musical questions, Joyce brought up for discussion those concerning style and grammar. In his opinion, these matters could not be separated from one another. During the entire period of our relationship he was busy with his new work, in which such problems, as we all know, assume a constantly increasing importance.

"In *Ulysses*," he told me once, "in order to convey the mumbling of a woman falling asleep, I wanted to finish with the faintest word that I could possibly discover. I found the word *yes*, which is barely pronounced, which implies consent, abandonment, relaxation, the end of all resistance. For "Work in Progress," I tried to find something better if possible. This time I discovered the most furtive word, the least stressed, the weakest in English, a word which is not even a word, which barely sounds between the teeth, a breath, a mere nothing, the article *the.*"

This way of finishing, *piano, pianissimo* and going one better than the absence of sound, what a lesson of taste to us who never tire of pointing up, of fixing the barb, of elaborating upon the final word. As a matter of fact, *Finnegans Wake* begins and ends in the middle of a phrase, and this phrase is the same one. The final *the* is to be connected to the initial *riverrun*—at the last line the reader has to resume the first. Thus the shackle is buckled and the circle is closed. All is finished and all begins anew. All that fills the interval, the whole development of this dream or poem is contained between the beginning and the end of a single sentence. Time is no more. Vico's circle is complete, and complete is the feeling of eternal return. Everything starts again *da capo.* Such was the subtlety, the depth of effects that the ingenious artist was able to draw from his art.

Since *Ulysses* one can hardly keep track of the novels in English literature taking place in one day (like the classical tragedy, but in a

43. Joyce translated this Verlaine poem while in college. The translation is reprinted in Gorman's biography, p. 59.

precisely opposite sense): *Mrs. Dalloway* by Virginia Woolf, *Twenty-Four Hours* by Louis Bromfield, etc. "The Prince of Wales seems to have passed through here," Joyce used to say; the Prince of Wales having the privilege of launching the fashion in England: a trouser pleat, a grey felt high-topper for the races. He enacts the role that Beau Brummel used to play of old.

I knew the direction of Joyce's research for his new book. Now and then, without speaking to me about the work in general, he confided some *trouvaille* of detail which satisfied him. I came thus upon some of his methods. I was astounded by what he could achieve in matters of acrobatics. Sometimes, it was a simple jest, with no significance. Nothing more droll than the arrangement of the phrase *A tache of tch* (a spot or tea) [*FW* 111.20]! where the conjunction of a French word and a Russian word produces a comic effect, a sort of tickling, an unexpected *Atishoo*! The same process is used in the description of a meal where some spoonerisms, some reversed syllables, *naboc* (bacon), *kingclud* (duckling), *eaps* (peas), represent the act of chewing, while the onomatopoeia *xxoxoxxoxxx* is a funny portrayal of a mouth occupied by a gruel of potatoes [*FW* 456.22–23]. This kind of verbal humbug gave him exceeding pleasure.

Sometimes it was a proverb, a popular saying (of which he possessed an inexhaustible stock), whose terms he found amusing to reverse. One day he recited to me with a certain complacency the following arrangement: *If time enough lost the ducks, walking easy found them* [*FW* 449.05] (after the French saying "Si Jean qui s'en-fait a perdu les oies, Jean qui s'en-f—— les a retrouvées"), and he seemed very pleased with this prank.[44] Sometimes I would be the first to hear one of his new lines, as the following: *They lived and laughed and loved and left*[45] —only four words of song, but they comprise all living. If one is sensitive to the rhythm of a phrase, to the winged grace of a cadence made of four liquid consonants with an interior variation of vowels, one has to admit that no one since the divine Will has ever written a similar line.

I was surprised sometimes that an artist gifted with such a feeling for beauty had restricted himself to the role of a clown. He admitted it himself: "Such a book, all in puns!" It is true, among these jokes and jests there are some excellent ones, which also make you think. Once he delivered his new calendar of the week days: *Moansday, Tearsday,*

44. "Honeys wore camelia paints (*FW* 113.17), "Honey swarns where mellisponds" (*FW* 238.33–34) (after the French "Honi soit qui mal y pense"). "To me or not to me. Satis thy quest on" (*FW* 269.19–20). "And trieste, ah trieste ate I my liver!" (*FW* 301.16). "Walhalloo, Walhalloo, Walhalloo, mourn in plein!" (*FW* 541.22). One could quote a hundred examples of such pleasantries and parodies. [Gillet's note]

45. "They lived und laughed ant loved end left" (*FW* 18.21).

Wailsday, Thumpsday, Frightday, Shatterday [*FW* 301.20–21], a true almanac of Jeremiah, a calendar for Lent, for penitence and hardship, which moreover is not too badly made for our days of *De profundis*.

In the last few years he showed himself very much occupied with a certain Jesuit priest, whose name unfortunately escapes me.[46] Joyce had heard him at the Salle de Géographie in a very curious lecture on comparative phonetics and linguistics, and these new ideas expressed seemed to him most daring. According to this clergyman, all languages constitute a system of the Revelation, and their history in the world is the history of the Logos, the history of the Holy Spirit. Perhaps this is somewhat of a logomachy. I do not guarantee that the speaker really said all that Joyce quoted of him. One feels, however, that such a speech offered Joyce material for long reveries.

Moreover, as time went by, he paid increasing attention to the opinion of the clergy. The attitude towards him had slowly changed. Rome never hurries—what are twenty years for her? I imagine Joyce was glad to count at last in the esteem of some grave people; Voltaire too attached importance to the praises bestowed upon him by his old teacher, Father Porée. In the main, ecclesiastics were people of distinction, a sort of tribunal whose suffrage was worth having—they constituted a serious public. Their consideration withdrew the author of *Ulysses* from the mob of novelists. These severe judges had ended by recognizing in Joyce a man of their own kind, experienced in dialectics, a psychologist without illusions, a poet disenchanted from all vanities and concerned solely with eternal problems. They were connoisseurs. Joyce made me read, not without satisfaction, here an extract from *Etudes*, there a cutting from *Osservatore Romano*, where he was treated with visible caution and deference.[47] What a change since his books had been scorched at the stake, and since the day when he was only a rascal savouring of heresy! Did the poet see in these evident advances a sign of the time when it would be permissible for him to make an honourable return to his fatherland? Perhaps he flattered himself that some day . . .

But Joyce died unyielding, without being reconciled, though if only by word, with the Church, and even without arranging a final return for his ashes to the land where his dead lie.

46. This would have been Marcel Jousse. Eugene Jolas ("My Friend James Joyce," *Partisan Review*, 8 [March-April 1941]: 90) mentions and Mary Colum (*Our Friend James Joyce* [Garden City, N.Y.: Doubleday and Co., 1958], pp. 130–31) describes in more detail Joyce's interest in Jousse's theory about language growing out of gesture.

47. The *Etudes* article is probably Armand Petitjean's "Signification de Joyce," *Etudes Anglaises*, 1 (Sept. 1937):404–17, an analysis of the language in "Work in Progress." Regarding the *Osservatore Romano* article, see above, p. 88 and note.

✠

One day I spoke to Joyce about a charming book on Ireland that I had just read. It was written in Irish by a man named Sullivan, a simple peasant who knew no other language than his native tongue. It goes without saying that I read a translation of it, not having the pleasure of understanding Gaelic. The English title is *Twenty Years A'Growing*.[48] It is impossible to have more charm and wit than this author; the rustic seems to be swelling with talent. He writes like Pliniak, Chekov, Gorky; today only the Russians have so many gifts, so much naturalness and spontaneity; but in this Irishman there is more gaiety and good-nature, certainly less bitterness, an experience less cruel. These are the memoirs of a happy man.

The story takes place on a lost islet, off the south-west tip of Ireland. I forget the name of this rock, the largest of a rosary of reefs prolonging the cape like blocks of dislocated sea-wall. This rock measures almost one mile in length and fifteen hundred feet in width. The population is two hundred and fifty inhabitants.

For the natives of this quite wretched isle, Ireland is the main land, it is almost the continent. Their life on this outcast rock is precarious at all times—storm after storm, squall after squall, poor soil, scanty crops, no cattle except for a few goats, chickens and rabbits; to this they add some fishing whenever the weather allows it.

The war changed all this; I speak of the First War, of course. Ireland was already quite outside the scuffle and could not complain too much about the conflict. For the islanders it was rather a blessing. Each storm that smashed a ship, each submarine that sank a commercial or supply cargo-boat, was working for these hermits. The sea became a warehouse, a horn of plenty; each day brought its wreckage. The entire universe seemed to have no other care than to fatten and clothe this society of anchorites. Meat, victuals, clothes, canned food, coffee, flour, spirits, anything you wanted—there it was! Before long, everybody was going around with two watches in his waistcoat pockets. It was a life of milk and honey. Only sugar, says the author, was missing from the menu; hurry as they might, they arrived too late; they always found it dissolved.

The reader will forgive me for these quite long details. They are necessary in order to describe the stage and place the setting for the story that will follow.

Joyce listened to me. He put on a smile of awareness and began telling what I have been getting at. Here now is his tale:

48. *Twenty Years A-Growing* (1933), by Maurice O'Sullivan, describes life on the Blasket Islands.

Your story does not surprise me. I have heard tell of this island. A few years ago, one of my friends spent a fortnight there in order to observe its flora and fauna, not neglecting to gather all that seemed picturesque, whether in the detail of the landscape or in the manners and costumes of these poor peasants.

Soon his supply of film was used up. He had to go to the city to renew his stock. The city was a mediocre port, some seven hundred feet from the islet. One went there by boat. The sailor used as ferryman was an old sea-dog with the face of a gardener, a sort of amphibian resembling a seal, half-human and half-fish. While my friend went shopping, the seal wandered in the bazaar—he had never seen so many things. There was one object especially that tempted him: a small pocket-mirror in the shape of a medallion almost as big as the palm of his hand. It was a great novelty to the simple man. For thirty years he had shaved without a mirror, even without a pail in which to look at himself. He didn't know what his face looked like. The idea of seeing his snout had never occurred to him. For a long time he fondled the object in his hands, examined it, put it back in place, walked away, sighed, then came back. Finally, he thought, it didn't seem to cost too much, he could satisfy his fancy. The old seal made up his mind. He took his courage in both hands, made his way towards the counter, and paying one shilling, pocketed the mirror.

The return trip was as easily accomplished as the going, but it was twice as long. The oarsman was so entranced by his lucky find that every few moments he forgot to row and fingered in his pocket to see if the mirror was still there. He couldn't keep himself from pulling it out now and then, became furtively absorbed in the contemplation of the face that he saw portrayed. He let the oar go and looked at the image. His tanned-leather face lighted up with a smile, his wrinkles beamed with tenderness, and my friend heard him murmuring as if he spoke to the mirror, with a voice moistened by happiness: "Oh Dad! Dad!"

Here mere words are not enough, one needs the aid of pictures. One had to see Joyce mimicking the scene with all his body! He drew his cupped hands near to his face, smiled into them as if he were holding a mirror, moved aside, then quickly bent making a spittle-like noise as if he were swallowing a draught of water. He was himself the character, imitating the gestures, the tone, with a delightful voice. It was a cascade of "Dad! Dad!" repeated on all notes of the scale, with small looks, small pouts, small cries, with expressions that showed surprise, reproach, love, as when one meets a beloved person whom one didn't hope to see again: "It had been such a long time! How you made us wait! Where were you hiding?" The old man believed that he was seeing the image of his father. Not knowing the usage of mirrors and never having seen his own features, he thought that the mirror contained a portrait of the one he loved; it was enough to bring the magic disc to his face in order to see at once this beloved face appear in the enchanted circle. All this corresponded so well to the intimate thoughts of the poet that it was no effort for him to play the part. In this role Joyce was plainly a perfect picture.

Once they had arrived, the man rushed to his home like someone carrying a treasure in his pocket, and the same stratagem started afresh. His wife found in him at first a radiance that she had forgotten existed, and said to herself; "That's it, my man has been drinking!" As for him, any time he thought he was unobserved, he would pull the mirror out half-way and secretly sneak a look, always with the same appearance of rapture. But now, restraining himself, so as not to be heard, he only moved his lips silently (and Joyce moved his like two leaves, not a sound coming from them) as when one says a prayer: "Dad! Dad!" It seemed as if he were talking to himself.

His wife, while looking to her household work, watched him slyly from the corner of her eye and said this time: "That's it! He's crazy!" She was asking herself, however (women are suspicious), what could be seen in this unknown object that had the power to make her husband lose his wits. She didn't know any more about mirrors than he did; it was an accessory ignored on this primitive island. She tied up her mop of hair in a harum-scarum sort of way, being not so particular as to looks. She was troubled nevertheless by this disc which her husband wouldn't show her and only ogled stealthily. Naturally, she was curious, and curiosity had soon turned into jealousy. "Oh, now I see," she said to herself, "someone must have cast a spell on him; it must be some wench picked up in town with whom he is all infatuated."

She was on fire to learn more; but the less she succeeded in dissimulating her distrust, the more the old man increased his affectations of mystery. This supernatural image belonged to him—it was a sacred thing, a secret between his father and himself. "Stay back, woman! Hands off!" But passion and ruse aided by patience always end by finding prudence napping.

On a hot day the couple was working in the fields. The man hung his jacket on the hedge. His wife seized her chance. She knew that the enchanted object never left her husband's pocket. In two leaps she was at the hedge and searched quickly in the jacket, overjoyed to be able to see at last the head of the rival who held her man bewitched. She took out the mirror and glanced into it—instead of a graceful little phiz the magic mirror reflected only a hideous pack of wrinkles. Instead of the face of love, she saw the grin, the nag of hatred. "Faugh! an old woman!" she cried out, and angrily threw the mirror which broke against a stone on the ground.

Readers, what do you say to this story? One could make a fabliau of it. One would entitle it *The Mirror of Marriage* or perhaps *The Mirror of the World.* Why not? We find in things only what we put in them. They give us back only our own image.

What had to be seen, however, was this life, this style, mimicry, devilment: what a zest, what a humour, what a talent for a tale! It was the genius of a race, the grace of a story-telling people, the gift for creation of fables and myths, the spell of a savage island, of a fatherland of novelists and poets who have created in mass the most beautiful legends that ever charmed the world. For one hour, I saw functioning for me alone this exquisite poetic machine. By what cruel and teasing demon had this mind of a charmer made the perverse choice of changing itself into a mechanism for riddles, of changing its talent for story-telling into the toilsome manufacturing of a tiresome scrawl and sibylline text which could be no more than *caviar to the general,* as the Prince of Denmark says, that is to say, a puzzle, an enigma to the public? How strange this need to revenge oneself on the world and to make it pay for an indefinable despair and misfortune in life! [49]

I had not seen him since the outbreak of the war. I knew that he had left Paris and had settled in La Baule, near the nursing home where his daughter was tended. The sick girl vegetated in a state of gentle madness, she had become a child again. Her father spent some moments with her every day, waiting patiently for some gleam of reason to come back to her. He believed he knew more about the girl than the doctors did— he hoped for a miracle from paternal love.

The rest of each day wore away in walks on the beach. They reminded him of the time when on the seashore of Ireland, in the customs tower, he had spoken about matters of heaven and earth with his friends Haines and Mulligan, and where the waves had brought him the smile of Nausicaa. He remembered also the quays of Trieste and the sails on Ulysses' sea. Now his work was done. He was on vacation. But the waves roared as ever; another war had started, the Ocean continued beating the shore and chafing on its edges. Genesis pursued its course. And in his mind was rising the idea for a new poem whose fundamental theme would be the murmur of the sea.[50]

49. Gillet reveals here that in spite of his sympathetic treatment of *Finnegans Wake* in print, he shared the opinion of many of Joyce's other friends that the book was a mistake. It is odd, however, that he should have seen only the differences between the story Joyce told and *Finnegans Wake*, since the attempt at total expressiveness that characterized Joyce's telling of the story also characterizes the book and often acounts for the very difficulty Gillet objects to.

50. This is one of several suggestions as to what Joyce might have had in mind for his next book. To Stanislaus he said the next book would be "The Reawaken-

During this time his grandson, *the child we all love to place our hope in for ever*, was entrusted to Mme Jolas. For the war period she had sheltered the school she used to direct in Neuilly, in a château of the Allier. When the downfall came, the Joyce family gathered there. There I saw Joyce for the last time.

I finish these pages far from Paris, where I had the happiness to associate with him for ten years, and where he was one of the glories, at the same time, world-wide and secret. I close my eyes. Again I see the small café on the corner of the Rue Fabert where I used to meet him, where he confided in me and liked to pour out his heart. It is evening. The windows are blurred, the trees of the esplanade are only a dim design where he wends his way, feeling the ground with the cane of a blind man. He moves away, he has disappeared. And now, in that scattered and half-extinct Paris it seems to me that I am barely less of a ghost than he and that we are both only shadows.

June 7, 1941

TRANSLATED BY GEORGES MARKOW-TOTEVY

---

ing" ("James Joyce: A Memoir," *Hudson Review*, 2 [Winter 1950]:514). See Paul Léon's recollection, p. 291, for a similar idea, and Dr. Giedion-Welcker's, p. 279 and note, for a quite different one.

Jacques Mercanton

THE DIFFICULTIES OF Finnegans Wake *have led many people to
accuse Joyce of not caring about his readers. But in fact, few writers
have shown as much concern over their readers as Joyce did. One of the
best illustrations of this concern is his friendship with Jacques
Mercanton (b. 1910). Whereas the most impressive credentials could
not gain journalists access to Joyce, Mercanton's interest in* Finnegans
Wake *brought him a ready welcome and willing explications of the
book. These explications were given not simply to enlighten Mercanton
but, since he planned on writing about the book, to enlighten a wider
audience as well.*

When asked why he did not provide an explanation of Finnegans
Wake, *Joyce replied that people did not value things that were handed
to them free. "Even an alley cat" he said, "would rather snake an old
bone out of the garbage than come up and eat a nicely prepared chop
from your saucer."* [1] *Supplying guidance indirectly, through people
such as Mercanton, diminished this problem, made for better propaganda,
and also satisfied his fondness for having collaborators. He had begun
giving indirect guidance to his readers in 1921, when he sent the "schema"
of* Ulysses *to assist Carlo Linati in writing about the book. He continued
the practice with Budgen's and Gilbert's books on* Ulysses *and with*
Our Exagmination. *He contributed significantly to these and other
studies of his work, indicating directions they should take, offering explanations, reading manuscripts, and even suggesting titles.*

Next to the Letters, *Mercanton's recollection contains the most
extensive record of Joyce's comments on* Finnegans Wake. *Joyce seems
to have discussed the book with him in more detail than he did with
anyone else but Miss Weaver, perhaps intending him to be its official
explicator, as Gilbert was of* Ulysses.[2] *These comments are especially
important because they come from a time when the book was nearing
completion, whereas most of those in the* Letters *are from much earlier.
They represent Joyce's last major attempt at explaining it.*

1. Max Eastman, *The Literary Mind* (New York: Charles Scribner's Sons, 1931), pp. 103-4.
2. Ellmann makes the suggestion (*JJ* 723).

The recollection also gives an intimate and sympathetic portrait of Joyce during his last years. This portrait shows a much more forgiving or accepting man than appears in the previous recollections. He exhibits no rancor even toward his old antagonist Oliver St. John Gogarty. More surprising yet, he defends Ireland and Dublin, while his wife attacks them. The effects on him of Lucia's madness, the impending war, and other worries are fully apparent in Mercanton's account, but so, too, are sudden transformations of mood once he began discussing or reading aloud Finnegans Wake. *Those changes make it clear that the book was not just the obsessive burden he described to Vinding but also was a source of delight and solace.*

The Hours of James Joyce

By Jacques Mercanton

PREFACE

I KNEW JOYCE only in the concluding years of his life, at the time he was completing his last work, *Finnegans Wake*. The portrait the reader will find in these pages is of that Joyce.

I have arranged nothing, composed nothing, added nothing, taken nothing away from the writer's moments or hours, on vacation and at work. The words I have put in his mouth are those he spoke. The reader will not be surprised to learn that I jotted them down at the time. Moreover, as I mention later, Joyce's company forced me to train my memory: he expected people to recall things precisely, and in detail.

It was enough to make a choice among details: certain recollections should not be allowed beyond the intimacy of the memory; others, depending on the hours and on the meetings, concern only the man and not the author. Though touchy, suspicious at first, Joyce revealed himself in the confidence of friendship just as he did in his work, with the same sincerity. But precisely that: the same inviolable sincerity.

SOUND THE TRUMPET

When his wife showed me into the living room, he was sitting on the floor in front of a radio, legs stretched out, looking for a station with the help of a magnifying glass. He got up in one easy, sliding movement, fixed his gaze on me for a second through his thick glasses, extended a dry hand. "Do you have one of these sets?"

He was trying to get the Regional London program, to pick up an aria by Purcell; he excused himself, tried again, asked me the time, pulled out a pack of cigarettes and offered it to me negligently. "An aria for tenor, or counter-tenor: 'Sound the Trumpet.' It must be part of a cantata. But if this bores you, I'll turn it off."

The voice was curt, peevish, but delicate, with a rather strong English accent. He was wearing a smoking-jacket over a blue woolen vest, tight trousers without a crease, slippers. His eyes were invisible behind his glasses, one lens of which was thicker than the other, almost opaque. His forehead, high and bulging, dominated the lean, sad, ailing face. His complexion was florid. He talked immediately about the art of song, about his son's voice studies, asked me if I played—if I sang, what was my register? "So, you are a bass, then."

Next, giving up the radio, still mute: "Well now, what can I do for you?"

He talked briefly about Switzerland, where he had lived during the war, about Lausanne, which he knew from a tour with the English Players, about Geneva, where Edouard Dujardin had given a talk on him, about Zurich especially and his oculist, Vogt. "You know, my eyes have been operated on ten times. And I can't see your face."

He sat down near the window, solitary, not making the least effort to establish contact. But he grew somewhat livelier when he talked about his work. " 'Work in Progress'? A nocturnal state, lunar. That is what I want to convey: what goes on in a dream, during a dream. Not what is left over afterward, in the memory. Afterward, nothing is left." He shrugged his shoulders. "Afterward, nothing will be left."

Then, in answer to my questions: "The hallucinations in *Ulysses* are made up out of elements from the past, which the reader will recognize if he has read the book five, ten, or twenty times. Here is the unknown. There is no past, no future; everything flows in an eternal present. All the languages are present, for they have not yet been separated. It's a tower of Babel. Besides, in a dream, if someone speaks Norwegian to you, you are not surprised to understand it. The history of people is the history of language."

When I brought up Michelet's *Vico*: "I don't know whether Vico's theory is true; it doesn't matter. It's useful to me; that's what counts."

It was plain to see he had no wish to return to *Ulysses*; it no longer interested him. Nevertheless, when I spoke of the artist's nature of the hero, Leopold Bloom, he lent an ear: "You must be one of the first to have noticed it. In general readers have looked down on Bloom. Like the women who say to me about Marion Bloom: 'Yes, women are like that.' Then I stare at a corner of the ceiling."

His legs crossed high up; swinging one foot, he threw himself back with a mocking laugh and fixed his eyes on the ceiling. "Bloom Jewish? Yes, because only a foreigner would do. The Jews were foreigners at that time in Dublin. There was no hostility toward them, but contempt, yes, the contempt people always show for the unknown. Marion too, she is half-Jewish, on her mother's side."

What struck him most, he added, in the character of the Homeric Ulysses was how little he resembled the other heroes of the *Odyssey*. For them he was a foreigner. Subsequently, that view was confirmed or developed in the theories of Bérard, who makes a Semite of Ulysses.[3]

He referred in passing to the kind of artist's intuition that anticipates science, but not at all as a gift: rather as an accident, luck—an idea he toyed with often. Then he came back to "Work in Progress," to the problem of dreams, which occupy a third of our lives and about which we know almost nothing. He conjured up the two characters Shem and Shaun: the one who acts and the one who watches others act, and who between them make up the complete figure of the artist. That is, of man, since for him man is definable only under that aspect: *homo faber*, he who reflects and he who fashions. His thin countenance, with its bleak profile, lighted up as he recalled all the faces he had seen in his dreams, he who could hardly distinguish the people who surrounded him in life. This gesture, that detail of clothing, the reappearance of a character— all obey certain laws, and those laws were what concerned him. They were to form the structure of his work. His voice warmed, was almost confiding. Besides, I had reassured him by repeating that I was not a reporter, that I wasn't in the least interested in an interview, but rather in a study of his works.

Mrs. Joyce came in once or twice to answer the telephone. I took a look at the living room which was later to become familiar to me: sober and elegant furniture, a big reproduction of a Vermeer, photographs, fine editions of *Ulysses* in the glazed bookcase. In the embrasure of the window where twilight was deepening, Joyce sat in silence, half stretched out in his armchair, holding a cigarette between two fingers, his face glowing, lost in his dream, a dream without mirage or rest, his eyes dead to the light of day.

"We have forgotten the trumpet." He smiled, and in a high voice as fresh as his smile intoned Purcell's aria. "Bah! that is not the only song in the world!"

When I was on the point of leaving, he became almost cordial, noted carefully, magnifying glass in hand, my name and my address, pressed

3. See p. 194 and note.

me to send him my study as soon as it was finished, gave me the latest number of *transition* wherein fragments from "Work in Progress" appeared.

"Come back and see me. Or perhaps I shall come to see you in Lausanne."

At the time, I did not think he would keep his promise.

✣

What fascinated me, as well as so many others, about that work of Joyce—so closely knit for all of its universality, so isolated by its power— I have tried to account for elsewhere.[4] Without succeeding, no doubt, in setting forth the internal laws of its attraction, without perhaps seeking to do so: in a young man of little more than twenty, admiration will sometimes stifle a more profound voice.

Today he speaks to me across the memory of my first reading of *A Portrait*, of *Ulysses*, and of his "Anna Livia Plurabelle," the extraordinary music of which, emanating from numerous motifs, many of which escaped me, overwhelmed me like a sort of mystical chant, so sharp, so spare, so shimmering, such as I had perceived in no other poetry. "Omnis caro ad te veniet":[5] in the magical flow that bore along sounds and images, names and faces, ideas and form, it seemed to me that all flesh came to its soul, at a call filled with distress. A night so lucid, so awake and, as the psalmist says, "light in [its] pleasures," became a night of hope. Perhaps because to all doubts, all questions, all anxieties, all explanation, it responded with no more than the representation of a dream. That is, divested man of all his chimeras. Nothing could be more opposite to an intoxication of the spirit, or to a hallucination of the senses and of the soul than this patiently explored dream.

"I reconstruct the nocturnal life," Joyce was to tell me one day, "as the Demiurge goes about the business of creation, starting from a mental outline that never varies. The only difference is that I obey laws I have not chosen. While He? . . ."

He smiled then the evasive, suspended smile that I was to see on his lips often. But his remarks were seriously intended. He made the same demands upon his art for rigorous truth, of submission to the given, of *orthodoxy*, as T. S. Eliot has noted, that he imposed upon his view of life.[6] That is why art could, without danger to the artist, become his

4. In *Poètes de l'univers* (Paris: Editions Albert Skira, 1947). [Mercanton's note]

5. "All flesh will come unto thee" (from the Daily Mass for the Departed). This Latin phrase occurs in Stephen Dedalus' reflections early in *Ulysses* and he quotes it later on (*U* 48, 391).

6. Eliot emphasizes Joyce's orthodoxy in *After Strange Gods* (London: Faber and Faber, 1934), p. 41.

only morality; the man kept his integrity. This great virtuoso of language, endowed with all the tricks and subtleties of his craft, was sincere, sincere in the almost absolute sense he gave that very modest word to define a man. Sincere his total, terrible will to expression, pushed as far as the enormity of *Ulysses*. Yet, sincere too the always recognizable, intense, and reserved voice that traverses all of his work. There is a Joycean tone that is like no other: mysterious moral beauty in a universe of pure idea. More than he wished, the artist is present in his creation; it has the features of his face.

In *A Portrait of the Artist*, he evokes the fine figure of a young Irishman, Davin, the hero's friend at the University, a boy from the country with a country accent, a devotee of the Gaelic renaissance. The latter tells the author about a race in Galway County, where one night, at an isolated farm, he was made welcome by a young peasant girl who asked him to stay and offered him, in all simplicity, the hospitality of her bed. A very pure and bare account, filled with an ancient grandeur and bearing witness to an old race whose gestures have kept all the majesty of mankind. Like most of the characters in *A Portrait* and in *Ulysses*, this youth once existed. After becoming mayor of Limerick, Joyce told me, he was killed, and he died true to his dream during the revolution of 1916.[7]

Joyce's dream was not the same, but it had the same accent as that page of his work—so grave, so upright, so just. With the same sincerity he submitted himself to the moral truth of life, that which reigns over very simple things, the elementary, the quotidian, the eternal—sole subject of *Finnegans Wake* as it is of *Ulysses*: the paternal home, the native land, children's games, the mysteries of life and death, the universality of desire and the weakness of woman, the pleasure and the suffering of the flesh, the distress of the human soul, which imparts itself to all existence.

AN OLD CARDINAL'S WHIM

My first visit to Joyce in the Rue Edmond-Valentin, Paris, is dated October 21, 1935. I was not to see him again for more than two years. I had written him that my study of his work was finished, that Jean Cassou would publish it in the review *Europe*, which he edited in those days. Since publication was delayed, Joyce asked me to send him the manuscript of my essay. A few weeks later, a telephone call from his

7. Stephen recalls Davin's story in *A Portrait* (181–83). The episode with the peasant girl occurred after a hurling match, nor a race. George Clancy, on whom Davin was based, was shot by the Black and Tans in Limerick in 1922, as Joyce knew (*Letters* I, 357).

agent, Paul Léon, summoned me to the Hôtel de la Paix at Lausanne, where Joyce and his wife had just arrived. He was keeping his promise.

Mrs. Joyce was sitting in the hotel lobby with Paul Léon and a Russian friend. She greeted me warmly, as though I were an old acquaintance. Joyce was still in his room writing a letter. During these past months he had been working all night, until dawn, and she very much wanted him to take a rest, "I think he is going to be lazy for a few days."

He was to repeat the same thing to me several times, asking insistently how I found him, forgetting I had seen him only once up to that time.

He appeared at the top of the staircase, slightly bent, hesitant, feeling his way, his great hat set back on his forehead, his scarf floating, a cane hanging from his arm. He came down cautiously, walked with one hand stretched out toward a mirror that sent back his own image. When I stepped in front of him, I felt for a second the pressure of his gaze and knew he recognized me. A friendly smile lit up his tired face. Taking my arm at once to go out, he told me about a recent broadcast from Radio Dublin, February 2, his birthday, during which a professor from the University of Dublin spoke in praise of his life and of his work; this was followed by the reminiscences of a school friend and a reading of poems from *Chamber Music*. He was deeply moved. This homage was more precious to him than any he might receive from anywhere else in the world. "It is the first time in more than thirty years they have mentioned my name there."[8]

He attributed the event to an article in the *Osservatore Romano*, the author of which had praised him for having transcended naturalism by carrying it to its extreme limits, and for having, thus, with "Work in Progress," given a new impetus to an art that is essentially religious.[9] He cited that in a light, reserved tone of voice. Then, with a mocking laugh: "He must have written that under the influence of some skeptical old cardinal who wanted to amuse and mystify everybody a little. Even me."

The idea of a poker-faced old cardinal enchanted him: he would return to it several times: it suited his fancy and his sense of humor.

Then he talked about his arguments with his publisher, Faber and Faber, who insisted on knowing the real title of his book, which Joyce refused to divulge. "I have kept it to myself for sixteen years. I will supply it at the last minute, when I please. To be so exacting about a book like mine is absurd."

8. This radio broadcast was in 1938. The "school friend" was Constantine Curran (1883–1972), whose *James Joyce Remembered* (New York: Oxford University Press, 1968), pp. 90–91, includes an account of the preparations Joyce made for receiving and celebrating the program.

9. See p. 88 and note regarding this article.

He had hoped the book would be ready for July 4, his father's birthday. He hoped then to turn it over to the publisher in October, for the anniversary of his marriage. And he pointed out, as something obvious, how important those dates were to him.

At table he showed his gay side, was amused by stories, was interested by little, familiar things. "We will not talk philosophy, will we?" In fact, he didn't; he talked about cooking, wines, travel, and the voices of celebrated singers, which was one of his favorite subjects. He told of his first visit to London at the age of fourteen to hear Duse, and he couldn't understand the usher's English.[10] To his wife he spoke now English, now Italian, according to family custom. Then he sat quietly for a long while, looking tired, yet open and benevolent. He hardly touched the meal. But he drank the local white wine with pleasure and ordered more. At the last, he stopped his ears while one of the two Russians who had turned up that day told about a frightful storm he had once witnessed in the Ukraine.

"The thunder would torment me all night long," he said. "There are enough thunderbolts in my book."[11]

While we were saying goodnight, he handed me proofs he had just received and on which he planned to work with me the following day. "But don't put yourself out. We will have a look at that abracadabra together tomorrow."

Then, feeling his way with the cane, he slid into a taxi.

DARK NIGHT AND WORDPLAY

He wandered for a long time through the hotel lobby before deciding to pick out an armchair. That morning he wore a brown velvet smoking-jacket, and his hair, brushed back, seemed whiter. His hand, laden with three rings, one of which was silver and held a big, opaque, green stone, like a talisman, rested on his knee. He talked about the series of dreams he had had the night before, dreams troubled particularly by the Arab word "Kebir," a word his Russian guest had used yesterday as he was leaving the restaurant. He played with it, took it apart, searched for echoes of it, for assonances. Then, interrupting himself: "Did you see how fast that Russian was drinking? I thought I was a fast drinker, but he . . ."

10. In 1900, when Joyce was eighteen, he traveled to London, using money earned from his Ibsen article. There he saw Duse in *La Gioconda* and *La Città morta*.

11. There are ten thunder words spaced throughout the book, the first nine are 100 letters long, the tenth, 101.

He returned to the broadcast from Dublin and to a question posed by the Irish professor about "Work in Progress": a new path, a discovery in the domain of art, or sterile wordplay? He stopped at this term, cross-examined himself: "It is I who could draw up the best indictment against my work. Isn't it arbitrary to pretend to express the nocturnal life by means of conscious work, or through children's games?"

He thought of one friend who considered that after having reinvigorated the art of the novel, Joyce had lost his way; of another who accused him of having destroyed "what he was pleased to call my talent"; of those who assured him that no one would read his book; of his wife who had wished for such a long time that the work would be finished. And he himself felt weary. "A book like that has no ending. It could go on forever. But I must finish. It will be impossible after more than fifteen years of work on it to avoid repeating myself."

He asked which languages I spoke or could read. "Isn't it arbitrary of me to make use, as I do, of forty tongues I don't know in order to express the dream state? Isn't it contradictory to make two men speak Chinese and Japanese in a pub in Phoenix Park, Dublin? Nevertheless, that is a logical and objective method of expressing a deep conflict, an irreducible antagonism."

But when we read the page I had recopied, having interpolated additions he had noted in the margins, his mood changed. The terrible question about the value of his efforts, about the rigor of his method of invention, about the ultimate truth of his work, seemed to vanish before his eyes. Nothing stood but the magical text with its multiple and subtle significations, some of which he explained to me as we read along, modulating certain phrases as though they were to be sung.

"Every English reader will remember that song and will know what that means." Or else: "There is not an Irishman on earth who won't laugh at that allusion." Or again, at a passage full of Hebrew words, intended to introduce a solemn, religious accent, he psalmodized softly. "I should like to hear a rabbi read that sentence."

His face lighted up with enchantment at the idea, with an expression of secret and melancholy gaiety. The shadows crept back after the reading. He pushed away the page, shrugged his shoulders.

"Why should I regret my talent? I haven't any. I write with such difficulty, so slowly. Chance furnishes me what I need. I am like a man who stumbles along; my foot strikes something, I bend over, and it is exactly what I want."

He mimed what he said to make it sound funny. But he spoke again of the many operations on his eyes, to which he had submitted over those long years of work, and of the state of his daughter's health. He no longer knew what to do for her. "Let us talk about something else. Nothing we can say will help her."

Yet there were tears in his voice; he couldn't talk about anything else. In that night wherein his spirit struggled, that "bewildering of the nicht," [12] lay hidden the poignant reality of a face dearly loved. He gave me details about the mental disorder from which his daughter suffered, recounted a painful episode without pathos, in that sober and reserved manner he maintained even in moments of the most intimate sorrow. After a long silence, in a deep, low voice, beyond hope, his hand on a page of his manuscript: "Sometimes I tell myself that when I leave this dark night, she too will be cured."

FIRE AND WATER

Good Friday, 1938: Two days before, on arriving in Paris, I went round to see Joyce, in the Rue Edmond-Valentin. He was deep in his work, tired but in a rather gay mood. He could see the dawn, he said, even though his book was not yet finished. For the first time, he talked about political conditions and asked me what was the reaction to the *Anschluss* in Switzerland, so close to the scene. He invited me to come and see him again on Good Friday, in the afternoon when he expected to work with Stuart Gilbert.

That day I found him installed in his bedroom, half-reclining in a chaise longue, Stuart Gilbert seated near him at a little table. They were going over a passage that was "still not obscure enough," as Joyce said, and inserting Samoyed words into it. "Dog tongue," said Stuart Gilbert. "Bitch of a tongue," replied Joyce. His face looked very soft that day, with an almost feminine softness, a bit red under the gray hair. He joked, slid over the bed to reach the door with the suppleness and agility of a dancer, asked me to serve the tea, nibbled a piece of toast, and said with a frightened look on his face, "We are sinning against all the rules of the Church today." Then he told me that Good Friday and Holy Saturday were the two days of the year when he went to church, for the liturgies, which represented by their symbolic rituals the oldest mysteries of humanity.

"I am going to work until 5:00 in the morning. Then I will go to

12. "Wildering of the nicht" (*FW* 244.33).

Saint Francis-Xavier's for the office. If you want to join me, you will have to rise early."

Notebook in hand, he dictated a series of terms to Stuart Gilbert, who, apparently, had almost guessed the still secret title of the book—but accidentally, and without Joyce's batting an eyelash.

"I didn't even smile. I thanked the good fathers who trained me so well," Joyce said later.

"Some," he said, "have put the title in an envelope, but they will be disappointed." He seemed to take a pleasure, both childish and magical, in this game, prolonged for so many years, as though it were essential that his mysterious book be veiled with one mystery the more before making its appearance in the world. Then, handing me the prospectus from Faber and Faber: "The only thing that gives me the courage to finish is Blake's proverb: If the fool would persist in his folly he would become wise."

The following day, Holy Saturday, I reached Saint Francis-Xavier's at the moment of the blessing of the baptismal fonts. Joyce was standing among the group of men who had accompanied the priest into the side chapel. He was enveloped in a thick cape and carried a cane over his arm. His face was sad under his gray hair. He was following the ritual from very close. When the procession regained the altar, he walked slowly as far as one of the lateral aisles of the church and rested there, leaning against a grill. I joined him. He looked frightened, recognized me in the shadows by my voice, slipped his frail hand into mine. Then, as soon as the Mass began, he made a nervous, impatient gesture and murmured in English, "I have seen the rebirth of fire and of water.[13] Enough until next year. The rest is without interest."

And he walked rapidly away, his face set, while the Gloria burst out from the bell-towers.

Joyce promised me another visit at Lausanne toward the end of summer. My study of *Ulysses* appeared in *Europe*.[14] He ordered some twenty copies to send to friends, in Ireland especially. Since I had made

13. The Easter vigil on Holy Saturday begins with the blessing of the "new fire" that is to provide light for the office of Vespers during the year. Later in the service the water that is to be used for baptism during the year is blessed.

14. "James Joyce," *Europe*, 15 April 1938. [Mercanton's note]

known to him my wish to study in detail, as an example, one page from "Work in Progress," he proposed the admirable fragment just published by the art review *Verve*, "A Phoenix Park Nocturne," promising at the same time to help me in my enterprise.[15]

August 22, 1938: a telephone message from Paul Léon informed me that Joyce and his wife were in Lausanne and that they intended to stay for a while. Shortly after, Joyce himself called and asked me to come up and join them.

In his lustring jacket—bought in Lausanne five years ago and put on in honor of my native city—very short flannel trousers that made him look like an English schoolboy, white shoes, a straw hat turned yellow, pushed back above his ears, he was not so majestic as he had been last winter. He made me think of the photographs taken of him as a young man, and his slim figure, at once poised and gangling, recalled the figure of Stephen Dedalus as he appears in the first pages of *Ulysses*. He leaned on, or rather seemed to wrap himself around, his cane, a cane of black wood with great jutting knobs that he held up for my admiration. "It's a real Irish cane, made from a wood that grows only there." A symbol of his country that he always carried with him on the roads of the world. Whenever he seated himself, he slid it between his legs; then he remained motionless, like a bird hooked onto a branch, his eye on the lookout and yet distracted. One never knew what he was looking at or what he saw.

Mrs. Joyce was happy, smiling: at last a vacation, after so many terrible days and nights of work. And the work itself, that had dragged on for such a long time, was moving toward a conclusion.

"Watch him," she said, laughing, "I leave him in your care. He must not be left alone for a minute."

A moment later I grabbed his arm to keep him from throwing himself against an automobile.

LAZZARONE

At the end of the afternoon, we strolled along the lake, already tinged with autumnal hues. Boys were diving into the waves. Joyce watched them with horror. "Did you ever dive into the lake like that?" He shivered at the thought and continued slowly along the bank, calmer

15. *Finnegans Wake*, pp. 244-46, published in *Verve I*, No. 2 (March-June 1938), p. 26.

and calmer, happy, rested. "My wife has fallen in love with your countryside. Look at her!"

Mrs. Joyce, who was walking in front of us with Paul Léon, stopped to contemplate the bathers, the boats, the mountains veiled by the fine weather; flowers in the gardens moved her to cries of enthusiasm. Joyce spoke excitedly about an article that had just appeared in the *Irish Times* and had to do with the University of Dublin, "sanctified" by Cardinal Newman, Gerard Manley Hopkins, and himself.[16]

"Just ten years ago, no one would have dared to print my name in an Irish newspaper. And it is an item released by the university itself."

He paused at the word "sanctified," which surprised and amused him; he thought it applied to the other two, but hardly to himself. He expressed admiration for Newman, the greatest of English prose writers in his opinion—not in the *Apologia*, which he thought rather badly written, but in his sermons. Even in the *Apologia*, I said, there are passages that have the same rather tremulous and spare melancholy one finds in passages of *A Portrait of the Artist*. "I have read him a great deal," Joyce said, "and in the 'Oxen of the Sun' in *Ulysses*"—he always used the Homeric title to designate the episodes of his book—"where all the authors are parodied, Newman alone is rendered pure, in the grave beauty of his style. Besides, I needed that fulcrum to hold up the rest."

And he told me, laughing, that John Eglinton thought he had "put his finger on it" when he took the passage for Ruskin.[17] He defined Gerard Manley Hopkins as a sort of English Mallarmé, though he had never read that writing of Hopkins' which some critics had compared with "Work in Progress." But that was hardly a justification for the word "sanctified"! He returned to Newman, about whom he spoke with great respect: "The Church will surely decide to make a saint of him, if only for the numerous conversions that have followed in the wake of his own. At least a Blessed, if they don't succeed in finding a miracle." And his tone bore no trace of the bitterly ironical mockery that was habitual with him when he alluded to the Church.

He questioned me incessantly about the names of places we passed through, of the mountains on the horizon, of the wines whose vineyards

16. John Henry Newman founded University College, Dublin, in 1853, as the Catholic university. Hopkins was professor of classics there from 1884 until shortly before his death in 1889.

17. Eglinton (W. K. Magee) made this identification tentatively in "The Beginnings of Joyce," included in *Irish Literary Portraits* (London: Macmillan and Company, 1935), p. 148. The Newman passage is on p. 241 of *Ulysses*, the paragraph beginning, "There are sins. . . ." "*Habent aures et non audient*" ("They have ears and do not hear"), Joyce remarked to his son apropos Eglinton's misidentification of the passage (*Letters* III, 365).

lay before us, above the lake. He repeated the words, came back to them, compared them, toyed with their sounds, their assonances, his mind constantly active. His wife, he said, would like him to rest completely during these few days in Lausanne, but he hadn't the slightest inclination to do so. With a comically furtive look, and lowering his voice for fear Mrs. Joyce might hear us, he confided in me that, since Paul Léon was going back to Paris to look after his own affairs, he counted on me to help him. At the same time, he asked me to get him the books he needed, *Le Rime* of Petrarch, Spenser's "Epithalamion," so he could enrich the pages of "Anna Livia Plurabelle," as well as the last pages of the book, with extra allusions to rivers. "Oh, you will see; those last pages are simple, banal. The mystery is gone. It is daylight again."

From time to time he whistled, hummed, or launched a few clear notes. He told me about new difficulties with his editor, objectively moreover, knowing full well himself that his book was a monster. Yet, that monster was his only pleasure, and his face brightened as he explained the meanings of words in the passage he had proposed I should study: Nancy Hands, the name of a pub in Dublin with an echo of Anna Livia in it; Laohun, "the tiger" in Chinese, and Sheutseuyes, the lion, which is much less ferocious in Asia and is said to have its eyes almost always closed. Joyce, stumbling among the pebbles on the shore, closed his eyes.

The rest, apart from "Work in Progress"? Worries, which he did not try to escape, being the most human of men: his daughter ill, his daughter-in-law not much better, his son in trouble about his career, his Jewish friends (whom he was doing his utmost to help) having to flee from Austria. He had obtained a permit for Hermann Broch to enter England, and permits for others to enter Holland.[18] He didn't dwell on the Nazi nightmare, which bore, alas, not the least resemblance to that of "Work in Progress." He would say only, pityingly, "Those poor Jews!" He was especially indignant about the fact that Hebrew first names had been prohibited in Germany. "First names that all of us bear."

On the Quai de Lutry, after having looked at the house of Edmond Jaloux,[19] whom he expected to see again during his stay, he installed himself on the little wall at the harbor's edge, stretched out his legs, pulled

18. Joyce knew the Austrian novelist and critic Broch (1886–1951) through a long essay, "James Joyce und die Gegenwart," the latter had written. Other Jews he helped were a nephew of Edmund Brauchbar and a son of Charlotte Sauermann. Like Brauchbar, Mrs. Sauermann was a friend from the Zurich years during World War I.

19. The critic Jaloux (1878–1949), whom Joyce met shortly after arriving in Paris, was probably next in importance to Valery Larbaud and Louis Gillet as a champion of Joyce's work in France.

his straw hat down over his forehead, closed his eyes like the lion of Asia, and basked in the last sunlight "like a lazzarone." So he sat there quietly, peacefully, at the water's brink, at the edge of the world, pondered over "Work in Progress," spoke of Saint Patrick, whose intercession was indispensable if he was to complete his book, wherein he has the saint carry on a dialogue in Chinese and Japanese with a druid; for time and space cancel out one another in his dream. He made no move to leave until the cool evening air began to chill him: "I follow Saint Patrick," he said, pointing to Mrs. Joyce, who was motioning to us from the platform of a streetcar. "It is the title of an erudite book by my friend Gogarty, the Buck Mulligan of *Ulysses*.[20] It would interest you."

Then, with a sigh, "Without the help of my Irish saint, I think I could never have got to the end of it."

DEAR DIRTY LITTLE DUBLIN

Thursday, August 25: the market of Saint Louis spread out its dahlias and roses under Joyce's windows. "But," he said, "this homage means nothing to me, since it is not in honor of my Jesuit protector, Saint Louis of Gonzaga." He mentioned Saint Patrick again, who was very much in his thoughts those days, informed me that Saint Lawrence was the patron saint of Lausanne as well as of Dublin, was astonished that Saint Denis meant nothing to the French. Nevertheless, in "Nausicaa" he put an invocation to Saint Denis in the mouth of one of the young girls on the beach [*U* 350], just as he had once heard it, for he made up nothing.

That night he was in a good humor and full of plots and ruses to delay the dinner hour. "He is full of tricks," said Mrs. Joyce, while Jim, as she called him, kept coming and going through the lobby, looked for misplaced letters, asked for stamps at the hotel desk, showed me curious passages in Gogarty's book. He was wearing a thick overcoat with a great, light beige, felt hat, very much turned down at the brim, elegant in a somewhat fantastic way that suited him marvelously. On the strength of an alluring advertisement, he had eaten lunch in a vegetarian restaurant and considered himself so poorly served that he took back the tip and filled his pockets with bread to make up for what he had spent. He gave me a detailed account, hoping to waken my sympathy, which was rather somnolent. It was no advice of mine that brought him to such a pass.

At the table, as usual, he picked absent-mindedly at every course and

20. Oliver St. John Gogarty's *I Follow St. Patrick* was published in 1938. A copy of this book was found on Joyce's desk after his death (see p. 279 below).

hurried to light his long cigar while he drank with great relish one of the local white wines. He spoke of Linnaeus, whom he compared to a second Adam giving names to everything. He showed me a sonnet by Petrarch, composed from the names of rivers, Non, Tesin, Po, Varo, which he meant to use. But he had no great admiration for the illustrious poet, who, he said, lacked intellect: an aesthete. There is far more beauty, he declared, in the poems of Michelangelo, despite their faulty forms. Then I realized that, though fascinated by its beautiful music, this pure artist of language required much more than that of poetry. He extolled the marvelous music of Spenser's "Epithalamion," [sic— "Prothalamion"] repeating softly the refrain, of which he never tired: "Sweet Thames, run softly, till I end my song." River music bathed his imagination, occupied as it was with that one object.

When I questioned him about Ireland, Mrs. Joyce protested against his eulogy: "A wretched country, dirty and dreary, where they eat cabbages, potatoes, and bacon all year round, where the women spend their days in church and the men in pubs." Joyce smiled: "Dublin is the seventh city of Christendom, and the second city of the Empire. It is also third in Europe for the number and quality of its brothels. But," he added, "for me it will always be the first city of the world." He described the Liffey, the color of tea without milk. He had a horror of bathing in it when he was in secondary school. "Wretched, muddy little stream," said Mrs. Joyce, "worthy of dear dirty little Dublin . . ."

"And I have put the most magnificent rivers of the world at its service," Joyce went on, "the Nile, the Amazon, and Socrates' Ilissus." Then, pointing to his wife, "How can you expect my compatriots to understand me?" But his tone was one of tender amusement. All the same, it was to them, his compatriots, that his thought turned most often.

THE CREATION OF THE WORLD

Joyce gave me some notes to complete my analysis of the fragment published in *Verve*, "A Phoenix Park Nocturne." And he asked me to recopy a number of pages in his manuscript for him, typewritten pages in which it was necessary to incorporate numerous additions. He was bringing the dialogue between Patrick (or Padraic in Celtic) and the druid to a close.[21]

"A Chinese puzzle," he said, putting both hands to his forehead. "That isn't surprising, since it's in Chinese. But you will see. Colors are showing through. Day is near."

21. The dialogue between Saint Patrick and Archdruid Berkeley occurs on pages 611–12 of *Finnegans Wake*. As Mercanton indicates further on, this passage was first drafted fifteen years earlier, that is, in 1923.

He guided me through his own work. Among the pages I was to recopy, one had been written that same morning; a page composed fifteen years before was supposed to follow it. He was still working on the second part of the book, though the third was already at the printer's.

As we read, he showed me the constant factors which, according to him, were intended to guide the reader. Thus, a Japanese word would always be followed by a Chinese word—an image for the antagonism that is the permanent background to the history of all men. Likewise, the "Sandhyas! Sandhyas! Sandhyas!"—a Sanscrit word meaning "the twilight of dawn"—that opens the last part of the book is a restatement of the Sanctus of the Mass, which reverberates throughout the whole work.

Using whatever examples came to hand, he later explained to me his method of working according to the precise laws of phonetics, the laws that rule over all languages and preside over their evolution, since to do that was, in his opinion, to obey the laws of history. It followed that a rigorous submission to the phenomena of language should guarantee the truth of his knowledge and of his representation of events. "The only difference," he declared, "is that, in my imitation of the dream-state, I effect in a few minutes what it has sometimes taken centuries to bring about."

So too, in his minute and exhaustive researches, he forced himself to avoid all arbitrary choices.

"Nevertheless," he concluded on a note of skepticism, "my whole book is shaky. There is only one thing that keeps it on its feet: the author's obstinacy." And, making an allusion to what doctors call an "ideal case": "This book has to do with the ideal suffering caused by an ideal insomnia. A sentence in the text describes it in those terms.[22] When you say it in advance yourself, you silence the critics."

When I perused a page of the manuscript of "Work in Progress," I did not imagine the unfolding of history but rather a foreshortened image of the creation of the world. Certain passages remained intact, just as they were written at the beginning, like particles instantaneously crystalized and fixed in their eternal forms. Other areas were in a state of continual flux and fusion, and it seemed that nothing would work to stabilize them; one sentence had recently been split up by a few new words, which in their turn had engendered a new sentence; or still others had just been interpolated according to the promptings of a growing understanding and complexity. Thus two words, consecutive at

22. "That ideal reader suffering from an ideal insomnia" (*FW* 120.13–14).

first, might eventually be separated by a whole page, or even more, as though certain active passages called out endlessly for new develop-ments, as though some areas of the text were volcanic by nature, while others were constituted at the very beginning with a static equilibrium: an image of the creation such as it might have been effected in the course of millennia, such as it is prolonged under our very eyes by various upheavals.

Just as I was about to go, taking the copy with me, Joyce called me back. "No, don't take all of it. Leave part with me, until tomorrow. I may have some revisions to make."

Deprived of his work, he was bored. In vain he would ask himself over and over if the pleasure he gained from it was proportionate to his fatigue; that fatigue alone could divert and rest him. On the way back from our walks, he would suddenly quicken his pace, slip quickly into his room before I could say goodbye to him, then emerge and detain me in a corner of the lobby so we could go over a few pages together. And his thin face, often tired or worried, would liven up and look rested.

FINN AGAIN

Those days Joyce was relaxed and communicative. Leisure and exercise had done him a lot of good. At the table, or in the course of our walks, he would tell me stories about his Dublin youth, about the years he spent in Trieste, and he spoke also about his Parisian friends. He expressed his affection for Valery Larbaud, for Philippe Soupault, for Edmond Jaloux, whom he had just seen again in Lausanne, and whose sensitive and refined epicureanism impressed him without making him envious. Joyce liked the more exuberant forms of pleasure, and Jaloux, he said, was so little *Marseillais*. He also told me about amusing evenings he had spent with Fargue, whose verve dazzled him. "But I don't see much of him. You have to stay up all night if you want to meet him. He is a night-prowler: his whole life is but the prelude to the aftermidnight of a Fargue."[23]

He smiled benevolently; distantly, too. He felt no real attachment except to the small and intimate circle of those who accompanied him in his labors. He dreaded and avoided all social and literary affairs. Mrs. Joyce was more direct. "Ah, all those people, they bored us to death!"

He didn't know much about contemporary French literature, admired Gide, *The Pastoral Symphony* or *Lafcadio's Adventures*, but

23. In the original, "*prélude à l'après-minuit d'un Fargue*," a pun on Debussy's *Prélude à l'après-midi d'un faune*. Léon-Paul Fargue was famous for his late hours.

not what he had written about Russia, which Joyce considered slight and sentimental. As for *Corydon*—he looked toward the sky, with the look he would assume when he meant to mock the universe: "Will you explain to me how an intelligent man could have written that!"

He loved Valéry's verse, but reproached him for reading it badly, as if, he said, Valéry couldn't hear it himself. And he told me about a party at Sylvia Beach's where Valéry "massacred" "The Serpent," which Joyce had asked him to read. "I couldn't recognize the poem. Yet it's the one I like best."

In his accounts of Ireland, he maintained his objective point of view. The English were very violent in their suppression of the uprisings, but the Irish were no less so in their rebellion, and no less so to one another during the civil war. He narrated this or that episode, old or recent, as though it were a scene from "Work in Progress," without the humor or the symbolism. He took no side. All the same, when Mrs. Joyce spoke of the cantankerous character of the Irish, he said, "My wife detests her race and her nation. I am loyal."

Curled up in an armchair, almost lying down, he appeared slim and slight, and his delicately jointed limbs lent him an adolescent grace. He had been reflecting, and, when the conversation languished, he turned eagerly to "Work in Progress." After a little while, we went for a short walk in the Parc de Mon-Repos, where he mistook the fracas made by a tree being cut down for a thunder-clap. Frightened, he made a half turn, dragging me along in his pirouette, and it would have been useless for me point out that the sky was blue, the atmosphere calm. We hurried to take shelter in the hotel lobby.

"*Ulysses*... I made it out of next to nothing. 'Work in Progress'... I am making it out of nothing. But there are thunderbolts in it." He shivered, looked at the ceiling as though to make sure the lightning couldn't reach us there, and expatiated on the character of Finn MacCool, the legendary Irish hero, the universal protagonist of his book. He had just read a work by a German scholar, Heinrich Zimmer, who saw in that Celtic hero a Scandinavian, thus confirming the liberty taken by Joyce (one he considered audacious) of ascribing to him precisely such an origin. "Besides," he concluded, "it matters little to me whether Finn is Scandinavian or not. There is no historical document to certify he really existed. For me it is enough that he lives in my dreams." With a playfully mysterious air, he announced that he would use Zimmer's beautiful phrase, "a great shadow," to designate Finn MacCool. "I do not often come across an expression as fine as that.[24] In Shaun's sermon, I use

24. Joyce described his hero as a "great black shadow" (*FW* 626.25). Zimmer (1851–1910) was a German expert in Celtic studies. Joyce compared Zimmer's scholarly confirmation of the Scandinavian origin he gave to Finn MacCool with

a term I heard an Englishman in Zurich use to designate the wine-waitress. He called her 'the virgin.' Why not?" He cited other examples of his use of common locutions. In one part [*FW* 569.05–11], he has introduced a series of saints' names "that you will have a hard time finding in the calendar." They are the names of streets in Dublin, for Dubliners have a habit of naming their churches after the streets in which they stand. " 'She plays the organ in Gardiner Street.' Naturally, you think of a hand-organ. Or else, 'She has gone to confession in Wicklow Street.' One imagines her kneeling in the middle of the road."

He got up and, gazing at the sky, pretended to turn a handle. Then, bending his knees, he joined his hands, and with an air of contrition whispered, ear advanced to catch the priest's questions. "So, I have taken you behind the scenes." Then, suddenly grave: "Good old Coleridge would call that fancy, not imagination."

I don't know what critic had recently cited in evidence against him those pages of the *Biographia literaria* wherein Coleridge establishes his crucial distinction. In a state of doubt and worry, Joyce referred to it several times. Because of it, all of his efforts were accompanied by a feeling of malaise. That day, with a slight shrug of the shoulders, he threw off his misgivings. "Let us turn to Finn again."

Faithful to the condition he had imposed upon himself, neither his face nor his voice betrayed anything. I didn't suspect that that phrase was nearly the title of the book.

IRISH TIMES

The tenseness of the political situation hung heavily over the summer's end; we were a few weeks away from the Munich Pact, and Europe was sliding toward the abyss. Joyce seemed to pay no attention. When I spoke to him about it, he limited himself to a few remarks about his general antipathy to the Germans and their language, the confusion of which he considered insufferable. He cited a letter from his oculist Vogt as an example of an absurd and barbarous syntax. Notwithstanding, he had a German friend, Ernst Robert Curtius, whom he had met during a stay at Wiesbaden, to whom he asked me to send my essay on his work.[25] But that day he asked me right off to get him a copy of the *Irish Times* so he could read the latest news.

Very doubtful that I should find that paper in Lausanne, where there

Victor Bérard's scholarly confirmation of the Semetic theme in *Ulysses* (*Letters* I, 401).

25. Curtius was an eminent German scholar and critic. He wrote extensively on Joyce, his major work being *James Joyce und sein Ulysses* (1929).

could not have been many Irish readers, I started to suggest other newspapers. But Joyce would not hear of them. In any case, I couldn't leave him in the dark about events that threatened us. Finally, after a good deal of searching, I managed to uncover a copy of the *Irish Times*. Rather proud of myself, I took it to him at once. His face lit up.

"You will see how indispensable that paper is to me." And half unfolding it in one supple gesture, he slid it under his coat, against his back. "Nothing will keep you warmer than that. Provided it's a good newspaper." Then he reassured me, "It doesn't hurt the paper. When you are ready to read it, you will find that no harm has been done."

He seemed to be in no hurry to do so himself. But he promised to give it back to me so that I could look up the addresses of laundries, which he needed for "Work in Progress."

Nevertheless he did read it. He passed on to me a recent number that contained a long article on the Abbey Theatre Festival, wherein his name was cited only once, but which gave a glimpse into Irish literary life at the turn of the century, with Yeats, O'Casey, Synge, and A.E. He asked me to send it to Gorman, who was planning to republish his biography of Joyce after bringing it up to date. In his objective way, careful not to encroach upon their freedom of judgment or of taste, he helped those who were concerned with him and his work.[26]

THE LITTLE NEGRO'S DANCE

Joyce was tired, nervous that morning. The night before he and his wife had been to a bar where a little Negro was dancing, "like Jim," said Mrs. Joyce, "when he drinks on holidays." He had gone to bed late, got up in the night to work, dreaming about the young Negro dancer whose performance had charmed him. He asked for the manuscript I had brought him, looked anxiously to see what the weather was, smoked another cigarette before going out, gave up the idea of going out, and set a time to meet me in the afternoon.

The sky was gray, cloudy, twilight already at 4:00 in spite of the season. In his light raincoat, half on, face a little red under his big, light, felt hat, umbrella in hand, he went on in his undulating walk, his eyes vague but sometimes curiously attentive to details. We climbed the Avenue de Chailly. He spoke little, preoccupied as he was again by Coleridge's observations about fancy and imagination, also by his

26. This description fits Joyce's procedure regarding those concerned with his work, but he maintained careful control of the Gorman biography, intending it in part to correct the damage he believed had been done by Michael Lennon's scurrilous attack on him and his family (see *JJ* 735–38).

recollection of a talk Jaloux had given on Blake, in which he compared the imagery of that visionary poet not with the images of a dream but rather with those born on the threshold of a dream, at the approach of night or of waking. The last pages of "Work in Progress" take place in the same region. Hence Joyce's effort toward a more perceptible coherence among his images, toward a clearer, more translucent language, one that would allow his reader to guess the light of day.

At Chailly, he flung himself into an almost deserted café, slumped down on the wall-seat, a melancholy expression on his face, ordered herb tea, and listened attentively to a high, thin voice singing on the radio: "Take Love When You Can Get It." He smiled, sighed, wondered if he too couldn't make his living as the little Negro at the bar made his, or by singing on the radio. "I could have made a fortune with my voice. And what have I done?"

He was delighted that he still had the voice of a young man, even of a child, for he could not remember if it had ever changed. Again he sighed. "That is because I didn't develop. If I had matured, I should not have had the folly to write 'Work in Progress.' "[27]

This was the way to get back to his book and the problems it posed. He was concerned about one cardinal objection that might be raised against him: that of having translated dream imagery, which is proper to sight, into auditory impressions. "But," he said, "otherwise I should have had to go at a frightfully slow pace . . ." And he cited descriptions by Flaubert and by Walter Scott which, poorly supported by the rhythm of the text, resulted finally in making it impossible for the reader to see anything at all. "That kind of transposition—from sight to sound—I insist, is the very essence of art, which is concerned solely with the effect it wishes to obtain. On the other hand, one hears more in a dream than one might think, often more than one recalls." I assured him that my most beautiful dreams were musical. He was surprised to hear that. His love of music, especially of song, had not given him that gift. Although his sight was so poor, he had extraordinarily precise and complete visions in his dreams. But the idea that transposition was one of the essential means of art seemed to convince him. "After all, the interior monologue in *Ulysses* is just that. I laugh at it today, now that I have had all the good of it. Let the bridge blow up, provided I have got my troops across." He laughed, but he was anxious. "Nonetheless, that book was a terrible risk. A transparent leaf separates it from madness."

Then: "It is absurd to say I have no skill. I have too much. But,

27. Joyce spoke of his prolonged juvenility to others, also. In a letter to Valery Larbaud, for example, he described himself as "inflicted with the incurable levity of youth" (*Letters* I, 284).

fortunately, no intellect. Otherwise I should have gone mad a long time ago."

He listened to me closely when I pointed out that Coleridge's distinction, so important for aesthetic considerations, had little bearing on poetic emotion. Illustrations were not hard to find in "Work in Progress": pages filled with such a learned fancy that they rouse the imagination infinitely.

Finally, after a few anecdotes about Parisian literary life, one about a meeting with Proust at a party a long time ago—the latter spoke of nothing but duchesses, "while I was far more interested in their maids"— he said again, apparently consoled, "After all, that book is nothing but a game, or a dance, like the one the little Negro did at the bar. That's what I was made for, a little Negro dance."

He laughed his juvenile laugh and stretched out along the wall-seat. It was a restful, pleasant moment, with a background of music to lull one's reverie, night falling, a few passersby lingering on the square, memories approaching silently. Then Joyce roused himself. "I am tired. I wonder if I shall do your native city the honor of finishing my book here."

Yet, never weary, he made me repeat names on the way back, inquired about my study, asked me to come the next day and read a few pages of Linnaeus to him, proposed an excursion to Fribourg, where he had never been and where, he said, there was an Irish secondary school. Children playing in the street fired a water pistol behind us and made him jump; he thought it was a thunderbolt.

ANCIENT AND MODERN LITERATURE

We strolled through Montreux and Joyce shared his wife's enthusiasm for the fine stores, the big hotels, the promenade beside the lake, the swans to which the old maiden ladies threw bread. He wondered if the swan's song was a fact or a legend, he recalled Fénelon, recited one of Horace's odes:

. . . abi
quo blandae juvenum te revocant preces.
   tempestivius in domum
Pauli purpureis ales oloribus
   comissabere Maximi,
si torrere jecur quaeris idoneum.[28]

28. The poem is "Ad venerem," *Odes*, book 4, no. 1. The passage Joyce quoted is as follows in English: "Go where fond prayers invite of younger men; / Fly hence on thy bright swans upstayed, / And for young Paulus Maximus enquire; / There richer feast is for thee laid; / If thou dost seek a fitting heart to fire" (*The Odes and Epodes of Horace*, trans. John Marshall [New York: G. P. Putnam's Sons, 1907], p. 193).

He contemplated one, motionless on the water, rocked by the waves, and admired its indifference. "It's all the same to him whether there are three or thirty-three persons in the trinity."

He delighted in Horace, whom he preferred to Vergil because of his minute perfections, his diverse meters, his rarest music. He cited other poems, among them "O fons Bandusiae," of which he had made a rather good translation at sixteen.[29] But, he said, the Jesuits who had educated him had no sense of literature, and he did not think they had changed. They held up Louis Veuillot as a great writer and scorned Voltaire, who has nevertheless given them their due.[30] "As I have. But nothing will satisfy them. They are old coquettes."

However, he spoke of the Jesuits with a certain admiration: a distinguished order, efficacious, remarkable educators, far more likeable than the Dominicans, whom he considered narrow, obtuse, tangled up in their own theology, truly the barking dogs of the Lord. Then he expatiated again on Coleridge—so troubled, unstable, and penetrating—whose "Kubla Khan" might have been the most beautiful poem in the English language if he had been able to finish it. On Spenser too, bard of the Thames, who lived for a time in Dublin. Still preoccupied with rivers, he asked me if I knew "a little book for boys" by Mark Twain, the title of which had escaped him—something that happened rarely—and the hero of which is the Mississippi.[31] "What do you like best in English poetry?" he then asked. Without hesitating, I told him "Keats's 'To Autumn' or the 'Ode on Melancholy.'"

He seemed surprised. "At your age, naturally, you are romantic."

I protested, as was befitting my age. I like Keats for his mystery, for that riddle of the soul, for the same reason I like "Work in Progress":

For shade to shade will come too drowsily
And drown the wakeful anguish of the soul.

I remembered a phrase Joyce had commented on the day before in a voice full of nostalgia: "Forth from his pierced part came the woman of his dreams, blood thicker than water, last trade overseas" [*FW* 130.31–33].

29. Joyce's translation of this poem is given in Gorman, *James Joyce*, p. 51.
30. Louis François Veuillot (1813–83) was a highly reactionary Catholic propagandist and writer of religious romances. In *A Portrait* (156) Stephen recalls a priest saying, ". . . There are many eminent French critics who consider that even Victor Hugo . . . had not so pure a French style as Louis Veuillot." And in *Ulysses* (44) he thinks, "*Un coche ensablé*, Louis Veuillot called Gautier's prose."
31. In 1937 Joyce sent a copy of *Huckleberry Finn* to David Fleischman, his daughter-in-law's son by a previous marriage, and asked him to make an abstract and to mark the key passages in it for use in *Finnegans Wake* (*Letters* III, 401–2).

Anna Livia, the river, the woman born of man's rib, and, through the proverb, the blood mixed with water that spurted from Christ's side at the blow of the spear, "fluxit unda cum sanguine."[32] Last voyage and last return over the sea where every life comes to an end. There is the art of fancy for you, one that stirs the imagination in its most secret and intimate recesses.

"I am very fond of that sentence," said Joyce.

Next, while Mrs. Joyce as usual slipped into a tearoom to have a light lunch, there was the long, tardy, and wearisome search for a restaurant that Joyce would consent to enter. Once there, he would choose a table, nibble something hastily without appetite, as though acquitting himself of a duty, and give many a sigh, at which he begged me to take no offense, since it was a habit that dated from childhood. After the meal he felt better, lingered, drolly mimed the way Italians eat; their virtuosity, offhandedness, and lack of manners enchanted him. Again he related his memories of Trieste, spoke Italian brilliantly, praised that beautiful language for its wealth of profanity: evidence of a devout, civilized, and ancient people.

He felt so well disposed that, raincoat over his shoulder, his great hat in the wind, he proposed to his wife that they go on foot as far as Vevey. He was glad to jump onto a streetcar halfway there, yet very proud to have covered, as he said, four kilometers. At Vevey, he asked me to take him to the little river, the Veveyse. Bent over, his hat pulled down over his eyes, he contemplated it for a long time, in that strange, restless reverie of his, without happiness, anxious on the contrary, and as though secretly agitated. Later, sitting at the tea-table, he was mute, his head inclined, body lopsided, mouth open, eyes staring vaguely and filled with a mocking sadness, directed not at men, nor even things, but at the order of things. It was what he called—giving the word its original meaning—"the idiotic character of the universe." "I am nothing but an Irish clown," he said, "a great joker at the universe."

FOLLOW ME UP TO CARLOW

Joyce telephoned me early the next morning to tell me about the frightful night he had spent in an armchair in the hotel lobby, because of a newly-established workshop under his window that did night work.

32. Source of quote unidentified. See John 19.34, ". . . et continuo exivit sanguis et aqua" (". . . and immediately there came out blood and water"). See also below, p. 246 and note.

He begged me to go up as quickly as I could and reassure his wife. "It would be just like her to pack her bags this afternoon," he told me, in the same tone he would have used to announce that Hitler was on the point of invading Switzerland.

I found both of them on the hotel steps, facing the mountains veiled in mist, worn out and pitiful, looking like victims of a shipwreck. After another account of their dramatic night, they allowed themselves to be cheered up a bit and the idea of leaving was dropped. They sent out an inquiry in hopes of finding a quieter hotel where they could stay. When the various choices were presented, they found one in particular that pleased them—on the basis that it was exactly in the center of things and a good place from which to observe the movement of the city.

Nevertheless, Joyce's tone of voice on the telephone had betrayed a real anxiety: the noise in the street reminded him of war, and he held himself ready to re-enter France, to go his daughter, at the slightest warning.

A ray of light in the autumn sky: from an Irish friend he had just received a copy of an old song that he had been trying to find for thirty-five years, "Follow Me up to Carlow," a war song with a martial rhythm.[33] He asked me to run through it once, so I could play it for him later. He related some of the adventurous passages in the life of one lord of Carlow, father or grandfather of his friend, who flung a bar of soap at a French admiral's head at Dieppe and who, from his bed in his Irish castle, would fire on birds that flew past his window. "Ah, if I were stronger and if I could see better, I would have done the same thing last night."

At the end of the afternoon, after our walk, we went up to the drawing room of the hotel. Joyce made me go over the song several times, sat down beside me at the piano, played a harmony in the bass, took up the refrain:

> Curse and swear, Lord Kildare!
> Feagh will do what Feagh will dare;
> Now, Fitzwilliam, have a care—
> Fallen is your star, low!
> Up with halbert, out with sword,
> On we go; for by the Lord!
> Feagh MacHugh has given the word:
> Follow me up to Carlow!

He looked to see what key it was in, would have liked to transpose it to a higher key, tried to play the song again from memory. Then,

33. The friend probably was Constantine Curran, whom Joyce often appealed to for help in locating Irish songs. "Follow Me up to Carlow" is referred to in *Finnegans Wake*, 379.10, and numerous other places throughout the book.

carried away by his own delight in it, and especially by the emotion of the song, he sat at the piano alone, and in a voice melodious and vibrant, though a little ragged, accompanying himself with a few chords, he sang a sweet, nostalgic, old Gaelic lament. Moved as he was, his face took on an expression that was both juvenile and sorrowful; his eyes closed, his fine hands with their heavy rings floated over the keys. He went on to a beautiful song by Grieg, set to Ibsen's works, something out of his youth, interrupted himself, rose impatiently, buttoned the raincoat he had not taken off, grabbed his umbrella. Then, since I asked him for something more and since Mrs. Joyce, seated at the end of the room, urged him to go on, he sat down at the piano again, hesitated an instant, and in a restrained, pathetic, and extraordinarily simple voice, intoned a melody he had composed himself for a poem in *Chamber Music*:

> Bid adieu, adieu, adieu,
> Bid adieu to girlish days.
> Happy love is come to woo
> Thee and woo thy girlish ways—
> The zone that doth become thee fair,
> The snood upon thy yellow hair . . .

Twilight invaded the drawing room. His fingers sliding over the keys, playing with the soft pedal, Joyce turned toward the rainy windowpane his almost emaciated face, imprinted with a mysterious pity, that which lingers in the secret places of the heart when it has listened to its own desire. "He felt the sufferings of women, the weaknesses of their bodies and souls . . ." [P 245]. In that melody, a bit sentimental, ragged in the high notes, smothered like a sob in the depths, the soul sang on alone above the desolation of memories, above the suffering of bodies and souls. Brusquely, as if he were chasing away a bad dream: "*Andiamo!*"

He straightened out his coat, put on his hat with its wide brim that extended like wings on either side, and went down the staircase so quickly we had difficulty following him.

Standing on the platform of the streetcar that was bringing us back from the lake to the center of Lausanne, Joyce slipped dexterously into a woolen vest that he had been carrying rolled up under his arm. Then he asked me point-blank if I was afraid of dogs. I confessed that I was—the more readily since I had seen him on the avenue one day give wide berth (as I had, too) to a big dog that stood in our way.

"They are cowardly beasts," he said. "They can sense when you are afraid of them, and that makes them bold." The truth is that dogs, in that respect, are like most men; and in Joyce's remark I did not find his usual objectivity. He invited me, nevertheless, to accompany him to a dog show being held on the esplanade of Montbenon, assuring me that we ran no risk: the dogs would be tied up. Agony in our faces, and describing wide curves around the stalls from which our enemies looked out at us with no ill will, we walked the garden's length at nightfall; *entre chien et loup*,[34] said Joyce. He circulated in the crowd, his battered hat down over his forehead, and slipped behind me while I read the names on the placards; then, keeping a respectful distance, he would lean forward to catch sight of the brutes, while I in turn would slip behind him. At closing time we took up positions on a bench from which we could watch the dogs pass by, going down the walk on their way home, somewhat excited by the ceremony and pulling their masters by the leashes.

Joyce was cheered up by our visit and noted how small a part animals, including the dog and the horse, play in his book—particularly the horse, glory of Ireland and first concern of every true Irishman.

"In the days of the hackneys, an Irishman who wanted to hire a carriage at the depot for a ten-minute ride would always begin by choosing the horse."

He was surprised that the English, who claim to love dogs, use the names of dogs for some of their worst insults. He loved animals apart from man, for themselves, he said, which is the contrary of the Englishman's sentimental love and also of Kipling's. I pointed out to him that he talked about animals just as he spoke of the English, with the same respect and the same distant curiosity.

"It's true," he said, "but, all the same, I understand animals better."

He cited as proof the marvelous page of "Work in Progress" that we were studying together at the time, a nocturne filled with the calls, the sighs, the uproar, and the prayers of animals going to sleep.

Then, one by one, we summoned them up: the dog on the beach at Sandymount that frightened Stephen; the Citizen's terrible dog in the episode of Circe; Garryowen, a big dog with red fur that, he said, belonged to one of his aunts and was the terror of his childhood; finally, the only one that is close to me, Athos, old Virag's dog, whom he entrusts to his son when he is dying: "Be good to Athos" [*U* 90].

When I reminded him of that sentence, Joyce smiled his melancholy smile—compassionate and mocking—that I liked so much. Then he told me how he had once been attacked by a big, red mastiff, one like Garryowen, in Holland.

34. Literally, "between dog and wolf." It means, however, "the evening twilight." [Translator's note]

"A descendant perhaps," he said, "who had read that page of
Ulysses and recognized me."

He shuddered to think of it.

ALL THIS OUR FUNNAMINAL WORLD

Sunday: the day when people are bored. Joyce asked me to pick them
up rather early, so we could go and have lunch together at the
lake. It was a radiant day, softened by the coming of autumn. I
joined Mrs. Joyce at Mass, and then we went to the hotel together. On the
way, she told me in her charming manner about their life in Paris, so
tiring when Joyce, more out of nervousness than for the pleasure of it,
insisted on going out to dine in a restaurant every night.

"I have put up with him for thirty-four years," she said, on a note of
mocking tenderness that corresponded exactly to his. "I deserve some
credit, don't you think?"

It was a credit she had no intention of foregoing, to judge from the so-
licitous questions she put to me about Jim's frame of mind, his rest, the
good he was doing himself with this stay in Switzerland. Next, having
despaired, it seemed, of ever learning how to conjugate French verbs, she
sighed: "We used to be [*nous étaient*] so happy before all our troubles;
so gay." She was thinking of her daughter's illness that cast such a heavy
shadow over their life, perhaps about her son's marriage, too. It had
taken him far from them.

Joyce committed the *Irish Times* to my care and charged me to read
passages of it to him in the afternoon. It would serve him as a second vest
when the night dew began to fall. He also handed me a letter, postmarked
Vienna and addressed to Mr. James Joyce, *Verfasser von Ulysse*,
Paris, which had reached him by luck. It was a naïve letter that listed
The Dubliners, A Portrait, Ulysses in a column. The writer professed
his admiration of Joyce and his pleasure in reading him—an inner refuge
im abendländischem Chaos. Joyce listened closely, obviously touched.
"But," he said, "I never answer letters, on principle." Still, that one
struck him as "sincere."

During our trip to the lake, he retold, with the same pleasure he
always took in it, an episode from "Work in Progress": a new one that
had to be read between the lines. It was obscene and philosophic at the
same time, as life is, especially in a dream. The obscene side, of course,
required a less subtle wit than the philosophical. When I objected to
the obscurity of the meaning, he answered: "It is night. It is dark. You can
hardly see. You sense rather."

To prove his point, he gave me the example of a dream he had had the
night before: a half-naked woman dancing, from whose breasts long

flames arose. The spectacle did not frighten anyone, for it was obviously a trick. "A premonitory dream, if you like." (We had been talking about the Sakharovs, who were visiting Lausanne at the time.) [35] "But what is the philosophical import of it?" he asked.

Mrs. Joyce too had had a dream, a charming one: thousands of little yellow birds fluttering around her and caressing her face with their wings. "See," said Joyce, satisfied, "you can't explain that one either."

During lunch on a narrow terrace overhanging the lake, he showed me a photograph in the *Irish Times* of O'Connell's statue in Dublin. In it, by chance and probably without his being aware, a tramp leaned with his back against the base in the same pose as the tribune, his arms crossed, his head bent forward, heavy with energy and eloquence. Joyce was delighted with it. "Altogether the meaning of 'Work in Progress': history repeats itself comically; this is our funnaminal world" [*FW* 244.13].

What saves the book, he continued, is precisely its "comicity," which is also its "cosmicity," like that in the newspaper photo. When the owner of the pub draws a beer that carries the trade name O'Connell, he is at the same time making the gestures of pouring out the wine of the Mass, for O'Connell liberated the Catholics who had truly been outcasts. He is also an embodiment of the hero of the book, H.C.E., Here Comes Everyone, or Haveth Childers Everywhere, since O'Connell peopled Ireland with his numerous children; which deed, noted Joyce, brought him none of the terrible censure incurred by Parnell for his one intimacy.

The conversation turned inevitably to Finn MacCool, whom Ossian-Macpherson had made his Fingal, and who, toward the end of the century, gave his name to all the movements for the liberation of Ireland: the Fenians, Sinn Fein, and so on. Joyce was afraid the Irish might bear him a grudge for appropriating their national hero. At least the Greeks could not offer any objections to his Ulysses.

It seems that already some of those in the Auden-Spender circle, "big boy scouts without any brains," had accused him of writing hermetic works "for the rich." As though he didn't write for everyone.

"You are not Irish," he said, "and the meaning of some passages will perhaps escape you. But you are Catholic, so you will recognize this and that allusion. You don't play cricket; this word may mean nothing to you. But you are a musician, so you will feel at ease in this passage. When my Irish friends come to visit me in Paris, it is not the philosophical subtleties of the book that amuse them, but my recollection of O'Connell's top hat."

35. Apparently the well-known dance team of Alexandre and Clothilde Sakharov who toured Europe frequently in the twenties and thirties.

Grave, dreamy, exact, he went on handing out parts. I murmured in answer: "Haveth Childers Everywhere" [FW 535.34].

He laughed gaily. "Not only living creatures. My paternity extends to the vegetables, the minerals, and even to algebraic signs. You will see."

When the meal was coming to an end and we were sitting back to enjoy the beautiful, golden light that turned the lake to sparkles, he opened the *Irish Times*. In it he had caught sight of a curious article on the stork.

"Jim is a tyrant," sighed Mrs. Joyce.

She urged me to protest. But he made a conciliatory gesture: "Don't read all of it to me. A resumé will do."

This meant that I would have to read the article at least twice, both times with the closest attention, so that my resumé would not leave out anything essential. Since the chances were that I would omit some detail and forget some of the terms, I would probably end up by reading the article a third time, aloud, repeating all the important passages.

"You will meet those storks again," he told me, as a kind of reward.

"Nothing is created, nothing is lost."

I was worried about encountering them again too soon, through some unexpected question that would find me at a loss. For Joyce was always surprised when anyone did not know by heart everything he had heard or read, even unfamiliar names and telephone numbers. He frowned when I pulled out a notebook.

After lunch, while Mrs. Joyce was resting, he proposed a stroll along the shore at Lutry. He went on at his nimble, rambling gait, extremely elegant in bearing, head thrown back and his fine face meditative under the brim of his big hat. He took an interest in the group of soccer players who were practicing in a meadow, sent back their ball with a lively kick, asked if they played association football and what were the French names for the positions. For once he was satisfied with my confused answers. Then, not even looking for a likely spot, he let himself glide slackly down onto the pebbles of the beach, two steps away from the gently lapping water. There he stretched out to his full length, put his hat over his face, and declared he would not budge for anything less than a thunderbolt—which nothing in that pure sky might lead us to expect. So we remained, recumbent on the small stones, lulled by the easy rhythm of the lake.

The first snow shone on the mountain ridges, the contours of which were blurred by a diffuse light. A small boat was advancing slowly along the shoreline. Their game finished, two or three soccer players had come to take a quick bath and were splashing in the waves a few yards from us, their bodies tanned by a fine summer. By mid-afternoon, the autumnal lake was already shaded with twilight hues. Joyce stood up, ran his tongue over his lips, as if he were searching for a taste of salt, and looked upon the bathers with his usual dread. I thought of Stephen Dedalus on the beach at Sandymount, measuring time and space, hostile and alone in a universe his obstinate will had not yet dominated. But years had gone by. Joyce contemplated with a friendly and mocking smile this sad and comic world, all the appearances of which he had absorbed by the power of his artistry: this is our funnaminal world.

He mentioned the humblest of his books, the tiny folder of poetry, *Pomes Penyeach*, a copy of which he had given me the day before. After *Ulysses*, he said, he wanted to persuade authors to write small books, so he had collected thirteen poems in that notebook: thirteen to the dozen, the way they sell fruit in the market, or milk in Ireland, always adding a small, extra measure, a tilly (no connection with the general), the title of the first poem. *Pomes Penyeach*, like the cry of a woman who sells her wares in the street, a poem or a pome, another old English word (derived from *pomme*), an "m" dropped, as the "n" in penny, to make it smaller. This little punning game amused him, and it is much like the games in "Work in Progress," if a bit simpler.

> Frail the white rose and frail are
> Her hands that gave
> Whose soul is sere and paler
> Than time's wan wave.
>
> Rosefrail and fair—yet frailest
> A wonder wild
> In gentle eyes thou veilest
> My blueveined child.[36]

A distant echo of his days in Trieste: a flower given to his little daughter. All the mockery had left his face, caressed by the night wind. There was nothing in it now but a mysterious pity for human life that flowers, is enchanted with itself, and declines in tears: in it the same sparse tenderness that fills the song from *Chamber Music* he had sung the other day:

> Bid adieu, adieu, adieu,
> Bid adieu to girlish days . . .

MADONNA BLOOM

We had walked the length and width, and from top to the bottom, of the little city of Fribourg. Joyce was interested neither in places nor in things, but, as usual, in their names. He inspected with some curiosity

36. "A Flower Given to My Daughter" from *Pomes Penyeach*. The lines from *Chamber Music* quoted further on are from poem XI.

the old lime tree of Morat and the last suspension bridge, though he had no desire to venture onto it. In the cathedral of Saint Nicolas, he sent forth a few resounding notes against the arches. In his opinion, there was nothing like a church to bring out a voice. Then, while Mrs. Joyce was admiring the stained-glass windows, he called to her *andiamo*, as though the atmosphere had suddenly become oppressive. From the lower part of town, we took a taxi to the University, which he had counted on seeing, and in which he was disappointed. Weary, turning his back on the world, he flung himself into the slow local that would take the rest of the afternoon to get us back to Lausanne. He stretched out full length on a seat, and asked me, timetable in hand, to tell him, as we came to them, the names of all the stations at which the train stopped.

Once at the hotel, he was like the victim of a shipwreck who has won his way back to solid ground. There he found pages of manuscript inviting him to more work, clippings of articles about Dublin, letters, a resumé in English of Zimmer's book on Finn MacCool, "a great shadow," and the pocket notebook in which he made entries while I read aloud. Revived by that activity which was his whole life, he showed me how he worked—seeking out the richest, the most intense concentration of multiple significations in order to bring together in a sentence, or a phrase, in a single word sometimes, all of the space and duration of great and of slight events; yet he was always careful to observe the phonetic laws and the semantic phenomena of the languages that he combined, since that was his only guarantee of truth. He had seemed inattentive, withdrawn, and aimless during the course of the day, but now he was alert and intense, his eyes burrowing into the big magnifying glass he used to reread his notes. Suddenly:

"I regret that we didn't wait two more days before we made our trip to Fribourg. Our visit would have coincided with the feast day of Madonna Bloom, September 8. There might have been a procession."

He was amused at my surprise. "Didn't you know that she was born on the same day as the Virgin Mary? You haven't read *Ulysses* very well."

As a matter of fact, that detail is carefully hidden. Bloom thinks about the present he would like to make his wife on her birthday and calculates how much time he has left to get it: July, August, September [*U* 168]. Elsewhere, Marion declares that her lover did the right thing in bringing her eight roses [sic—poppies], since that is the number of the day on which she was born [*U* 747]. A hidden detail, yet discoverable without great effort: the puzzles in "Work in Progress" require more discernment, since they are involved with the meaning of the whole book. Joyce called *Ulysses* "a little prelude to 'Work in Progress.' "

On Christmas Eve he brought up Madonna Bloom again, and Mrs. Joyce cried out: "He is always blasphemous!"

Joyce smiled sweetly. "The comparison," he said, "is perhaps sacreligious, but perfectly orthodox: Madonna Bloom is the mother of all the vices, just as the Virgin is the mother of all the virtues. Together they make the world go round."

He was joking; yet the sense of what he said was seriously intended. Although a connoisseur of blasphemies, he remained always within the most orthodox frame of reference, his mind curiously closed to every form of heresy, in the moral as in the religious order. He was, though not severe, rigorously precise in his moral judgments; moreover, a sect was to him inconceivable. He spoke of Protestantism in general as an arbitrary and bizarre choice in the Christian faith, made at the expense of coherence. He noted it often: he had no taste for the absurd.

Speaking next about Russian churches, where he loved to hear the deep, bass voices of the officiants, he said he could not understand my fervent admiration for the Oriental ritual; too slow, he said, lacking in articulation, in concentration, and in expressive structure. I thought then how Occidental the nature of his genius was, how Roman in its need of fixed forms, clearly defined, of a sharp and imperious design. In *Finnegans Wake*, the misty Celtic lore of Ireland is made to undergo a vigorous reworking by the intellect that orders, determines, and shapes. A poetry of clear images elaborated at great length, a song made up of controlled sounds and accents: there was no place for dreaminess in his methodical representation of the dream. At that time, I knew neither the plan of it, the architecture of which is so skillfully conceived, nor the title; but I could see plainly that a dream explored to that extent is a vigil, or a *wake*.

PORTRAIT OF THE ARTIST AS AN OLD MAN

One evening, while we were waiting for him in the hotel lobby, Mrs. Joyce described Joyce to me as he was when she met him for the first time in Dublin, many years before: his expression strange and severe, an overcoat that hung down to his feet, shoes down at the heel, a big, white sombrero. She drew his portrait with tender irony, astonished that a long life together, every instant shared (for they were seldom apart), had not effaced that fleeting image. "He is old," she said gently, "but he has not changed much. In so many ways, he is a little boy, as you have noticed."

One sensed that, at the end of so many years, she still relied in full confidence on that "little boy" and asked for nothing better. In practical matters, in the quotidian details of life as well as in the important decisions, it was he who took charge, who settled things. A great artist wrapped up in his work, he was, nevertheless, the most attentive of men when it came to the care of his family, to the material and moral problems of life. He was the sincerest of men, as he might have put it, and the most faithful.

He was that, too, in his literary life. He had just received a letter from a young poet in Belfast, who wrote him that, at the recent festival of the Abbey Theatre, there was a movement afoot among the young to "dethrone" Yeats in his, Joyce's, favor. He was upset when he told me about it: "You can well imagine that I will keep my distance. Yeats is a poet of the first order, and the immortality of his books is assured, which is hardly the case with mine. And today he is an old man, seventy-five."

He calmed down as he recalled his early meetings with Yeats. But he begged me to answer some of the letters myself, and in very formal terms: he had no intention of entering into any dispute, not by so much as a word.

I brought him *The Centaur* by Maurice de Guérin—which he did not know—for its evocation of rivers: "Melampus! My old age misses the rivers. . . ." He found the poem fine enough, but rather grotesque in its imaginings. (Besides, he said, the Centaur was born in a grotto.) "I would like to ask the poet if his centaur has twice the number of organs in his chest." The language bothered him too: "He multiplied his course," for example. Or: "Often I bathed in the bed of the rivers." How can you bathe in a bed?

He came back to the poem several times, as though to disburden himself of some uneasiness. However, the bold innovations of a Guérin looked timid beside his own. He did not think of them as such, for they were not the same kind.

He recited a page from Quinet, which satisfied him completely, a description on which he embroidered for several pages in "Work in Progress": the whole atmosphere of the Mediterranean is in it, he said, its ports, its flowers, the azure sky, the sun on the sea. In that passage he felt at home.[37]

He spoke once more about Newman's sermons and about his prose that he esteemed so highly. "But he bores me when he tries to make his reader believe the impossible. Saint Thomas is more entertaining: he proves far too much to convince anyone."

37. This passage, by the French historian Edgar Quinet, is doubtless the one quoted with some minor changes in *Finnegans Wake* (281.4–13), where it is given in the original. Other versions of it appear also (14.35–15.11, 236.19–32, and 354.22–36). Ellmann reprints the passage along with a translation and cites another instance of Joyce quoting it (*JJ* 676).

Religious matters always provoked him to mockery and excited a note of defiance in his laugh that it did not carry otherwise. His denial always had a personal accent. Thus it was that he spoke disdainfully about writers who portray priests without having known them, without having been subjected to them: Anatole France, for example, had had no experience of them. Renan, on the contrary, knew them, and his portraits are true.[38] When I mentioned the figure of Father Conmee in *A Portrait* and in *Ulysses*, he softened: "He was a humanist and a human priest of whom I was very fond. I tried hard to make him likable. The story of the glasses in *A Portrait*, for instance: it is the kind of thing that marks the soul of a child forever. It makes him believe there is justice in the world—a false assumption, but it gives him confidence. It couldn't have happened in an English school, with their abominable system of fags, that makes a boy the slave of older boys."

He repeated again: "But the Jesuits were not satisfied even with that. They are tarts. They want you to flatter them, to fondle them. A heartless order that bears the name of Jesus by antiphrasis. But, I spent sixteen years of my life with them, and I owe them a great deal."

That night, we dined together for the last time. I was to leave Lausanne the next day; Joyce and his wife would soon return to Paris. Their sojourn in Lausanne had done them a great deal of good, despite family worries, the threat of war, the noisy nights in the hotel. They talked about their home, the gaiety that reigned there once. "We sang, we danced all day long," said Mrs. Joyce, while he shook his head indulgently. "My wife exaggerates. It happened that I worked sometimes, too." In his turn, he described the charm and the grace of his daughter Lucia and mimed the way in which she played with some oranges on her saint's day, in a sort of mysterious dance, before she fell sick. The image still overwhelmed him. "In those days," he said, "I was never melancholy."

His face was suffused with an extreme gentleness and his voice was warm with humanity, forgiveness, and righteousness at the recollection of those happy days. No bitterness, no malice. It was no longer the arrogant, solitary, young and rebellious artist of *A Portrait* who sat across from me, his hand heavy with rings and turning a glass of white wine to make it sparkle under the lamplight. It was a man despoiled, very serious in his love of the few good things in life, very humble in the exercise of his art, and soon to be acquitted of his crushing task.

It seemed to me sometimes that the dawn that shines on the last pages

38. Joyce read Ernst Renan's *Souvenirs* and *Life of Jesus* while in Trieste. He read Anatole France during the same period.

of his book rose also that he might see better. This man, once suspicious and reserved, had learned the meaning of trustful affection.

I telephoned him the following day to say goodbye. He told me of his concern over his Jewish friends, whom he was trying to save from an Austria ravaged by the Nazi fury. One, who had reached Lausanne, had joined us the night before at the end of our dinner party. "You saw the state he was in. I am very much afraid for him."

I listened to that delicate voice coming over the phone, so serious in its expression of human sympathy, so perfectly sincere.

FOR AULD LANG SYNE

Europe had reached its lowest ebb in the autumn of 1938. Joyce watched nervously as the threat of war loomed over the forthcoming publication of his book. Indifferent to the event itself, as some have claimed? Rather, like the rest of us, he was thinking of what he had of his own to save. Though back in Paris by mid-September, he sent me a few words on the twenty-first from Dieppe, where, he explained, his wife wanted to relax for a few days more.

> We have closed our apartment, for we have been through some very anxious days. Even here, we do not know from one moment to the next when we might have to return to Paris, then leave with our daughter for La Baule, where the whole hospital will be transferred if necessary [*Letters* III, 431].

During the days of Munich, they did, in fact, move to Nantes until the emergency was over. Toward mid-October I went to see him again in Paris.

I found him deeply disturbed, incapable, he said, of getting back to work, which in itself was very significant to him. "During the World War, I was able to write *Ulysses*. It was altogether different then. We were not in the war. Today you are plunged into it even before it starts."

While we were having tea in a tearoom on the Rue de Cambon, and after Mrs. Joyce had told me about their grim stay in Nantes, he made a detailed analysis of events leading up to the crisis, without any illusions about its fatal outcome, dwelling particularly on the English maneuverings, and insisting on all the curious aspects of Chamberlain's foreign policy. He was surprised too at the incredible defeatism of "nationalist" France.

"In a year France will be Fascist. But there is reason to believe that she will not have to call in fascism from the outside; it will come to her from within."

I have retained no clear image of that hurried day in the moral twilight of the times. I was getting ready to leave for Florence, as a lecturer in French at the University, and I was not looking forward to my departure with any pleasure: the kind of government in Italy offered small occasion for joy. But Joyce encouraged me: he hardly knew Florence, but he had an old friend there [Francini Bruni], one from his Trieste days, and he asked me to go to see him. He loved Italian ways, their style of living, their language, the opera, and, contrary to most Frenchmen, he foresaw little danger from that quarter. "I doubt that there are many Fascists in Italy. The Italians are capable of a great deal of foolishness, but of little harm."

Some glimpses from those last days in Paris: Joyce at home, at the table with his grandson Stephen, a little boy of ten for whom he showed the tenderest regard. Another day, waiting for his daughter's nurse, anguish in his face. Walks in the late afternoon beside the Invalides or on the Champ de Mars, always worried about the fate of his Jewish friends in Central Europe. Finally, a long evening at Fouquet's, then at Francis's on the Place de l'Alma, with a few friends. Joyce was relaxed that night, and Mrs. Joyce so happy to be in Paris again after the gloomy days in Nantes—"We were [*nous étaient*] so bored." She was still delighted by the memory of their stay in Switzerland.

Music alone could cheer those anxious hearts. Mrs. Jolas sang a few Negro spirituals, Joyce, old Irish songs in that warm voice of his, capable of such gentle modulations. Seated around the table, we took up the refrain in a chorus, or else accompanied his light singing with our humming, "Loch Lomond" or "Drink to Me Only with Thine Eyes," which he sang in a restrained, an almost interior, voice, his face illuminated by the grace of the moment.

It was the last of a happiness that would soon be exhausted. Night was coming on, a dreamless night: a vacuum surrounding the publication of his book amid the tumult of war, more misfortune for his family, flight, exile, worry, and, too late, asylum in Switzerland, to which he would return only to die.

FINNEGANS WAKE

Holy Thursday, 1939. I had just come back from Florence, and I brought Joyce news of his friend from Trieste, Francini Branci [sic], whom he had not seen for many years. The latter had given me a cordial welcome. A smiling courteous Italian, a man of great finesse, he spoke, though with some reserve, about the long evenings he had spent with Joyce. His Catholic faith having evidently grown fervent with age, he looked sadly upon the evolution of his friend's thought: Joyce's work had become alien to him. "I used to hope," he said gently, "that as a result of experience, of having a family, of misfortune, he would become reconciled with the Church. That is not what has happened."

Joyce had commissioned me to ask him for a pamphlet he had written in their journeyman days: *James Joyce spogliato in piazza*, a satirical portrait of the Joyce of the Trieste days, useful for Gorman's biography. Francini surrendered it—his last copy, I believe—reluctantly, as a personal favor. He wrote a dedication in my name and begged me not to let it fall into the hands of the original. Perhaps he had scruples about having written those rather uninhibited pages, or perhaps he feared that Joyce might expose them to publicity. I did not hold to my promise: Joyce kept the brochure to reread at his leisure, passed it on to Gorman[39] and other events befell us.

I found Joyce in a half-empty apartment, on the eve of moving, Mrs. Joyce ill, himself very agitated, worried about his daughter-in-law's health, his son's difficulties, his grandson's future, and especially the fate of his daughter in case of war and evacuation. Later, pointing to two young priests, he said bitterly: "There are two fellows without a care in the world. They know nothing about such troubles."

He was uneasy too about delays in the publication of his book, about its coincidence with the war, which he couldn't see from any other angle at the time.

"Let us leave the Czechs in peace and occupy ourselves with *Finnegans Wake*." The title was revealed: "that," he said, "of an Irish music-hall ballad, very low comedy."

He did not want to give out the title in advance for fear of irritating the American-Irish. But the editor's delay allowed them time to mount a campaign against him, and Joyce was losing all the benefit of his caution.

He showed me the first copy of his work—bound in boards with a huge title. "Take it," he said, "if you want to look at it tonight. You will bring it back tomorrow."

His first smile of the day. A single night is not much time to read the 600 pages of *Finnegans Wake*; but it was long enough, he thought, to give me an idea of the book's composition, of the balance among its parts. At least I would have time to read the last pages, those on which he

39. This booklet appeared in the catalogue of the James Joyce Exposition, October-November 1949, La Hune. . . . The catalogue mentions the dedication to me; the copy must be the one I passed on to Joyce. [Mercanton's note]

Joyce should have had another, since Stanislaus apparently sent him one (*Letters* III, 59 and 102). See note 4, p. 6, regarding the references in Gorman's biography to the lecture.

was working last summer at Lausanne. I was still ignorant of the most beautiful among them, Anna Livia's last song, her last adventure.

First we took a walk along the Seine in the direction of the steel bridge of Passy. He quizzed me about Florence, life in Italy, his friend Francini, and was attentive to my answers, exacting about detail, and as curious and precise as ever. We took a taxi up to the Rue des Vignes, where he had rented an apartment, and he showed me the house, the view, the neighborhood. We continued our walk in a shower that had darkened the day's end. Joyce seemed to have gone into a trance. Pulling in one direction while I pulled him in the other, he narrowly missed throwing himself against every car that passed us. Finally he hailed a taxi to take us out to the Bois de Boulogne.

> So klammert sich der Schiffer endlich noch
> Am Felsen fest, an dem er scheitern sollte.[40]

Slouching on the seat, his cane between his legs, he laughed over the appropriateness of those lines. But the rain discouraged him from continuing his walk, and he found a still firmer rock in a little bar, deserted at that hour.

Suddenly, in a low voice, he began to recite from the concluding pages of the book. Its tonality is tragic, he said, yet it has its comical side. His face, austere, grown thin from the worries of these last months, shone with delight, and his voice vibrated on certain words.

"And it's old and old it's sad and old it's sad and weary I go back to you, my cold father, my cold mad father, my cold mad feary father, till the near sight of the mere size of him, the moyles and moyles of it, moananoaning, makes me seasilt saltsick and I rush, my only, into your arms" [*FW* 627.36–628.4]. Then he went on: "A hundred cares, a tithe of troubles, and is there one who understands me? One in a thousand of years of the nights? All me life I have been lived among them but now they are becoming lothed to me" [*FW* 627.14–16].

With angelic tenderness, so moving in that rebellious angel, and on a tone of confidence and wonder, Joyce evoked the last voyage of his heroine. She wears her most beautiful gown, all leafy; but, behold, little by little the fiancée's moving dress is coming apart: one leaf and then another flees toward the sea on the fugitive waters; one leaf glides on a wave that goes to mingle its foam with eternal waves. "A leaf, just a leaf, and then leaves" [*FW* 619.22–23]. Here she murmurs again: "I only hope whole the heavens sees us. For I feel I could near to faint away. Into the deeps. Annamores leep. . ." [*FW* 625:36–626.2].

Joyce murmurs with her, softly and more softly, his delicate hand

40. "So the shipwrecked mariner clings at last / To the rock, whereon his vessel struck." (These are the concluding lines of Goethe's drama *Torquato Tasso*.)

caressing the fleeting robe of the waters. Across his leaning face passes the irremediable shadow of farewell.

QUIA FRIGUS ERAT

Holy Friday: I came to pick up Joyce at his place, an apartment almost emptied of its furniture. Mrs. Joyce was still sick. When I told him about the Fascist invasion of Albania, he only shrugged his shoulders. A sad event, and ridiculous. He imitated Mussolini: *Volete una vita comoda?* And the crowd answers enthusiastically, *No!* When you know the Italians!

He referred again to some of his Jewish friends, including Zimmer, and his translator Goyert, for whom he continued his efforts.[41] But he had to move cautiously. In the first war, he told me, the English consul at Zurich had accused him of being a spy in the service of Germany, because he refused to write propaganda for England. "That is not my job." Brauchbar, the friend we had seen at Lausanne, had gone mad under the pressure of events. Joyce told me then that he was worried about him. "I foresaw it," he said. Then out of his repugnance for any abuse of language, he corrected himself immediately: "I was afraid it might happen." No rhetoric in what he said, no side taken; in fact, no hatred. Only a deep sense of humanity that made him seek to help others to the extent of his feeble means. I thought of Leopold Bloom: "No hate. Hate. Love. Those are words. Soon I am old."[42]

He returned an article I had written on *Finnegans Wake* for the *Nouvelle Revue Française*, and which Jean Paulhan had asked me to cut. "Do as he says. What is left is the important part. It is important too that it appear."[43]

He was very much concerned about the articles that were to be published in support of his book. Louis Gillet had promised him a few pages for the *Revue des Deux Mondes*, and he was delighted at the prospect of seeing his work presented to the readers of that venerable review. "Of course, it may not be the sort of thing they are used to reading."

We walked the terrace of the Invalides in the vernal gloom of a Parisian Good Friday. Birds in the foliage were silent. The sad waters

41. Heinrich Zimmer was the son of the Celtic expert. He had helped Joyce by sending him an extract of his father's work bearing on the Scandinavian origin of Finn MacCool. Georg Goyert (b. 1884) was the first German translator of *Ulysses*.

42. "He bore no hate. Hate. Love. Those are names. Rudy. Soon I am old" (*U* 285).

43. *"Finnegans Wake," Nouvelle Revue Française*, May 1, 1939. [Mercanton's note]

of the Seine drifted slowly onward. The cupola of Saint Louis was
blotted out. In the mist that enveloped us, Joyce went on at his undulating gait, questioning me again about Italy. He enjoyed my account
of a visit to Saint Clement's, in Rome, where Irish Dominicans officiate,
and my report of a conversation with a very talkative young monk who
had turned pale at the mention of Joyce's name.

"He was from Cork? So was my father. People from Cork are particularly loquacious." He smiled indulgently. "After what he has been
told about me, he must take me for the devil himself. He is not alone
among my compatriots."

Then he was silent. Prompted by the night wind, both of us buttoned
up our overcoats, and, to comfort us in the cold weather, I imagined the
Oriental warmth of the first Good Friday.

"Warm? Oh no," he said, "they lighted a fire in the courtyard of the
praetorium, *quia frigus erat*."[44]

Stretching out his hands, he bent over an invisible fire. And I repeated
that consecrated phrase: "Forth from his pierced part came the woman
of his dreams, blood thicker than water. . . ." "That's true," he said,
"today . . ." And, as in *A Portrait of the Artist*, he began to sing softly
in a deep slow voice:

Quae vulnerata lanceae
Mucrone diro, criminum,
Ut nos lavaret sordibus,
Manavit unda et sanguine . . .[45]

I listened to that wonderful chant, the most distressing, the most
consoling, in the whole liturgy, for it celebrates the grief of God himself.
It was the last time I was to hear Joyce sing.

There was nothing more to say. Ah! I knew full well that his great
book, with which I was still barely acquainted, was a work of reconciliation, but not in the sense of a return to the Church, still less in that
of a kind of spiritual substitution, a function that might conceivably
be assigned to the poetry. One cannot replace the Christian faith, and
there is no mask for the face of Christ. Besides, nothing could be more
alien to Joyce's spirit than the idea that his work should carry a
message, nothing further from his mind than the comfortable assumption
that the one thing can replace the other, or that there is no such thing

44. "Because it was cold" (John 18.18). This passage also appears in the Good
Friday service.
45. This passage is verse 2 of the Catholic hymn "Vexilla Regis," which is often
sung during the Easter period. It has been translated as follows: "[Christ's side]
rent open with a cruel spear / Of blood and water poured a stream / To wash us
from defilement clear." In *Portrait* (210), Lynch sings another verse of this hymn.

as total sacrifice. A Catholic cannot be mistaken in these matters. If *Finnegans Wake* is a book of reconciliation, it is so because a great poet—without regret, without a return, without ending his revolt—by means of his art alone, and with tireless love, has represented in it the daily and mysterious goodness of life.

There was nothing more to say. Under the mute trees, in the melancholy din of the Angelus at the day's end, Joyce, swinging his cane, was content in his turn to listen while I repeated softly a beautiful passage from Newman: "They do not take away the winter of my desolation, or make the buds unfold and the leaves grow within me, and my moral being rejoice . . ." Image of a world where neither reason nor ideas nor most faiths held out any promise for the future.

WILLIAM TELL

The next night, Easter eve, in the island formed by the still livable drawing room at the center of an otherwise empty apartment, a flask of Chianti between us (with no hard feelings, said Joyce, about the attack on Albania), we had the last tête-à-tête before our long separation. We talked about everything—music especially—and about nothing. After a few sarcastic remarks about English ministers who go fishing in the fine weather of a wartime spring, Joyce sighed; he was thinking of the operas I would have the opportunity to see in Florence. In that respect, at least, Italy remained dear to his heart.

On my return to Florence, and in response to my sending him a program of the *Maggio Fiorentino*, I received this card, dated May 7, 1939, 34 Rue des Vignes, his last domicile in Paris. I cite it as an example of his charming manner, naïve and spontaneous, when he spoke of things he loved:

> If you go to hear *William Tell* on the 9, the 11, or the 14, or better
> (as I would do) every night, I should like very much to have your opin-
> ion of it, especially of the Bulgarian tenor. I hope he can sing it,
> Arnold's role, without any cuts. I have heard a lot about him. During
> the third act, go out and smoke your pipe, but come back for the fourth.
> Above all, don't miss the terzeto of the second. I have heard the other
> singers on the radio. They are all good, but it is a devil of a part for
> the tenor. Send me also, s.v.p., the reviews in the papers. I surely wish
> I could be there. Perhaps it will be broadcast. . . .

Who was that Bulgarian tenor? His name has slipped my mind. Joyce had spoken to me about him in Paris, and especially about the role of Arnold, which was dear to his heart.[46] Often at the end of an evening's visit, at the moment of least constraint, we had exchanged our opinions about music, though our tastes were not alike. I had the narrow tastes of my age and liked only the "classical" operas, Mozart, *Boris Goudonov*, *Pelléas*, but chiefly Wagner, whom Joyce could scarcely tolerate, or at the most *Die Meistersinger* and, in *Tristan*, "the chambermaid"; that is to say, Brangwyn's call in the night. How should he have taken pleasure in a form of musical drama that assigns meaning and accent far more often to the orchestra than to the voices? And how should he have borne with a system of myths that was arbitrary in his opinion and opposite to the true and daily myths of the dream and of history, which he was exploring so patiently and so methodically?

But there was more to it than that. It was not only the brilliance and the virtuosity of the singing that attracted him to Rossini, Verdi, and to other Italians (he was the first to speak enthusiastically to me about Monteverdi) whose music one heard rarely in those days. It was the truthfulness and the purity of his own soul. He recognized in them the "sincerity" which is the secret behind all of the secrets of his own art, and which he valued so highly. That brilliant, subtle, sonorous, and cordial music, so generous to the voice, so speakable, so singable, corresponded to his own humanity, to his own good faith. Religious at times, but never metaphysical, it did not upset the order of the world and did not seek to interpret the mystery of life. In it Joyce felt free: such is the condition of pleasure. When, at the end of 1940, he succeeded after many efforts in entering Switzerland, he immediately announced to me that he had reserved a ticket in Zurich for a performance of *La Forza del Destino*. His joy dominated his misfortune and suffering; it was perhaps the last in his life.

BRIEF ENCOUNTER

I was to see him once more in the course of that agonizing year. Previously I had been corresponding with Paul Léon about the article Jean Paulhan had accepted for the *NRF*, and about the persons to whom Joyce wished me to send the study we had written together, which had just appeared in Lausanne: among them his brother Stanislaus Joyce in Trieste, Ernst Robert Curtius, T. S. Eliot, Louis Gillet,

46. The tenor Joyce spoke about, especially in connection with the role of Arnold, would have been John Sullivan. The transcription of this letter in *Letters* (III, 441) gives "Sullivan" rather than "Bulgarian," but the context within the letter makes "Sullivan" an unlikely reading.

Viscount Carlow, Professor Lévy-Bruhl, Padraic Colum. At the moment when his chief work was making its appearance, he was eager to provide letters of credit for it. No one could have been more desirous of being understood, in his intentions and in his effort, than that difficult author, and, though incapable of any concession where his art was concerned, his attitude toward serious readers was very humble. In short, he was emerging from seventeen years of solitude.

In August 1939 I returned by car from a stay in the mountains of Valais. Stopping at Montreux for lunch, I chose a table on the terrace of the restaurant where Joyce and I had lingered so long on a fine, late-summer day the year before. Suddenly I saw his tall form standing there before me, and I heard Mrs. Joyce cry out in delighted surprise. They had been drawn there by the same memory. Joyce, trying to reach me in Lausanne, had decided that I had left again for Florence. They were spending a few days in Montreux with their daughter-in-law —a final pause before the commotion of war set in.

Enchanted, suspended pause—the memory of it is poignant. A bright sun shone over the lake, and the tourist-filled town simmered with happy animation. A group of young Americans rode past on bicycles in peaceful innocence, dressed for tennis or the beach. Joyce told amusing anecdotes about the publication of *Finnegans Wake*, about the stupefaction of some readers. But he was waiting impatiently for the critics' reactions. When I alluded to the possibility of another project in a still distant future, he answered: "For the moment I am taking a rest. Now it is time for the others to do a bit of work."

The next day, or the day after, in Lausanne, his mood had changed. He confided to me his new worries: the apartment in the Rue des Vignes did not suit them at all; his daughter-in-law's health was more and more disturbed; and, always, there was the question of his daughter's fate in case of war. Then, once more: "Let them leave Poland in peace and occupy themselves with *Finnegans Wake*."

MESSAGES

That advice, as the reader well knows, was not followed. Joyce's last vacation was soon cut short. A card from La Baule dated September 8—the feast day of Madonna Bloom—brought me news of him.

> We are here now and have been waiting a good twelve days for my daughter's arrival. I can't imagine what is keeping that psychiatrist, why he doesn't move his hospital from Paris to La Baule as he said he would, and we are beside ourselves with worry. For three weeks now, everyone who can, or who isn't kept there by business, has been leaving Paris, but he stays on with his patients. He thinks, so I hear, that

the night alerts have a beneficial effect on the most nervous. It's hard to believe.

There is a long article on me in the *Revue de Paris*. Nothing in *NRF*: that is, your second article is not in it. The number is dedicated to the memory of Charles Du Bos, whom I knew. [*Letters* III, 454–55]

In January 1940, after a long silence that made me apprehensive of fresh trouble, I received a card from Saint-Gérand-le-Puy, and it proved that my fears were not groundless. In it Joyce told me about the illness of his daughter-in-law, whom he had had to have confined, and about the desperate case of his son, still in Paris and looking for work. He himself had the care of his grandson and was dividing his time between Paris, La Baule (where his daughter had finally arrived), and Saint-Gérand, where he had taken refuge with his wife and young Stephen and where he was to remain until he went to Switzerland. About his book:

> Here no one has breathed a word of its existence. I have received a few reviews of it, among them a very bizarre counter-attack from Helsinki. . . . There was another of the same kind in the Roman review *Panorama*, for November 12. Because the book is based on the work of an Italian thinker? In short, a total fiasco up to now as far as the European reviews are concerned. I haven't even been able to collect my royalties, because of laws about the exportation of capital. . . . [*Letters* III, 463]

In March his news, on the first score at least, was better: two articles in the Italian review *Prospettive*, with his own translation of "Anna Livia" into Italian; the publication of the biography by Herbert Gorman in New York; and, finally, "a very long and remarkable study," [by Harry Levin] published in the United States by *New Directions*.[47] To this information he added a nostalgic greeting to the vineyards of Villeneuve, near Montreux, the wine of which was so dear to him. That greeting would turn up in other messages.

The rest does not come under the heading of literary recollections but has to do with a private life that Joyce was at pains to conceal from the public. Since the occupation in France, he had tried in every way to arrange, first for his daughter and then for himself and his family, an asylum in Switzerland. At that time this was not an easy thing to do. The steps he himself took at the Swiss consulate, those of his friends in Zurich, my own in Lausanne, were all calculated to join at a point on the other side of the tangled forest of bureaucracy. Neither Joyce nor his son was willing to exchange his English passport for the Irish one

47. Joyce talked to me with admiration about this article by Harry Levin. . . . [Mercanton's note]
It is partially reprinted in *James Joyce: The Critical Heritage*, 2:693–703.

to which he was entitled: thus they were citizens of a belligerent country. At Saint Nazaire, Lucia Joyce was in the occupied zone, and the state of her health required the most elaborate preparations for the trip to Switzerland. At the last minute, the difficulty of changing money raised further obstacles. The Swiss authorities too invented one, unexpected enough, by taking Joyce for a Jew, as he wrote me in his stupefaction. They had confused him with Leopold Bloom. There is no reason to quote passages here from the urgent correspondence we exchanged in the last months of that terrible year. Perhaps one should, nevertheless, mention that despite his worries Joyce remained energetic, clear-eyed, and calm, the master of himself and of his purpose. His appearance, due to nervousness and fatigue, was haggard, but he seemed to me as lucid, thorough, and moderate as I had seen him at his work. The absent-minded, fantastical, crotchety Joyce is a legend, though one to which he sometimes lent himself. But, like all great artists, he knew perfectly well how to distinguish art from life. It is true, of course, that the times were instructive in that respect. And when, during that ordeal, he found time to call my attention to an article or to ask me for a new book on Vico for which he had seen an advertisement, it was a sign of his wonderful equilibrium.

LAST TRADE OVERSEAS

In mid-December 1940, all obstacles removed, the transportation of his daughter scheduled to take place in a few days, a card and then a telegram from Joyce announced the time of his arrival in Lausanne.[48]

I can still see his slender silhouette on the railway platform, in the shadow of a wintry twilight, his face very pale, aged, marked by fatigue. He advanced through the crowd, which his tall figure dominated, holding onto his wife's arm like a blind man. His hat was turned down over his eyes, his cane hooked over his wrist. He seemed to have come from very much farther away than neighboring although cut-off France, from very much farther even than his native Ireland, at the frontier of the sea. "Last trade overseas." He had entered into eternal exile.

I should not record the hours of that last evening for the reader, but the minutes. Minutes of grace and respite when I rediscovered in his weary and emaciated face the luster of a friendly and youthful gaiety that had always touched me to the heart. He was happy that

48. The card is dated 10 December, Saint-Gérand-le-Puy; the telegram from the Geneva train station, 15 December. The same day Joyce went to Corcelles-Chavornay to see the sanitarium where he intended to place his daughter. He left Lausanne for Zurich the following day, 16 December, late in the afternoon. [Mercanton's note]

night, despite the serious worries that still persisted. He drank in quiet pleasure the wine of Villeneuve that he loved to mention in his letters and postcards. But on several occasions, while he was chatting with his son or playing with young Stephen, Mrs. Joyce confided to me her constant worries about his health. He ate poorly, and less and less: there had been days when he was so exhausted she thought she would lose him. I noticed again in that peaceful and smiling face, under the hair turned white, the pallor, the wear, and as it were a nocturnal transparency. Proudly, the little boy showed me a photograph of himself in the copy of Gorman's book that Joyce had brought me, while Joyce smiled tenderly.

The following day, before he left for Zurich, I joined him at the Hôtel de la Paix, where he had agreed to meet Edmond Jaloux. But because of a misunderstanding on the phone, Jaloux was waiting for us somewhere else.

When he finally appeared, there was time for no more than a brief conversation on the sidewalk. Joyce asked the great critic insistently if he had received and read his "latest book." With exquisite politeness, Jaloux sought to evade the question. Though a fervent admirer of Joyce, as he told me afterward, he had experienced a kind of shock when confronted with the job of reading Joyce had thrust upon him.

"He seemed rather embarrassed," said Joyce thoughtfully, as we went down to the railroad station. "Perhaps the book took him by surprise." Then, looking aloof and malicious: "Perhaps, too, he was not the only one."

A few days after that, I received one last card from Joyce. He called my attention to an article on *Finnegans Wake* by Louis Gillet in the *Revue de Deux Mondes*[49] and wished me a happy new year [*Letters* III, 506]. I expected him to return to Lausanne for his daughter's arrival. We had made plans for reading and working together in Lausanne and in Zurich. January 13, I heard on the radio about his death.

TRANSLATED BY LLOYD C. PARKS

49. Louis Gillet, "The Extraordinary Adventure of James Joyce," *Revue des Deux Mondes*, December 1940; reprinted in *Stele for James Joyce*. [Mercanton's note]

Carola Giedion-Welcker

ONE OF JOYCE'S CONSOLATIONS while struggling with "Work in Progress" *was the appearance of young converts to his cause. Hence the delight over Armand Petitjean that he expressed to Ole Vinding. In 1928 he met another young supporter of his work, the Zurich art critic, Dr. Carola Giedion-Welcker (b. 1893). She was to become his closest friend among European women. In a moment of pique he told Mary Colum, "I hate women who know anything,"*[1] *a prejudice seemingly confirmed by his choice of an uneducated woman as wife and as heroine of* Ulysses. *But Dr. Giedion-Welcker, the daughter of a Cologne banker who took pains to provide her a distinguished education, was when Joyce knew her and still is a very knowledgeable woman as well as a highly accomplished one. She has written extensively about Paul Klee, Giacometti, Kandinsky, Mondrian, Picasso, Brancusi, Max Ernst, and other modern artists, many of whom she knew personally and championed long before they were widely recognized. Attracted to the avant garde in literature as in art, she also was an early translator of Alfred Jarry's drama* Ubi roi, *and has written several studies of Joyce's work in addition to her recollection of him.*

She knew Joyce chiefly in Zurich, which he often visited in the thirties, partly for consultations with Professor Vogt, whose surgical skills she had joined Georges Borach in recommending. Several times on these visits she accompanied him to local museums and galleries but found him indifferent to contemporary art, except for Max Ernst's relief, Europe après la pluie. *This work, she said, "thrilled" Joyce,*[2] *one suspects largely because it suggested a parallel to the flood motif prominent in* Finnegans Wake. *There were also numerous evenings together with her and her husband, Siegfried Giedion, an expert on European architecture. With the deepening of their acquaintance Joyce turned to her, as he did to other women, for help in the care of his daughter. She responded by inviting Lucia for a visit and, at his suggestion,*

1. *Our Friend James Joyce* (Garden City, N.Y.: Doubleday and Co., 1958), p. 132.
2. "Interview with Carola Giedion-Welcker," *Yeats, Joyce, and Beckett: New Light on Three Modern Irish Writers,* ed. Kathleen McGrory and John Unterecker (Lewisburg, Pa.: Bucknell University Press, 1976), pp. 110–12.

*introduced her to some eligible young men, the only result being painful
silence on all sides.³ She also served as his agent in a complicated scheme
to have Lucia's handwriting analyzed by the Zurich graphologist,
Max Pulver, one of Joyce's more desperate attempts at finding some
clue to his daughter's malady. In assisting Joyce with Lucia and in
various other efforts in his behalf, Dr. Giedion-Welcker proved herself
as loyally devoted as his other women friends, Maria Jolas, Sylvia
Beach, and Harriet Weaver.*

*Her recollection focuses on her encounters with Joyce in Zurich.
August Suter and Georges Borach deal briefly with his sojourn there
during World War I, but she gives a much more complete picture of his
relationship with the city. Zurich, as she demonstrates by repeated
examples, had a strong impact on his imagination, influencing his work
in a variety of ways. It also appears to have had an exhilarating effect
on his spirits, as though he found there a temporary escape from the
gloomy atmosphere that Nino Frank says characterized the Joyce
household in Paris during the thirties. The other recollections contain
few instances of his gaiety to compare with several that she describes.
She also captures the Paris atmosphere in her account of a 1938 Saint
Patrick's Day party at Paul Léon's flat. This party, dominated by strained
talk about Hitler and the Nazis, contrasts vividly with the Zurich outings. It also contrasts with the carefree Saint Patrick's Day celebration
in Trieste thirty years earlier, recalled by Francini Bruni, poignantly
dramatizing a trajectory in Joyce's life.*

*During conversations such as that at the Léon party Joyce often sat
quietly listening, but this time he broke in with a detailed analysis of
Hitler. Dr. Giedion-Welcker's summary of his remarks provides a rare
glimpse of his attitude toward the German leader, about whom he
refused to take any public stand. That refusal made him the subject
of increasingly intense criticism, but she makes a shrewd defense of his
political quietism. His concern, she says, was always for individuals,
not groups, and was expressed in direct assistance. She cites his aid to
Jews during this period and his almost overwhelming solicitude when
her daughter became ill. Her description of the latter episode gives a
striking example of Joyce's Bloom-like sympathy with parental
anguish, sensitivity to the suffering of children, and inclination to "Good
Samaritanism."*

*According to Dr. Giedion-Welcker, Joyce assumed that her daughter's
illness, as well as Lucia's, was related to the trauma of puberty, which
she says he defined as a time of "sickness, of feverish, often eruptive
awakenings, realizations, and transformations." She also says that he
discussed with her the ways this difficult period had been treated in*

3. Ibid., p. 114.

various "*puberty dramas*," *including* The Wild Duck. *Hedvig's puberty is hardly the central issue of that play, but given Lucia's problems and his admiration for Ibsen's genius, it is easy to understand the special significance Hedvig must have had for him. His own puberty drama,* A Portrait of the Artist, *gave him additional reasons for being interested in this form. Indeed, his definition of puberty sounds very much like a description of Stephen's experience in* A Portrait.

In spite of Lucia and ominous political developments, Joyce's vein of humor survived in his private life as in his work. Occasionally it emerged in engaging bits of comic verse, two fine examples of which Dr. Giedion-Welcker quotes. Often his humor was directed at his own misfortunes, as in a letter she quotes where he comically denounces a Zurich hotel for having refused to accept his check. This letter leads her to a discussion of Joyce's comic sense, an important trait not particularly noted in the other recollections. With Joyce, she says, sooner or later everything ended in laughter. This observation should not be taken as careless exaggeration, considering that in the "Cyclops" section of Ulysses *Joyce could base a comic episode on the grisly execution of Robert Emmet.*[4]

An odd feature of Joyce's humor in his letters and conversation, during his later life at least, is the absence of the scatological strain prominent in his work. He was especially opposed to the use of off-color language or the telling of off-color stories in the presence of women. But if he had any special attitude toward women that affected his personal relations with them, it is not apparent in Dr. Giedion-Welcker's recollection. Nor does her recollection contain any sign that he disdained her intelligence and knowledge. On the contrary, it shows that he spoke to her as to an intellectual equal and in addition that he recognized his special debt to women. In a footnote she recalls him commenting, "Again and again in life it has been women who were most active in helping me." Mrs. McCormick, Sylvia Beach, Maria Jolas, Harriet Weaver, all came to his aid at various crises. So, too, did Dr. Giedion-Welcker. When in 1940 he sought refuge in Switzerland, it was chiefly her efforts in overcoming the barriers to his emigration that allowed him to spend his final days in the relative peace and stability of Zurich. Thus the last of the debts that he owed to women he owed to her.

4. In a recent interview Dr. Giedion-Welcker told a story about Joyce's laughter while composing *Finnegans Wake*: "Nora and Joyce were in Zurich, and Nora complained. Speaking of the time she'd just spent in Paris, she said, 'I can't sleep anymore, I can't sleep anymore.' I said, 'Why?' And she said, 'Well, Jim is writing at his book.' I said, 'But what does it matter to you?' She said, 'I go to bed and then that man sits in the next room and continues laughing about his own writing. And then I knock at the door, and I say, now Jim, stop writing or stop laughing'" ("An Interview with Carola Giedion-Welcker and Maria Jolas," ed. Richard M. Kain, *James Joyce Quarterly*, 11 [Winter 1974]: 96).

Meetings with Joyce

By Carola Giedion-Welcker

THE FIRST TIME I saw and spoke with James Joyce was in Paris, in
Sylvia Beach's bookshop, 12 Rue de l'Odéon.[5] It was in the spring of
1928, several months after a lengthy essay of mine on *Ulysses* had been
published.[6] I wanted to present a copy, in person, to Miss Beach, whom
I had met some time previously. In the back of her shop she had a little
room devoted to documents bearing on modern English literature,
above all on Joyce's work and its reception in newspapers and periodicals.
Whenever the knowledgeable guardian of this select material and
atmosphere sensed in visitors a genuine interest in current writing or a
particular interest in the career and work of James Joyce, she gave
careful attention to all their special questions, placed her own knowledge
at their disposal, or encouraged them to undertake studies in this
direction or that. Without ever sliding over into intimate anecdotes,
she spoke about Joyce, his character, his life, his method of work, and
his work itself. Instinctively recognizing in Joyce a writer of great
importance, she personally had taken over the manuscript of *Ulysses* in
1921 after its long odyssey among various publishers, and held on to it
until she could entrust it, at her own risk, to the best French printer
in Dijon. Above all, it was her courage and her vigilant collaboration
in the publishing that, along with Miss Harriet Weaver's financial help,
made possible the unmutilated publication of this epochal work.[7]

Because of my article on *Ulysses* I now seemed to her enlisted in the
ranks of those who fought for the understanding and recognition of the
poet. The pamphlet was carefully added to the other documents in
that small room, and then the hidden treasures of manuscripts, documents, and photographs were brought out for the visitor. Once again the
great importance of the brilliant bookshop became apparent as a source
of information, stimulation, and guidance on subjects generally given less
care and attention than they deserve from the official side of the literary
world. As yet unsanctioned literature found here a home and a haven.
The manuscript of *Ulysses* with its endless corrections and with key

5. This text is the result of several essays. The first was published in *Die
Weltwoche* (Zurich) 388, 18 April 1941, under the title "James Joyce in Zurich,"
the last as an appendix to Herbert Gorman's biography, *James Joyce: His Life
and Work* (Hamburg, 1957, pp. 367–75). [C. G.-W.'s note]

6. Vol. 1, 1928, of the *Neue Schweizer Rundschau*. . . . [C. G.-W.'s note]

7. "Again and again in life it has been women who were most active in helping
me," Joyce said once later on. [C. G.-W.'s note]

lines underscored by colored pencil, as well as a first edition, were now pulled out and leafed through. Literature? Was it not something quite different that emanated from this Joycean Odyssey? Did not its multilayered contents expressed in appropriately polyphonic language add to life a new dimension, different from one's everyday sense of time and environment, just as it added a new dimension to artistic expression? Here was a bird's-eye view of the world and people and at the same time the revelation of a microscopic reality, which opens before us in its thousandfold intertwined details, only to fit back again into the entire frame where it is held by tight structural ties. Not only was art and particularly poetry showing its changed, intense contemporary face, but also, after one read the book, life itself seemed changed and newly recreated in larger dimensions.

While I was deeply absorbed in the British and American magazines and new publications that filled the front section of this extraordinary bookshop, a light from outside suddenly seemed to break into the back room. A summer lightness now dominated the atmosphere. The silhouette of a head, distinguished by the arching curve of tightly-brushed-back hair, but most of all the intense blue of tragic, motionless eyes that looked out from thick, sparkling glasses confirmed that the figure, now turned to enter the front room, had to be James Joyce. I was introduced to him, and, with an aloofness and cool politeness that I later observed repeatedly, he invited me to his apartment (then in the Rue de Grenelle) for that afternoon. The Eiffel Tower would guide me in the right direction, the poet added with a brief, final gesture.

During the subsequent tea at his flat, a place that was thoroughly bourgeois Parisian, though marked by a number of personal touches, the talk first turned to Switzerland, specifically to Zurich and the period of the First World War that Joyce had spent there. His talk consisted of short remarks and friendly questions, followed by retreats into the isolation of his private thoughts. It was a strange succession of openness toward his guest and drawing back into his own solitude. We touched on the subject of increasing mechanization in the world, and suddenly Joyce asked—as if finally to make a sharp verbal clarification of this development's current status—"Tell me, what sort of an idea do you think the word 'automobile' would have aroused in the Middle Ages?" "Certainly only that of a divine being," he added without waiting for my answer, "a self mover, thus a god." He left me to draw my own conclusions regarding the present.

Later, at the "In Memoriam" exposition held in Paris (Galerie La Hune) in 1949, I found a reference related to our first conversation. In the manuscript of *Exiles* (1919) the central characters of the play, Richard and Robert, were distinguished as "auto-mystic" and "automobile." "Language-Landage," as it was later called in *Finnegans Wake*, seemed to resonate here already. From a key word and the conception it aroused, Joyce wanted to crystalize a cultural state, or better yet the cultural crisis of a century. For god and technology had moved critically close to each other. At that time I thought of those strange poetic creations which stemmed from the same perspective and which were given prophetic shape by an artist who, just like James Joyce, came from the mystical period of symbolism and who wove that symbolism into a new realism—Alfred Jarry. Jarry introduced the catastrophe of the dominating "auto-mobile" by means of an auto-monster and then, using the form of a burlesque motorcycle race, demonstrated it by the victory of a Superman ("Surmale"). The victory was a technological triumph, which then—through a fatal "vicious circle"— biologically destroyed the auto- and sex-hero.[8]

Joyce was almost totally blind by this time—it was his "darkest" period. But he felt for things and found his way around the room with peculiar skill, showing none of the painful hesitation commonly associated with people suffering his disability. Joyce seemed to possess another mysterious, invisible instrument of perception that helped guide him. His appearance and manner gave the impression of something in suspension. The white summer suit; the be-ringed left hand (for Joyce gems were not only decorative objects but also radiations from other spheres and at the same time symbols recalling certain events in his life); the melodious Irish accent with the rolling "R," which often lends to English a nearly Italian plasticity; the quick, elastic movements of his hands that at the same time revealed an overriding composure; and all the time the imminent threat of total blindness that hung over his existence—all this left me, after our first meeting, with a vague, deeply disquieting impression that only gradually would become clear and crystalize.[9]

The next time I met James Joyce was in Switzerland, in the Zurich Red Cross Hospital, where on May 15, 1930, he had undergone an eye operation performed by Dr. Alfred Vogt, the ninth, but finally successful such operation. Concerned as always, Sylvia Beach had told me of his arrival in Zurich in order to mobilize all help within reach. Because of the strong *Föhn* wind, which Joyce had suffered from during

---

8. See Alfred Jarry, "Le Surmale," *Œuvres complètes* (Monte-Carlo: Editions du Livre), 3:117–229. For the reference to *Exiles*, see "Notes by the Author" (*E* 113).

9. Speaking of this first meeting with Joyce, Dr. Giedion-Welcker later said, "His eyes were then in a very bad state, and I was terribly touched by this. When I left, I stood in front of the house and cried a little. And I called, 'Taxi, taxi,' and the taxi-driver stopped and waited, and he saw that I was filled with emotion, and he said, 'Madame, ne pleurez pas. Il y en a d'autres' ('Madame, don't cry. There are others')" (Kain, ed., "An Interview with Carola Giedion-Welcker and Maria Jolas," p. 104). Ellmann placed this episode after Joyce's funeral (*JJ* 754), but silently omitted it from the paperback edition.

James Joyce. Drawing by Lucia Joyce
(courtesy of Jane Lidderdale)

earlier days in Zurich, the surgery had to be postponed for a short time. Zurich had always brought him luck in the past, and once more he trusted his lucky star and the spirit of the place. When I entered the hospital room he was sitting in a comfortable chair with his left eye bandaged. He told me slyly that his friend Georges Borach had secretly smuggled him some garlic, the flavor of which he loved and the healing powers of which he believed in, though it definitely did not accord with Professor Vogt's therapy.

This was some time after the surgery and an especially happy day for Joyce because while in the hospital garden he had "seen" a red rose that his daughter-in-law Helen had pinned on herself. He had seen it differently, more clearly than he had perceived objects before his operation. The relieved family was gathered around him and seemed full of this event. Nora Joyce was there, along with the newly-wedded couple, Helen and Giorgio Joyce. The radiant and blooming nature outside seemed to penetrate into the hospital room, and I told him of my recent hike through the mountains, during which we had walked not only upwards in space, but also, as it seemed to me considering the flora, backwards in time—from forget-me-not back to crocus, from June to March, a paradoxical reversal of calendar order. Joyce seemed to be interested and inquired precisely about the names and shapes of the flowers that we had seen at the various stages of the trail. For the first time I noticed this curiosity about the tiniest details, this precise, almost scientific observing and collecting of details, this constant probing and classifying of fragments of reality as phenomena of life and, at the same time, as material that, filtered and transformed, would later find renewed life in his poetry. Sublime transfiguration of experience and knowledge into a free world of the fantastic . . . this is to be found as a leitmotif throughout the poet's life and work. It was the same thing that Paul Klee accomplished as a painter in *Rebirth of Nature on Canvas*.

Joyce wore a lilac necktie—a color that he loved and whose Passional significance this former Jesuit student believed in[10]—and a soft jacket, above which his head with bandaged eye seemed to be set firmly, in proud resistance to all expressions of sympathy. His appearance made me think of the portrait of Guillaume Apollinaire in the Val-de-Grâce hospital in Paris, where underneath the white turban of a head bandage the beautiful and gentle face of the *porte blessé* reveals itself to the viewer, sorrowfully and smilingly.

That day the poet gave me as a present a copy of "Anna Livia Plura-

---

10. Here, as with many other instances in his life, a symbolic reference was made that hovered between the personal and the ritualistic. Thus Joyce observed and celebrated certain days according to his own calendar, on which ecclesiastical and historic dates as well as personal memories were marked. [C. G.-W.'s note]

belle," a fragment from his last work, at that time still called "Work in Progress." In later years a record was added in which he himself reads from this passage. Except for a recording from *Ulysses*, it is the only document of his voice left to us. It is a linguistic work of art fashioned by a trained voice that is able to make the listener understand acutely the magic density of a spoken word, that makes a word seem as if touched by a magic wand, and that knows how to awaken through the sensuous power of sound and modulation the whole of that under-lying and richly associative sphere of language, that "pan-aroma (panorama) of all flores of speech" [*FW* 143.3–4], as it is called in his last work. In Joyce's reading the Dublin dialect of the washerwomen is mystically interwoven with the ceaseless murmur and rustling of nature, uniquely conveyed by that singing and at the same time precisely articulating Irish timbre which at the end glides over into a stammering and reverberating echo.

Professor Vogt's operation was successful beyond all expectation. In the following years this *coup de génie*, which Joyce was not to forget for the rest of his life, brought him and his family back to Zurich repeatedly for check-ups, a city he felt a certain affinity with and where Nora Joyce enjoyed staying also. Perhaps he would have preferred more frequent vacations at the seashore, because he was an "ocean man" and also had been born under the sign of Aquarius, but a combination of attractive features made Zurich the choice again and again for short or longer stays. " What a city!" he would exclaim. "A lake, a mountain and two rivers are its treasures." As is said of Ireland, "It has two voices, one comes from the mountains and the other from the sea." In this remark about Zurich he sought to capture characteristics and generally accepted tendencies that sprang from its geographical features.

James Joyce had a deep interest in towns, whether large or small, and in their design and history. They appeared to him as collective individuals, history turned into shape and space, large reservoirs of life. He saw them in the past and in the present as manifold units growing with time, as self-determining identities, as living history. Even if only passing through he always tried to penetrate into their special "nature" and into the secret laws of their complex substance, and to listen to their current and eternal heartbeat. He thought that being a mayor of a city, holding all the threads in one's hand, involved a more direct and real relationship than being king of a nation. Just as he mastered and continually studied countless languages and dialects, so he also knew the wines, special dishes and candies and pastries of many European regions. His interest extended even to the special cakes of a small provincial town in France. Carefully he exposed them as characteristic of the locale, rather than seemingly accidental features, and integrated them into the regional and historical context. Dublin—Paris—Trieste—Zurich, these cities played a fateful part in his life. And Zurich's role was hardly less important than that of the other three. As early as 1904, on their honeymoon, the twenty-two-year-old and his beautiful Galway wife came to Zurich for the first time. On October 11, 1904 they moved into the modest hotel Hoffnung ("Hope")—now Speer—for a short stay. As Joyce told me later, the auspicious name of the inn attracted him more than the zealous recruiting by hotel porters at the Zurich train station. Nevertheless, the outcome he "hoped" for did not materialize because he did not get the promised position as English teacher at the Berlitz School. Instead he was referred to Trieste, where the couple then moved.

But eleven years later the same inn was to accommodate the four members of the Joyce family when they returned (on June 30, 1915), the inn by that time having a new owner named, much to Joyce's amusement, Doeblin. The sound of that name had, of course, rich associations for Joyce. Italy's entry into the war led to an almost four-year stay in Zurich.

It was to become a decisive phase in his life with regard to the development of his work. At that time Joyce wandered through Zurich as if leading a double life. His official job was that of English teacher, but deep inside he was all poet and absorbed in the creation of his *Ulysses*. There was the husband (already suffering from his eyes), concerned with practical matters and caring for the welfare of his family, and at the same time there was the free Celtic visionary on a peaceful European island who was fusing Homer's myth with the contemporary epic of twentieth-century life. Present-day Europe emerged from the proto-cell of Greece, a nation linked with his Irish island since prehistory. This highly polished mind, sharpened and trained early through the study of history and philosophy, illuminated everything. The large city became the locus of all events, the human settling place, eternal nucleus of all civilization.[11] Even though its dimensions in time and space were immense, it was still a comprehensible unit of life. Dublin itself

11. Le Corbusier, the city designer, felt that the method of *Ulysses* related to the principles of his own work. As he wrote me once in 1938, "Un champ de proportions neuves et une grande découverte de la vie que—dans un métier différent—je foule aussi passionnément." [C. G.-W.'s note]

Dr. Giedion-Welcker arranged a meeting of Le Corbusier and Joyce at the latter's flat, expecting profound discussions of "man and the city." Instead, they spoke desultorily about things to do on Sunday outings and about Paris traffic, which caused Joyce problems because of his bad eyesight. The conversation became animated only when Corbusier noticed a cage with some parakeets in it, and the two began discussing birds, which topic occupied their remaining time together ("A Winged Dialogue in 1938 between Le Corbusier and James Joyce," *Schriften*, pp. 52–53).

appears again and again in his late work as the mythical city, city of all cities, focal point of time and the world, of civilization and nature. From the center of a fantastic universe it now emanates a mysterious light.

The Joyce family lived in several different apartments during their four-year stay in Zurich: on Kreuzstrasse and Seefeldstrasse (no. 73) and on Universitätstrasse (no. 38 and no. 29). Among their closer Zurich friends were the assistant conductor [Ferruccio] Busoni, Philippe Jarnach, and the soprano Charlotte Sauermann, with whom they shared their living quarters on Seefeldstrasse.[12] Among the "students" and later friends of the Berlitz School teacher was the silk manufacturer Edmund Brauchbar, whose outstanding characteristics—vitality, sense of reality, spontaneous human warmth and wit were woven into the traits of the central figure in *Ulysses*, Leopold Bloom.[13] Georges Borach also was one of Joyce's students at that time and maintained a friendly relationship with him later on. They discussed encyclopedic questions, details from various scientific fields, which reappeared poetically transformed in Joyce's work. Like Paul Léon later on in Paris, Borach became a kind of Eckermann with whom the poet entered into exhaustive dialogues during frequent walks along the lake in Zurich. The small, deformed man followed Joyce on his daily walks with the same energy and unreserved interest that he followed the strange Joycean mental journeys, and up to the end provided him sympathetically and unselfishly with whatever material he desired.

Borach's sudden death in an automobile accident in 1934 obsessed his friend's mind for days. It happened on Good Friday, and the circumstances under which he died, in a sporty racing car on the Riviera, appeared to Joyce especially grotesque for a man who had moved through his whole life with the painful steps of a cripple. I will never forget the way Joyce pronounced the word "Pietà" after having met the sorrowing mother who had lost her only son. That night as usual we were sitting in the Kronenhalle. While Joyce intensively considered the recent happening, now and then alluding to the biblical Passion and humming quiet passages from Bach's *Passion*, this whole fantastic and tragic world, wherein the extraordinary is closely mixed with the trivial, was suddenly interrupted by a piercing call, "Closing time!" The rational voice of public order and tyranny penetrated unexpectedly and just as inexorably into the free domain of his bold associations

12. For a glimpse of Joyce's relations with these members of Zurich's musical world, see *JJ* 422–23, 434–35. Joyce helped Mme Sauermann's son escape the Nazis.

13. As Dr. Giedion-Welcker explains later, Brauchbar (1872–1952) helped Joyce obtain residence in Zurich in 1940 (see also Paul Ruggiero's recollection, p. 283 and note). Brauchbar's niece was another of those whom Joyce assisted in finding refuge from the Nazis (*Letters* III, 430).

and interpretations, which had elevated this individual case to an "epiphany." The sudden paradoxical clash of contrary worlds corresponded precisely with Joyce's *humour noir*. "Loud, heap miseries upon us yet entwine our arts with laughters low!" [*FW* 259.07].[14] This is how the frightened children pray in *Finnegans Wake* when the threatening thunder comes rumbling down from the sky. That this passage contains a word association with wine is significant, since many of the profound and witty comments that Joyce made about the happy and tragic events of life often sprang from moments when he was elated by wine.

Wine actually played an important part in his life. It did not burden him, but elated him, and wine also, in the end, triggered the stroke of death. The Vallois wine, which he had baptized "Erz-Herzogin" (archduchess) because of its earthy taste (*erzgeschmack*),[15] and later the Neuchâtel, which he called a "true Midsummer Night's dream," would always effervesce through those evening gatherings. His remark, "Red wine is liquid beef steak, but white wine is electricity," had its analogue in his assessment of the human voice. The tenor struck him as a "sublime, divine blessing, a supernatural sound," while the bass with its "healthy stability" and the baritone with its "beautiful naturalness" remained for him more earth bound. Only after sunset did he seem to feel free to imbibe the luminous, golden earth-spirit of our country.

Between 1926 and 1928 the Rhein-Verlag (Basel) published German translations of all the poet's prose up to that time: *Dubliners, A Portrait of the Artist, Ulysses*. Again Switzerland was a starting point for the forwarding of his work. In 1919 the Rascher-Verlag in Zurich published a German translation of his only play, *Exiles*, one year after the English edition had appeared. Stimulated by his work on that play, Joyce undertook to introduce English plays to the Swiss audience. The "English Players" were founded under his direction. Plays of Oscar Wilde, Shaw, and Synge were performed at the "Kaufleuten," at the Pfauentheatre, and at the Municipal Theatre in Lucerne. *Exiles*, modestly placed last in the Irish series, was not staged because of an internal dispute between the actors and the director. The battles during this theatre period in Zurich found their poetic transformation in the "Circe" chapter of *Ulysses*. The district court of Zurich finally settled those differences and in James Joyce's favor.

During the Irish exile's walks beside the Zurich lake, Dublin, *la cité*

14. Entwine—ent-wine, to free from wine, which played such an important role in Joyce's life, and from whining. [C. G.-W.'s note]

15. Regarding Joyce's fondness for this wine and his play on the name "archduchess," see Frank Budgen, *James Joyce and the Making of "Ulysses"* (1934; rpt., with "Other Writings," London: Oxford University Press, 1972), p. 172; *Letters* (I, 126, 131); and *Finnegans Wake* (171.23–28).

suprême, probably appeared to him frequently, in eternal transformation and eternal beauty, just as Paris, the distant beloved city, *l'inoubliable*, seemed to emerge from the sea before the French exile Victor Hugo on the beach of Guernsey. But it was also part of the Joycean manner of thinking and experiencing that while being fully aware of their idiosyncracies, he would discover repeatedly a continuity and similarity in people, destinies, and regions. The Zurich Bahnhofstrasse at noon, filled with the living details of his present experience, was permanently superimposed over the rememberd image of Dublin and merged with the twelve o'clock life of his native city in that masterly chapter of his Odyssey.[16]

He observed the life of waters, the ocean and above all the rivers, as he observed the life of people. River-nature, river-myth merged with that "river-civilization" which seemed to him fundamental. Repeatedly he sought out regions with rivers, the lovely idylls of Luxembourg, the harsh beauty of the Dauphin near Grenoble with its rivers, woods, and mountains, or the broad epic flow of rivers in France. Even the rushing of the little Wolf Creek behind our garden could charm him. Referring to this little creek he implored us never to give up a house that was suffused with such a sound of nature. "Here I experienced the illusion of an eternal peace," he once said after having spent a long time in the part of the garden where the creek flowed by. "Probably an illusion of old age," he added ironically. To him the confluence of the Limmat and Sihl was an elemental and dramatic meeting, and when I once wanted to take a picture of him in Zurich, it had to be exactly at this spot and with this river background.

The broad surface of the lake meant something different to him. In contrast with the active life of a river, it was a great, self-evident being, which stretched out calmly at the edge of the city. The lake enticed him to frequent boat trips, especially in latter years. We found out only later that these trips were taken not only to experience nature but also to serve his art. These were moist word-expeditions, which he took by motorboat. From the water, the fish smell, the blue-green color, the misty haze, from this bouquet of associations he hoped one word would be born, one word that would encompass all these things and when heard would evoke them simultaneously. This multiheaded creation could be discovered only close to the lake's surface and its radiating life and could be captured only with help from the genius of the place and the time. As to whether he ever fished such a comprehensive word pearl out of the Lake of Zurich, the poet remained stubbornly silent.

He already had interlaced the fragment of "Anna Livia Plurabelle" with word plays related to Zurich. Again and again these grotesque

16. See also "Bahnhofstrasse" in *Pomes Penyeach*.

poetic blooms were stimulated by the circumstances in which he chanced to be living. They grew from human contacts, from things he saw and heard, as well as from the landscape. Describing the small river Limmat he said, "Well, that's the Limmat" (for limit). The stolid building of the Sihlpost inspired the question, "You don't say, the sillypost?" [FW 200.21–22], or "Legging a jig or so on the sihl" [FW 200.23–24] (to do a little dance on mud). Referring to the spring festival in Zurich: "There's the Belle for Sexaloitez!" [FW 213.18–19] (There's the beauty for sexual people [leute]. At the same time the "bell" is that of the Sechseläuten).[17] Through these word burlesques, rich in associations, where the word inspired the listener visually as well as auditorily and where the tension of suggested meanings induced manifold metamorphoses of the core word, Joyce created a poetic game while at the same time accomplishing his aim of incorporating mosaics of real life into his work. In this sense even the slightest event could become the starting point for a fantastic visual and auditory experience. He achieved the sort of "totalization of the object" that Paul Klee strived for in painting. This totalization, with which he sensuously and intellectually surrounded things, people, and events, never permitted a single-layer picture.

When the Japanese edition of Ulysses appeared in 1932, he showed it to me with special interest. He believed that, because the Japanese mentality was used to an indirect and fragmentary symbol language and also because their form of poetic expression was close to his, they were well prepared for his way of thinking and writing. A Japanese poem which he recited to me in English translation showed the different "I's," which changed according to the situation. It dealt with an abandoned sweetheart whose multifaceted and fluctuating psychic state was expressed through symbolic allusions (mist, clouds, jewels, etc.) thereby also revealing the personality of the lamenting sweetheart.

Joyce also used grotesque symbolic details for joking characterizations of his friends. Once when we missed meeting him at the train station in Herrliberg for a planned walk, Nora Joyce gave the stationmaster a matter-of-fact description of us two "lost ones." Joyce himself was standing nearby and reported later with a grin what a different description he would have given: "She: a flash in her eyes, a dash in her steps, attractive, but a little giddy" (weaving together the idea of giddiness and the name Giedion).[18] "He: a Nizzam, with a blue turban around

17. The Sechseläuten, or "Six o'clock Festival," occurs in Zurich at the end of April in celebration of spring. The festival is marked by bell ringing, a procession of the historic town guilds, and a huge bonfire on which a papier-mâché figure representing winter is burned. The figure is called the Böögg (also spelled Bögg).
18. In a letter to Lucia, Joyce alluded to this "giddiness," remarking of Dr.

his head, Kohinor diamonds as vest buttons, in his hand a Swiss alarm clock that causes a gold coin to drop from his mouth every time it rings." This referred to "Nizzam's" (Siegfried Giedion's) recent invitation to teach at Harvard University (1938), which Joyce had dwelt on in previous conversations as offering an impressive economic reward for intellectual work.

The same kind of fantasy was apparent in Joyce's response to folk plays and all historical cults, which in his view revealed a simultaneity of the past and the present. They confirmed his belief in the continuity of history. Because he often was in Zurich during the spring, he frequently attended the Sechseläuten, whose name he used for his audacious word plays in *Finnegans Wake*. From his window on Bellevue-Platz he registered precisely all phases of the ceremonial burning. The mixture of genuine commonplace reality with the fantastic rituals around the winter symbol struck him as highly amusing, especially when the watchmen with their wolf hounds extinguished the last flicker of fire that burned the mystical "Böögg." The most banal present-day event penetrated into history. Thus once in a gay vinous mood he wanted to restage the last act of Rossini's *William Tell*, making it an apotheosis of Switzerland celebrated by countless hotel porters, so that the "happy ending" would be illuminated and concluded by the present.

Swiss hotel porters were altogether something special to him. They were living information centers about small and big events, the *faits divers* of the city where he happened to be living, and most of all a rich source of jokes. But things could go wrong here, too. Thus there were unpleasant incidents in a respected Zurich hotel, incidents which Joyce, who in money matters was always extremely generous and reliable, considered disloyal and which affronted his sensitive and stubborn sense of justice. There were padded bills and a cashier at a hotel where he always stayed who refused to accept his check as he was leaving, so that he had to call on his friends at the last minute for funds. This was the spring of 1938 when Austria had been conquered by Hitler in the "Cold War," and because of this event people had an acute sense of Switzerland's endangered position. In a characteristic flight of imagination he now mixed his resentment over the embarrassing hotel incident with political eventualities. From Paris his friend and secretary Paul Léon sent me a letter, for my information, once again itemizing in careful detail the long list of the hotel's sins, and the poet had added in his own hand a peppery afterword: ". . . All I would say about the future in Zurich is as follows: I hope that whoever marches

---

Giedion-Welcker, "She is a nice woman even if a little hysterical" (*Letters* III, 357).

into the city will respect the Giedion's villa, likewise Othmar Schoeck's[19] as well as Prof. Vogt's clinic and the Kronenhalle. But as far as I am concerned, they can stuff the entire staff of that 'crooked dive' into sacks and hang them out the window, prepared, for all I care, to be hauled away. As for the cashier, heaven help all poor Jews who fall into his hands."[20]

Everything ended—as it usually did with Joyce—in fantasy and laughter. "Funferall, fun again, Finnegan" is the leitmotif throughout his late work. Joking, all the way from nonsense to gallows humor, the joke in all its shades, meant a sort of release for this man whose life was filled with personal tragedy and yet who up to the end believed in his lucky star. It meant release from all complications and it meant liberation from the burden of reality into the more sublime regions of the intellect and imagination. It embodied a deep love of life and at the same time an aloofness and discipline. Those who considered Joyce a crafty Jesuit, somber nihilist, or a cold, insensible observer like the moon,[21] viewing the world indifferently, misjudged the distinctive and essential in him, the humane traits of his character. His ability to shift over into the sphere of the comical and unreal enabled him in his special way to master the world, to relieve its tensions and to brighten it. "The most intelligent person," is the way Sylvia Beach first described him to me. Or as Paul Léon shortly before his arrest said of Joyce in writing to Jean Paulhan, "His exquisite sweetness stems from his infinite understanding."[22]

"Nomen est omen" applied to his own name, too. As he explained to me once, his name was derived from "joy," genealogically from the

19. Much earlier James Joyce had recognized that among modern composers Othmar Schoeck had great importance and special merits as a preserver of song, the lyrical side of music and the one that particularly appealed to Joyce. He wrote to me from Saint-Gérand-le-Puy, "J'ai écrit un petit mot à Schoeck lui disant que j'ai entendu l'autre jour soir son œuvre magistral, 'Lebendig Begraben' (Gottfried Keller) à la radio et qu'on m'avait défendu à moi de fouler le sol de son Zurich où je voulais aller le féliciter. . . ." (I have written a little note to Schoeck telling him that the other evening on the radio I heard his majestic "Lebendig Begraben" (text by Gottfried Keller) and that I have been prevented now from setting foot on the soil of his Zurich, where I wanted to congratulate him. . . .) [C. G.-W.'s note]

In 1935 Joyce accompanied Professor Fehr to a concert of songs by Schoeck (1886–1957) and was so impressed by them that he bought the music, had Schoeck autograph it, and then sent it to Giorgio. He told Giorgio that Schoeck stood "head and shoulders over Stravinsky and Antheil as a composer for orchestra and voice" (*Letters* I, 356).

20. See *Letters* III, 416–418, for a slightly different version of this correspondence.

21. Lecture by C. G. Jung, given in Zurich in 1930, and printed with slight changes in 1934. [C. G.-W.'s note]

22. Léon's letter to Paulhan is included below, pp. 286–91.

old French name "de Joyeuse." By his response to various circumstances of life he often confirmed this derivation. In contrast with his broad sophistication, he also had in his nature a streak of the primitive sense of cosmic threat. In a sense the first human being and the last were joined in him. During the thunderstorms that early summer lavishes on Zurich, panic would seize him and he would hide away dispiritedly in his hotel on the Bahnhofstrasse, "like the Pope in the Vatican." Even the modest Zurichberg seemed to him a powerful Mont Noir when the sky discharged electricity around it, behaving, as he said, "like a drunken sailor indiscriminately throwing dynamite around." Later on he showed another side of himself, appearing utterly indifferent to imminent danger at the time of the bombing raids in France, as Nora Joyce reported. Likewise, the stoic calm and patience with which he endured his many eye operations revealed an astonishingly disciplined and courageous side of him.

The opinion which the English poet Stephen Spender expressed (in the periodical *Comprendre*, 1951), that Joyce's antisocial and arrogant attitude toward the war reflected an individualism inappropriate to the times, was not even partly true. During and just before World War II he proved himself extremely helpful and concerned toward all those who for political reasons had become homeless. However, it was not his nature to believe that he should engage in any kind of meddling or become actively involved in politics. His vocation lay in the fulfillment of a poetic mission, and he wanted to carry that mission out to the last detail, conscientiously and freely. In this sense he cursed "the disturbance of a war," not because he overvalued his cultural role and saw his special poetic work endangered but because to him, in the final analysis, war meant the victory of barbarism, with the result that any kind of cultural work—and therefore his, too—could become involved in a bloody power struggle and be destroyed.[23] C. P. Curran, an old Irish friend of James Joyce, who had been very close to him ever since they were students together in Dublin, remarked on this very aspect of Joyce's nature and outlook. Taking a position the reverse of Spender's and absolutely to the point, Curran said,

> In Ireland we had many artists who did not hesitate to interfere in public matters. Joyce was not among them. To maintain total independence from all such matters for the sake of his art became a passion with him. This aim cost him many sorrows aside from a painful separation. It led him through much suffering. But with a wonderful heroism

23. See the account by Maria Jolas, "James Joyce en 1939-40," *Mercure de France*, 309 (May 1950): 45-58, where this topic is dealt with in a revealing way. [C. G.-W.'s note]

he followed his ideal unperturbed through poverty, exile, physical pain, in good times and bad. It is even expressed in the way he wrote, a way that is perhaps hard to understand but certainly is not often encountered. The integrity and freedom of the artist may be degraded by a cheap slogan. For Joyce that integrity and freedom was everything.[24]

His attitude toward political groups and personalities was strikingly revealed during a Saint Patrick's Day celebration at the home of Paul Léon in Paris the evening before I was to leave for the United States. At that time the political sky in Europe seemed to be growing steadily darker, and so the discussion touched, of course, on National Socialist Germany, whereupon fears, suspicions, and curses were voiced by several of those present. James Joyce had assumed a calm, pensive attitude, but suddenly he began to talk and declared in his objective and cool manner that Hitler was surely a historical phenomenon of colossal force that wouldn't be easy to cope with. The detached and emotionless way he spoke, as though referring to a personal adversary, particularly bothered the women present. Nora Joyce, who had listened to him intently, now suddenly jumped up, and, while Joyce continued his calm, interested analysis of Hitler's personality from the point of view of its immense force and drive, she grabbed her knife, which she had just then been using on a *poulet de bresse*, rushed toward him and shouted, "Jim, another calm word about that devil and I will murder you!" Her response had a strange mixture of genuine anger and burlesque acting, and such a beautiful élan that I suddenly wished I could see this high-spirited Irish woman, who was now standing at the head of the table with her drawn knife, confronting Hitler not Joyce, like an armed and fearless Charlotte Corday. The poet seemed to accept her outburst, just as he always admired the natural behavior of his wife and listened in fascination when she intuitively and spontaneously decided matters that he had scrutinized carefully from every angle, *sine ira et studio*.

Hitler interested Joyce as the personification of demonic powers and at the same time as an example of an individual's rise. To him he was the reverse side of the individualism that generated and maintained the world of art, the destructive power that was related to the world of art yet had an independent existence, like that dualism of figures representing good and evil found linked together on the pilasters and façades of medieval churches. "Changes are in the offing. The satanic must be fused into a simultaneity with the heavenly, the dualism not

24. From Joyce's obituary in the *Irish Times*, 14 January 1941; reprinted in *A Bash in the Tunnel: James Joyce by the Irish*, ed. John Ryan (Brighton: Clifton Books, 1970), p. 245.

being treated as such but as complementary parts of a unity." So Paul Klee wrote in a letter during World War I. Joyce, too, had an intense awareness of this two-sidedness in things. For him every potent event, negative and positive, stemmed from the highly active cells of individualism. "The movements which work revolutions in the world are born out of the dreams and visions in a peasant's heart on the hillside. For them the earth is not an exploitable ground but the living mother." So it says in *Ulysses*.[25] Kierkegaard's "category of the individual" did not mean for Joyce, any more than it did for Kierkegaard, isolation in an ivory tower or resignation to the spirit of the times but restraint which became transformed into inner activity.

His respect for individualism also was apparent in his everyday behavior toward people. His acts of helpfulness were never aimed at an unknown collective. Only direct assistance mattered to him, one individual helping another in a situation that could be assessed personally. As a simple matter of course he turned his great intellect and sure instincts to the problems and sorrows of others. Once when my daughter was seriously ill, having made a surprisingly correct medical diagnosis, he took the time to locate the proper specialist in Paris and through him instigated the medical treatment that was decided on in Zurich. His whole correspondence with me about this illness was conducted on post cards. Though brief, his notes not only laid the groundwork for my daughter's cure but also provided intelligent, restorative injections of friendly sympathy and assurance.[26]

In connection with this event he often would talk about the intense spiritual battles during puberty, a period of physical and psychic threats that he vividly portrayed in his *Portrait of the Artist*. He considered the time of maturing almost as one of sickness, of feverish, often eruptive awakenings, realizations, and transformations. He thought that the deep psychic mysteries of this time had been portrayed most poetically and dramatically in *Hannele's Ascension* and in *The Wild Duck*. Wedekind's *Spring Awakening* struck him as the weakest of the

25. A.E. speaks these lines (*U* 186–87).
26. Dr. Giedion-Welcker explained this episode more fully to Kathleen Mc-Grory: ". . . My child was once sick with an illness of the glands. They thought perhaps she had a tumor. Joyce immediately gave me books about glands. . . . Then he went to Paris and didn't tell me that he was working for me. He . . . visited *the* doctor for glands. La Fagulière was the great man at that time. And then suddenly I received a card saying, 'I've arranged everything for you. You can come with your daughter to Fagulière. He will accept you.' Then another card came a day later: 'You don't need to come. I spoke with him and have a man in Zurich. . . . ' He did all that very quickly and accurately. . . . He always wrote, 'How is she doing? Is she better?' " ("Interview with Carola Giedion-Welcker," p. 112).

"puberty dramas." In Gottfried Keller's *Memory of Youth*, which he recited fluently, he found a bright, clear resonance sounding above this —in general—deeply threatening zone of human development. A word like *"Lindenwipfelwehn"* [27] could enchant him completely and seem to him a concentrated "aroma of the whole."

His opposition to ecclesiastical or political forces interfering with an individual's freedom expressed itself positively in a respect for the individual activities and modes of life of his fellow men. One sensed that from whatever level of daily life people encountered Joyce, he granted their activities, though entirely different from his, the same freedom that he allowed himself in his own sphere. Only on rare occasions was he inclined to discuss literature or art with his friends, but he loved to carry on a dialogue about Dickens with some unknown attendant at the post office window or to discuss the meaning and structure of Verdi's *La Forza del Destino* with the person at the box office. It fascinated him to overhear the resonances of a more naïve walk of life and to trace its psychological limitations and pattern. In large gatherings he always was reluctant to express his views about art, and he was stubbornly silent on this subject before curious reporters when they attacked him.

But he could present his views with force and precision and did so on rare occasions when some incident had happened to stimulate his thoughts. Once when we were alone together at the Kronenhalle he spent the entire evening comparing Shakespeare and Ibsen as dramatists. He analysed Ibsen's late work *Little Eyolf* in detail, stressing the brilliant exposition in the play and claiming that as regards dramatic technique Ibsen was the greater master and artist. He thought that with Shakespeare the superabundance of worldly wisdom and the radiance of the language, with its grandiose formations and deformations, puns and wonderful zaniness, dominated, leaving the dramatic construction of the whole far behind. While still a high school student I had visited London and seen Beerbohm Tree play Hamlet. When I described my impressions of the performance, Joyce suddenly recalled the powerful way this actor had thrown himself with "chattering teeth" before the Ghost. He thought it Beerbohm Tree's most brilliant performance, aside from his great rendition of Antony's funeral oration. Then with lowered voice he repeated the oration passage, clearly articulating every word. Following that suddenly came the unexpected—a fantastic question: What would Shakespeare have thought of Joyce's current

27. "Swaying of the Linden tree top." Joyce proposed as an epigraph for *James Joyce and the Making of "Ulysses"* the passage from *Memory of Youth* in which this word occurs (*Letters* III, 284).

work, at that time still called "Work in Progress"? The only response I could come up with was to remind him of Goethe's attitude toward Kleist; however, there the time span was different, involving only a generation's change in perspective.

On another occasion he attempted this same retrospective method of juxtaposing contemporary art with the ways of the past, this time regarding prose style. The point was to evaluate his work in relation to Cardinal Newman's, whose "silver-veined prose" he deeply admired and whose sublimely simple and evocative style owed itself, Joyce believed, to the faith of the convert. His mental play following this animated evening crystalized into "An Epilogue to Ibsen's *Ghosts*," which he wrote down after returning late to his hotel and read to me the next day several hours before he left for Paris.[28]

Another evening at a cafe (the Seerose) in Tiefbrunnen in the Tessin seemed destined to produce literary discussion since the small group of friends gathered there included a poet and a professor of English literature, James Joyce and Bernhard Fehr. However, the two, who were great connoiseurs of opera and lovers of Verdi's music, would not allow the least bit of "shop talk." The dialogue was exclusively about music, and the two partners, unconcerned about the others in the cafe—probably to their delight—sang to each other part after part from various of the master's operas. As we were leaving the mood of gaiety reached its peak when the poet lay down on the roof of our car and, pointing to the stars, insisted on being driven to our house in Zurichberg in that precarious horizontal position. After an elegant balancing act on the way up, we landed safely in the Doldertal with our precious load. There the discussion turned to lighter kinds of music, while Professor Fehr began playing dance tunes. After executing an original waltz step—more with himself than with me—Joyce then took the stage as solo dancer, belaboring the inside of his stiff straw hat with wild jumps and kicks so that in the end, after these rhythmical and astonishingly acrobatic exercises, he was left with only a straw wreath in his hand, which he triumphantly held aloft and then as a finale placed on his head.

The grotesque flexibility of his long legs, which seemed to fill the room, and the bizarre grace with which he executed all movements of this strange dance, made him appear part juggling clown and part

28. Ellmann says that Joyce wrote the "Epilogue" on the train returning to Paris from Zurich (*JJ* 681). But in a note dictated for Gorman, Joyce said he wrote it "in 1934 while staying in Switzerland and after having seen for the nth time Ginette Faccone in . . . *Ghosts* at the Théâtre des Champs Elysées in Paris before leaving [for Switzerland] . . . " (note on Gorman typescript in the Croessmann Collection at Carbondale).

mystical reincarnation of Our Lady's Tumbler, who would like to have continued the performance endlessly, urged on by the constantly changing musical variations of the tireless piano player. Hardly had the dance interlude ended, however, when the singing began, with Joyce delivering Irish folk songs and some he himself had composed.

To hear Joyce sing with his beautiful tenor was an enchanting experience. It meant access to the sound of his innermost being. Voice and language remained for him mankind's most wonderful and humane instrument of communication, springing from the depths of the emotional life. Like Klee with his paintings, Joyce linguistically humanized the world of things and creatures. The human voice, when elevated into song, seemed to him the highest and purest manifestation of music. In this connection he once laughingly maintained that most instruments were made of animal skins and guts, the drum, for example, being made from the stomach of an ass. It wasn't enough that this animal was beaten perpetually during its life; even after its death this cruel treatment continued uninterruptedly.

In September 1940 in answer to our alarmed urging that he come to Switzerland, Joyce agreed and said that he wanted very much to leave France as soon as possible. At the time he was in Saint-Gérand-le-Puy (Allier). Maria Jolas, who had moved her school there from Neuilly (Paris), insisted that he come and spend Christmas. Due to the events of the time, the spontaneous visit had to be extended for almost ten months. Maria Jolas has vividly described this period from her own experience.[29] A small community of friends (Paul Léon and his wife, the Joyce family with son and grandson, and, for a short time, the writer Samuel Beckett), had fled to this remote place from all directions.

At the end of the summer in 1940 the question of a refuge in Switzerland became increasingly urgent for the Joyce family, who stayed behind while the others left. Having helped Joyce make important corrections for the American edition of *Finnegans Wake* in this remote little town, Paul Léon returned to Paris, in spite of his friend's warning. There he salvaged most of Joyce's library from the Rue des Vignes and then was deported, dying miserably in 1942. Maria Jolas, along with her daughters, returned to the United States. Eugene Jolas, another helping hand and first publisher of Joyce's final work, was already there. In spite of urgings from every side, Joyce did not want to remove his family to the United States, especially since that would have meant leaving his daughter behind in a sanitarium in the occupied zone (Pornichet-Bretagne). He wanted to stay in Europe, and Switzerland, a place where he felt at home, seemed therefore to be the best choice.

29. In "Joyce en 1939–40." [C. G.-W.'s note]

However, since there were not only the Joyce couple, but also his son Giorgio, and his grandson Stephen, settling in Switzerland involved numerous difficulties. In addition there was the problem of his daughter Lucia still being in the occupied zone.

Wanting to fulfill his wish and recognizing that since he, as well as his son, had English passports an extension of the occupied territory could result in their both being classified as political enemies, we realized the necessity of doing everything possible at our end to rescue him from the danger zone. This meant spending weeks appearing before various city or cantonal administrative officials. Loaded with documents about his world-wide fame, we had to walk from office to office demonstrating to the different departments the urgency and moral obligation of providing this Swiss refuge. An old friend of James Joyce, Paul Ruggiero, whom he had known since the first war years in Zurich, had also been alerted and helped me, especially with the complicated question of Joyce's citizenship, while the mayor (Dr. Klöti) and the director of the University Medical Clinic (Professor Löffler) rendered their energetic help by going to various offices to speak in support of the entry request. Following the initiative of the University Rector, Ernst Howald, a number of professors, as well as prominent members of the Association of Swiss Authors headed by the poet Felix Moeschlin, supported a petition to the immigration officials demanding asylum for Joyce. At the end of November, after weeks of negotiation, we finally reached the financial kernel of the issue—a guarantee of twenty thousand Swiss francs was needed to open the gates to Switzerland.

Now reduced to figures, the rescue of this prominent European personage seemed to reach its absurdest point. But in spite of great cultural enthusiasm, when the time came to make up the sum there was little eagerness in Zurich circles to come forth with money. The only one who helped promptly and reliably was Joyce's former student and friend, Edmund Brauchbar in New York. He contributed one-fifth of the sum needed to satisfy the strange requirement of a guarantee for such a sublime being. Other Americans had at first shown great enthusiasm for the cause but at the last moment sent a negative reply, probably because of a justified fear about the approaching financial isolation of Switzerland. Time was pressing because his French emigration visa had expired once already and was extended only through the intervention of several well-known people, among them Jean Giraudoux. After all these administrative experiences and human disappointments, we had to deposit the bulk of the money ourselves, the dangerous delays having elicited increasingly agitated special delivery letters from the otherwise extremely patient and polite Joyce.

Then came the next problem, to find a suitable place for Joyce and his family to stay in Zurich. The Pension Delphin seemed a satisfactory temporary answer. It was an old house (torn down a year later), surrounded by a beautiful garden. In view of the coming poet, the name could have been considered a favorable omen, since nobody then could know that a *"de la fin"* was secretly resonating under ground. A little bitterly he indicated that he did not want to experience once again the difficult and troubled time of World War I, as though caught in a vicious circle. Nevertheless, shortly after getting off the Geneva train at the Zurich terminal on that gray December 17, looking, it seemed to us, more fragile and preoccupied than in earlier times, he had stressed again and again how happy he was to stand on such solid ground. The next morning on his first outing he went to the French bookstore near the lake in order to buy a French edition of the Greek epics for his grandson. The boy was just the age Joyce had been when the *Odyssey* made its first strong impression on him. It was a memorable sight to see him walk through the snow, hand in hand with the lively little child, to whom this radiantly white element was an exciting novelty. Joyce followed slowly, his posture and gestures seeming more tired than before. Or was it only the strong, blinding effect of the wintery blanket that delayed his step?

And then followed the last Christmas with him as that sinister year drew to a close, the year of the *"drôle de guerre"* that never existed. They were the last days of a great "individual" who bore within himself an immense world of knowledge, experience, and fantasy, which he revealed poetically, yet without the universal recognition due him. Joyce was wearing his grandfatherly vest with the green embroidered hunting scenes, as he usually did on such festive occasions, and was sitting at the head of the family table where the different generations down to the eight-year-old Stephen had gathered. A snow-white Christmas day was to be celebrated with religious and secular songs and with songs sung in Irish and Latin, during which the father's sublime tenor often united beautifully with the son's strong bass. The recording of the Irish singer John McCormack doing a lilting text from *The Rubáiyát of Omar Khayyám*, "Ah, Moon of My Delight," was also played.[30] It was a gentle song, dreamy and twi-lit, reminiscent of Joyce's early lyrics. He was especially fond of it and had given me this rendition as a present many years before.

And then, like a partial finale to years of friendly ties, came his last invitation for a gathering in a restaurant, since torn down, on the Kreuzplatz. Here in this rustic, wood-paneled room the old wanderer, sitting in front of a carafe of golden Fendant, seemed to inhale Swiss

30. "Moon of My Delight" is a song from the 1930s musical *Chee Chee*, by Rogers and Hart.

stability from the locale and climate, while outside was the chaos of world events. The old-fashioned, plain setting emanated an unperturbed peace and quietude, which seemed extinguished in the rest of the world. After having been witness to a chaotic migration and flight of people in the small French town and having felt his own feet to be on a kind of *trottoir roulant*, he had finally found stability. Switzerland, which in 1917 the poet Hugo Ball had called a "nature sanctuary for the mind," seemed to the Irish poet in the present politically uncertain hour like a shelter in the storm, fending off a hurricane. "Here one still knows where he stands, here life has remained constant," he said, looking around the room. He seemed to mean that what characterized this moment and this place applied to the country as a whole. We, who for months had lived in a thoroughly unsettled state, with our rucksacks packed, accepted his optimistic and prescient assertion with surprise and pleasure. It was not his habit to make vague predictions. Usually he construed possibilities carefully and precisely from existing facts. This habit seemed to us the reaction of a man who in the domain of his work was used to reaching out repeatedly into the future and into new dimensions beyond all experience. That probably also explains why his attitude and remark in that almost medieval setting exerted a strangely reassuring effect.

But with Joyce the reverse side of the coin always followed immediately. So vis-à-vis this peacefulness and security he touched sarcastically on the Swiss preoccupation with cleanliness and orderliness, associating this concern with an impulse toward self-complacency that Joyce thought had an almost sterilizing effect, in the country's modern architecture, for example. On leaving he returned to this subject and even began to eulogize dirt: "You have no idea how wonderful dirt is," he said, as though putting an end to the subject. We were already standing on the street. Instead of the cosy warm room the cold winter night and the dreadful "blackout" of modern war isolated us now. These strangely burlesque words were the last that I heard directly from him. Already they issued like a murmur out of the darkness. Then we parted, because we wanted to drive into the mountains for a short stay.

We left the next day and in the mountains only his New Year's wishes made their way to us over the telephone. They were spoken with special sincerity and yet were filled with sad concern for what the future would bring. Since it was the last direct one, that brief earlier remark in the dark of the night remained especially engraved on my mind, although it probably was not meant to be quite so full of implication. Later, however, it seemed spoken with the presentiment of one who soon would have to return to the earth.

Several times during his last years and also in Zurich in 1938 Joyce had suffered from abdominal cramps. He had especially severe attacks when he arrived in Saint-Gérand-le-Puy in 1939, at which time a doctor diagnosed them as due to nerves. Previously, a Swiss doctor had suspected something serious and had strongly recommended that he have X-rays taken. But working intensely to complete *Finnegans Wake* and deeply concerned by his daughter's illness and with finding appropriate treatment for her, Joyce had not found time to follow this advice. The outbreak of the war with all its various effects on his family, including the constant excitement and strain over emigration and immigration, had undermined his health severely. The shock that precipitated the catastrophe must have been caused by the white wine which, in spite of its irritating effect, he had not stopped drinking during the last months in France and later. The birthday of his friend Paul Ruggiero was celebrated in the Kronenhalle on that fateful Friday (January 10).[31] That night he was seized with cramps, and was given superficial treatment by a doctor who was rushed in from the neighborhood. Two days later he underwent surgery, which, had it been initiated immediately, would probably have saved him. A perforated ulcer had led to peritonitis and had poisoned the entire body. An overall physical weakness set in that even a transfusion did not remedy. The donor was a soldier from Neuchâtel, an area that at first seemed a good omen to us, sitting in the anteroom of the clinic and participating in the distressing events of the sick room as they were relayed to us. His body, which had become so fragile as to make even the technical side of the transfusion a problem, succumbed to the poison. A feverish delirium set in, and with increasing urgency he repeated the same command—that Nora Joyce, who was sitting beside him, should set up her bed next to his. On January 13 at two o'clock in the morning he died, without having regained consciousness. It was that thirteenth which Joyce had always avoided for taking trips or making important decisions. It strangely moved and deeply impressed all who were close to him that he died on just that day.

And then came the funeral high above the city in the Allmend cemetery, where the poet Georg Buchner also lay. Nearby is the Zurich Zoo, where Joyce had walked so often during the last years. It had been his studio for the portrayal of that nocturnal "Phoenix Park"—or Garden of Eden—and at the same time an ordinary zoo where a dark murmur surges through a sleepy animal world, and from the grotesque words and shorthand descriptions the primitive form and being of the animalistic rises in this "funnaminal world." It was a cold

31. The date was Thursday, January 9, according to Ruggiero (see below p. 285).

winter day. The sun was like a dull milky eye, shining softly through a haze. The roaring of the animals could be heard in the distance. An oddly mixed funeral procession had gathered to honor the great poet: there was no representative from Ireland, but the British envoy, Lord Derwent, had come. His understanding appreciation and great admiration for Joyce and Joyce's work were vividly apparent in his farewell address. The poet and translator of Joyce's early lyrics, Max Geilinger, representing the Association of Swiss Authors, and Heinrich Straumann, Professor of English, representing the University of Zurich, also were there. The wreath with the Irish emblem of a harp, entwined with grass-green ribbons, recalled not only Joyce's native land but also his poetic mission. The musical part of the ceremony, Monteverdi's "Addio terra, addio cielo," sung by the tenor Max Meili, was like a lonely lamentation. However, the most striking part of the ceremony came at the end when Nora Joyce had to part from the lowering coffin and with a simple, impulsive gesture spread out her arms for a farewell, while she bent lovingly over the wooden coffin as though to prevent the final lowering. And almost simultaneously there was an indistinct mumbling from an ancient Zuricher, nearly a century old, who also stayed at the Pension Delphin and therefore had attended the funeral. Hard of hearing, he had his neighbor repeat again and again the poet's name, trying unsuccessfully to pronounce it himself.[32] This burlesque episode, following immediately after a moment of pathos, seemed entirely in Joyce's vein. The sun gradually brightened, broke through the haze, and turned the snow into shining white. The earthly remains of James Joyce slowly sank into the ground, where he had set his foot again and again on his many wanderings.

People may wonder what had been in the poet's mind during the last weeks, apart from the everyday problems, apart from the worries about his daughter, whom he had had to leave behind in occupied France. Were there poetic ambitions for the near future and in what direction? There were two books lying on his table: a Greek dictionary and next to it the book *I Follow St. Patrick* by Oliver St. John Gogarty. The courageous struggle for freedom by the Greeks against the Italians had impressed Joyce deeply and occupied his mind. Thus the Greek theme returned once again, now under a new aspect.[33] The other book, however, concerned part of the unforgettable country of his youth,

32. See Armin Kesser, *Neue Schweizer Rundschau*, vol. 2, 1941. [C. G.-W.'s note]
33. In an interview Dr. Giedion-Welcker said, "When I went to see him at [the Pension Delphin] I saw that Joyce had a notebook and I asked, 'Are you going to work on something?' . . . He said, 'Yes the Greek revolution.' That time against the Italians, you know, had made a great impression on him, and he said,

the exile's native land. It was a mosaic rich in the topographical references and legends that are woven about the national saint and the beloved Ireland.

And the dead man's face? It rests in a sublime sleep, as not only the closed eyes of the death mask reveal, but also the relieved, spiritual glow emanating from it . . . "Au-dela de la mort ce sont ses rêves qui sont le paradis" (Beyond death are his dreams, which are his paradise).[34]

TRANSLATED BY WOLFGANG DILL

'I would like to write a drama on the revolution of the modern Greeks' " (Kain, ed., "An Interview with Carola Giedion-Welcker and Maria Jolas," p. 97).

34. *A Jarry*, by Rachilde (Paris: Gosset, 1928). Letter to Rachilde before his death (1906). [C. G.-W.'s note]

Paul Ruggiero and Paul Léon

THE FINAL TWO recollections are short and best dealt with in a single introduction. The first, by Paul Ruggiero (1887–1972), describes the difficulties in getting official permission for Joyce's entry into Switzerland and gives a detailed account of the last days of his life. The second is a homage by Paul Léon (d. 1942), the man who probably was closer than anyone else to Joyce during the last part of his career.

Ruggiero, an employee in a Zurich bank, was one of the nonliterary and relatively unknown people that Ellmann says Joyce favored. The two seem to have become friends almost from their first meeting in 1916. Ruggiero knew modern Greek, having lived several years in Greece, and thus offered Joyce a chance for occasional exchanges in the language, which he had learned slightly while in Trieste. Ruggiero also was a fairly accomplished musician, providing an even more important mutual interest. One episode growing out of that interest gives an insight into a curious side of Joyce's taste in music.

In 1938 he listened to a French version of a song that he had heard Ruggiero sing in Greek. Enchanted by the song, he wanted a record of it, but couldn't find one since he lacked the title and the name of the composer, so he wrote Ruggiero asking for information. Ultimately he located and bought two records of the song, sending one to Ruggiero and playing his own over and over. He also asked Ruggiero to send him the Greek words, since he wanted to sing both versions at a party. The song, titled "A Dream," goes:

> I walked out all alone on the strand
> To remember how we had wept together
> When I kiss you, you remember it too.
> When I kiss you, you remember it too.
> Now I love another, a blonde
> Much prettier than you.
> But at the bottom of the heart
> First love keeps its deep roots. [JJ 727]

Joyce told Ruggiero that Nora cried while listening to it. He went on to ask, "What the deuce is there in music, and above all in singing, that moves us so deeply?" (Letters I, 403). A more interesting question is, What was there in himself that caused him to be moved by such banal little songs as this one and the one Nino Frank mentions him taking pains to learn?

The devotion Joyce aroused in people is illustrated once again in Ruggiero's struggle to arrange his entry into Switzerland. But few exemplified that devotion to the degree the Russian emigré Paul Léon did. Léon met Joyce in 1930 and almost immediately became involved in helping with Finnegans Wake. Though a man of distinguished scholarly achievements in both law and literature, he was dazzled by the genius he saw at work. Shortly after they met he told Joyce, "... I do feel I cannot ever thank you enough for having allowed me to observe the formation of your thoughts which is, I confess, both captivating and meaningful" (JJ 643). In a letter to his brother, he was equally enthusiastic, claiming Joyce to be "the greatest writer of our time" (JJ 643).

Ultimately Léon began assisting Joyce with nearly every phase of his work as well as with innumerable private matters, and continued to do so for nearly ten years. Miss Weaver, who was in a position to know, remarked that "in the later years . . . Mr. Léon was Mr. Joyce's staunchest and most loyal and devoted and understanding friend."[1] In 1939 there was a brief estrangement, but Léon followed Joyce to Saint-Gérand-le-Puy, and the two were soon strolling together, exchanging bitterly whimsical remarks about the war (JJ 745). There Léon helped with the corrections to Finnegans Wake and then, against Joyce's urging, returned to Paris. Léon's last act of devotion to Joyce was to rescue many of his books, papers, and pictures, which were about to be auctioned by an unscrupulous landlord. Protecting his friend's privacy with a care that has caused some frustration among Joyce scholars, Léon arranged for the papers to be deposited in the National Library of Ireland under a fifty-year seal. Though as a Jew he was in constant danger in Paris, he remained there hoping to see his son graduate. The day that event was supposed to take place, he was picked up by the Germans and sent to the concentration camps, where he died.[2]

1. Jane Lidderdale and Mary Nicholson, *Dear Miss Weaver: Harriet Shaw Weaver 1876–1961* (New York: Viking Press, 1970), p. 397.
2. For a fuller account of the relationship between Joyce and Léon see Lucie Noël, *James Joyce and Paul L. Léon: The Story of a Friendship* (New York: Gotham Book Mart, [1950]).

James Joyce's
Last Days in Zurich

By Paul Ruggiero

ON AUGUST 4, 1940, Joyce expressed the wish to come to Zurich with his family and begged me to do anything I could with the relevant authorities. In the meantime, however, on the recommendation of Mr. Zumsteg,[3] he had written to an attorney in Geneva, Mr. Haldenwang, asking him to take the steps necessary for their return to Switzerland. But Mr. Haldenwang had not succeeded. Joyce wrote asking me to contact the Giedions,[4] whom I didn't know at the time. I immediately went to the Giedions and for several hours we discussed what could be done for Joyce. For my part, as Joyce had been one of my best friends since 1916, I decided to inquire of the Zurich immigration officials about obtaining a residence permit for Joyce and his family. Knowing, however, that Mr. Haldenwang officially represented Joyce, I wrote Joyce that I could help him on condition that Mr. Haldenwang relinquish his part and send me the dossier. Joyce immediately telegraphed Mr. Haldenwang, who, in a letter of November 7, 1940, turned matters over to me. There followed exchanges of letters, telephone calls and personal visits with the immigration officials. Finally they demanded the deposit of 50,000 francs as a guarantee. An impossible demand. Where could one get such a sum?

Mme Giedion offered 15,700 francs (deposited at the Crédit Suisse) and Mr. Brauchbar $1,000 (= 4,300 francs). I finally managed to persuade the immigration officials to reduce the required sum from 50,000 to 20,000, on condition that Joyce would make a declaration of assets. This was really the last straw. I telegraphed Joyce to draw up this declaration so it would reach me as quickly as possible, and Joyce, believing that he had found a better way to send it than by express, gave it to Mr. Augsburg,[5] who was leaving for Lausanne. Feeling no need to hurry, Mr. Augsburg traveled leisurely to Lyons, etc., with the

---

3. Joyce had written of his problem to an old Zurich friend, Edmund Brauchbar, mentioned later in the recollection. Brauchbar then wrote to Zurich urging his son and his son's business associate, Gustave Zumsteg, to give Joyce any help they could. Zumsteg's mother, also mentioned later in the recollection, managed the Kronenhalle in Zurich.

4. Siegfried Giedion and his wife Carola Giedion-Welcker.

5. Given as Gia Augsbourg in *Letters* III, 498. Otherwise unidentified.

declaration in his pocket, while I waited and waited. I sent a second message to Joyce telling him, "Declaration not yet arrived. Send another by express," which he did, and the declaration reached me at the same time that Mr. Augsburg telephoned from Lausanne saying that he had a letter for me from Joyce and asking me if he should send it on. Mr. Ellmann is mistaken in writing that the immigration officials refused Joyce's declaration.[6] My account is the true one, as documents in my possession prove.

Finally the immigration officials consented to authorize residence in Zurich for Joyce and his family, and thus Joyce arrived in Zurich on December 17, 1940, at eight o'clock in the evening, finding Mme Giedion and myself at the station. Joyce's first words were, "Ruggiero, we can never repay what you have done for us." Foreseeing that after so much turmoil Joyce would need rest and knowing that he disliked hotels, I had arranged two rooms for them at the Pension Delphin, Mühlebachstrasse, which was surrounded by a large park where Joyce could rest. It was a family pension with ten or so well-furnished rooms. Since it was his habit never to dine where he was staying, room with breakfast was agreed on, and they were very happy and satisfied with all I had done for them.

After several days of well-earned rest, Joyce went out into the city with Stephen.[7] For my part I went to see them almost every evening after work, and I reported anything new that had come from America regarding their finances. On entering his room where he awaited me, I had the bad habit of placing my hat on their bed, and each time he said to me, "Ruggiero, take that hat off the bed. I am superstitious and they say that means someone will die." What a presentiment . . . Joyce was really very superstitious. I remember one time when we were walking together, we met two nuns, and immediately he said to me,

"Do as I do. 🤙 Those women bring bad luck."

On Noel, that is to say December 26, Saint Stephen's Day, I invited the whole family to tea at our house. He looked very well and we spent a very pleasant afternoon together. I played two pieces on the cello accompanied by my son on the piano. Following that Giorgio sang with his beautiful bass voice "O vulnera doloris" by Giacomo Carissimo, accompanied by my son on the piano. Then around seven o'clock they left to have dinner at the Kronenhalle, promising me to return some evening to dine with us, when we would have fish and white wine, which he liked very much.

6. Ellmann says, "Joyce . . . composed one declaration which was not accepted, then another which at last the authorities took" (*JJ* 750).
7. Joyce's grandson.

On January 9 (it was a Thursday and not January 10 as Richard Ellmann writes and has no connection with my birthday, which I celebrate on February 8) after my usual visit, Joyce said to me, "Come have dinner with us."[8]

"With pleasure," and we went to the Kronenhalle. The weather was gloomy, damp, and rainy, half snow, half rain. Joyce was not as well as he had been a few days earlier. He ate almost nothing in spite of Mme Zumsteg's great efforts at exciting his appetite—ham, fish, etc.—but nothing appealed to him. He only drank and smoked his long Virginia cigarettes. During the whole evening Joyce kept praising me for the work I had done to allow their entry into Switzerland, and said to me, "You should have been a diplomat."

At 11:30 we decided to go home. On leaving the restaurant, Nora Joyce slipped on the steps and almost fell to her knees, except for the support I gave her. Then she said, "Why do you make me go out at night in such terrible weather?" Fortunately, she was not hurt. Having arrived before the door of the Pension Delphin, I took leave of them and said, "Now I am going home to make some rum grog to warm myself a little," and Joyce said to me, "Good night, Ruggiero," and recommended the grog. (When the weather was damp and cold Joyce enjoyed drinking one and even two glasses of gin or rum grog.)

The next day, Friday, January 10, Giorgio telephoned me at the bank and said, "Papa is very sick: he had severe stomach pains all night."

"Very well, I will go see him." In the meantime, Joyce had been taken to the hospital. Saturday morning, since the bank was closed, I went to the hospital and saw Joyce with whom I exchanged only a few words because he was very weak. Seeing him in that state I immediately had an inspiration, "If he dies during the operation, neither Giorgio nor Nora will be able to draw on the account he has at my bank." I went down to the hospital office and wrote out a power of attorney for his son Giorgio. I went back upstairs and talked with him explaining, that just in case, it would be a good idea if he signed a power of attorney giving Giorgio access to his funds at the bank. I gave it to him and without reading it, he signed and said to me, "Ruggiero, make the best out of it." These were the last words I heard from him because after the operation it was impossible to talk with him. I was at the hospital until Sunday evening, January 12, then returned home distressed and sad.

The next day, Monday morning, January 13, Giorgio telephoned me at the office and said, "Papa is dead."

8. According to Ellmann, on January 10 Joyce "came again to the restaurant [the Kronenhalle] after visiting an exhibition of nineteenth-century French painting; this time he was celebrating Paul Ruggiero's birthday" (*JJ* 754).

The funeral has been described by Richard Ellmann [*JJ* 755]. There were a number of wreaths but the most beautiful was one from his wife, who had ordered a wreath in the form of a harp. She told me, "I had it made in that shape for my Jim because he loved music so much."

I had found it impossible to convince Nora that it would be good to have a priest come for the final benediction.

After various remarks and the singing by the tenor Meili of "Addio terra, addio cielo" by Monteverdi, the procession was led toward the grave, and all took their positions several yards from the edge. Only Nora, accompanied by me, moved up before the coffin, and after I had made the sign of the cross with my hand, along with a "Requiem aeternam dona ei Domine," we withdrew and Nora left accompanied by Mme Giedion.

Sic transit gloria mundi.

TRANSLATED BY CARLETON W. CARROLL

In Memory of Joyce

By Paul Léon

Dear Monsieur Paulhan,[9]

Eight months have now gone by since I saw Mr. Joyce for the last time, and it will soon be four months since the papers announced his death. Your little note can only add to my sadness and regret that I should never have set down any of the conversations I had with him during this last twelve years, when we met at least once or twice a day, except if one or the other of us was on holiday, or traveling. Time has already taken its toll; memories become blurred and fade . . . I consider, however, that I owe you a reply. But my reply will necessarily be of a more general nature than I should have wished it, especially since it is no longer possible for me to refer to the letters that passed between us

9. Jean Paulhan, publisher of the *Nouvelle Revue Française*, asked Léon to write an article about Joyce shortly after the latter's death. At first Léon refused, then decided to write Paulhan a letter instead, leaving his signature off so as not to attract the attention of German authorities (*James Joyce and Paul L. Léon*, p. 38).

during our various separations or occasionally even, in the interval of two meetings, from one street to another. It will also, perhaps, seem more personal than it should which I hope you will forgive, for therein lies the great danger of all memoirs written after the event.

The most general and lasting impression I shall always retain of Joyce the man is his exquisite gentleness, together with his infinite power of comprehension. By this I do not mean a quality of heart, which I should like to bring out one day, but which touches too personal, too intimate a side of his nature to be discussed now. I am referring to a more general characteristic, one that partakes, as it were, of the elementary forces of his make-up. For gentleness and comprehension, in his case, did not spring from weakness or indifference, but were allied to an inner strength, a directed spiritual activity, such as I have never seen in anyone else. Fate decreed that he should be obliged to put his strength and activity to daily use. The time will come when the story of his life may be written, and it will be possible then to estimate to what extent he was pursued by misfortune, how much courage he needed to combat and dominate events . . . Today I simply mention this fact, for the guidance of future biographers.

Meanwhile, however, the student of the human soul should read attentively Joyce's writings in which it is mirrored, for Joyce made no distinction between actual life and literary creation. His work is one long self-confession, and in this respect he is akin to the greatest of the romantics. I well realize that all writing, even the most objective, is self-revealing. But I also realize that in the desire to describe and portray ourselves, we only misrepresent ourselves, and the description and portrayal are never quite faithful or complete. The influences of time and environment, daily life, chance acquaintances, as well as more durable ties, tend to conceal us from ourselves. Joyce, however, seeks to attain to absolute sincerity, to all that is most human within us; he seeks to do away with writing that merely aims at covering the blank page, to do away with conventional self-expression, to do away with the very body which intervenes between the most secret "I," Pascal's "I beyond the soul," and the exterior world. He also seeks to do away with the writing hand, the listening ear, the seeing eye . . . and on this last point a pitiless fate met him more than half-way . . . But should one then be silent? Joyce's work offers brilliant proof of the contrary, but it serves also as proof that he had the necessary courage, perseverance, inner strength and energy of mind—any one of which might easily have been insufficient—to overcome all obstacles, all suffering, and to attain perfection. When his work comes to be judged according to its true value, as posterity will judge it, it will appear overwhelming, if only because of the crushing labour that it obviously represents, and one man's life will seem to have been conceived on too small a scale in comparison with the immensity of the effort involved.

There exists yet another aspect of the intimate and indissoluble tie between Joyce's life and work, which it is perhaps even more important to mention here, since it will necessarily be something of a closed book to posterity, and that is the influence of his work on his life. Continuous self-confession, for Joyce meant continuous creation; it was he who created the atmosphere and general conditions that surrounded him, and he never stopped creating them. There has been much talk of disciples, of a coterie, of an ivory tower in which he was supposed to have lived in an inaccessible retirement. Nothing could be more inexact. I know no one who was more averse to preaching, teaching, and every kind of pose than he was. With rare exceptions, too, his followers were persons who did not know him and did not get to know him—here we come to a phenomenon which belongs to literary history, one which concerns his friends and what, for the sake of precision, we may call his acquaintances. Meeting new people, or creating new ties, was always for him a difficult problem to be solved, something to be created. For this reason I fear that very few sensed how much ripe reflection and infinite precaution, warm kindliness and genuine respect for humanity was hidden by his silence. As one grew to know him, one became as it were enveloped by a fine network of half-expressed thoughts and feelings that created an atmosphere of such suavity that it was difficult to resist, all the more so since it contained no element of constraint. But in order to partake of this atmosphere, a personal effort was necessary, and it was a mistake to enter into it without due reflection. For its only reward was that of unfailing friendship, disinterested attachment, the delights of the mind. It did not offer what the majority of people were looking for: neither, as in some cases, the direct road to truth, nor, as in others, social relations. These disappointed hopes may perhaps account for the fact, which was noted by his most recent biographer, that in the course of his lifetime, many friendships gave way to undying hatred. Without any doubt, too, they explain the fact that he had the reputation of being unapproachable.

There is no disputing that this continuous creation, this unremitting effort of the mind, entailed hazards for him as well as for those near him. This explains in part his tendency to take infinite precautions, his close outward observance of convention, and his exquisite politeness; for he was conscious that this creative effort was generated by an almost titanic force, one that was capable of dominating all conventions and revolutionizing the most deep-rooted traditions, the most accepted "truths." Many celebrated writers have retained mastery over their work; others have been mastered by it. I believe that Joyce provides the most perfect example of unremitting and supremely successful effort on the part of an artist to give equal value to his life and to his work. Indeed, despite the anxiety and suffering, the doubt and passion, the cruelty and heartbreak which fate did not spare him and which he in turn did not hesitate to manifest in his work, I shall always retain a memory of his serenity, a serenity that was all gentleness and comprehension like that of nature itself, whose enchanted observer he was, and with whose serenity his whole spirit was imbued.

I recall a day in late September 1930. I was leaving for a holiday and Joyce had insisted on walking with me part of the way towards the Gare de Lyon. I am a very poor walker, just the opposite of Joyce, and our strolls aroused in me only moderate enthusiasm. I believe, however, that he felt safer crossing the streets when I held his arm. But the two of us must have made a sorry pair in the streets of Paris and, in fact, Philippe Soupault had baptized us "the halt and the blind." That day, as we walked quietly along the Boulevard Raspail, Joyce was suddenly stopped by a young girl who, somewhat awkwardly but charmingly, complimented him on his work. Joyce lifted his unfortunate eyes towards the still-sunny sky, then brought them back to the boxed trees growing along the Boulevard: "You would do better," he said to the girl, "to admire the sky or even these poor trees." Should that young girl chance to read these lines, she will perhaps recognize herself, but I should like [her] to know how great a truth lay behind this apparently banal suggestion. This was not false modesty, but a genuine admiration for the natural universe; for its colours which he could hardly distinguish, but which he appreciated all the more fully in consequence; for the constant mobility of its forms, whether pleasing or unshapely; for its sounds, to which only recently we listened together, stretched out on the grass in the Allier;[10] for the human beings who people and quicken it with their thoughts, their passions, whether good or evil, noble or base, harmonious or discordant.

Joyce's feeling for all bodies of water amounted almost to nostalgia, and he was drawn to the seashore by an irresistible attraction. Wherever he went on holiday, he immediately looked for a river, a stream, or even a brook,[11] and his first walks led him along its banks. How many

10. That is, at Saint-Gérand-le-Puy.
11. This recalls a line from Lady Gregory's *Gods and Fighting Men*: "And then he said farewell to Crimall and went on to learn poetry from Finegas, a poet that was living at the Boinn, for the poets thought it was always on the brink of water poetry was revealed to them." [Maria Jolas' note]

hours we passed together, watching the calm flow of the Seine from the Pont de l'Alma or the Pont Royal!

The mystery of this attraction towards water has been revealed to us by Joyce himself in his revolutionary, astonishing, Pantagruelian, romantic *Finnegans Wake*, especially in the last dozen or so pages, which are composed of short, choppy, restless, rippling, flowing sentences that follow each other in rapid, turbulent succession. Here we have the homecoming of the river Liffey, as it rushes swooning into the arms of its father the Ocean, there to become transformed by the heat of the sun's rays into a cloud which, in turn, floats back upstream and dissolves into raindrops that swell the river as it flows down to the sea.

Among the innumerable critical reviews that I have gone through, I recall no mention of a point which, it seems to me, should strike us immediately: and that is, the fact that the amazing postscript which concludes the work ends on an unfinished sentence, with the article "the"; and the noun that follows this article is the first word of the book, that is to say, "riverrun." It is not for me to spell out all the meanings of what people are inclined to consider as a cryptogram; this task belong to future generations of critics and literary historians. All I should like to do here is to introduce the testimony of one who witnessed the growth of this work. This postscript had probably been carried in its completed form for many years in the prodigious brain that engendered it.

The first version, which was only about two and a half pages long, was written in one afternoon, in December 1938. It was a veritable deliverance. Joyce brought it with him when we met that evening for our usual half-past-eight *rendez-vous* in Mme Lapeyre's pleasant *bistrot*, on the corner of the Rue de Grenelle and the Rue de Bourgogne. He then left to join Mrs. Joyce for dinner at Fouquet's, where he was accustomed to go quite regularly, and where I met him a little later. While at dinner his daughter-in-law read the fragment to us for the first time, and Joyce's pleasure at hearing his written words come to life and take on consistency and colour through this agreeable rendering was very evident. This occasion, when to an orchestral accompaniment of clattering dishes and clinking glasses, his own words created harmony in the surrounding discordance, was one of the rare times when I sensed that he was either satisfied or proud of himself.

Then began a period of feverish labour, which filled every hour and every minute of both day and night. I am afraid Joyce got little sleep during that month or six weeks. We were being pressed by the printer, who had promised to send a copy for Joyce's birthday on February 2nd, and we had even to give up reading a third proof. Meanwhile the postscript was growing in length and consistency, so that from two pages of manuscript it developed into a dozen printed pages.

And then the countless misadventures . . . All Joyce's friends were pressed into helping with the typing. Mrs. Jolas was typing in Neuilly, Mr. Gilbert was typing in his Rue Jean-du-Bellay apartment, and I was dictating in our flat in the Rue Casimir-Perier. Around seven in the evening, the different fragments were assembled at the headquarters of the masterbrain in the Rue Edmond-Valentin. One day, having gone to fetch Mr. Gilbert's *pensum*, I returned to the Rue Edmond-Valentin, and had reached the fourth floor when I suddenly realized that I had left the envelope in the taxi. I rushed home and called London to ask for another set of proofs, because we were already making additions on the galleys. But this would mean a delay of three days, three days lost, since it had happened on a Friday evening and the only person I had been able to reach in London was a lone secretary. Fortunately, my taxi-driver proved to be exceptionally honest, and two hours later the envelope was returned to us unopened. Those two hours were difficult ones for Joyce, but he neither complained, nor reproached me during that time.

When the proof was finally posted, it was not yet the end. Additions and corrections poured in, and there was no longer time to send them by post, with the result that there were telephone calls to the publisher in London and even to the printer in Glasgow. Both the telephone and telegraph wires, in fact, were kept humming, and I fear that for a month I must have made life intolerable for Messrs Faber & Faber's literary director, Mr. Richard De la Mare. Finally the book appeared on February 2nd, and only commercial reasons kept it from being put on sale before May 4th. *Finnegans Wake* was now out of Joyce's hands and launched on a life of its own . . .

But the man himself is gone . . . It is hard for me to write this, and I wish I could not believe it. Events had separated us, and as this separation lengthens it becomes all the more difficult to believe that I shall never see him again . . . But the loss is greater than that, because his indefatigable brain was about to give birth to something new . . . to a new confession . . . a new creation . . . to the awakening of *Finnegan*: "Wait until Finnegan wakes," he used to tell me.

Very sincerely yours,

L——

TRANSLATED BY MARIA JOLAS

Index

61; wide knowledge, 62; joins J in doggerel game, 63; J tells of Gillet, 164, 165; mentioned, 66
Busoni, Ferruccio, 263
Byrne, Davy: J on, 31n

Candide (periodical): reports on J party, 98
Carlow, Lord (George Lionel Seymour): J has tea with, 99; stories about his family told by J, 230; J sends article to, 249
Carr, Henry, 56n
Cassou, Jean (editor), 210
Catholic Church: J's opinion of, 29, 37, 71, 199, 238; J on popes of, 29, 38; J sings music of, 32, 36, 41, 58, 246; J won't baptize children in, 35; J interested in the Vatican, 99 (see also Osservatore Romano); J intends to attack, 172; place of Newman in, 217; in FW, 221; Nora attends, 233; J on Daniel O'Connell and, 234
—Holy Week: J attends Mass during, 63–64, 214–15; liturgical color of, and J, 260; mentioned, 246
—priests: J on literary portrayal of, 240; have no worries, 243; not at J's funeral, 286. See also Jesuits
Cervantes, Miguel de: Don Quixote, 69
Chamberlain, Neville: J on foreign policy of, 241
Chamber Music: basis of J's future work, 181; J sings his setting of poem in, 231; mentioned, 50
A Chaucer ABC: J anticipates, 143; Gillet helps with, 165
Chee Chee (musical): J likes song from, 276
Choux, Jean: J sees film of, 99
Clancy, George (model for Davin in P): death of, 210
Coleridge, Samuel Taylor: definition of fancy and imagination worries J, 224, 225, 227; J admires "Kubla Khan," 228
Colum, Padraic: J talks of, 185; J sends article on FW to, 249
Commercial High School. See

Scuole Superiore di Commercio Revoltella
Communists. See Marxists
Compagni, Dino (writer), 40
Comprendre: attack on J in, 269
Conmee, Father: J remembers fondly, 240
Cooper, James Fenimore: J sees movie inspired by, 99
Crémieux, Benjamin: J recommends Confessions of Zeno to, 81; lunches with J and Svevo, 82; at PEN reception, 100; works on translation of "ALP," 102n
Croce, Benedetto, 71
Crosby, Harry and Caresse: at the Joyces', 89
Cunard, Nancy: J short with, 156n
Curran, Constantin: J arranges for Gillet to meet, 186, 187n; and radio program on J, 211n; obituary on J, 269–70
Curtius, Ernst Robert: study of U, 196; J has articles on FW sent to, 224, 248
Czech language: and J, 126, 134, 135
Czechoslovakia: J's work in, 128–32 passim, 136; J's brother-in-law from, 135

Danish language: and J, 57, 140, 141, 143, 147
D'Annunzio, Gabriele: J's knowledge of, 45n; J talks of, 99; J praises, 149
Dante Alighieri (Divine Comedy): J admires, xv, 29, 37; J quotes from, 12, 41n; J knows from memory, 40; moves J to tears, 45; less human than Odyssey, 69; J identifies with, 70, 158; J wants to talk about, 80; J on number in, 129
De la Mare, Richard (Faber and Faber): and FW, 291
Denmark: J's interest in, 137–52 passim
Derwent, Lord (British envoy): at J's funeral, 279
De Tuoni, Dario: recollection of J, xvi; J recites Verlaine to, 43n
Dickens, Charles, 272

Dostoevsky, Feodor, 34, 62
Dubček, Alexander, 119
Dubliners: difficulties in publishing, 32, 184; read to Prezioso, 54; Stanislaus brings copy to Benco, 56; and *U*, 70; and J's work as whole, 131, 132; and Ferrero, 156n; mentioned, 55
Du Bos, Charles, 250
Dujardin, Edouard: at "Déjeuner *U*," 85; mentioned, 207
Dunsany, Lord: J encourages publication of, 87
Duse, Eleanora: J visits London to see, 212

Eglinton, John: errs about *U*, 217
The Egoist, 59
Ehrenburg, Ilya: introduced to J, 80
Eliot, Thomas Stearns: J's attitude toward, 87; essay on *U*, 153; emphasizes J's "orthodoxy," 209; J has article on *FW* sent to, 248
Ellmann, Richard: biography of J, xiii, 5, 6, 14, 33n, 40n, 139, 164, 258n, 273n, 284, 285
England: water closet makers, 28; J keeps British passport, 185; J on treatment of Irish by, 223; leaders of behave strangely, 241, 247; J refuses to write propaganda for, 245
English language: and the Irish, 28; J cannot understand, 212
English literature: made by Irish writers, 28
English people: sentimental about dogs, 232
English Players, 56, 264
"An Epilogue to Ibsen's *Ghosts*": composition of, 273
Erigena, John Scotus: J's knowledge of, 37
Ernst, Max: J likes "Europe après la pluie," 253
Europe: J's "spiritual father," xiii; J's response to, xiv
Europe (periodical): study of *U* in, 210, 215
Exiles: "Author's Notes" to, 257–58;

scheduled for English Players, 264; mentioned, 56
Eyers, H. J. (Berlitz School), 14

Fargue, Léon-Paul: at J parties, 85, 114; gives up on *FW*, 178; J likes wit, 222; mentioned, 180
Fascists(-ism): at 1937 PEN meeting, 153, 155–56; J on, in France and Italy, 241, 242; mentioned, 102. *See also* Hitler, Adolf; Mussolini, Benito
Fehr, Bernard: J sings Verdi with, 273
Fénelon, François: J alludes to, 227
Ferrero, Guglielmo: at 1937 PEN Congress, 155–56 and n
Finnegans Wake: J's chief discussions of, 64–65, 129, 131–32, 149–51, 159–61, 178, 197–99, 207–45 *passim*; like mountain, 64; sound in, 65; J begins, 73; J's attitude toward reception of, 73, 104, 132, 150, 234, 243, 245, 249, 250, 252; publication of, 87, 103, 177, 178, 181–82, 212, 218, 243, 274; hold on J, 87, 138, 149, 213, 222, 223, 233; J reads aloud, 88, 244–45; J's reading for, 92; J keeps title secret, 98, 161–62, 181, 211, 215, 243; Soupault lectures on, 106; and surrealism, 107–8; reception of, 117, 131, 161, 178, 203, 248, 250, 252; constantly changing, 129, 221–22; and *U*, 131, 149, 207, 237; J insists on wide appeal of, 131, 213, 234; J gives general explication of, 132, 178–79; pleases J, 150; J's doubts about, 150, 153, 160–61, 179, 213, 221, 224, 226; Gillet shows to Parandowski, 161; and Valéry, 178; J knows by heart, 179; on finishing, 181, 215, 219, 290–91; last pages of, 197, 218, 226, 244–45, 290; J deprecates, 198, 226, 227; J anxious to have understood, 205; J's aims in, 207; J follows laws in writing, 209, 237; J works at night on, 211, 214–15, 216, 225, 255n; Nora anxious for completion of, 213; linked with Lucia's illness, 214;

not obscure enough, 214; Gilbert helps with, 214–15; Saint Patrick/ Archdruid dialogue in, 220–21; made out of nothing, 223; and Blake, 226; a favorite sentence in, 228–29; J on obscurity in, 233; scope of, 235; and WW II, 243, 249; J has articles on, sent to friends, 248–49; J laughs while writing, 255n; and Shakespeare, 272–73; correcting American edition of, 282

—*Elements in*: trouvailles, 65, 198–99, 223–24; Petrarch, 93, 218, 220; Dublin, 97, 224, 225; singers, 107n; Francesco Soave, 107n; number, 120, 129–30; Denmark, 137–38; dreams, 149, 207; Hebrew, 213; Japanese and Chinese, 213, 218, 219, 220–21; Spenser, 218, 220; the Liffey, 220; Finn MacCool, 223, 234; laundries, 225; *Huckleberry Finn*, 228n; animals, 232, 234; Daniel O'Connell, 234; Quinet, 239; Zurich, 265–66, 267

—*Major figures in*
ALP: and Mrs. Svevo, 87; J finds representation of, 179–80; Gillet explicates, 180
HCE: J on, 178, 180, 234
Shem and Shaun: significance of, 208

—*Sections of*
"ALP": J and translating of, 96–98, 101–2, 114–15, 132–33; translations of, 106, 136, 150, 193, 250; J gives copies to friends, 179, 260–61; J's recording of, 196 and n, 261
"A Phoenix Park Nocturne": J helps with article on, 213, 216, 218, 220

Fitzgerald, F. Scott, xiv
Flaubert, Gustave: J looks for German writer like, 62; J recites from, 159–60, 226
Fleiner, Fritz (professor): on Budgen, 62
Fleiner, Mrs. Fritz: friend of Nora's, 62
Fleischmann, Marthe: and *U*, 60

Fock (Berlitz School), 19–20
"Follow Me Up to Carlow": J sings, 230–31
France, Anatole: portrayal of priests, 240
Francini Bruni, Alessandro: J at flat of, 58; J asks Mercanton to visit, 242; J obtains copy of lecture, 243; J asks about, 244
French, Percy, 141n
French language, 124, 196
Fribourg: J visits, 227, 236–37

Gautier, Theophile: J cites, 160
Geilinger, Max: at J's funeral, 279
German censors: pass articles on J, 104
German language, 196, 224
German writers: J seeks one like Flaubert, 62. *See also* Goethe, Johann Wolfgang; Hauptmann, Gerhart; Keller, Gottfried
Germany: J on treatment of Jews in, 218; J on Hitler in, 254, 270
Gibraltar, 124
Gide, André: J on, 146, 222–23
Giedion, Siegfried, 253, 266–67, 283
Giedion-Welcker, Carola: helps with J's Swiss visa, 283; meets J, 284
Gilbert, Stuart: book on *U*, 57, 84; and French translation of *U*, 76; reads D. H. Lawrence to J, 87n; manner, 89; praises Gillet's recollection of J, 165; helps with *FW*, 214, 215, 291
Gillet, Louis: quoted on J, 143; J praises his introduction to *ABC*, 143; shows parts of *FW* to Parandowski, 161; to review *FW*, 245, 252; J has article on *FW* sent to, 248
Giraudoux, Jean: work of, bores J, 156–57; helps J with Swiss visa, 275; mentioned, 90
Goethe, Johann Wolfgang: J on *Faust*, 65, 69; quoted, 244
Gogarty, Oliver St. John: in *U*, 63n; book on Saint Patrick, 219, 279
Goll, Ivan: and J's association with *900*, 75–76

Gorman, Herbert: biography of J, 6n, 31n, 32n, 67, 225, 243, 250, 252

Goyert, Georg, 75n, 245

Greece: flags from, for *U*, 126; J plans to write about, 279

Greek language: and J, 44n, 57, 127, 279, 281

Greek literature. *See* Homer

Gregory, Lady Augusta, 172n, 289n

Grieg, Edvard: J sings song by, 231

Grosz, George: J likes caricatures by, 120, 126

Guérin, Maurice de (poet), 239

Haldenwang, Georges, 283

Halper, Nathan, 69

Hansen, Mrs. Kastor: J cautions, on translating *U*, 149n

Hauptmann, Gerhart: J praises work of, 271

Heiberg, Gunnar: J read, 141

Hemingway, Ernest: J's attitude toward, 79, 148

Hitler, Adolf: J on, 254, 270

Hohenlohe, Prince, 43

Homer: J's knowledge of, 44, 157; J discusses, 57; J's reasons for basing *U* on, 69–70, 153–54; is sole composer of *Odyssey*, 158; J's debt to, 158; his Ulysses J's childhood hero, 168; J's etymology for Odysseus, 194; Ulysses different from other heroes, 208; chapter titles of *U* from, 217; J buys for grandson, 276

Hopkins, Gerard Manley: J linked with at UCD, 217

Horace: J recites, 227–28; prefers to Vergil, 228

Horniman, Annie B., 172n

Horthy, Lord (ex-Regent of Hungary): student at Berlitz School, 39

Howald, Ernst: helps with J's Swiss visa, 275

Huxley, Aldous: J prefers to D. H. Lawrence, 87

Ibsen, Henrik: J talks about, xv; shared J's dislike of Rome, 29; J does not idolize, 34; influence on J of, 41, 56, 137; J learned Danish to read, 141; J writes to, 147; J compares with Shakespeare, 147, 272; J sings Grieg setting of, 231

—*An Enemy of the People*: J sees Zacconi in, 30

—*Ghosts*: J tormented by Zacconi in, 30 and n; J writes "An Epilogue to . . . ," 273

—*Hedda Gabler*: not a feminist play, 147

—*Little Eyolf*: J praises, 148, 272

—*When We Dead Awaken*: J writes about, 35 and n, 147

—*The Wild Duck*: J on performance of, 147–48; and Lucia, 254–55; J praises, 271–72

"Ibsen's New Drama": J on composition of, 147; mentioned, 35

Ireland: J's preoccupation with, xiv, 179–80, 237; J's attitude toward, 3, 27–28, 33, 41, 88–89, 172, 220, 223, 234, 269–70; J tells stories about, 31, 222; importance of, in J's work, 97, 132, 159; J's reasons for not returning to, 116, 146; Danes in, 141–42; response to J there, 146, 211, 213, 246; J seldom discusses, 184; Nora visits, 184; independence of, unimportant to J, 185; J urges Gillet to see Howth in, 186–87n; attitude toward Jews in, 208; J sends articles to friends in, 215; Nora dislikes, 220, 223; J on English treatment of, 223; clippings on, sent to Gorman, 225; J will not apply for passport from, 250–51

Irish Academy: J will not join, 146

Irish-Americans: J worries about reaction of, to *FW*, 234, 243

Irish language (Gaelic): J studied briefly, 44n; J scorns, 185

Irish Times: article on UCD in, 217; J reads, 224–25, 233, 235

Italian language: and J, 12, 40, 44, 49, 52–53, 65, 80, 83, 157

Italian literature: J's knowledge of, 41–42, 45, 193. *See also* Dante Alighieri

Italians: excessively proud of culture,

29; are greatest actors, 30

Italy: J's fondness for, 45, 149, 157, 192, 242, 247; J thinks few Fascists in, 242. *See also* Trieste

Jaloux, Edmond: J expects to meet, 218; J's affection for, 222; lectures on Blake, 226; J queries on *FW*, 252

Japan: and J's work, 50, 266

Japanese language, 213, 219, 221, 266

Jarnach, Philippe, 263

Jarry, Alfred: compared with J, 258

Jesuits: J's debt to, 64, 240; no sense of literature, 228; are "tarts," 240

Jews: J quotes Talmud on, 71; in Ireland and *U*, 208; J's concern for during WW II, 218, 241, 242, 245, 263n; J mistaken for one, 251

John, Augustus: J praises, 144; mentioned, 188

John, Saint: J admires, 37, 62

Jolas, Eugene: part of J's circle, 92, 98; publishes J, 178; in U.S., 274

Jolas, Maria (Mrs. Eugene): her recollection of J, xvi, 269n, 274; gives party for J, 98; on Beckett and Lucia, 104n; cares for Stephen J, 204; sings spirituals, 242; returns to U.S., 274; helps with *FW*, 291; mentioned, 98, 254

Jousse, Marcel: J interested in his theory of language, 199

Joyce, Giorgio (son): J's attitude toward, 63; manner toward J, 89; J anticipates grandson from, 92; sings on radio, 93–94; has party for J, 93–94, 182; J wants to return from U.S., 106; known for girl friends, 127; J sends telegram to, 141; tells of J's last days, 170; J concerned about, 218, 243, 250; visits J, 260; emigration in WW II, 275; his singing, 284; reports J's death, 285; mentioned, 181

Joyce, Helen Kastor Fleischman (daughter-in-law): appearance and manner, 89, 93; scorns J's taste, 142; is ill, 218; J worried about, 243; health worsens, 249; is con-

fined, 250; visits J, 260; reads aloud *FW*, 290; mentioned, 181

Joyce, James: and languages, xiv, 12, 40, 44, 49, 52–53, 57, 62, 65, 80, 83, 124–27, 134, 140, 141, 143, 147, 157, 159–60, 185, 196, 224, 266, 281 (*see also specific languages*); superstitions, 26, 284; associates people with animals or vegetables, 26–27, 31, 93; rejects church and state, 27, 38, 71, 272; drinking habits, 27, 31–33, 40–41, 43, 63, 86, 144, 182–83, 192, 212, 264; and Bible, 27, 37, 62; interest in theater, 30, 54, 56, 113, 141, 147–48, 264, 272; as storyteller, 31, 50, 144, 146, 150–51, 200–3, 223, 227; and music, 32, 36, 41, 49, 58, 62, 64, 67, 72, 89, 99–100, 107n, 113, 149, 168, 180–81, 195–96, 226, 230–31, 242, 247–48, 264, 274, 276, 281–82 (*see also specific composers*); family heritage, 33, 44, 135; and religion, 35–38, 62, 71, 228, 240 (*see also* Catholic Church; Jesuits); keeps anniversaries, 42, 60, 113–14, 181, 212, 260; dress, 45, 57, 78, 127, 143, 207, 212, 216, 219, 276; fears thunderstorms, 46, 66, 142, 212, 269; eyesight, 49, 56, 88, 112, 126, 128, 146–47, 151, 168, 207, 213–14, 216, 258–60; youthfulness, 49, 78–80, 85–86, 90–91, 139, 216, 226, 238, 273–74; and politics, 50, 53, 66, 80, 146, 153, 156n, 185, 224, 269–70; writes aphorisms and paradoxes, 56; reserve, 63, 71, 78–79, 134, 208; thoughtfulness, 60, 66, 84, 271; comic sense, 62, 255, 266–68; sets puzzles, 65; flats, 76–78, 208; dines out, 91, 98, 151, 170, 182; interest in cinema, 99; conversation, 99, 183–84, 212, 257, 272; and WW II, 102–3, 214, 241, 243, 245, 267–71 *passim*; assigns errands, 106–7; moodiness, 114, 138, 141, 164; energy, 114, 140; fondness for caricature, 119–20; curiosity, 140–41, 217, 235–37, 260; interest in names, 142, 236–37, 272; not a hero, 165;

name, 167, 268–69; memory, 179, 235; daily schedule, 183; concern for children's illnesses, 192, 271; expressiveness, 201–3, 213, 224, 229, 240, 246; and dreams, 207, 208, 212, 226, 233–34; handles all family matters, 238–39; attitude toward women, 253, 255, 256n; his rings, 258; interest in towns, 261–62; attraction to water, 261, 265, 289–90; courage, 269
—*As artist*: lacks imagination, 60; believes few original themes exist, 71; has no interest in literary theories, 79–80; response to words, 115, 132, 212, 217–18; anticipates science, 208; doubts talent, 213; has no intellect, 226–27; is clown, 229
—*His work*: effect on J of difficulties with, 32; J does not discuss, 47, 50, 54; J anxious to have translated, 50 and n; J's commitment to, 92–93, 108–18, 138, 149–50; next after *FW*, 93, 203, 249, 279, 291; continuity of, 109, 120, 131; J's response to criticism of, 115; J's attitude toward readers of, 117; J offers to autograph, 126; J wants to rewrite, 129; time in, 129; J wants to escape from, 151; J's habits in writing, 151, 183; place of women in, 190–91; influence of *Hamlet* on, 191; quotidian in, 210; animals in, 232–33; compared with Klee, 266, 270–71; and Newman, 273; self-confession in, 287; J deprecates, 289
Joyce, John Stanislaus (father): urges J to go to Europe, 3; his portrait, 86–87; J's admiration of, 167; *FW* to be published on his birthday, 181, 212; J wants children to meet, 184; and J's work, 187–88; his response to Brancusi impression of J, 188; reconciliation with J, 188–90
Joyce, Lucia (daughter): resembles J, 46; takes voice lessons, 65; appearance and manner of, 89, 90, 104–5; J's response to her illness,

91, 92; Beckett's concern for, 104–5; and *ABC*, 143, 165; J speaks of her illness, 182; J blames self about, 192; J believes he understands, 203; her illness linked with *FW*, 214; J's concern over, 218, 230, 240, 243, 249–50; and Nora, 233; in *Pomes Penyeach*, 236; problem with during WW II, 251, 274–75; J seeks help from women with, 253–54; connection with Hedvig in *The Wild Duck*, 254
Joyce, Mary Jane Murray (mother), 135
Joyce, Nora Barnacle (Mrs. James Joyce): J's elopement with, 3; unhappy in Trieste, 4; speaks little Italian, 4, 27; notes change in J, 5; cries, 14n; runs up bills, 27; J uses in Berlitz exercises, 27, 28–29; miscarries, 29n; and *U*, 59–60, 64, 138; is friendly with Mrs. Fleiner, 62; becomes Wagnerite, 64; her portrait, 76, 91; at "Déjeuner *U*," 86; likes J's poetry, 88; appearance and manner of, 89, 91, 104; and J, 138–50 *passim*; won't carry umbrella, 143; responds to beauty, 143, 217, 237; knows title of *FW*, 181; visits Ireland, 184; wishes *FW* finished, 213; jokes about J, 216; J eludes her eye, 218; dislikes Ireland, 220, 223; is bored by formal occasions, 222; attends Mass, 233; on her life with J, 233; has difficulty with French, 233, 242; dreams, 234; calls J tyrant, 235; recalls J as young man, 238; is nostalgic, 240; is ill, 243, 245; worries about J's health, 252; loses patience with J, 270, 285; and J's last illness, 278; and J's funeral, 279, 286; cries over music, 281
Joyce, Stanislaus (brother): on Francini lecture, 6; quarrels with J, 40–41; in aliens' camp, 43; J wishes to talk with, 47; brings copy of *Dubliners* to Benco, 56; J has article on *FW* sent to, 248; mentioned, 46n, 135

Quinet, Edgar: J quotes, 239

Radek, Karl: attack on J by, 119
Renan, Ernst: his portrayal of priests, 240
Reumert, Poul (actor), 148
Revue de Paris, 163, 250
Revue des Deux Mondes: notice of U in, 163; importance to J, 245; article on *FW* in, 252
Ribemont-Dessaignes, Georges: launches *Bifur*, 87
Richards, Grant, 59
Romains, Jules: at "Déjeuner U," 85; at PEN reception, 100
Rome: a mortuary, 29; J robbed in, 31; J's stay in, 43
Rossini, Gioacchino: *William Tell*, 64, 248, 267; J likes music of, 168
Roth, Samuel: protest against his piracy of U, 83, 123, 155
Ruggiero, Paul: helps J, 275
Russian Orthodox Church: J dislikes ritual of, 238

Saint-Gérand-le-Puy: J at, 74, 104, 165–66, 204, 250, 274
St. Leger, Baroness: provides material for U, 60, 62
Sakharov, Alexandre and Clothilde, 234
Sargent, Louis, 62
Sauermann, Charlotte, 218, 263
Schaurek, Eileen Joyce (J's sister): J sends Czech translation of U to, 135
Schaurek, Frantisek (J's brother-in-law): suicide of, 135
Schildt, Runar: J sees his *Gallows Man*, 148
Schmitz, Ettore: and U, 33n, 48, 81, 193–94; J's friendship with, 47–48, 112; J moved by his death, 50; visits Paris, 81–82
Schmitz, Livia Veneziani (Mrs. Ettore): her portrait, 87
Schoeck, Othmar: J admires his music, 168
Scott, Walter: J quotes, 226
Scotus, John Duns: J's knowledge of, 37

Scuola Superiore di Commercio Revoltella, 43, 55
Settanni, Ettore: and translation of "ALP," 101–2
Shakespeare, William: *Hamlet* and J's work, 69, 191; J compares with Ibsen, 147, 272; J wonders about, 272–73; J recites from *Julius Caesar*, 272; mentioned, 62
Shaw, George Bernard: J writes on, 53n; mentioned, 7, 127
Silvestri, Tullio, xvi
Simoni, Renato, 54
Slowacki, Juliusz, 160
Soave, Francesco: J wants copy of his *Moral Tales*, 107n
Socialism: in Berlitz School, 16
Solaria, 83
Soupault, Philippe: at "Déjeuner U," 85; J's affection for, 222; on J and Léon, 289
Spanish Civil War: J will not comment on, 156n
Speck, Paul: makes death mask of J, 170
Spender, Stephen: attacks J, 269; mentioned, 234
Spenser, Edmund: J's interest in, 218, 220, 228
Stein, Gertrude, 79
Stiernstedt, Marika, 155
Stoppard, Tom, 56n
Straumann, Heinrich: at J's funeral, 279
Strauss, Richard: J likes *Der Rosenkavellier*, 195
Stravinsky, Igor: J does not care for, 149, 268n
Strindberg, August, 57
Suckert, Kurt. See Malaparte, Curzio
Sullivan, John: J's enthusiasm for, 64, 68, 89, 113, 248; at parties with J, 180; J envies, 194
Surrealism: J dislikes, 99; and *FW*, 106–7
Suter, Mrs. August: gives Lucia singing lessons, 64–65
Suter, Paul, 59, 63
Svevo, Italo. See Schmitz, Ettore
Swift, Jonathan: J admits influence of, 131